TOURING ATLAS
OF SOUTHERN AFRICA

MICHAEL BRETT

ALAN MOUNTAIN

Struik Publishers (Pty) Ltd
(a member of The Struik Publishing Group (Pty) Ltd)
Cornelis Struik House, 80 McKenzie Street
Cape Town 8001
Reg. No.: 54/00965/07

ISBN 1 86825 928 5

Copyright © in published edition: Struik Publishers
(Pty) Ltd 1997
Copyright © in text: Michael Brett & Alan Mountain 1997
Copyright © in photographs: as credited below 1997
Copyright © in maps: Struik Publishers (Pty) Ltd 1997
Copyright © in Mountain High Maps TM 1993 Digital
Wisdom Inc

First edition 1997
Also available in Afrikaans as *Reis-Atlas van Suider-Afrika*.

Managing editor: Annlerie van Rooyen
Editors: Glynne Newlands and Alfred LeMaitre
Designer: Gillian Black
Cover design/Design manager: Janice Evans
Design assistant: Lellyn Creamer
Cartographers: Desiree Oosterberg, Caroline Bowie
and Mark Seabrook
Cartographic illustrators: Malcolm Porter and
Caroline Bowie
Cartographic editor: Lesley Hay-Whitton
Indexer and proofreader: Alfred LeMaitre

Repro co-ordinator: Andrew de Kock
Reproduction: Unifoto (Pty) Ltd, Cape Town
Printing: South China Printing Co. Ltd, Hong Kong

Road signs reproduced with the kind permission of the
Department of Transport.

Every effort has been made to ensure factual accuracy in
this book, but with the rapid changes taking place in
southern Africa, information may become outdated.
The authors and publishers invite any comments or
suggestions for future updates. Please write to: The
Editor, Touring Atlas of Southern Africa, PO Box 1144,
Cape Town 8000.

Front cover: *The Drakensberg*. Insets from top to bottom
Vygies, Basotho man, Clifton beach. Spine: *Cheetah*. Title
page: *Great Brak River Island*. Back cover: *Penguins at
Boulders beach*.

AUTHORS' ACKNOWLEDGEMENTS

In writing a book of this nature, a great deal of research is required and many
people, too numerous to mention by name, have been involved in helping me to
acquire relevant and up-to-date information. To them all I would like to express
my gratitude. I would like to especially thank Glynne Newlands for her patience
in editing my work. Michael Brett's suggestions and comments are greatly valued
and appreciated. To Struik and their enthusiastic staff I would like to express my
gratitude for the positive way in which this book has been managed from inception.

Alan Mountain

In researching and writing my contribution to this book, I travelled some 23 000 kilometres across southern Africa, visiting all nine provinces at least once. During these
wanderings I encountered hundreds of friendly and supportive people who enthusiastically assisted me. Although their names are too many to mention, the valuable contribution that they made is greatly appreciated. I am indebted to the staff of the

provincial conservation departments, the National Parks Board, botanic gardens,
private nature reserves, wine farms and over 50 publicity associations. Alan Mountain
made many valuable suggestions; Gurling and Sue Bothma provided a base in Pretoria,
and Robert Daphne and Sharon Kallis one in East London – Robert accompanied me
on a journey through the Karoo, Kalahari and Highveld, and my son Andrew assisted
me on a visit to Gauteng. My wife Ros eagerly supported this project, even when it
took me away from home for long periods. Finally, a special word of gratitude to the
staff of Struik Publishers. Although a project of this magnitude demands the creative
energies of a team of editors, designers and cartographers, in particular I would like to
thank Annlerie van Rooyen and Glynne Newlands. Annlerie provided professional
guidance and direction, and demanded excellence at all times. Ever-patient, cheerful
and committed, Glynne carefully crafted the text, brought the various pieces together
and managed hundreds of queries, amendments, deletions and last minute alterations.

Michael Brett

PHOTOGRAPHIC CREDITS

Copyright for the photographs rests with the following
photographers and/or their agents.
SA = Shaen Adey; **DB** = Daryl Balfour; **MB** = Michael
Brett; **DB** = David Bristow; **RDLH** = Roger de la Harpe;
ND = Nigel Dennis; **WD** = Wendy Dennis; **GD** =
Gerhard Dreyer; **JDP** = Jean du Plessis; **CF** = C Friend;
AF = Albert Froneman; **LH** = Leonard Hoffman; **AJ** =
Anthony Johnson; **WK** = Walter Knirr; **JM** = Jackie
Murray; **JN** = Jackie Nel; **JP** = John Paisley; **CPJ** =
Colin Paterson-Jones; **PP** = Peter Pickford; **CP** = Carol
Polich; **HP** = Herman Potgieter; **AP** = Alain Proust; **MS**
= Mark Skinner; **DS** = David Steele; **NS** = N Sutherland;
ET = Erhardt Thiel; **FVH** = Friedrich van Hörsten; **HVH**
= Hein van Hörsten; **LVH** = Lanz van Hörsten; **PW** =
Patrick Wagner; **KY** = Keith Young; **ABPL** = Anthony
Bannister Photo Library; **NPB** = Natal Parks Board; **PA** =
Photo Access; **SIL** = Struik Image Library

Front cover: main picture (**RDLH**), insets from top
to bottom (**LVH/SIL**), (**HVH/SIL**), (**LVH/SIL**), **spine**
(**ND/SIL**), **back cover:** (**AP**), **title page:** (**GD/SIL**).
Pages: 4 (**GD/SIL**), 7 (**HVH/SIL**), 10 (**WK/SIL**),
10 (bottom) (**HP**), 12 (**HP**), 13 (top) (**JM/SIL**), 13
(bottom) (**HVH/SIL**), 14 (**HP**), 15 (**HP**), 16 (**AF**), 17
(top) (**WK/SIL**), 17 (bottom) (**HVH/SIL**), 18 (top)
(**LVH/SIL**), 18 (bottom) (**WK/SIL**), 20 (top) (**LVH/SIL**),
20 (bottom) (**HVH/SIL**), 21 (**HVH/SIL**), 22 (top) (**ND**),
22 (bottom) (**MB**), 23 (**HVH/SIL**), 24 (**DB/PA**), 25
(**JN/PA**), 26 (top) (**WK/SIL**), 26 (bottom) (**ND/SIL**),
28 (top) (**LVH/SIL**), 28 (bottom) (**WK/SIL**), 29 (top)
(**HP**), 29 (bottom) (**WK/SIL**), 30 (**ND/SIL**), 31 (top)
(**ND/SIL**), 31 (bottom) (**ND**), 32 (top) (**WK/SIL**), 32
(bottom) (**LVH/SIL**), 33 (left) (**LVH/SIL**), 33 (right) (**MB**),
34 (top) (**PP**), 34 (bottom) (**HVH/SIL**), 35 (top) (**ND**),
35 (bottom) (**AF**), 36 (**LVH/SIL**), 37 (**LVH/SIL**), 38 (**ND/
SIL**), 39 (**LVH/SIL**), 40 (**WK/SIL**), 41 (top and bottom)
(**WK/SIL**), 41 (centre) (**MB**), 42 (**LVH/SIL**), 44 (top)
(**DS/PA**), 44 (bottom) (**WK**), 45 (top) (**RDLH/SIL**),

45 (bottom) (**HP**), 46 (top) (**WK/SIL**), 46 (bottom) (**WK**),
48 (top) (**KY/SIL**), 48 (bottom) (**RDLH**), 49 (top) (**RDLH/
SIL**), 49 (bottom) (**SA/SIL**), 50 (**RDLH**), 51 (top) (**MB**),
51 (bottom) (**LVH/SIL**), 52 (top) (**RDLH**), 52 (centre)
(**FVH**), 52 (bottom) (**KY/SIL**), 53 (top) (**WK/PA**), 53
(bottom) (**ND/SIL**), 54 (**SA/SIL**), 55 (top) (**WK/SIL**),
55 (bottom) (**RDLH/SIL**), 56 (right) (**ND/SIL**), 56 (left)
(**WD/SIL**), 57 (left) (**WK/SIL**), 57 (right) (**SA/SIL**), 58
(top) (**HP**), 58 (bottom) (**RDLH/SIL**), 60 (**RDLH/SIL**),
61 (top) (**ND/SIL**), 61 (bottom) (**HP**), 62 (top) (**RDLH/
SIL**), 62 (bottom) (**MB**), 63 (**RDLH/NPB**), 64 (**SA/SIL**),
65 (**RDLH/NPB**), 66 (top) (**WK/SIL**), 66 (bottom)
(**RDLH**), 67 (top) (**RDLH/SIL**), 67 (bottom) (**RDLH**),
68 (top) (**PW/PA**), 68 (bottom) (**FVH**), 70 (**JP/PA**),
71 (**LH/SIL**), 72 (top) (**PW/PA**), 72 (bottom) (**ND**),
73 (**PW/PA**), 74 (top) (**MB**), 74 (bottom) (**WK/SIL**),
75 (**MB**), 76 (top) (**KY/SIL**), 76 (bottom) (**MS/SIL**),
78 (top) (**LVH/SIL**), 78 (bottom) (**ET/SIL**), 79 (top)
(**ND/SIL**), 79 (bottom) (**HVH/SIL**), 80 (top) (**HVH/SIL**),
80 (bottom) (**KY/SIL**), 81 (**ET/SIL**), 82 (top) (**ET/SIL**),
82 (bottom) (**AJ/SIL**), 83 (top) (**MS**), 83 (centre) (**HVH/
SIL**), 83 (bottom) (**LVH/SIL**), 84 (top) (**HVH/SIL**), 84
(bottom) (**HP**), 85 (top) (**AJ/SIL**), 85 (bottom) (**ET/SIL**),
86 (top) (**HP**), 86 (bottom) (**MS/SIL**), 87 (top) (**LVH/SIL**),
87 (bottom) (**HP**), 88 (top) (**LVH/SIL**), 88 (bottom)
(**KY/SIL**), 89 (top) (**ET/SIL**), 89 (bottom) (**HVH/SIL**),
90 (**GD/SIL**), 91 (top) (**ET/SIL**), 91 (centre) (**HVH/SIL**),
91 (bottom) (**SA/SIL**), 92 (top) (**GD/SIL**), 92 (bottom)
(**WK/SIL**), 94 (top) (**KY/SIL**), 94 (bottom) (**KY**), 95
(**GD/SIL**), 96 (**HVH/SIL**), 97 (top) (**HP**), 97 (bottom)
(**HVH/SIL**), 98 (top) (**HVH/SIL**), 98 (bottom) (**LVH/SIL**),
99 (top) (**WK/SIL**), 99 (bottom) (**HVH/SIL**), 100 (top)
(**GD/SIL**), 100 (bottom) (**LVH/SIL**), 101 (top) (**WK/SIL**),
101 (centre and bottom) (**LVH/SIL**), 102 (top) (**HVH/
SIL**), 102 (bottom) (**GD/SIL**), 104 (top) (**ND/SIL**), 104
(bottom) (**GD/SIL**), 105 (**GD/SIL**), 106 (top) (**WK**), 106
(centre and bottom) (**GD/SIL**), 107 (**GD/SIL**), 108 (top)
(**GD/SIL**), 108 (bottom) (**PP/SIL**), 109 (**GD/SIL**), 110 (top)

(**CF/SIL**), 110 (bottom) (**MS/SIL**), 112 (top) (**HVH/SIL**),
112 (bottom) (**SA/SIL**), 113 (**HVH/SIL**), 114 (top) (**KY/SIL**),
114 (bottom) (**SA/SIL**), 115 (top) (**HVH/SIL**), 115 (bottom)
(**SA/SIL**), 116 (**HVH/SIL**), 117 (**LVH/SIL**), 118 (**HVH/
SIL**), 119 (**HVH/SIL**), 120 (top) (**HP**), 120 (bottom)
(**HVH/SIL**), 122 (top) (**HVH/SIL**), 122 (bottom) (**HP**),
123 (**HVH/SIL**), 124 (**HVH/SIL**), 125 (top) (**FVH**),
125 (bottom) (**WK/SIL**), 126 (**HVH/SIL**), 128 (**LVH/SIL**),
129 (top) (**LVH/SIL**), 129 (bottom) (**MS/SIL**), 130 (top)
(**LVH/SIL**), 130 (bottom) (**HVH/SIL**), 131 (**GD/SIL**),
132 (top) (**ND/SIL**), 132 (bottom) (**HVH/SIL**), 134
(**HVH/SIL**), 135 (top) (**WK/SIL**), 135 (bottom) (**HVH/
SIL**), 136 (**ND/SIL**), 138 (**ND/SIL**), 139 (**ND/SIL**), 140
(**WK/SIL**), 141 (top left and top right) (**ND/SIL**), 141
(bottom) (**SIL**), 142 (top) (**NS/SIL**), 142 (bottom) (**KY/
SIL**), 144 (**NS/SIL**), 145 (**KY/SIL**), 146 (**HP**), 147 (top)
(**WK/SIL**), 147 bottom (**HP**), 148 (**HVH/SIL**), 149 (left)
(**WK/SIL**), 149 (right) (**RDLH/SIL**), 150 (top) (**WK/SIL**),
150 (bottom) (**KY/SIL**), 152 (**LVH/SIL**), 153 (top left)
(**HVH/SIL**), 153 (top right) (**LVH/SIL**), 153 (bottom)
(**HVH/SIL**), 154 (**HVH/SIL**), 155 (top) (**LVH/SIL**), 155
(bottom) (**HVH**), 156 (**CP/SIL**), 158 (**JDP**), 159 (**JDP**),
160 (**JDP**), 161 (**JDP**), 162 (**KB/SIL**), 164 (top) (**RDLH/
SIL**), 164 (bottom) (**MS/SIL**), 165 (top) (**PP/SIL**), 165
(bottom) (**MS/SIL**), 166 (top) (**RDLH/SIL**), 166 (centre
and bottom) (**KB/SIL**), 167 (**RDLH/SIL**), 168 (top)
(**LVH/SIL**), 168 (bottom) (**ND/SIL**), 169 (top and centre)
(**ND/SIL**), 169 (bottom) (**HVH/SIL**), 170 (**GD/SIL**), 171
(top) (**LVH/SIL**), 171 (bottom) (**HVH/SIL**), 172 (**RDLH/
NPB**), 173 (top) (**RDLH/SIL**), 173 (bottom) (**SA/SIL**),
174 (**LVH/SIL**), 175 (**SA/SIL**), 176 (**LVH/SIL**), 177 (top)
(**HVH/SIL**), 177 (bottom) (**LVH/SIL**), 178 (right)
(**LVH/SIL**), 178 (left) (**HVH/SIL**), 179 (top and centre)
(**LVH/SIL**), 179 (bottom) (**PP/SIL**), 180 (**WK/SIL**), 181
(top) (**KY/SIL**), 181 (bottom) (**LVH/SIL**), 182 (**RDLH/
SIL**), 183 (top and bottom right) (**HVH/SIL**), 183 (bottom
left) (**GD/SIL**), 184 (**LVH/SIL**), 185 (top) (**MS/SIL**), 185
(bottom) (**DB**), 186 (**ET/SIL**), 187 (**HVH/SIL**)

CONTENTS

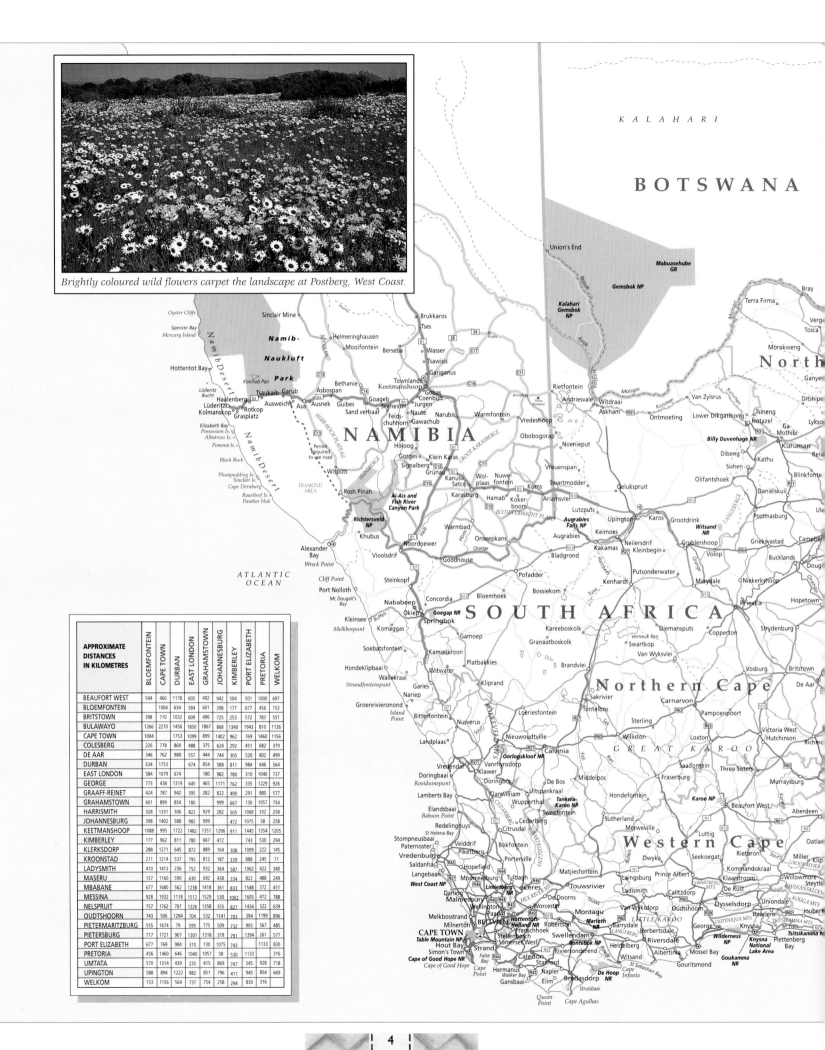

Brightly coloured wild flowers carpet the landscape at Postberg, West Coast.

APPROXIMATE DISTANCES IN KILOMETRES	BLOEMFONTEIN	CAPE TOWN	DURBAN	EAST LONDON	GRAHAMSTOWN	JOHANNESBURG	KIMBERLEY	PORT ELIZABETH	PRETORIA	WELKOM
BEAUFORT WEST	544	460	1178	605	492	942	504	501	1000	697
BLOEMFONTEIN		1004	634	584	601	398	177	677	456	153
BRITSTOWN	398	710	1032	609	496	725	253	572	783	551
BULAWAYO	1266	2270	1456	1850	1867	868	1340	1943	810	1126
CAPE TOWN	1004		1753	1099	899	1402	962	769	1460	1156
COLESBERG	226	778	860	488	375	624	292	451	682	379
DE AAR	346	762	980	557	444	744	305	520	802	499
DURBAN	634	1753		674	854	588	811	984	646	564
EAST LONDON	584	1079	674		180	982	780	310	1040	737
GEORGE	773	438	1319	645	465	1171	762	335	1229	926
GRAAFF-REINET	424	787	942	395	282	822	490	291	880	577
GRAHAMSTOWN	601	899	854	180		999	667	130	1057	754
HARRISMITH	328	1331	306	822	929	282	505	1068	332	258
JOHANNESBURG	398	1402	588	982	999		472	1075	58	258
KEETMANSHOOP	1088	995	1722	1482	1351	1296	911	1445	1354	1205
KIMBERLEY	177	962	811	780	667	472		743	530	294
KLERKSDORP	288	1271	645	872	889	164	308	1009	222	145
KROONSTAD	211	1214	537	795	812	187	339	888	245	71
LADYSMITH	410	1413	236	752	932	364	587	1062	422	340
MASERU	157	1160	590	630	692	438	334	822	488	249
MBABANE	677	1680	562	1238	1418	361	833	1548	372	451
MESSINA	928	1932	1118	1512	1529	530	1002	1605	472	788
NELSPRUIT	757	1762	707	1226	1358	355	827	1434	322	639
OUDTSHOORN	743	506	1294	704	532	1141	703	394	1199	896
PIETERMARITZBURG	555	1674	79	595	775	509	732	905	567	485
PIETERSBURG	717	1721	907	1301	1318	319	791	1394	261	577
PORT ELIZABETH	677	769	984	310	130	1075	743		1133	830
PRETORIA	456	1460	646	1040	1057	58	530	1133		316
UMTATA	570	1314	439	235	415	869	747	545	928	718
UPINGTON	588	894	1222	982	851	796	411	945	854	669
WELKOM	153	1156	564	737	754	258	294	830	316	

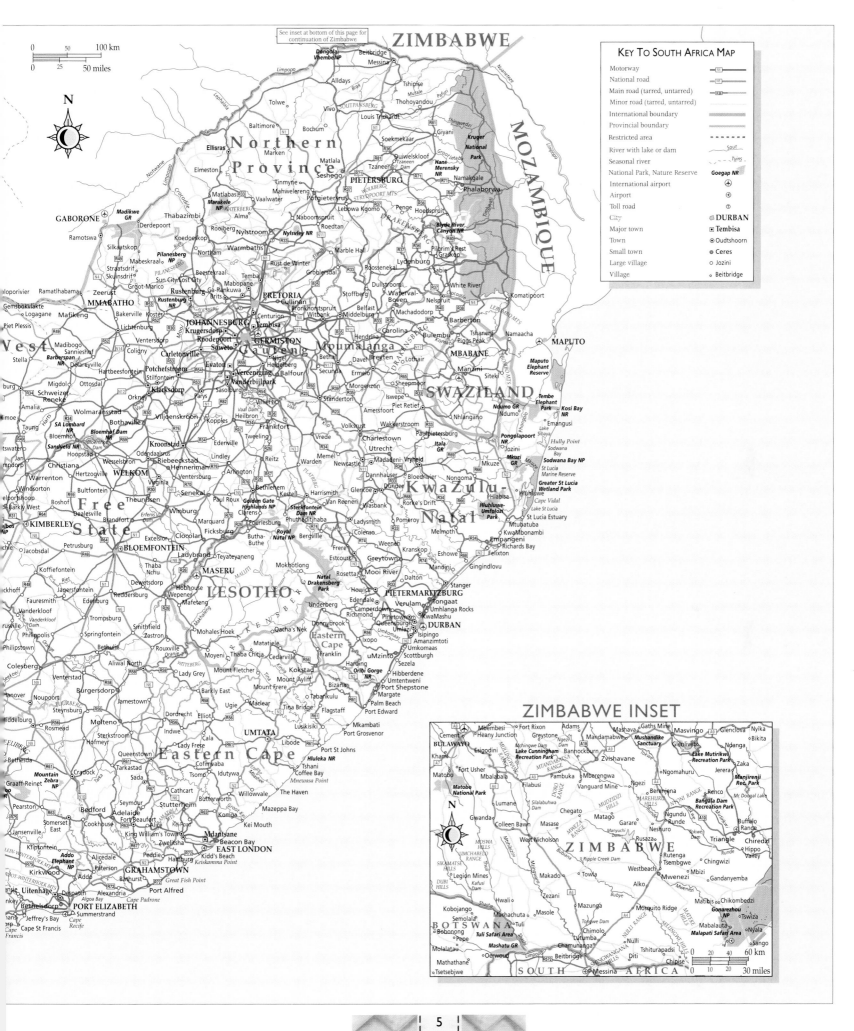

See inset at bottom of this page for
continuation of Zimbabwe

MOZAMBIQUE

KEY TO SOUTH AFRICA MAP

Motorway
National road
Main road (tarred, untarred)
Minor road (tarred, untarred)
International boundary
Provincial boundary
Restricted area
River with lake or dam
Seasonal river
National Park, Nature Reserve · **Goegap NR**
International airport
Airport
Toll road
City · **DURBAN**
Major town · **Tembisa**
Town · Oudtshoorn
Small town · Ceres
Large village · Jozini
Village · Beitbridge

Northern
Province

PIETERSBURG

Kruger
National
Park

GABORONE

MMABATHO

PRETORIA

JOHANNESBURG
GERMISTON

Gauteng Mpumalanga

MBABANE

MAPUTO

SWAZILAND

West

Free
State

KIMBERLEY

BLOEMFONTEIN

MASERU

L'ESOTHO

KwaZulu-
Natal

PIETERMARITZBURG

DURBAN

Eastern Cape

UMTATA

EAST LONDON

GRAHAMSTOWN

PORT ELIZABETH

ZIMBABWE INSET

BULAWAYO

ZIMBABWE

BOTSWANA

SOUTH AFRICA

0   20   40   60 km
0   10   20   30 miles

HOW TO USE THE BOOK

The *Touring Atlas of Southern Africa* consists of two sections: Atlas and Tours, and a Leisure Guide. In the first section, southern Africa is divided into 19 geographical regions, each with a detailed map. To enable readers to explore just beyond South Africa's boundaries, excursions into Swaziland, Zimbabwe and Namibia have also been included.

Regions

ATLAS AND TOURS: Atlas section

The locator map highlights the detailed regional map on the opposite page. Overlapping regions and their respective page numbers are supplied for ease of reference.

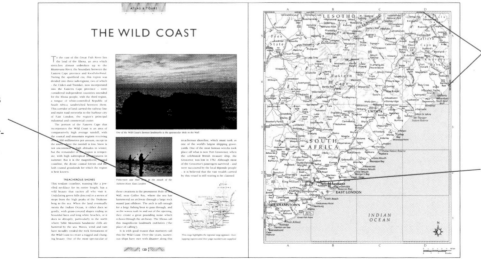

To locate destinations on the regional map, a grid reference system is supplied and used in the index e.g. East London *121* (page number) *B2* (co-ordinates).

Readers can see at a glance which tours are covered in a region as they are shown in yellow on the regional map. The tours include page references.

The Atlas and Tours section consists of a general overview of a particular region, including a detailed regional map and a city map, or maps, where applicable. This is followed by a description of the most scenic tour(s) in that region, also with a comprehensive tour map, or maps.

ATLAS AND TOURS: Tours section

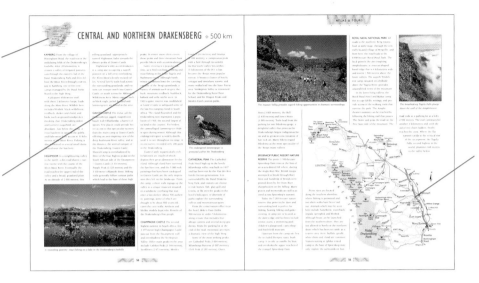

The region in which the tour is situated is indicated by a block on the southern Africa locator map.

In order to assist the reader in planning his or her trip, the estimated length of the tour is given next to the heading.

The tour map (marked in orange) shows the route discussed in the text, and the starting point of the tour is indicated by an arrow. All the main roads and rivers are also shown.

LEISURE GUIDE

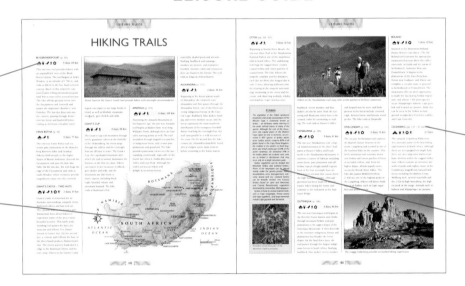

Symbols indicate at a glance what facilities and attractions are available. A definition of each symbol is given in the box below.

The Leisure Guide map clearly shows the location of each destination and activity discussed.

Where a place is referred to in another section of the book, the relevant page number(s) are given.

Topics of special interest are highlighted in tinted feature boxes.

SYMBOLS

1. Rest camp/accommodation
2. Camping site
3. Restaurant/refreshments
4. Wildlife
5. Birdlife
6. Game drives
7. Walks/hikes
8. Horseback trails/horse riding
9. Hot-air balloon trips
10. Flora/botanical gardens
11. Live music
12. Wine-tasting
13. San rock art

The N2 freeway near Riviersonderend forms part of South Africa's excellent road network.

GETTING ABOUT

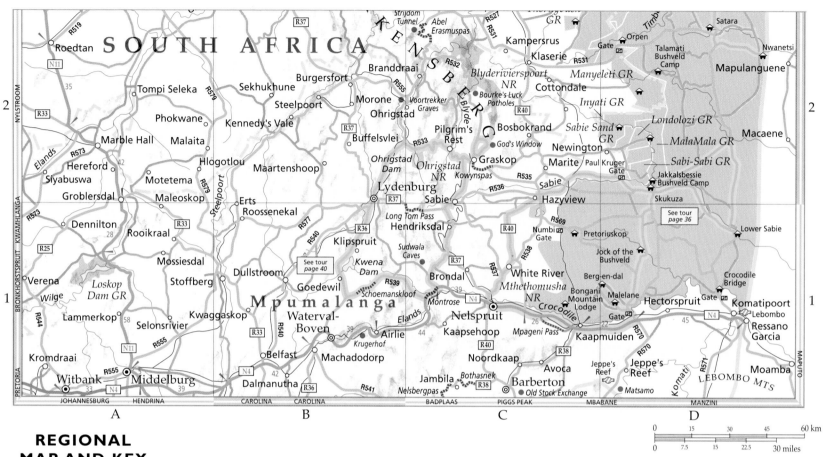

REGIONAL MAP AND KEY

Motorway	N4
National road	
Main road	R79
Main road untarred	
Minor road	
Minor road untarred	
Tour route	
Toll road	T
Route number	R539
Distance (in kilometres)	100
Railway	
International boundary	
Provincial boundary	
River	Nossob
Lake or dam	
Place of interest	Blockhouse ●
City	
Major town	
Town	◉
Small town	◎
Large village	○
Village	○
Peak	▲
Gate	
Province name	North-West
National park or reserve	
Airport	✈
Camp	
Border post	
Directional	Nelspruit→
Restricted area	

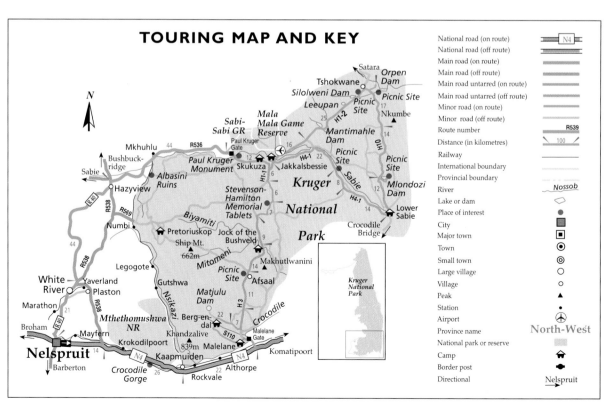

TOURING MAP AND KEY

National road (on route)	N4
National road (off route)	
Main road (on route)	
Main road (off route)	
Main road untarred (on route)	
Main road untarred (off route)	
Minor road (on route)	
Minor road (off route)	
Route number	R539
Distance (in kilometres)	100
Railway	
International boundary	
Provincial boundary	
River	Nossob
Lake or dam	
Place of interest	●
City	
Major town	
Town	◉
Small town	◎
Large village	○
Village	○
Peak	▲
Station	
Airport	
Province name	North-West
National park or reserve	
Camp	
Border post	
Directional	Nelspruit→

RULES OF THE ROAD

The general speed limits on South African roads are:

- 60 km/h on a public road in an urban area;
- 100 km/h on a public road, other than a freeway, in a rural area;
- 120 km/h on a freeway.

However, a road sign may indicate a speed limit that is lower than the general limit.

In South Africa, the rule of the road is to drive on the left-hand side, and the general rule for freeways and main roads is to keep left and pass right. Seat belts must be worn at all times, and both drivers and passengers of motor cycles must wear protective helmets.

Remember to always carry your driver's licence with you when you are driving.

 Regional routes.

 Metropolitan routes.

 Provincial routes.

 National routes.

 Direction to a transport terminal.

 Exit signs show interchange numbers and distances, plus the services available.

 The top sign confirms the direction and distances of the route. The sign below gives advance information.

 This direction shows the junctions ahead, the route numbers, the destinations and a toll road.

Ostrich farm	Museum	Bird sanctuary	Wine cellar
Accommodation	Caravan park	Camping	Bed & breakfast	Rooms

Ostrich farm — Museum — Bird sanctuary — Wine cellar — Accommodation — Caravan park — Camping — Bed & breakfast — Rooms

Restaurant — Police — First aid post — Petrol & workshop — Public telephone — Hospital — National Parks Board — Inland water resort — Hot springs

Beach resort — Mountain resort — Waterfall — Snake park — Scenic route — Viewsite — Crocodile farm — National monument — Botanical garden

Hiking trail — Rest area — Golf course — Emergency phone 500 m ahead — Parking — Toilets — Tourist information — Facility for the disabled — Roadside stall

---

USEFUL ADDRESSES AND TELEPHONE NUMBERS

EMERGENCY NUMBERS
Police – Flying Squad 10111
Ambulance 10177
Directory enquiries 1023

AUTOMOBILE ASSOCIATION
South Africa:
(24-hour service) toll-free
080001 0101
Zimbabwe:
Bulawayo, tel. (263) 9-70063
Namibia:
(24-hour service) (011) 403-4400

TABLE MOUNTAIN AERIAL CABLEWAY CO.
7 Bree Street, Cape Town, tel.
(021) 24-5148, fax. 21-4619

FLOWERLINE
Cape Town, tel. (021) 418-3705

NATIONAL PARKS
South Africa:
Pretoria, PO Box 787, Pretoria 0001, tel. (012) 343-1991, fax. 343-0905
Cape Town, PO Box 7400, Roggebaai 8012, tel. (021) 22-2810, fax. 24-6211
Zimbabwe:
Bulawayo, 140a Fife Street, tel. (263) 9-63646

Masvingo, Shop 5, Robert Mugabe Street, tel. (263) 39-62563
Namibia:
Ministry of Environment & Tourism (to book state-owned rest camps and resorts), tel. *Windhoek* (264) 61-33875, or *Lüderitz* (264) 63331-2752.

NATIONAL BOTANICAL INSTITUTE
South African Head Office, Kirstenbosch, Rhodes Drive, Newlands 7700, Cape Town, tel. (021) 762-1166, fax. 701-1399

NATURE CONSERVATION
Head Office, Private Bag X209, Pretoria, tel. (012) 201-9111, fax. 201-3741
Western Cape, Private Bag X9086, Cape Town 8000, tel. (021) 483-3170, fax. 483-4158
KwaZulu-Natal, Private Bag X9024, Pietermartizburg 3200, tel. (0331) 94-6698, fax. 42-1948
Eastern Cape, Private Bag X3, East London 5252, tel. (0431) 41-2212, fax. 41-3200
Free State, PO Box 502, Bloemfontein 9300, tel. (051) 447-0407, fax. 447-5240

Mpumalanga, Private Bag 11233, Nelspruit 1200, tel. (01375) 94000, fax. 759-4089
North-West Province, PO Box 5396, Kockpark 2523, tel. (0148) 297-7428, fax. 294-6008

WILDLIFE SOCIETY
South Africa:
National Office, 31 Oxford Street, First Town, Johannesburg, tel. (011) 486-3294
Zimbabwe:
National Office, PO Box HG996, Highlands, tel. (263) 4-700451

SA TOURISM BOARDS
• *Tourism South Africa*, 442 Rigel Avenue, Erasmusrand, Pretoria, tel. (012) 347-0600, fax. 45-4889
• *Western Cape*, 3 Adderley Street, Cape Town, tel. (021) 21-6274, fax. 419-4875
• *Eastern Cape*, Phalo House, Phalo Avenue, Bisho, tel. (0401) 952-115, fax. 956-4019
• *Northern Cape*, Kimberley Library, Chapel Street, Kimberley, tel. (0531) 82-7298, fax. 82-7211
• *KwaZulu-Natal*, 160 Pine Street, Durban, tel. (031) 304-7144, fax. 305-6693

• *Free State*, 2nd Floor Midland Street, Bloemfontein, tel. (051) 407-1137, fax. 448-8361
• *Mpumalanga*, cnr Louis Trichardt and Henhall Streets, Nelspruit, tel. (013) 752-7001, fax. 752-7013
• *Northern Province*, cnr Dorp and Suid Streets, Pietersburg, tel. (0152) 295-9300, fax. 295-5819
• *Gauteng*, cnr Market and Kruis Streets, Johannesburg, tel. (011) 333-8082, fax. 336-4965
• *North-West Province*, Royal Building, Lombard Street, Potchefstroom, tel. (0148) 293-1611, fax. 297-2082

PUBLICITY ASSOCIATIONS
South Africa:
Johannesburg, cnr Market and Kruis Streets, tel. (011) 336-4961, fax. 336-4965
Sondela Central Reservations & Tourist Information, 71 Main Street, Sabi, tel./fax. (013) 764-3492
Captour, Adderley Street, Cape Town 8001, tel. (021) 418-5214, fax. 418-5227
West Coast, Oorlogsvlei, Van Riebeeck Street, Saldanha, tel. (02281) 42088, fax. 44240
Garden Route Tourism Office, 54 York

Street, George, tel. (0441) 73-6314, fax. 74-6840
Durban Unlimited Tourist Information, 160 Pine Street, Durban, tel. (031) 304-4934, fax. 304-6196
Pietermaritzburg, 177 Commercial Road, tel. (0331) 45-1348, fax. 94-3535
Drakensberg, Tatham Street, Bergville, tel./fax. (036) 448-1557
Dolphin Coast, next door to BP Service Station, Ballito Drive, Ballito, tel./fax. (0322) 61997
South Coast, 126 Scott Street, Scottburgh, tel./fax. (0323) 21364
Port Elizabeth, Donkin Reserve, Central, tel. (041) 52-1315, fax. 55-2564
Zimbabwe:
Bulawayo, adjacent to Jairos Jiri Craft Shop, between Takawira and 8th Streets, tel. (263) 9-60867/72969, fax. 9-60868
Masvingo, PO Box 340, tel. (263) 39-62643
Namibia:
Keetmanshoop, Southern Tourist Forum, tel. (264) 631-2095, fax 3818.
Lüderitz, Ministry of Environment & Tourism, tel. (264) 6331-2752

GAUTENG

South Africa's smallest province is dominated by a low ridge that the early pioneers named the Witwatersrand (the 'ridge of white water') in whose rock strata the world's richest deposits of gold were bedded. These riches powered the early development of South Africa's secondary and tertiary industries and gave rise to an arc of settlement which stretched from Randfontein in the west to Springs in the east; today the fulcrum centres around Gauteng's sprawling city of Johannesburg, the economic heart of the country.

It was in this region many millions of years ago that nature laid down a fine carpet of gold particles along the shores and floor of what was either a vast lake or river delta. The particles were carried in the silt brought down by a river, or rivers, which drained from the north and northwest. In time, the gold became locked into the surrounding sedimentary rocks. When gold was discovered along certain creeks and ridges of the eastern Escarpment in the 1880s, prospectors widened their search for the precious metal to the Highveld of the then Transvaal.

The city of Johannesburg – viewed here from a disused mine dump (above) – was built on gold. Gold still forms the backbone of the country's economy. The refined molten metal is poured into gold pan moulds (below).

In 1886, prospector George Harrison stumbled upon a small weathered outcrop of gold-bearing sedimentary rock. He immediately staked his claim, but, strangely, did nothing to develop it. Instead Harrison sold it for a mere £10, thereby turning his back on an opportunity to acquire fabulous personal wealth from what became one of the world's richest treasure chests.

At first, shallow mining was possible, and many small-scale mining operations proliferated along the reefs. But it was not long before the shallow deposits were exhausted, necessitating deep mining. Corporate capital was essential to fund the enormous costs involved. This gave rise to the development of giant mining corporations and stimulated the growth of supply and service industries. Gold mining thus provided South Africa

This map highlights the regional map opposite. Overlapping regions and their page numbers are supplied.

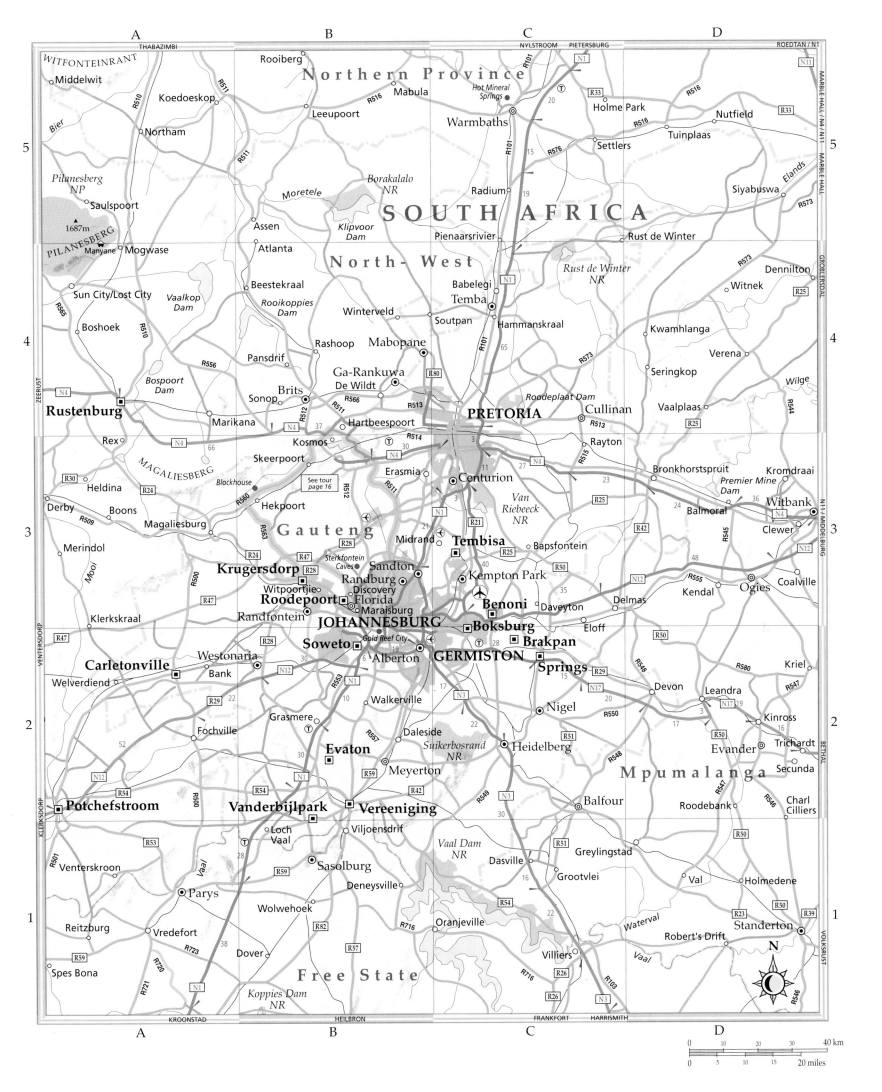

Typical of Johannesburg is this futuristic building in Diagonal Street, site of the country's only stock exchange..

SOUTH AFRICA'S FINANCIAL HEARTLAND

After the war, the Witwatersrand's growth and development resumed. In a little over a century, an uninhabited ridge had been transformed into the largest urban sprawl and industrial complex in Africa. Today it has spread along two axes – the one unbroken for 80 kilometres running east to west, and the other, broken in a few places, between Pretoria in the north and Vanderbijlpark in the south, a distance of some 130 kilometres. Approximately 10 million people live within the neighbouring cities, towns, and suburbs, including the bleak dormitory townships that were specifically designed to house the region's black population under the apartheid regime. Interestingly, this extended metropolitan region is the largest in the world that is not situated around a harbour or on a navigable river with direct access to the sea.

While gold provided the stimulus, it did not alone account for the industrial development of the Gauteng region. The Witwatersrand has easy access to a wide variety of raw material and energy sources, and these have provided the essential ingredients for ongoing economic growth. Readily obtainable iron ore, coal, limestone, vanadium, chrome

with a vital engine of economic growth and focused the centre of the country's development on the cities and towns that sprang up along the ancient gold-bearing reefs. Within nine years of Harrison's discovery, the population of the dusty mining town of Johannesburg had grown from nothing to 80 000. By 1895, Johannesburg had become South Africa's largest town, far greater than Cape Town, established more than 200 years earlier.

THE ANGLO-BOER WAR

Outside the axis of frenzied mining development that took place on the Witwatersrand was Pretoria, at the time the capital of the Zuid-Afrikaansche Republiek (or ZAR). The different perspectives of the residents of Pretoria and the miners on the Witwatersrand eventually led to a physical clash of wills. In 1899, war broke out between Great Britain, which backed the miners and the moguls who financed them, and the ZAR, whose leaders resented the invasion of their territory by an ever-increasing wave of independent-minded foreigners. The Anglo-Boer War grimly continued until 1902, when the Boers finally surrendered. However, while the battles on the veld might have ended and the guns of war fallen silent, the conflict

left the Afrikaners with a legacy of hatred and insecurity. The results of the war therefore did much to fuel Afrikaner sectarian nationalism and the resultant development of the oppressive policy of apartheid.

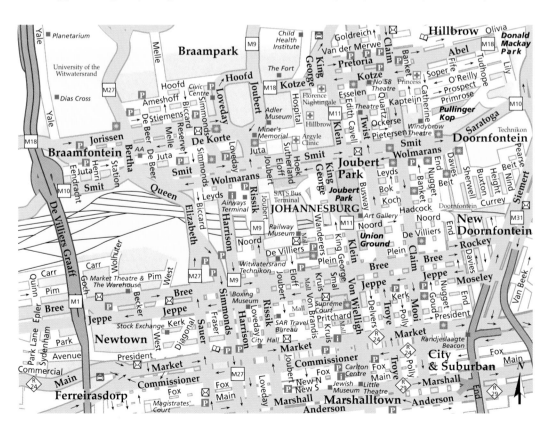

and nickel led to the development of the steel industry; a large steelworks was built by ISCOR (the Iron and Steel Corporation of South Africa) at Pretoria in 1934, and a second in 1944 at Vanderbijlpark, a town built to house the miners. Together these plants produce over two-thirds of the country's steel requirements. Manufacturing industries of all kinds have flourished in association with these major commercial enterprises, and tertiary and service industries have also mushroomed. Today the Gauteng region is undoubtedly the commercial, industrial and financial heartland of South Africa, the centrepiece being the Johannesburg Stock Exchange. Established in 1887 after the discovery of gold on the Witwatersrand, it is the country's only stock exchange.

JOHANNESBURG TODAY

Also known as Egoli, 'the place of gold', Johannesburg is the largest city in southern Africa and the capital of Gauteng. It is typical of most modern industrial cities – its skyline jagged and stepped by slender skyscrapers. Modern road systems ring the metropolis, and rail lines stretch out to surrounding cities and towns. Johannesburg is a restless

city – old buildings constantly give way to higher and larger ones, and the continuous sprawl outwards creates new urban centres, many to the city's north; major shopping centres have already been established at Rosebank, Sandton, Four Ways and Hyde Park, to name a few. Sadly, the growth of the suburbs has meant that much of Johannesburg's central business district, once the hub of city life, has become blighted, unkempt and unsafe. However, attempts have been made to bring life back to the city.

The old Market Precinct, not far from the glittering Johannesburg Stock Exchange, has been converted from a rambling produce market into an exciting and thriving arts centre. Taking centre stage is the acclaimed Market Theatre, established in 1975. The Market Precinct also houses art galleries, restaurants, live music, a wide range of specialty shops and an open-air flea market.

The exciting MuseumAfrica adjoins the complex. Using photographs, artifacts, recreations and music, the museum tells the story of southern Africa and its peoples from the earliest times until the present. South of the city centre, Johannesburg's mining past comes alive at Gold Reef City, a

An optimistic attitude to change has been adopted by many in the 'new' South Africa.

period mining town re-created around the old headquarters and shaft No. 14 of the historic Crown Mines. Visitors can tour the mine, watch demonstrations of gold-pouring and enjoy traditional gumboot dances.

THE EAST RAND

To the east of Johannesburg lies a series of towns and cities that developed as the traces of the main reef were followed east of Harrison's discovery. The area is collectively known as the East Rand. Germiston, the first city east of Johannesburg, is the sixth largest city in South Africa and has one of the country's highest concentrations of heavy engineering and manufacturing industry. It also has Africa's largest railway junction, the world's biggest gold refinery – the Rand Refinery – and the Witwatersrand's largest man-made body of water, the 57-hectare Germiston Lake.

East of Germiston lie the towns of Boksburg, Benoni, Brakpan and Springs. The more attractive of these is Benoni, which was laid out by the Transvaal government in 1881 to serve the surrounding farming community. After the discovery of gold, Sir George Farrar, the chairman of the mining company that acquired most of the land in the area, had many thousands of trees planted, while water from the mines was pumped into the region's marshes, thereby creating wetlands for waterbirds and fish. A number of dams were also built, generating a chain of lakes that today provide opportunities for a variety of water sports. Although Springs owes its origin to the discovery of coal in 1888, it was only when gold was

Traditional dancing is one of many attractions at Gold Reef City, a period mining town south of Johannesburg.

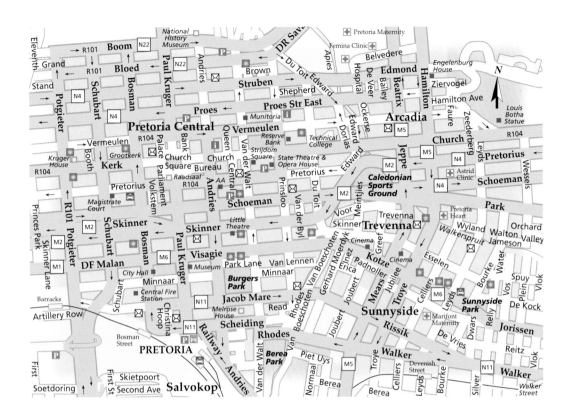

found that Springs was transformed into a rich gold-producing area. Today substantial secondary industries, producing foodstuffs, paper, glass and bicycles, have been created.

THE WEST RAND

A ribbon of towns sprung up on the West Rand following the discovery of gold. Roodepoort came into being after prospecting rights were secured by a certain Jan Bantjes on a farm called Roodepoort. Other settlements that later either grew into towns or suburbs in the area include Florida, Maraisburg, Witpoortjie and Discovery. Each took its name from one of the original farms that had been registered there.

Southeast of Roodepoort lies Soweto, an acronym for SOuth-WEstern TOwnships. Designed for exclusive occupation by black persons, according to the country's erstwhile apartheid policy, sprawling Soweto is the largest 'township' in South Africa. Much of the struggle against apartheid was waged from its dusty streets.

It was here, on 16 June 1976, that students rebelled against the government's demand that certain subjects be taught in Afrikaans. The Soweto riots set in motion a process that eventually culminated in the overthrow of apartheid. Guided tours of Soweto give visitors an intriguing insight into this vast city's everyday life.

Krugersdorp is the principal town of the West Rand, and dates back to the discovery of gold in 1884 in its rocky outcrops. Besides being a rich gold-mining town, Krugersdorp is also an important industrial and commercial centre. The town is the hub of an agricultural region that produces tobacco, dairy products, maize and deciduous fruit. In 1952 the world's first uranium recovery plant was opened at West Rand Consolidated Mines, which produces this material as a by-product of the gold-refining process.

Krugersdorp gained further international prominence for two significant archaeological sites discovered in the district: the Sterkfontein Caves, where *Australopithecus africanus* – the 'missing link' between ape and man – was found; and Kromdraai, 1,5 kilometres from Sterkfontein, where the Kromdraai Palaeontological Reserve has been established. Not far from Krugersdorp is Randfontein, named after the farm purchased by mining financier JB Robinson following the 1886 gold rush. In 1889 Robinson floated the Randfontein Estates Gold Mining Company and Randfontein was created to service the mine. At first it was administered as part of Krugersdorp, but in 1929 Randfontein acquired its own municipal status.

PRETORIA

Built on the bureaucracy of government and public administration, Pretoria has a character all of its own. Situated at a lower altitude than Johannesburg and the Reef towns (*see* p. 13), the city's climate is hotter and its natural vegetation subtropical in nature. Famous for the more than 80 000 jacaranda trees that line its streets, Pretoria is quite aptly known as the 'Jacaranda City'.

From stone implements and the remains of iron smelting found along the banks of the Apies River, in whose two broad and well-sheltered valleys Pretoria is situated, it has been ascertained that people have lived here for at least 350 years. Both Sotho and Ndebele have dwelt here, and, in 1825, Mzilikazi, the renegade Zulu chief who deserted Shaka with a number of followers, established a stronghold on the banks of the Apies. After Shaka located Mzilikazi's whereabouts, he sent his armies to obtain retribution for his desertion. Mzilikazi warded off the attack but left his stronghold and fled to the Marico district.

The jacaranda-lined streets of Pretoria; the city boasts more than 80 000 of these lovely trees.

The magnificent Union Buildings provide offices for the President, senior cabinet ministers and officials. From its elevated site it commands sweeping views over Pretoria.

In 1837 the Voortrekkers discovered the fertile valleys and abundant water of the Apies River and set up a number of farms along its banks. One of the Voortrekkers who was attracted to the region was Andries Pretorius, hero of the battle of Blood River (*see also* p. 42), who established a farm in the valley where the Apies and Crocodile rivers meet. Shortly after his death, the Apies valley was chosen as the site for the capital of the newly created Boer republic, the Zuid-Afrikaansche Republiek (ZAR). Marthinus Pretorius, son of Andries, selected a site for the new town on the farm Elandspoort, and on 16 November 1855 it was proclaimed and named Pretoria in honour of his father.

Pretoria grew up around Church Square, originally the marketplace and focal point of the Boer community, and it is still the hub of the city's social and political scene. Several impressive buildings have been built around the square, such as the Palace of Justice and the old Raadsaal (parliament) of the ZAR. Its centrepiece is the bronze statue of Paul Kruger, who was president of the ZAR. His modest home – Kruger House

Museum – is open to the public. Pretoria is a sedate but handsome city with sophistic-ated shopping malls, several museums and historic buildings, a variety of cultural and scientific institutions, and is home to one of the world's top zoos, the National Zoo-logical Gardens.

Today Pretoria is the administrative and diplomatic capital of South Africa. The most notable of the city's edifices is the Union Buildings, designed by Sir Herbert Baker and built like an acropolis on Meintjieskop above the city. Completed in 1913, this architectural masterpiece provides offices for the Presi-dent and senior government officials. The buildings are closed to the public but visitors can enjoy fine views of the city from the land-scaped, terraced gardens.

Overlooking Fountains Valley is the Uni-versity of South Africa (Unisa), one of the world's biggest correspondence universities. Pretoria's other major educational institution is the University of Pretoria, the country's largest residential university. On a low hill outside the city rises the monolithic Voor-trekker Monument, completed in 1949 to

commemorate the Voortrekkers' pioneering spirit. Some regard it as an important memor-ial to Afrikanerdom, others see it as a reminder of apartheid. Its interior frieze is said to be the second longest in the world.

Melrose House is one of South Africa's finest period museums. It was here that the Peace of Vereeniging was signed in 1902, for-mally ending the bitter Anglo-Boer War.

The huge Voortrekker Monument, commemorating the Great Trek, is a major landmark near Pretoria.

MAGALIESBERG CIRCULAR ❖ 200 km

Black eagles normally produce a clutch of one or two eggs.

WITWATERSRAND BOTANIC GARDEN

On the way from central Johannesburg to the Witwatersrand Botanic Garden, the road passes through Triomf, a suburban community that stands on the site once occupied by Sophiatown, a vibrant, multicultural township, now immortalised in books, plays and songs. In 1955, in keeping with the policy of creating racially-exclusive suburbs,

The spectacular Witpoortjie Waterfall at the Witwatersrand Botanic Garden.

the township was levelled, its inhabitants moved to Soweto and a new suburb called Triomf created. A permanent exhibition on Sophiatown can be viewed at MuseumAfrica. From Maraisburg, the route passes the attractive suburbs of Florida Hills and Constantia Kloof, set against the rocky slopes of the Witwatersrand.

Although the Witwatersrand Botanic Garden is situated in the heart of the country's most densely populated province, it is one of the finest floral reserves. The garden's focal point is the spectacular 70-metre-high Witpoortjie waterfall, formed by water cascading down a rugged ridge of alternating bands of shale and quartzite into a clear pool below. As land purchases and donations have secured the high ridges above the falls and the surrounding protea-covered hills, visitors can explore the 225-hectare garden, with its 500 species of indigenous trees, without being aware of nearby small-holdings and urban sprawl.

Near the entrance complex and gift shop, a path leads downhill to the Sasol Dam and bird hide; the garden is home to over 180 species of bird, including a nesting pair of

black eagles. An interpretative centre, situated near the cycad beds, contains mammal and bird displays, vegetation maps and a short history of the garden. On weekends, many visitors arrive at the garden's restaurant in time for an outdoor breakfast served under shady trees.

KRUGERSDORP

The road gradually ascends the Witwatersrand to Krugersdorp. The road skirts the main business district, but the curious traveller will find it appealing: tall trees grow down the centre of roads which are wide enough to have accommodated ox-wagons in the past, and the City Hall's white facade occupies a prominent place on the central square.

KRUGERSDORP GAME RESERVE

Barely 2 kilometres from the town's outskirts, a turning leads to the entrance of the Krugersdorp Game

Reserve. It is modest in size – only 6 kilometres long and 3 kilometres wide – but sustains a variety of habitats that include grassland, thornveld, riverine forest and rocky outcrop, as well as a great diversity of wildlife. Game – including buffalo, hippo, zebra, giraffe, white rhino and 13 antelope species – tends to concentrate on the lush grasslands in the north of the reserve. Apart from large herds of springbok, eland and blesbok, rare antelope such as tsessebe, roan, sable and black wildebeest are also to be seen. Also occurring in the northern half is a pride of lions, which frequents a separate enclosure set in a thornveld valley.

The Ngonyama Lion Lodge, in a secluded valley in the centre of the reserve, offers guided day and night game-viewing drives. Accommodation is available in rondavels and

The Hartbeespoort Dam, framed by the Magaliesberg's quartzite cliffs.

lodge units, with some overlooking a tranquil dam that is home to a small community of hippos. North of the lodge, a caravan park, restaurant and picnic area have been established.

STERKFONTEIN CAVES On a hillside above the road to Hekpoort, a tree-rimmed shaft leads down an incline into the mysterious subterranean Sterkfontein Caves, formed when dolomite rock was dissolved beneath the water table. A huge underground lake floods the bottom of the caves, and its level varies greatly depending on rain cycles. Discovered by an Italian prospector in 1896, the caves are regarded as one of the world's most important prehistoric sites.

Palaeontologist Dr Robert Broom began his search for apeman, or hominid, fossils at Sterkfontein as early as 1936. In 1947, Broom uncovered the perfectly preserved skull of 'Mrs Ples' – a female specimen believed to be two and half million years old. With over 600 hominid fossils unearthed and catalogued to date, Sterkfontein is the richest *Australopithecus* site in Africa, attracting scientists from around the world. The caves are owned by the

Witwatersrand University and guided tours are offered throughout the day. The soaring Hall of Elephants (23 metres high and 91 metres long) is the largest of Sterkfontein's caverns, some of which can only be accessed through narrow, muddy passages; walking shoes and casual clothes are advisable. On the crest of the hill above the caves, visitors can enjoy a meal at the restaurant, or inspect the excavation of fossils being carried out by university researchers.

RHINO PARK A private establishment on a 1 000-hectare tract of rolling grasslands and hills near Kromdraai, the Rhino Park offers visitors a glimpse into the past, when herds of game roamed the Highveld. A large camp at the park's entrance surrounds several dams where hippos can be seen, and lions inhabit a large hilly enclosure near the chalets. This park is home to a growing population of white rhino, and to big herds of wildebeest, eland, hartebeest and zebra. Animals such as giraffe, sable and buffalo are also present.

Driving along the park's sandy tracks, visitors will also delight in a profusion of birds, such as blue

crane, plover and widow bird; the picnic area – at the highest part of the reserve before the roads circle back to the entrance – has a swimming pool and takeaway outlet.

HEKPOORT VALLEY AND THE MAGALIESBERG Tucked between the parallel ridges of the Magaliesberg and a range of hills to the south, the fertile Hekpoort Valley is a favourite destination for weekend getaways – the bushveld vegetation, inviting river banks and lovely views of the Magaliesberg revive the city-dweller.

To enter the valley, the road passes through a narrow *poort*, or opening, guarded by an old fort. Known as Barton's Folly, it was constructed during the Anglo-Boer War. The fort's unusual architecture differs completely from other bulwarks built by the British, and has been declared a national monument.

Across Hekpoort Valley, the highest point of the Magaliesberg (1 852 metres) overlooks the famous Boer War battle site of Nooitgedacht.

HARTBEESPOORT DAM Completed in 1923, Hartbeespoort Dam (one of the country's oldest dams) is a favourite recreational spot for city-dwellers (*see also* p. 147). Set against the backdrop of the Magaliesberg's sheer quartzite cliffs, the 2 000-hectare lake

backed up behind the dam wall creates a striking scene. Visitors can enjoy a circular drive around the lake; a single-lane road passes through a short tunnel and then continues on top of the 59-metre-high dam wall, guarded by a sandstone arch. Although newer roads such as the N4 and R512 have shortened the journey over the mountains, the route over the dam wall is still the most scenic. Ample parking is available on the western side of the wall and visitors often buy fruit from the vendors there. After good rains have fallen, water cascades down a rocky channel into the Crocodile River below. Attractions at Hartbeespoort include a zoo and snake park, cableway, bird park, yacht clubs, freshwater aquarium, fishing and camping sites, restaurants and chalets.

In the hills above the southern shore, unusual concrete chimneys and several large buildings are evidence of Pelindaba, South Africa's first nuclear research facility. The station, in operation since 1965, achieved fame by developing a new method of enriching uranium; it also conducted advanced experiments in nuclear physics. The capacity to produce nuclear weapons was developed in the 1980s, but all research into the use of nuclear material for military purposes has been stopped.

The perfect weekend getaway, Hartbeespoort Dam offers many leisure options.

THE GREAT NORTH ROAD

A popular health spa and holiday resort, Warmbaths provides a variety of recreational activities.

Orth of Pretoria the country flattens and stretches out like a green carpet as far as the eye can see. The soil is red and rich and is farmed extensively, the main crops being maize, groundnuts, sunflower seed and sorghum. Known as the Springbok Flats, this landscape was created millions of years ago when a great tear ripped down virtually the length of the African continent, forming the Great Rift Valley. Starting at the Red Sea coast, the rift reached dramatic proportions in East Africa, continued south across Zimbabwe and eventually disappeared underground just north of Pretoria.

Molten rock, rich in minerals, was forced up by pressure from the earth's centre and oozed along the crack that the earth's tectonic forces had created. But when it reached the point where the crack disappeared, the molten rock had nowhere else to go but to force its way into every crevice and weak point of the sedimentary rock layers that made up the geological structure known as the Transvaal System. The foundations of the earlier landscape collapsed, causing mountains, hills and valleys to tumble into the gathering lake of molten rock.

When the earth's crust solidified, the smooth surface of a giant petrified lake ringed by distant mountains (the Magaliesberg, Strydpoortberg, Soutpansberg and Pilanesberg of today) remained. The new geological structure created became known as the Bushveld Igneous Complex, and it has presented man with a treasure chest of important raw minerals, among them nickel, tin, chrome, platinum, iron and tungsten.

Bright geometric designs, usually painted by the women of the village, adorn Ndebele homes.

THE SOUTHERN NDEBELE

Around Middelburg, and particularly at Botshabelo Mission Station, are the colourful villages of the Ndebele people. In these villages the walls and surrounding courtyards of the houses have been decorated with brightly painted and distinctive geometric patterns. The Ndebele women, who are invariably the painters and therefore the traditional custodians of the art form, wear colourful clothing made up of beaded skirts, bright blankets and ornate jewellery, fashioned from multicoloured beads, chromed metal, aluminium and brass.

ANCIENT HOT SPRINGS

The road running from Pretoria through the Northern Province to Zimbabwe (*see* p. 162) is commonly known as the Great North Road. On the outskirts of the Springbok Flats it passes through Warmbaths, named after the hot mineral springs found there. Early inhabitants saw a cloud of steam rising over the Bushveld and encountered a spring that yielded 22 000 litres per hour of warm, mineralized water, rich in sodium chloride, calcium carbonate and other minerals. Animals such as elephant and buffalo used to wallow in the mineralized mud, and the springs were later used by Iron Age man. In 1873 the Transvaal government bought the

This map highlights the regional map opposite. Overlapping regions and their page numbers are supplied.

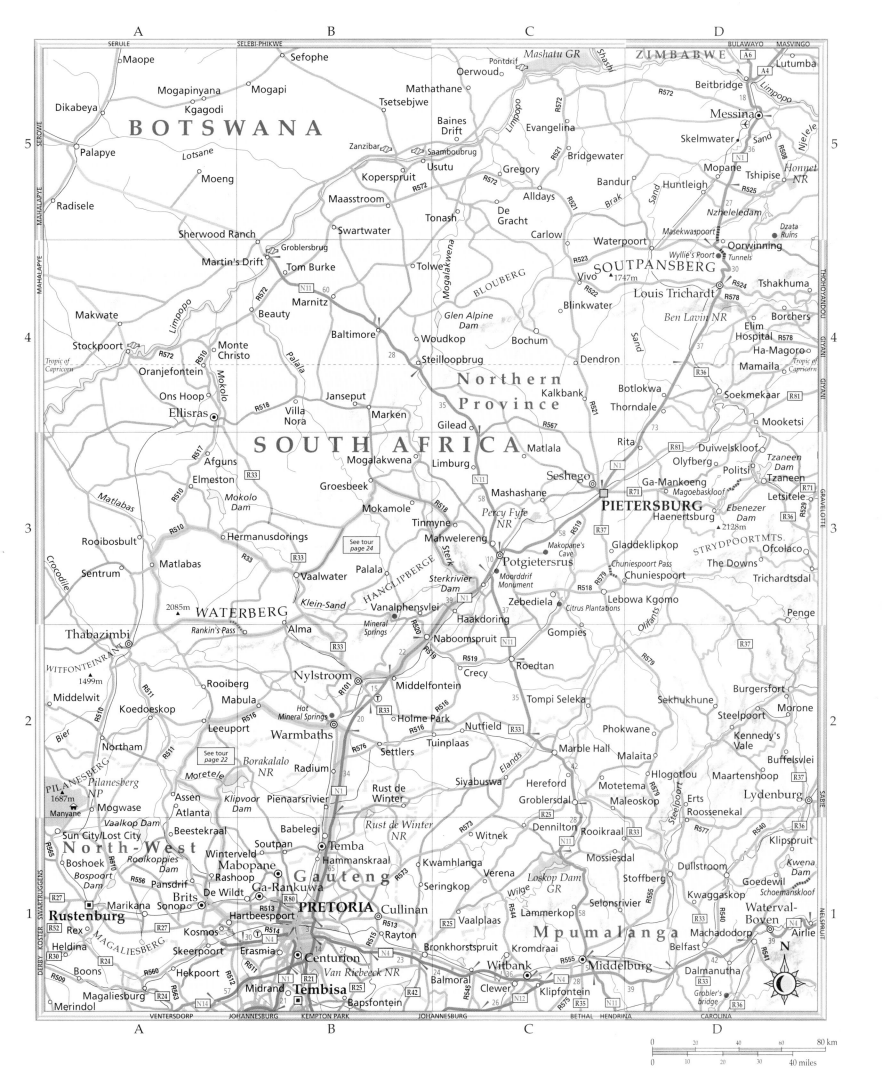

springs and Warmbaths has since grown into a popular health spa and holiday resort with over a quarter of a million visitors annually.

NYLSTROOM AND NABOOMSPRUIT

North of Warmbaths, at the foothills of the Waterberg, lies Nylstroom ('Nile Stream'). It was named in the 1850s by the Voortrekkers who, after consulting the maps in their Bibles, concluded that the north-flowing stream marked the beginning of the Nile River. Their conviction was strengthened by a pointed hillock nearby which these God-fearing pioneers took to be the remains of an ancient pyramid. The town soon developed into the principal centre of the Waterberg district and today serves a large cattle ranching and groundnut community.

Nylstroom is often associated with the gifted journalist, poet, lawyer, doctor, scientist and naturalist, Eugène Marais. After the Anglo-Boer War, Marais withdrew from society and sought refuge in the Waterberg. He studied a troop of baboons for three years and published *The Soul of the Ape*, the first scientific study of primates in the wild.

Flanking the Waterberg, the Great North Road proceeds northwards to Naboomspruit. After a prospector found a tin deposit here in 1910, fortune-seekers flooded into the area and established a settlement on the banks of the Naboomspruit. The tin deposits proved to be disappointing, but the little

Citrus, grown along the Limpopo River near Messina, is an important crop in the area's economy.

The fertile Potgietersrus district yields excellent crops of cotton, as well as maize, groundnuts, wheat and sorghum.

community remained and today serves the surrounding districts. The giant Zebediela Citrus Estate lies some 80 kilometres east of the town. A number of hot springs in the area have encouraged the growth of several popular holiday resorts.

MOORDDRIF MASSACRE

Between Naboomspruit and Potgietersrus the Great North Road passes the memorial at Moorddrif ('murder ford'). Here, in September 1854, a group of 12 Voortrekkers led by Hermanus Potgieter (brother of Andries Potgieter, the Voortrekker leader) were murdered by a band of Tlou warriors, a clan of the Pedi tribe. It is suspected that the Voortrekkers had unwittingly broken a Tlou taboo.

The Tlou chief, Makopane, realizing that revenge would be swift, fled with 2 000 of his followers into what is known today as Makapansgat (meaning 'Makopane's Cave'), some 25 kilometres northeast of Potgietersrus. These limestone caves opened to huge subterranean caverns where Makopane and his followers held out against a Voortrekker siege that lasted 30 days. Hunger and thirst eventually took their toll, and when the burghers stormed the entrance they found over 1 500 bodies. It is believed that the remaining 500 warriors slipped out of the cave under cover of darkness during the early part of the siege.

WATERBERG REGION

Named for its many streams, the Waterberg stretches 140 kilometres across the Northern Province and still retains much of its pristine bushveld quality. The ruggedly beautiful range encircles a high plateau of about 15 000 square kilometres, and has a diversity of habitats ranging from thick sourveld bush to flat, open plains with dense riverine vegetation, especially along the Palala River. These support a wide variety of bird and animal species, which has in turn encouraged a proliferation of game farms and lodges.

Set in a valley between the Waterberg and Strydpoort mountains, Potgietersrus was named after Piet Potgieter, the burgher leader who was killed during the siege at Makapansgat. It is a warm, attractive town, richly endowed with luxuriant subtropical gardens. The surrounding area is prime ranching country, and the most important crops include maize, groundnuts, sorghum, sunflower seed, wheat, cotton and citrus. Just outside town is the Potgietersrus Game Reserve and Breeding Centre, which breeds endangered animals such as tsessebe, black rhino, pygmy hippo and Madagascan lemur.

The capital of the Northern Province is Pietersburg (*see also* p. 30), founded in 1884 and named after Commandant-General Piet Joubert, acting president of the Transvaal at the time. Since then, Pietersburg has built

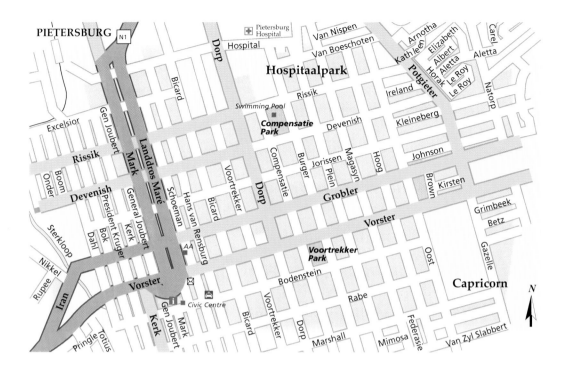

PIETERSBURG

Bold abstract designs decorate the exterior walls of many Venda homes.

up a comprehensive industrial, commercial and financial base. The district's mixed farming economy includes cattle ranching, dairying, poultry and pig-breeding, and the cultivation of green vegetables, potatoes, lucerne, sorghum, maize, beans, groundnuts, sunflower seed and tobacco. About 20 kilometres east of Pietersburg lies the main campus of the University of the North.

SOUTPANSBERG REGION

The Great North Road continues through flat, bush-clad country, occasionally broken by outcrops of huge granite boulders, until it reaches Louis Trichardt. In the distance the impressive Soutpansberg stretches for some 130 kilometres from east to west, with its highest point being Letsumbe at

1 747 metres. The range takes its name from a strong brine spring which has been a source of salt for the region's inhabitants since ancient times. Man has been attracted to the Soutpansberg from the very earliest days and the mountains are rich in history. San (Bushmen) people of the Late Stone Age lived in caves here, leaving rock paintings as a legacy of their passing. The Khoi built shelters on the mountain plateaus, but they were later driven out by the Rozvi-Karanga, an Iron Age people who migrated from the Zimbabwe region in the early 18th century. Attracted by the region's fertility, they called it Venda ('pleasant place') and built settlements that remain to this day.

Rainfall along the Soutpansberg is normally high – up to 2 000 millimetres annually in places – and this, combined with the rich red soil and the Soutpansberg's subtropical location, encouraged the growth of natural forests along the range's watercourses. Today patches of these indigenous forests have been cleared for agriculture or to make way for pine and eucalyptus plantations.

Louis Trichardt (*see also* p. 34), the main commercial and industrial centre of the Soutpansberg region, has a long and bloody history. In 1835, the first Afrikaner settlers from the Cape, led by Hans van Rensburg and Louis Trichardt, trekked further north. But the leaders quarrelled and Van Rensburg

trekked ahead to the Soutpansberg. In 1836, the Van Rensburg party continued eastwards along the Limpopo River only to be massacred by a Zulu regiment. Trichardt's party camped at the site of the present town before venturing on a hazardous route over mountains and uncharted bushveld. They arrived in Lourenço Marques in 1838, but out of 53 Voortrekkers, a total of 27, including Trichardt, died of malaria. It was only in 1899 that an administrative centre for the far northern Transvaal was established and named after Louis Trichardt. Today this vibrant town services a large agricultural district, the principal crops being subtropical fruit, tea, coffee and timber.

Winding through the Soutpansberg above Louis Trichardt, the Great North Road treats the traveller to ever-changing vistas of mountains, forests and distant plains. On the northern side of the range the road twists and turns as it rapidly descends, finally passing through Wyllie's Poort, a narrow gorge with two tunnels. From here the road suddenly opens onto flat, bush-covered plains occasionally punctuated by low-lying hills and baobab trees. Eventually the Great North Road reaches the hot Lowveld town of Messina and the Limpopo River, the frontier between South Africa and Zimbabwe. Rich copper deposits have been extracted in the area since prehistoric times, and several big copper mines have been developed. Iron ore and magnesite are also mined here. Game ranching and agriculture form other important economic activities; the main crops of citrus, subtropical fruit and vegetables are grown under irrigation along the Limpopo.

The monarch of the bushveld – giant baobab trees dot the landscape in the hot, dry Lowveld.

DISTRACTIONS ON THE ROAD NORTH ❖ 380 km

The magnificent king cheetah is marked in black bands instead of the usual spots.

DE WILDT CHEETAH RESEARCH CENTRE Close to Brits and beneath the northern edge of the Magaliesberg lies the De Wildt Cheetah Research Centre, internationally recognised as the world's leading cheetah breeding station. Before Ann van Dyk established the centre in 1971, cheetah births in captivity were virtually unknown. Not only did van Dyk succeed in unravelling the key to cheetah reproduction – with over 400 cheetah cubs born at the centre – but the mystery surrounding the legendary king cheetah was also solved.

Renowned for its beautiful coat marked in black bands instead of the usual spots, the king cheetah was believed to be a separate sub-species. However, in 1981 a king cheetah cub was born at De Wildt to common cheetahs, conclusive proof that this curiosity is caused by a rare recessive gene. Cheetahs bred at De Wildt have been released in the Pilanesberg National Park (*see also* p. 146), and in reserves in Mpumalanga and KwaZulu-Natal. Apart from breeding cheetahs, De Wildt has successfully raised endangered animals such as the suni, riverine rabbit, wild dog and brown hyena for reintroduction to parks throughout southern Africa.

BORAKALALO NATURE RESERVE This reserve lies 64 kilometres from Brits. As the route to Borakalalo is not signposted, follow the tarred road north of Jericho to a sharp left turn which leads along Borakalalo's boundary fence for 7 kilometres to the entrance gate. Borakalalo, meaning 'the place where people relax' in Setswana, is a picturesque 15 000-hectare reserve. It surrounds the sickle-shaped 760-hectare Klipvoor Dam on the Moretele River and boasts an astonishing variation in vegetation. Silverleaf trees and acacias are common in the south, combretums clothe the hills near the dam wall, and tall seringas grow on the sandy soils to the west. The eastern half of the park has been set aside as a wilderness area, but a network of game-viewing roads – which can be negotiated in a sedan car – crisscross the rest of the reserve.

Guided walks are available at Borakalalo, which is home to over 30 species of large mammals, including elephant, white rhino, giraffe, zebra, buffalo, sable, roan, eland, tsessebe and kudu. Elusive leopard, brown hyena, jackal and otter are also sometimes seen, and early morning and late afternoon are the best game-viewing times. The game-viewing hide at Sefudi Dam is an ideal spot to photograph animals coming to drink.

Klipvoor Dam is much favoured by fishermen. As boating on the dam is prohibited, hippos and water birds, such as hamerkop, spurwing goose, jacana and redbilled teal, are easily sighted. The main road leads along the western shore of the dam to an attractive picnic site.

Accommodation is available at the exquisite Moretele Camp, perfectly situated in dense woodland on the banks of the Moretele River. This unfenced camp consists of a number of camp sites and safari tents, and is a popular retreat for serious birdwatchers; over 300 bird species have been recorded in the reserve, including crested barbet, grey lourie, forktailed drongo, blackeyed bulbul and arrowmarked babbler.

After leaving Borakalalo, common forms of transport seen on the dirt road are donkey carts and bicycles.

MABULA GAME RESERVE Less than a 90-minute drive on the N1 from central Pretoria, the Mabula Game Reserve is an ideal destination for tourists on a tight schedule. Visitors are only permitted to drive from the entrance gate to the camps in the northern half of the 12 000-hectare reserve. But guests can join game drives led by rangers, or they can opt for a walk to a hide, a night drive or a bush walk through sour bushveld. Mabula offers the unusual opportunity to view game from horseback, which allows visitors to approach to within a few metres of the animals. Apart from 18 species of antelope, wildlife such as giraffe, elephant, hippo, crocodile, buffalo, zebra and white rhino can also be seen. Lions are housed in a separate enclosure, but the owners intend to enlarge the reserve until sufficient space is available to support these predators. Birdlife includes drongo, pearlspotted owl and bunting.

The comfortable main lodge and three smaller camps are operated as timeshare units. The Sunset Hill camp, on the crest of the Groenkop Hills that cut through the reserve, offers guests superb views towards the distant Waterberg.

One of the game-viewing options at Mabula is a guided bush walk.

MABALINGWE NATURE RESERVE

Situated 8 kilometres after the turn-off to Mabula and tucked into the foothills of the Hoekberg, Mabalingwe's 6 400 hectares supports a rich diversity of wildlife, including 17 antelope species, hippo, white rhino and elephant. Several dams have been constructed along the river flowing through the reserve, creating extensive water features, the main focus of Mabalingwe. A number of camps overlook these dams.

The largest camp, Ingwe, is ideally situated on the wooded crest of a boulder-strewn hill. A footpath leads down the hill to the swimming pool and squash and tennis courts, which adjoin a small dam inhabited by crocodiles. A secluded spa bath, set among the boulders at Ingwe camp, offers a commanding view over much of this lovely reserve.

Mabalingwe can be explored from open game-viewing vehicles provided by the resort and accompanied by a ranger, or visitors can stalk game on foot in the company of an experienced tracker. As the bushveld can be hot in summer, guests can cool off in a number of refreshing swimming pools at the camps.

WARMBATHS

A popular resort town that is renowned for its therapeutic mineral springs, Warmbaths is considered to be one of the most modern resorts in the world. It features a large indoor pool fitted with underwater jets, a plunge pool, a rheumatic bath and hydrotherapy section, and a fully equipped gymnasium. Large outdoor hot and cold swimming pools, wave pools, water slides and tennis courts cater for the energetic visitor. Accommodation consists of comfortable self-contained chalets and caravan sites, and several restaurants and takeaway outlets provide refreshments.

Although relatively small, the adjoining Warmbaths Nature Reserve conducts game-viewing drives where waterbuck, kudu and Burchell's zebra may be seen.

Warmbaths Spa, with its warm mineral springs, attracts more than a million visitors each year.

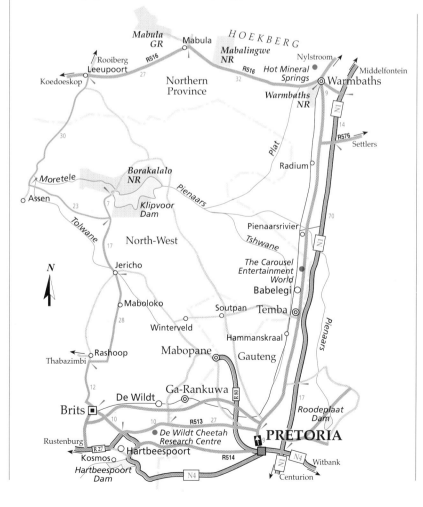

THE CAROUSEL

Extensive beds of colourful roses and cannas greet visitors at the entrance to the Carousel, a large casino and entertainment complex located just off the N1, about 50 kilometres south of Warmbaths. The resort takes its name from the magnificent carousel which occupies centre stage in the entertainment wing.

A large fountain and glass-roofed dome dominates the Carousel's foyer. Inside the Carousel, the cool interior, decorative floor tiles, pillars, soft lights and fountains create a wonderfully unusual blend of American casino and Victorian arcade. Aside from the slot machines, the Carousel contains a hotel, fast food outlets, restaurants, movie theatres, computer games, clothing boutiques and candy shops. Children can ride on the wooden horses of the carousel, and dozens of computer-generated rides, such as motorbike and helicopter adventures and Wild West shootouts, provide exciting entertainment for both young and old.

THE WATERBERG EXPLORER ❖ 520 km

DOORNDRAAI DAM NATURE RESERVE
From Naboomspruit, the Waterberg's densely wooded foothills make way for wide open spaces and a region embracing game farms, nature reserves and hot springs. Prickly pear hawkers and donkey carts are often seen along the way.

The tarred road to Sterkrivier leads off the N1 towards Doorndraai, curving through an unspoilt range of wooded hills with the 1 768-metre-high Hanglip peak dominating the horizon. Visitors will delight in Doorndraai's unhurried tranquillity. The 7 229-hectare reserve surrounds the Doorndraai Dam, which stretches upriver for 12 kilometres. Motor boats are restricted to the dam's eastern half, and waterskiing, windsurfing, canoeing and yachting are also allowed. Fishing is permitted, the most common catches being yellowfish, barbel, carp and kurper. Two camp sites are sited near the dam wall. A single track from the entrance gate follows the southern shore through sour bushveld of silverleaf, acacia and combretum trees. Wildlife present includes sable, tsessebe, kudu, wildebeest, zebra, giraffe and leopard. A two-day, 30-kilometre circular hiking trail traversing the scenic Waterberg foothills offers an easily affordable wilderness experience.

The D794 to the Waterberg leads through a rugged, mountainous area characterised by streams and a wealth of indigenous trees.

LAPALALA WILDERNESS AND TOUCHSTONE GAME RANCH
The 24 000-hectare Lapalala Wilderness and adjacent 17 500-hectare Touchstone Game Ranch include 40 kilometres of the beautiful Lephalala River which rises in the Waterberg to the south and cuts a scenic gorge across the Palala Plateau.

At Lapalala visitors overnight in small camps overlooking the Lephalala and Blockland rivers. Lapalala's wilderness philosophy encourages guests to explore the surroundings on foot and driving is therefore not allowed. Visitors can also stay at Kolobe Lodge to the south, which offers rondavel accommodation and a swimming pool, or at the Rhino tented camp on the Blockland River. These two camps are situated within a 5 000-hectare rhino sanctuary – where game drives are permitted – and it was in this area that five black rhino were released in 1990. Lapalala, the first private reserve in South Africa to obtain black rhino, now has 13 of these magnificent creatures and white rhino, hippo and the endangered roan antelope have also been released. Abundant birdlife includes goldenbreasted bunting, hamerkop, redcrested korhaan and grey lourie.

On the neighbouring Touchstone Game Ranch, three- to seven-day wilderness trails on horseback allow guests to observe wildlife from close quarters. Guided walks and game drives reveal tsessebe, elephant, giraffe, buffalo, waterbuck and leopard, and if exceptionally lucky, cheetah and wild dog. Birders should look out for black eagle, Cape vulture, hoopoe and secretarybird.

Touchstone has several intimate camps and future plans include the opening of a luxury game lodge.

MELKRIVIER TO VAALWATER
From Melkrivier the road crosses the Palala Plateau's sour bushveld and passes several reserves en route. Near Melkrivier the 400-hectare Waterberg Game Reserve caters for nature-lovers who may ramble freely over the property. The 1 400-hectare Nyathi Game Reserve, 17 kilometres from Melkrivier, protects antelope, white rhino and giraffe. Two small camps and an outdoor bar are added attractions. The extensive Triple B ranch, a cattle and game farm, offers horse and walking trails. Hikers' accommodation is available in rustic cottages, and the enchanting thatched guest cottages, Windsong and Rainbow, cater for other visitors.

Ten kilometres before Vaalwater, a road leads to Vier-en-twintig Riviere. Although there is only a trading store, it is well worth a stop, if only for a stroll or picnic in the silverleaf woodland. An anomaly in this isolated wilderness is the St John the Baptist Anglican Church near Vier-en-twintig Riviere. Built in 1914 on land donated by the Fawsett sisters, who commissioned Herbert Baker to design the church, it is reached along an avenue of bluegums and conifers.

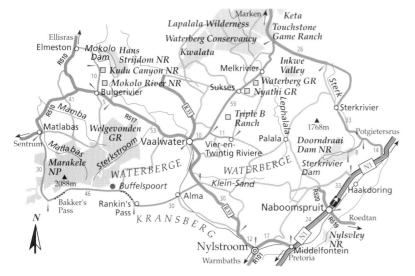

An unusual feature of Vaalwater is the spreading wild fig tree that has been left in the centre of Davidson Street (one block south of the Melkrivier road). The Zeederberg Cottage and Vaalwater Hotel are good venues to enjoy Waterberg hospitality.

VAALWATER TO BULGERIVIER From Vaalwater the R33 heads northwest and after 24 kilometres, passes the entrance to Welgevonden Private Game Reserve, a 25 500-hectare reserve which shares a 22-kilometre boundary with Marakele National Park. Three rivers flow across Welgevonden and the reserve supports a rich diversity of wildlife. The first adult elephants to be relocated from the Kruger National Park were released here. A few small camps offer accommodation, with one – Bobbejaan se Biertuin ('Baboon's Beer Garden') – on a ridge above the Suikerbos River.

After 26 kilometres Bulgerivier's sole building – a vibrant purple post office and trading store – suddenly appears. From here a dirt road leads to the Mokolo (formerly Hans Strijdom) Dam and the surrounding 3 600-hectare provincial reserve.

Upstream from the dam, two nature reserves occupy the rugged plateau country bordering the Mokolo River. The 2 200-hectare Kudu Canyon Reserve accommodates visitors in self-catering lodges and camp sites. Attractions include game-viewing drives to spot white rhino, buffalo and antelope, and cruises on the adjacent Mokolo Dam. The adjoining 7 000-hectare Mokolo River Nature Reserve provides an exclusive bush experience for up to 10 guests. It supports a small herd of elephant and many antelope.

MATLABAS TO MARAKELE The R510 crosses 30 kilometres of unspoilt bushveld before reaching the isolated community of Matlabas. In sharp contrast to the dry bushveld are the perennial Mamba and Matlabas rivers, and the source of these is in the distant, high Waterberg. Matlabas has just two buildings: the impressive Dutch Reformed Church, built in 1932, and the police station.

After Matlabas the thick bushveld plains are soon dominated by the Waterberg's rugged quartzite peaks. The two highest summits (2 088 and 2 004 metres) form part of the Marakele National Park. Halfway along the route the D928 skirts the dramatic table-top Kransberg, also part of Marakele. Marakele was developed as an alternative 'Big Five' destination to the Kruger National Park. Buffalo, giraffe, zebra, tsessebe, eland, hartebeest, roan, sable, hippo, white and black rhino, and elephant have been introduced. Birds to be seen include redbilled oxpecker and black eagle, as well as the country's largest breeding colony of Cape vulture. At present Marakele is accessible only by 4x4 vehicle, and it has a tented camp on the Matlabas River.

BAKKERS PASS TO ALMA At the four-way intersection 30 kilometres from Matlabas, the D794 traverses some of the Waterberg region's most spectacular scenery. After ascending densely wooded terrain to the crest of Bakkers Pass, the road follows the base of the Waterberg's imposing cliffs for 12 kilometres. After 17 kilometres, the Kransberg Hiking Trail's comfortable

The Mokolo River carves a craggy chasm through the Kudu Canyon Reserve.

overnight hut can be seen on the left. Walkers can choose between three one-day trails which explore the surrounding mountain slopes.

The road then curves through a magnificent amphitheatre, dominated by towering quartzite cliffs. Further on lies the farm Buffelspoort, known for its fascinating *skilpad*, a hill resembling a giant tortoise. Izell's Cottage, set on Buffelspoort, is ideal for a peaceful weekend getaway. Hippo occupy the dam on the farm, and guests can relax while birdwatching or by walking on the farm.

Herds of blesbok roam the grasslands bordering the D794 before the road negotiates another scenic pass. At the T-junction, 6 kilometres further, a left turn leads to the two-store hamlet of Rankin's Pass. Unobstructed views of the Waterberg range are afforded en route to the tiny village of Alma. From here, a road marked Heuningfontein leads for 29 kilometres to the main R33 to Nylstroom.

NYLSTROOM The town of Nylstroom has nurtured several prominent Afrikaners, among them General Christiaan Beyers; architect Gerhard Moerdijk (designer of the Voortrekker Monument, *see also* p. 15); and the naturalist and writer, Eugène Marais. When Prime Minister DF Malan retired in October 1954, JG Strijdom, MP for the Waterberg and a Nylstroom advocate, succeeded him. Strijdom's residence in Church Street has been preserved as a museum.

Where the N1 crosses the Klein-Nyl River, a concrete dam forms an attractive water feature, and is the focal point of a tree-lined park that houses a bird sanctuary, swimming pool and caravan park. The steam locomotive *Nylstroom*, one of the first to haul carriages along the *Spoorwegtmaatskappij Beperkt* railway line from Pretoria to Nylstroom, can be viewed at the town's railway station. Every January a grape festival promotes the local table grape industry, and visitors can tour a groundnut factory and a peanut butter factory.

THE EASTERN ESCARPMENT AND LOWVELD

South Africa's northeastern corner is defined by two very different landscapes: the eastern Escarpment, a dramatic mountain wall of great beauty and soft edges; and the Lowveld, a densely covered, flat bushveld plain, blasted by the sun's intense heat, lying less than 600 metres above sea level. With an annual rainfall of more than 1 000 millimetres in places, the subtropical Lowveld becomes a humid oven at the height of summer.

Together the rolling mountains of the Escarpment and the sweeping carpet of game-rich Lowveld bush a thousand metres below present the traveller with an ever-changing kaleidoscope of scenic masterpieces. This is the land that inspired Rider Haggard's famous book *She*, and which provided much material for *King Solomon's Mines* and *Allan Quartermain*.

Here, over many exciting and adventurous years, hunters, slave raiders, itinerant traders, prospectors, warrior armies, transport riders and others passed, left their sometimes imperceptible imprint and disappeared into history, legend or mystery.

The triplet peaks of the Three Rondavels dominate the breathtaking Blyde River Canyon.

As many as 2 000 lions are protected in the Kruger Park. A lion sighting is a highlight for most visitors.

EASTERN ESCARPMENT

Rivers and their tributaries winding down from the Highveld plateau, some 200 kilometres north (*see also* p. 10), have eroded deep and twisted valleys through the Escarpment's edge, creating vistas of majestic beauty along its entire 300-kilometre length. In places these rivers tumble over cliffs and down rocky walls as spectacular waterfalls and cascades, many of which were held sacred by the region's early inhabitants.

One of Africa's scenic gems is the dramatic canyon of the Blyde River, a rugged gorge some 800 metres below the Escarpment's crest. The river winds its way downwards to the Blyderivierspoort Dam where the 22 667-hectare Blyderivierspoort Nature Reserve has been established. Dominating the canyon are the triplet peaks known as the Three Rondavels, and in the distance lies the flat-topped summit of Mariepskop (at a height of 1 944 metres).

Another highlight in the area is God's Window, a gap in the Escarpment that gives visitors unforgettable views across the broad sweep of the Lowveld. Close by is the Lowveld Panorama and Nature Reserve, where paths wind through indigenous flowering

This map highlights the regional map opposite. Overlapping regions and their page numbers are supplied.

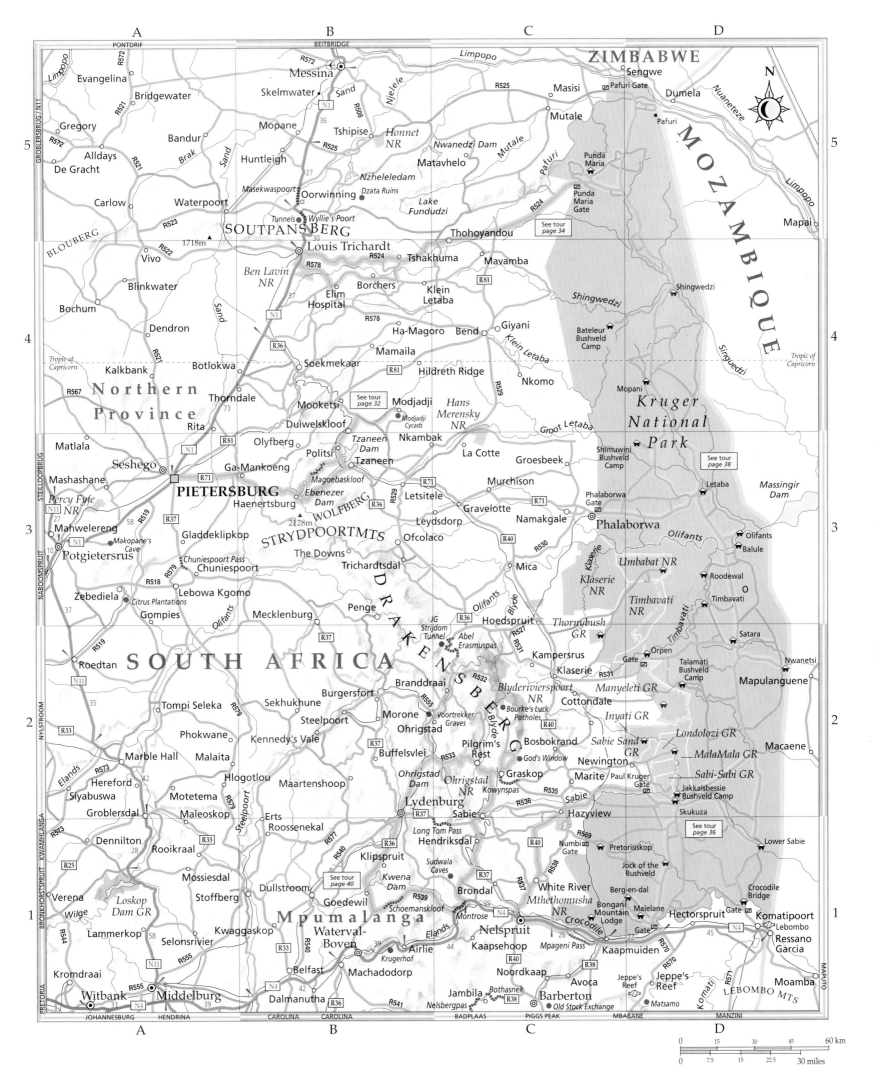

plants and trees. Further north, at the confluence of the Blyde and Treur rivers, the scouring of water-borne pebbles over countless centuries has carved out a collection of surreal rock shapes known as the Bourke's Luck Potholes – named after a miner, Tom Bourke, who struck it lucky at a mine he opened nearby.

The picturesque forestry town of Sabie, situated on the edge of the Escarpment at an altitude of 1 060 metres, began as a wood-and-corrugated-iron gold mining camp. In 1895 a group of friends picnicking on a farm owned by Henry Glynn indulged in some carefree target practice along the Sabie River, where they discovered traces of gold. A mining company was quickly formed and the town's first streets were laid out. By the time the mine closed nearly 60 years later, the town had also become the centre of the most extensive timber plantations in the country. Today Sabie's lush greenery, ideal climate, spectacular waterfalls and many outdoor pursuits stimulate a booming tourist industry.

Much of the indigenous vegetation of the Escarpment – the riverine forests in the valleys and the grasslands on the mountain slopes – has been cleared to make way for extensive plantations of exotic trees destined to feed the country's pulp and paper mills.

A region of unrivalled scenic splendour: Mpumalanga boasts the surrealistically shaped Bourkes Luck Potholes (top) and the beautiful Forest Falls (above) near Sabie, as well as a host of other natural wonders.

IN SEARCH OF GOLD

The discovery of alluvial gold in the streams of the eastern Escarpment provided South Africa with one of the most fascinating chapters in its history. From the time the first Europeans landed on the shores of this subcontinent, the belief grew that a fabulous treasure trove of the yellow metal lay waiting to be discovered in a hidden corner of the 'Dark Continent'. In 1658, only six years after landing at the Cape, Jan van Riebeeck commissioned the first gold-seeking expedition. From then on the hunt for gold was a constant preoccupation for those who journeyed into the interior.

In 1853 the first systematic search for the precious metal took place in the then Transvaal. Traces were found along the banks of the Crocodile River, which drains the northern slopes of the gold-rich Witwatersrand (*see also* p. 10). A motley army of prospectors scoured the rivers of the Transvaal intermittently for the next 20 years, often finding just enough to stir fortune-seekers into frenzied gold rushes. All too often these rushes were short-lived, and the frustrating search for the mother lode would resume.

PILGRIM'S REST

On 6 February 1873 a Scotsman named Tom McLachlan found his El Dorado. While prospecting along a small creek in the Spitzkop area near the Blyde River, he panned a 2,5-ounce nugget of gold. McLachlan's find triggered a massive gold rush centring on a place, it is said, that he and his partner William Trafford called Pilgrim's Rest. There are no records to confirm the origin of the town's name; some say it was not McLachlan who found the original gold, but an irascible loner, Alec 'Wheelbarrow' Patterson (named because he carried all his possessions in a wheelbarrow), who panned the first gold in the area. Patterson allegedly lamented 'Here comes another pilgrim to his rest' when each newcomer invaded his world. Others say it was Trafford who exclaimed 'The pilgrim is at rest' when he saw the incredible riches lying in his pan.

Pilgrim's Rest soon became a bustling town with a number of inns, several bawdy bars and general dealer shops. The infant town even had its own newspaper, *The Gold News*, later renamed *The Gold Field's Mercury*. By 1876 most of the alluvial gold had been found; prospectors then went underground, excavating along the leaders and reefs from which the gold had originally been eroded. Few of the prospectors could tolerate working within the confines of a structured mining company and so they moved on to try their luck along other rivers and valleys of the region. The Transvaal Gold Mining Estates Company continued to mine the deeper reefs at Pilgrim's Rest until 1972. After the mine closed, the entire village was purchased by the state and declared a national monument. It still supports a few hundred permanent residents and provides the visitor with a delightful living museum.

GOLD RUSH FEVER

Spurred on by the finds at Pilgrim's Rest, an ever-increasing band of prospectors scoured the rivers that drain the eastern Escarpment. It was not long before they struck gold once again. On 21 June 1884, Graham Barber discovered a rich reef in Rimer's Creek in the De Kaap Valley. Three days later, when the commissioner of mines visited the site, he broke a bottle of gin over the reef, named it Barberton (*see also* p. 74) and a boom town was born as more discoveries were made.

By 1886 over 4 000 claims were being worked and the town's population swelled daily as makeshift hotels and rowdy taverns mushroomed in the wake of the euphoria that accompanied each new find. At one time Barberton could boast of one tavern for every 15 citizens. New businesses were opened and two stock exchanges created to float new ventures and trade in stocks and shares.

The Barberton goldfields were the world's richest at that time. The town was the scene of frenetic wheeling and dealing as investors from all over the world (particularly Britain) vied for stock. Many unscrupulous rogues took advantage of this to float bogus companies. Mining results soon lagged far behind expectations, losses mounted and confidence in the Barberton goldfields sagged. But just as disillusionment set in came news from the Witwatersrand of the discovery of the fabulous gold reef that would establish the world's largest goldfields (*see also* p. 10). South Africa had found a new El Dorado and Barberton almost became a ghost town overnight.

Fortunately, the faltering town had other strengths and today Barberton is the centre of an important agricultural and forestry district, in which the main crops are subtropical fruit, tobacco, citrus fruit, vegetables,

Emerald-green tea bushes (top and above) *cover the lower slopes of the lush eastern Escarpment with its subtropical climate and abundantly rich soils. The area is also ideal for cultivating fruit and vegetables.*

*The striking impala lily (*Adenium obesum*) favours dry regions such as the Kruger Park.*

rice and pecan nuts. Large bluegum and pine plantations supply the forestry industry. Gold is still mined in a small way, and a variety of other minerals have also been identified in the area. These include nickel, asbestos, titanium, copper, mercury, magnesite, chrome, barytes, verdite and a variety of semiprecious stones.

THE SCENIC ROUTE

Farther north, where the Wolkberg crosses the Escarpment, lies Magoebaskloof. Here the road from Pietersburg crosses the mountains on the way to Tzaneen, and the sheer beauty of the countryside makes it one of the most popular scenic drives in South Africa. As the road winds through the often mist-covered mountains (hence the name Wolkberg, or 'cloudy mountains'), it passes through tall natural forests and pine plantations, broken in places to allow the traveller to stop and view the spectacular scenery.

At the foot of the Escarpment the road passes two large tea-producing estates, Grenshoek and Middelkop, which have been developed by the Industrial Development Corporation. The closely planted and neatly trimmed tea bushes cover the lower slopes of the mountains with a gently rolling carpet of dense green foliage.

REALM OF THE RAIN QUEEN

Just north of Tzaneen lies Duiwelskloof, where the Molototsi River has carved a deep valley in the mountains. In this valley Modjadji, the Rain Queen of the Lobedu tribe, lives and reigns in secrecy. Locals believe that for over 400 years she and her ancestors have held sway over the rain that falls in this part of the world.

According to oral tradition, a princess of the Karanga empire in Zimbabwe bore an illegitimate child and was banned from the royal household. She fled south with her followers, taking with her the tribe's rain-making equipment and the secrets of the ruling family. When the fugitives reached the fertile valley of the Mololotsi River, they settled there and the princess applied her power to make rain. Her success gave her and her descendants mystic powers with which not even Shaka's Zulu warriors dared tamper. Modjadji's mystique, the inspiration for Rider Haggard's *She*, was scoffed at by some but nevertheless lingers on in this bewitching valley.

Today, on the northeast-facing slopes above the Rain Queen's residence, the Modjadji Nature Reserve protects one of only two known cycad forests in the world, the cycads being the tallest in South Africa.

THE LOWVELD

World-renowned for the Kruger National Park (*see* p. 31), the Lowveld has abundantly rich soils and a climate that is ideal for the cultivation of subtropical vegetables and fruits, such as avocados, pawpaws, bananas, litchis, mangoes, granadillas, pecan nuts, tomatoes and citrus. Sugar cane, tobacco and even coffee is also grown in the region.

Nelspruit, the capital of the province of Mpumalanga, is a thriving, bustling town whose streets are softened by trees and shrubs which provide splashes of brilliant colour during the flowering season. The Lowveld National Botanic Gardens protects dense vegetation along the Crocodile River. The town provides a good stopover for visitors en route to the Kruger.

Another important and expanding centre in the Lowveld is the mining town of Phalaborwa, established in 1957 on the borders of the Kruger National Park to exploit rich mineral deposits. Here, a 20-square kilometre 'pipe' rich in phosphates, copper, vermiculite, iron and other minerals was created by volcanic action some 2 000 million years ago. Archaeologists have found from the remains of diggings in the area that copper and iron were mined there by Iron Age man for many centuries.

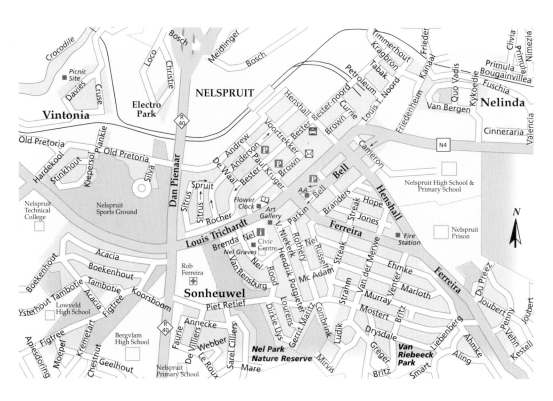

KRUGER NATIONAL PARK

On 26 March 1898, Paul Kruger, president of the Zuid-Afrikaansche Republiek, signed a proclamation declaring the area between the Sabie and Crocodile rivers a game reserve and nature sanctuary. The new Sabie Game Reserve (forerunner of the Kruger National Park) made a major statement for nature conservation. Greatly enlarged since its founding, the Kruger now covers 19 633 square kilometres, occupying an area about the size of Israel. It contains more than 200 species of trees, and is home to over 450 bird, 147 mammal, 115 reptile, 50 fish and 33 frog species, as well as a seemingly endless variety of insects. Kruger's ecological zonation and species diversity make the park an extraordinary place, well served by superb rest camps and a good road network. Despite the huge numbers of people that visit the park, it has many remote corners for those who seek the solitude and spiritual healing of the African bush.

The Kruger's impressive wildlife line-up includes the stately elephant (top), *and numerous herds of zebra and impala* (above).

Haenertsburg's landscape is coloured by a profusion of brilliant azaleas.

UNIVERSITY OF THE NORTH Just outside Pietersburg the countryside is dominated by the typical short grasses and stunted trees of the Pietersburg plateau, with the imposing peaks of the Wolkberg and Magoebaskloof in the distance. A little further on, near Turfloop, the University of the North occupies an extensive site, offering a fine view of the mountains and the surrounding rocky *koppies* (hillocks). One of three universities established exclusively for black students in accordance with apartheid policy, the now-multiracial institution came into being in 1960.

MORIA CITY Where the road begins to descend through a rugged landscape of boulders, hills and aloes, an orderly village and a giant star on the hillside denote the headquarters of the Zion Christian Church, one of South Africa's largest Christian denominations. Zionist members typically wear a silver star and a green ribbon above a shirt pocket. During the Easter weekend each year, almost 3 million worshippers converge on Moria for the open-air services, purporting to be the biggest annual gathering of Christian worshippers.

HAENERTSBURG Named after a German explorer who discovered gold in the nearby hills in 1880, the attractive, peaceful village of Haenertsburg was laid out on the edge of the Escarpment overlooking the wooded hills of Magoebaskloof. Situated at a lofty altitude of 1 400 metres, visitors can enjoy

lovely views from all over the village, and the near-perfect climate encourages the growth of a profusion of flowers. Extensive timber plantations cover much of the area.

Adjacent to the Town Board offices, a circular monument honours all South Africans who have died in war. In the centre of the monument, fragments of the last 155-millimetre Long Tom cannon used by Boer forces during the Anglo-Boer War point to the hillside across the valley where the artillery piece was once placed.

MAGOEBASKLOOF From Haenertsburg the road passes between the tranquil Troutwaters and Stanford lakes where fishing, canoeing and paddle-boating can be enjoyed. Beyond the Magoebaskloof Hotel, the breathtaking Magoebaskloof Pass – one of the most popular scenic routes in South Africa – enters a dense patch of lush indigenous forest before commencing the abrupt descent down the Escarpment.

The densely wooded Magoebaskloof boasts both indigenous and exotic forests.

Dropping a dramatic 610 metres in less than 6 kilometres, the road winds steeply through plantations of tall bluegum trees. Several outlooks near the top of the pass afford superb views over the surrounding countryside.

DEBEGENI FALLS AND WOODBUSH FOREST From the R71 a dirt road leads past experimental plantations of indigenous yellowwood and red mahogany, with signboards indicating the species and the year the trees were planted. The road then passes through patches of dense indigenous forest before reaching the dramatic Debegeni Falls, or 'place of the big pot', a reference to the deep pool at the waterfall's base. The Politsi River tumbles in a spectacular 80-metre cascade down a smooth boulder face, making Debegeni one of South Africa's most beautiful waterfalls. It is a popular picnic spot, and tables arranged below the falls can be reached by a footbridge crossing the river. Although visitors swim in the lower pools, it is wise to be cautious as the smooth rocks are very slippery.

Beyond Debegeni Falls, the road enters Woodbush, the largest indigenous forest in the Northern Province protecting over 40 species of tree, including Natal mahogany, yellowwood, redwood and ironwood. The only known sightings in South Africa of the blackfronted bushshrike were made here. From the old De Hoek Forest Station, the three-day Magoebaskloof Hiking Trail, traversing plantations and forests, begins.

A couple of kilometres beyond the turning to Debegeni, the road crosses Sapekoe's Middelkop estate, one of only six locations in South Africa where tea is grown. The company's name is derived from the Chinese word *pekoe*, meaning tea. Sapekoe conducts regular tours of the estate and factory, followed by a cup of freshly brewed tea.

DUIWELSKLOOF Early residents chose the name of Duiwelskloof – the 'devil's ravine' – after battling against the high rainfall and resultant sticky mud which hindered wagon traffic. This quaint town, with its compact business district, has attractive gardens surrounded by hillsides of timber plantations and indigenous forest. Higher up the slope on the edge of the town, a swimming pool, sports fields, rondavels and camping sites are some of the attractions of the Duiwelskloof Holiday Resort. Tall specimens of the red mahogany grow here and resound with the call of the beautiful purplecrested lourie.

The Debegeni Falls cascade into a pool known as 'the place of the big pot'.

SUNLAND BAOBAB Ten kilometres north of Duiwelskloof, a worthwhile diversion is to follow the signpost to the colossal Sunland baobab tree, one of the largest in the Northern Province. At the Sunland Nursery, a narrow doorway in the gnarled trunk of this hollow baobab leads into a cosy pub. An entrance fee is charged.

MODJADJI CYCADS Modjadji, the 16th-century Karanga princess and Rain Queen, was able to weave spells that brought or withheld rain. Her

direct descendants continue the royal line and have inherited her rain-making abilities. The Modjadji Nature Reserve is on a northeast-facing slope above the Rain Queen's residence. It protects one of only two known cycad forests in the world. Thousands of cycads of a single species, *Encephalartos transvenosus*, cluster together to form a dense forest. Often referred to as the 'Modjadji palms', these cycads are the tallest specimens found in South Africa and may grow up to 13 metres in height. A road through the reserve leads to a picnic site, kiosk and braai areas, where superb views over the forest and the Lowveld are afforded. The characteristic round, thatched huts of Lobedu settlements are visible in the valley below. From the picnic site, a network of walking trails leads through the cycad forest.

Had it not been for the Lobedu's reverence of the Rain Queen – for whom the forest is sacred – the Modjadji cycads would undoubtedly have been plundered long ago. A small museum houses a display on the Rain Queen, but photographs are strictly forbidden. A guard at the exit searches cars to ensure that nobody removes a cycad from the reserve.

TZANEEN The most likely origin of Tzaneen's name is the Pedi word *tsaneng*, meaning 'the happy land'. It is a pleasant, tropical town surrounded by mountainous countryside, and is situated on the ecological boundary between the Lowveld (woodland savanna) and Highveld (grassland).

Modjadji Nature Reserve, one of only two known cycad forests in the world.

Given its location, it is not surprising that Tzaneen is noted for its luxuriant gardens, abundant Lowveld trees and palm-lined main street.

LETABA VALLEY The fertile and intensively cultivated Letaba Valley – stretching from Tzaneen to the Ebenezer Dam – is one of the country's prime fruit-growing areas, producing such subtropical fruit as bananas, avocados, lichis, pawpaws and mangoes. Twelve kilometres from Tzaneen the R528 reaches

Tenby Garden. Surrounded by lush fruit and timber plantations, Tenby's well-stocked arts and crafts shop and restaurant overlooks a broad expanse of lawn and garden.

Near the crest of the pass which ascends the Letaba Valley towards Haenertsburg, the peaks of the impressive Wolkberg ('cloudy mountains') are visible across the deep valley. Encompassing some of the Northern Province's least-known wilderness country, many of the higher mist-crowned peaks and buttresses of this rugged mountain range are protected within the pristine 19 000-hectare Wolkberg Wilderness Area. Day visitors are welcome and there are a few hiking trails, but only experienced hikers are advised to tackle the mountains.

In recent years a previously unknown species of lizard, related to the common skink, was discovered among the secluded peaks. Other animals likely to be seen include bushbuck, baboon, samango monkey and thick-tailed bushbaby, while bat hawk, secretarybird and martial eagle are among the birds sighted.

LOUIS TRICHARDT Located some 45 kilometres north of the Tropic of Capricorn, the picturesque town of Louis Trichardt nestles against the southern slopes of the Soutpansberg. Its tropical climate encourages the abundant growth of trees, flowers and shrubs, and nearly 100 tree species are displayed in the town's Indigenous Tree Park. A reminder of the town's turbulent history (*see* p. 21) can be seen at Fort Hendrina, an unusual bastion constructed from iron plates during the pioneering days. Today Louis Trichardt has several hotels situated on the wooded slopes of the Soutpansberg.

At the 2 500-hectare Ben Lavin Nature Reserve, 12 kilometres southeast of Louis Trichardt, visitors are free to explore the reserve on foot. Game includes giraffe, tsessebe, sable and eland, and a total of 240 bird species, such as Wahlberg's eagle and paradise whydah, have been identified here, which can be observed from the two hides overlooking water holes. Accommodation is available in rustic huts or camping sites.

SCHOEMANSDAL Little remains of the nearby town of Schoemansdal, a settlement founded in 1848 by a group of Voortrekkers. It soon developed into a thriving community of about 1 800 citizens who established

trade links with Natal and the coastal Portuguese settlements. Ivory was the town's main source of income, and each year an estimated 30 tons of lead, brought in from the coast, was used to manufacture bullets.

However, Schoemansdal attracted a lawless bunch of renegades, and relations with the neighbouring BaVenda were never good. In 1867 the town was attacked and burnt to the ground by the BaVenda. Today a museum on the site of the old town offers candle-making, pottery and bread-baking demonstrations, and visitors can ride on ox-wagons. A few replica houses have been built, furnished as they would have been at the time of the town's foundation.

HANGLIP FOREST The forested southern slopes of the Soutpansberg are dominated by Hanglip, at 1 719 metres the range's second highest peak. From Hanglip Forest Station, 4 kilometres north of Louis Trichardt, two circular trails (part of the Soutpansberg Trail) lead through indigenous forest that protects trees such as the Cape chestnut, forest mahogany and green hazel.

The one-day trail covers 14 kilometres, leading to a pleasant picnic site set in a clearing. The longer trail requires two days, with an overnight stop at Hanglip Hut, and

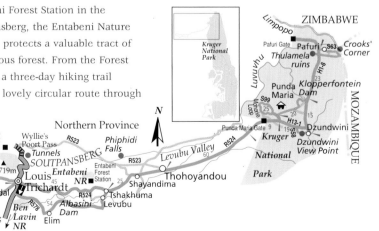

Nyala ewes, easily recognizable by their vertical white stripes, in the Kruger Park.

takes hikers on a scenic route through the forest and up the mountain to a plateau. This vantage point, 800 metres above a vast plain, provides superb views of the surrounding wooded valleys and Louis Trichardt in the valley below.

SOUTPANSBERG The 120-kilometre-long Soutpansberg forms a significant barrier separating the baobab-studded mopane veld of the Limpopo Valley from the open bushveld of the Pietersburg plateau. Some parts of the range receive an annual rainfall of 2 000 millimetres which, in places, encourages the growth of dense woods. Near the Entabeni Forest Station in the Soutpansberg, the Entabeni Nature Reserve protects a valuable tract of indigenous forest. From the Forest Station, a three-day hiking trail traces a lovely circular route through

forests and timber plantations. The Soutpansberg were originally occupied by San fleeing the BaVenda tribes but today the BaVenda inhabit most of the country from the Soutpansberg to the Limpopo River.

THOHOYANDOU Approximately 40 kilometres from Louis Trichardt, the characteristic conical huts and cultivated gardens of the BaVenda indicate the boundary of the former Republic of Venda. It came into being in 1979 and was the smallest of the four Bantustans (tribal homelands) to be granted independence by South Africa during the apartheid

Skilfully decorated Venda huts at the Venda Tourist Village near Messina.

era. Thohoyandou was the site chosen as the capital of Venda, and the name commemorates Thoho ya ndou, 'the head of the elephant', a distinguished chief who led the BaVenda away from strife-torn regions to the safety of the Soutpansberg. Government buildings, a casino hotel, shopping centres and a university are located in the town. Not to be missed is the Arts and Crafts Centre, where traditional crafts are displayed.

PUNDA MARIA The Kruger National Park's northernmost rest camp is Punda Maria, which owes its name to its first ranger, Capt. JJ 'Kat' Coetser, who was familiar with the Swahili language. As his wife, Maria, was fond of wearing black-and-white dresses, Coetser called the camp Punda Maria – a marriage of his wife's name and the Swahili *punda milia*, meaning zebra.

Surrounded by typical sandveld vegetation, the camp's thatched, rustic huts date back to 1933 and have been retained as part of its heritage. Rough wooden beams make up the verandahs (typical of *hartbees-huise*, or 'pioneer homesteads'), and spacious grounds enhance the uncluttered feeling of the camp.

Hikers will enjoy the Paradise Flycatcher Trail – named because of the many flycatchers seen en route – which leads up a steep hill beyond the restaurant before descending past some of the 80 tree species that have been identified within the

Paradise flycatchers are commonly seen at Punda Maria.

Thulamela archaeological site was once a sophisticated, precolonical city.

camp. These dense thickets attract many other birds such as robin and thrush. Just outside the camp, the Mahonie Loop offers one of the best game drives in northern Kruger and passes through sandveld forest that often reveals elephant, lion, leopard, nyala, kudu or buffalo.

THULAMELA Perched on a plateau a few kilometres west of Pafuri, the walled citadel of Thulamela flourished from AD 1200 to 1600, and its discovery is regarded as one of the most important archaeological finds in South Africa. Its open-air museum, opened in September 1996, is the second archaeological site in the Kruger made accessible to the public (*see* p. 38), and since 1993, the ruins of the citadel have been painstakingly excavated and rebuilt.

Research has shown that Thulamela was a highly organised mountain stronghold ruled by a king. Archaeologists now believe that Great Zimbabwe did not disintegrate but divided into smaller groups, one of which came south to Thulamela. Its inhabitants were skilled goldsmiths who traded in gold objects, and glass beads from India and

Chinese Ming Dynasty porcelain have been unearthed. The discovery of iron gongs is proof that there were trade links with West Africa. The king's inner royal enclosure bordered steep cliffs overlooking the Luvuvhu River, and the dwellings of the king's wives were nearby. After the death of the king around 1600 Thulamela was abandoned. The remains of the king and queen were recently found; the queen, buried around 1550, has her head facing the king's chamber.

PAFURI AND CROOKS' CORNER A secluded picnic site, Pafuri lies on the Luvuvhu flood plain near the confluence of the Limpopo. Pafuri's many uncommon species (such as nyala, suni, samango monkey and crested guineafowl), wild beauty, and fig and fever forests have earned it the reputation of being one of the most enchanting corners of the Kruger Park. Apart from its remoteness, Pafuri is noted for its sandveld vegetation – which includes sycamore fig and fever trees – and alluvial plains.

Pafuri is a favourite haunt of bird enthusiasts. The exquisite crimson-and-green Narina trogon is often sighted on the path that leads from

the picnic site to a sycamore forest along the river bank. Of the many birds which occur here, longtailed glossy starling is the most common but rare vagrants (such as the green sandpiper, banded martin and honey buzzard) may also be spotted.

From the picnic site, a 19-kilometre circular drive follows the river through dense riverine bush and fever trees before turning west to rejoin the main road. Nyala, kudu, bushbuck and buffalo are frequently sighted, and birds such as white-fronted bee-eater and wood dove may be seen en route. The road passes 'Crooks' Corner', the isolated hideaway created by the invisible point in the centre of the Limpopo River where South Africa, Zimbabwe and Mozambique meet. In the early 20th century the area was the stamping ground of ivory poachers, gunrunners and renegades, as it was easy for fugitives to slip over the border into a neighbouring territory.

About 51 kilometres south of Pafuri lies the lovely Dzundwini viewpoint. From the 600-metre-high summit, the golden hues of the mopane veld extend in every direction over northern Kruger.

LEVUBU VALLEY After leaving the Kruger, the route retraces the R524 for 85 kilometres to the tropical Levubu Valley. Watered by the Luvuvhu River, the valley lies in the fertile crescent of the Soutpansberg, where bananas, avocados and other subtropical fruits, coffee and nuts are grown. The Levubu Experimental Farm, open to the public on weekdays, develops new strains and methods of producing tropical fruits.

ALBASINI DAM Water from the Albasini Dam irrigates 1 800 hectares of crops in the Levubu Valley. It is a popular weekend venue for fishing (yellowfish, barbel and kurper, for example) and water sports, with slipways for boats and picnic sites along the shores. Overnight visitors will enjoy the quiet camp site.

In the Kruger Park, all the animals have right of way.

NELSPRUIT An attractive, tropical town surrounded by granite *koppies*, Nelspruit is Mpumalanga's capital and the breadbasket of the Lowveld. Orchards of tropical fruit abound, and the many roadside stalls tempt the tourist with succulent mangoes, paw-paws and avocados. The town's main attraction is the Lowveld National Botanic Gardens, and paths meandering through its dense vegetation along the Crocodile River lead to views of the Nelspruit Cascades.

BERG-EN-DAL From Punda Maria (*see* p. 35) in the north to Malelane and Crocodile Bridge in the south, eight entrances lead into the Kruger Park. The thatched Malelane Gate, completed in 1983, is the southern-most of these. From here, visitors can reach Berg-en-dal along a road leading through a broad valley bounded by mountainous terrain, with the Kruger's highest peak, 839-metre-high Khandzalive, visible in the distance.

The designers of Berg-en-dal took great care to retain the camp's natural vegetation, and it accommod-ates visitors in secluded chalets or caravan sites. The swimming pool is concealed behind landscaped banks, and a shady picnic site has been cre-ated for day visitors. The take-away

and restaurant, supermarket and information centre are located in a complex overlooking the Matjulu Dam, where crocodile are likely to be seen, with bushbuck, impala, baboon and elephant on the shore.

Berg-en-dal has a high concentra-tion of white rhino, and because of its mountainous terrain, is the ideal habitat for mountain reedbuck. Self-guided game drives and walking trails leave from the camp, or visitors can join guided bush or night drives. The Rhino Trail follows a paved path along the camp's fence and is suitable for the blind as it includes Braille in-formation boards and items such as animal skulls as points of interest.

In the surrounding granite coun-try, impala, kudu and warthog are common. White rhino are often seen at Matjulu windmill, 5 kilometres from camp. Other animals likely to be seen in the vicinity include elephant, giraffe, lion and wild dog.

AFSAAL PICNIC SITE Afsaal ('unsaddle') is a picnic site located on the old wagon route once used by transport riders between the Mozambique coast and Pilgrim's Rest. This intriguing period of his-tory is documented in Percy Fitzpatrick's classic book, *Jock of*

the Bushveld. Visitors will find the rest areas, tucked under shady tamboti trees, to be no less inviting than they were to early transport riders. Noisy francolins scurry about in the under-growth while breakfast is cooked on complimentary gas cookers. Boiling water is available in the central kitchen and a store is stocked with refreshments and curios.

Afsaal is situated in a narrow band of thornveld that differs greatly from the surrounding combretum country-side. Zebra and wildebeest are often seen. The nearby Jock windmill on the old transport route is worth inves-tigating for the game that drink there.

After Afsaal, the road passes between the rocky Makhutlwanini *koppies*. Klipspringer are often visible on the boulders, and the lucky visitor may even sight leopard.

JOCK-OF-THE-BUSHVELD PRIVATE CAMP This small camp has a tran-quil setting at the confluence of the Mitomeni and Biyamiti rivers. Its lounge, overlooking the rivers, con-tains mementoes from *Jock of the Bushveld* – such as Sir Percy Fitz-patrick's rifle – and in the camp's grounds stands a statue of Jock fight-ing a sable. Lion, wild dog, impala and kudu are the animals usually seen in the dense combretum veld.

STEVENSON-HAMILTON MEMORIAL An unblemished granite boulder and a tangle of vegetation may seem an unlikely memorial for a man who dedicated 44 years to establishing the Kruger Park. But James Stevenson-Hamilton, the park's first warden, could have chosen no better site than Shirimantanga ('the early gar-dener'). This was his favourite re-treat until his death in 1957, and when his wife, Hilda, died in 1979, the couple's ashes were scattered on Shirimantanga by their daughter. To the west the flat-topped Ship Moun-tain, is visible across a sea of bush; to the south the Malelane Mountains protrude above the horizon.

SKUKUZA More a large village than a rest camp, Skukuza is the headquar-ters of the Kruger National Park. Skukuza – 'he who sweeps clean' – commemorates James Stevenson-Hamilton. As the park's largest camp, it covers 30 hectares and can accom-modate over 500 visitors in chalets. Caravan sites and self-contained tents occupy the eastern end of Skukuza. It also houses a bank, post office,

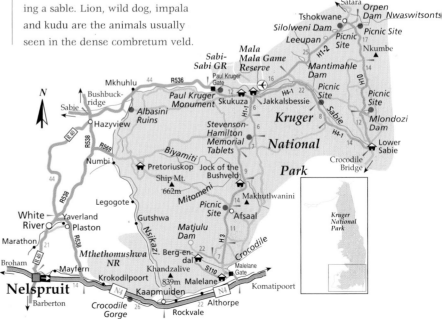

garage, restaurant, library, museum and a supermarket with a bakery. Although some visitors prefer the smaller camps, the Skukuza region is one of the best for game-viewing. Lion, leopard, hyena, wild dog, elephant and buffalo are often encountered, particularly along the river road that leads to Lower Sabie. Early morning and late afternoon drives are the best for game-viewing and kudu, bushbuck, giraffe and monkey are common along this route.

Near the river, an extensive picnic area, an outdoor restaurant and takeaway outlets have been established. Tall fig trees grow along the river bank, providing an ideal habitat for birds such as purplecrested lourie, masked weaver and blackheaded oriole. The airport, across the Sabie River, allows visitors easy access to this lovely camp.

The nearby staff village provides the over 3 000 employees with a golf course, rugby field and a primary

Vervet monkeys (top) *perch on the road sign that points to Skukuza* (above).

school. The park's conservation, research, construction and management divisions are also based here.

LOWER SABIE Many wildlife enthusiasts consider Lower Sabie to be the most rewarding game-viewing region in the Kruger. Set in the humid valley of the Sabie River some 42 kilometres downstream from Skukuza, it is something of a tropical paradise. The camp's lawns and beds of shrubs and flowers lead to the chalets, which survey an expanse of water backed up behind a weir on the Sabie.

Lower Sabie is a good base from which to explore southern and central Kruger. An early start on the road north could reward the visitor with a lion sighting. Other animals likely to be seen include elephant, wildebeest, kudu and tsessebe, while impressive migrations of zebra take place across the plains in winter. About 12 kilometres from Lower Sabie, a dirt road to the right leads to Mlondozi Dam. Reedbuck are frequently seen at the dam, and elephant, buffalo, impala and waterbuck often come here to drink, especially during droughts. From the shelter on the hill crest, there is a wonderful view of the dam in the valley below. The attendant at the shelter has soft drinks for sale, and picnic sites and braai areas are provided nearby.

The Kruger Tablets, south of Tshokwane, honour Paul Kruger, founder of the park.

NKUMBE MOUNTAIN The rocky crest of Nkumbe, about 25 kilometres on from Lower Sabie, provides one of the best locations in the park for the shy klipspringer. From the mountain's thatched look-out, visitors can enjoy an unparalleled panoramic view across a portion of the Kruger's 19 633 square kilometres of wilderness. To the southwest, the aptly-named Ship Mountain is visible.

ORPEN DAM Superbly situated on a hill summit overlooking Orpen Dam and the surrounding bush below, the dam's picnic site is an ideal spot to spend a few relaxing hours. Orpen Dam commemorates Eileen Orpen, whose generosity resulted in the addition of 24 529 hectares of land along the Kruger's western border.

Apart from the splendid scenery, it attracts large numbers of waterbirds, including Egyptian geese and heron. Visitors can also expect to see animals such as elephant, giraffe, waterbuck, kudu and impala, while enormous crocodiles often bask in the sun on the shore.

TSHOKWANE A popular picnic site at the junction of five major routes that cross the Kruger's central region, Tshokwane's focal point is a shady veranda surrounding a huge

sausage tree. Many of the ample picnic and braai facilities adjoin the palm-fringed Nwaswitsontso River. Tshokwane reverberates with bird choruses, and at times the noisy, demanding flocks of starlings and hornbills drown out human voices in their competition for a discarded morsel. After leaving Tshokwane, the road passes several important dams and water holes. Silolweni Dam is inhabited by hippo, while the shallow Leeupan is an excellent place for bird-watching – yellowbilled hornbill, blackwinged stilt and plover are common here. It also attracts a variety of game such as wildebeest, waterbuck, giraffe and jackal.

Further down the road, a parking area framed by marula trees gives visitors the opportunity to watch game drinking at Mantimahle Dam. Where the road runs parallel to the Sand River, it is wise to drive slowly as this area is known for sightings of leopard, lion and buffalo. Several stopping points have been provided under the lofty riverine trees.

KRUGER GATE The return route, connecting Skukuza with Nelspruit, was built in 1973. Where it crosses the Sabie, a statue of Paul Kruger honours the former president of the ZAR and founder of the Kruger.

PHALABORWA Founded in 1957, Phalaborwa is one of the youngest towns in the country. However, archaeological evidence indicates that the district's mineral-rich volcanic rocks were mined as early as 800. Much later on, in the mid-9th century, a group of metal workers, the BaPhalaborwa, began mining the rich deposits of copper and iron ore. Just outside Phalaborwa, part of their ancient workings have been traced to two *koppies* – Sealene and Kgopolwe – which have been declared national monuments. Because of their immense value, they are unfortunately not open to the public.

With a mean winter temperature of 26 ˚C, Phalaborwa is renowned for its profusion of bushveld trees and flowering plants. The town's golf course adjoins the Kruger National Park and is one of a handful of golf courses in the world where wild animals introduce an added handicap!

Since its establishment, the Loolekop outcrop outside town has been transformed into one of the world's largest open-cast mines. It measures 2 kilometres across, is 700 metres deep and is many times larger than Kimberley's Big Hole (*see* p. 144). Visits can be arranged.

MASORINI MUSEUM Near the Kruger Park's Phalaborwa Gate, the Masorini Iron Age village was carefully reconstructed from ruins that were uncovered on a steep, rocky *koppie*. Researchers believe that the village was established by people from the BaPhalaborwa tribe who surrounded their houses with stone walls as protection against enemies.

Iron ore was mined nearby and smelted at temperatures exceeding 700˚C. The iron was then worked into spears and hoes, and the village economy depended on the selling of these implements.

Today, visitors can walk to the crest of the hill and examine the ancient village site – which includes dwellings, iron-smelting furnaces and granaries – or enjoy the picnic sites.

LETABA RIVER Two kilometres before Letaba camp, the road heads through shrub mopane veld to the Letaba River and a viewsite overlooking the Mingerhout Dam. With abundant game seen en route, the 14-kilometre road along the river is rated as one of the top river drives in the park. Several side tracks lead down to the river and careful observation will reveal elephant, buffalo, kudu, waterbuck, bushbuck, and even leopard or

Buffalo trek long distances to drink in the Letaba River.

lion. At the intersection of the main H1-6 to Letaba, a loop leads along a high bank bordering a band of riverine trees. In the riverbed below, buffalo and elephant can often be seen.

LETABA CAMP Fifty kilometres from Phalaborwa Gate lies the archetypal safari camp of Letaba. Located on the southern bank of the Letaba River, the camp's 850 metres of river frontage provides excellent sightings of game, specifically bushbuck, elephant and buffalo. Thatched chalets are arranged in semi-circles along the river bank and can accommodate over 300 guests. The Elephant Hall in the Gold Fields Environmental Education Centre exhibits 16 colossal elephant tusks, believed to be the largest tusks ever found in southern Africa. A life-size statue of a bull elephant, 3,2 metres tall, guards the entrance to the building.

ENGELHARD DAM Kruger's largest impoundment was built in 1970 after it became apparent that water usage outside the park was seriously affecting the Letaba River's flow. The S46 runs along the southern shore of the Engelhard and several side tracks lead right to the water's edge where waterbuck, impala, buffalo, elephant, crocodile and leguaan are often seen.

In the arid mopane veld, the dam also provides a vital refuge for waterbirds, including duck, stork, heron, snipe or plover.

OLIFANTS CAMP Perched on a high summit above the broad sweep of the Olifants River, Olifants camp enjoys a commanding position unsurpassed in any other African park. From viewsites on the cliff edge – equivalent in height to a 20-storey building – guests can survey the river valley, where elephant, giraffe, hippo and bushbuck can be seen along the flood plain.

Accommodation is in comfortable chalets, over half of which adjoin the cliff edge, allowing visitors to enjoy the magnificent panorama over the wilderness. The restaurant and shop complex overlooks lawns which slope to a lovely viewsite.

OLIFANTS RIVER The largest river in the Kruger Park is the Olifants ('elephant'), so named because of the many breeding herds that congregate along its banks. As elephant breeding herds tend to shy away from humans, park managers restrict visitor access to a 20-kilometre stretch of the river in the vicinity of Olifants Camp. One of the most beautiful roads in the park is the one

Giraffe and impala are comfortable drinking partners.

which runs along the Olifants and heads towards Balule. It is renowned for sightings of four of the 'Big Five' (*see* p. 171), and leopard, lion, elephant and buffalo may all be encountered in a single drive.

BALULE The rudimentary huts at Balule, the smallest camp in the Kruger National Park, date back to the early years when a ferry was the only means of crossing the Olifants River. Balule can accommodate just 15 guests, but the camp has been extended to include camping facilities. Its old-world atmosphere is perfect for those who seek solitude. The camaraderie of the communal evening fire also brings nocturnal visitors to the camp's fence, and civet, hyena, elephant and hippo are often caught in the fire's glow. En route to Satara, the visitor drives

Waterlilies are found in the Kruger Park's quiet waterways.

through open, lightly-wooded plains where large herds of zebra and wildebeest are common, and sightings of buffalo, elephant, impala, lion and giraffe are frequent.

SATARA The second largest camp in the Kruger Park, Satara can accommodate over 400 visitors in attractive chalets. The restaurant, reception area and supermarket adjoin a wide lawn with an unusual birdbath crowned by a statue of a caracal. In summer, herds of wildebeest and zebra often gather at a small water hole below the boundary fence. Satara's central position allows the visitor to explore a region that is known for having the highest concentration of predators in the park: within a 20-kilometre radius from Satara, over 20 lion prides are present, and the chances of spotting a hyena, cheetah, jackal or leopard are excellent.

NWANETSI ROAD Widely regarded as one of the top game-viewing roads in the park, the dirt road running along the fig-lined banks of the Nwanetsi River traverses the territories of a few lion prides. Leopard are often seen in the fig trees fringing the riverbed, and cheetah are also regularly sighted. The reason for the concentration of predators is

obvious: large herds of zebra, impala, wildebeest, waterbuck and giraffe congregate in the open woodland bordering the river.

Where the dirt road joins the tarred H6, on a high bank above the Sweni River, a shaded picnic site is ideally located to escape from the heat of the day. From here, a short walk up a steep hill leads to a shelter perched on the edge of the cliff. From this vantage point, animals can be seen drinking at the pool below.

TIMBAVATI RIVER A lone baobab, an unusual sight in central Kruger, marks the entrance to the Timbavati picnic site where picnic and braai sites are grouped around a shady tree overlooking the bed of the Timbavati River. Human activity seems to attract a host of birds, particularly glossy starlings, and a pair of redbilled hornbills often raise their young in a tree nearby. To the north of the picnic site, visitors can

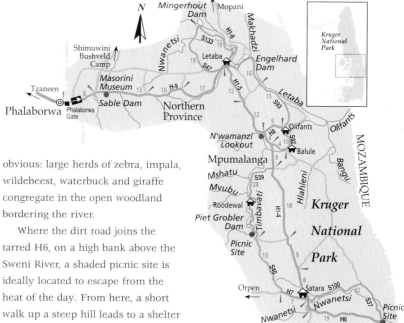

enjoy spectacular views. At the wall of the Piet Grobler Dam, a plaque commemorates the minister of the same name who pioneered the National Parks Act. The dam attracts elephant, buffalo, impala and kudu, and bird-watchers should look out for stork and fish eagle.

Apart from the occasional pool in the riverbed, three windmills along the route draw a variety of game that includes elephant, giraffe, buffalo and waterbuck.

N'WAMANZI LOOKOUT After crossing the high-level bridge spanning the Olifants River, the 8-kilometre stretch of road that runs parallel to the river offers some of the Kruger's finest game-viewing. Wildlife concentrates along the river, elephant and buffalo often cross the road on their way to the river, and leopard and lion sightings are common.

The road turns off to a parking lot on the crest of a small *koppie* (hill), where the vista over the Olifants is one of Kruger's most splendid: across a flat flood plain, the river cuts a course that leaves tree-crowded islands in its wake; on the opposite bank from the viewsite, elephant and buffalo often trek to water down footpaths between tall fig trees.

Olifants Camp occupies a prime position overlooking the Olifants River, the longest river in the Kruger Park.

VISTAS FROM THE ESCARPMENT ◆ 300 km

SABIE The lovely town of Sabie is bounded on its northern side by the Sabie River, and the lush surroundings provide a perfect setting for camp sites, motels and holiday resorts. Where tributaries tumbling down from the Escarpment's high peaks have met resistant rock shelves, spectacular waterfalls have been created, such as the 68-metre-high Lone Creek and 70-metre-high Bridal Veil falls. A tarred road leads to the more accessible Lone Creek waterfall, 8 kilometres from Sabie, while Bridal Veil is 4 kilometres away on dirt. There are four lesser cascades in the vicinity as well.

The more energetic could also walk to Bridal Veil Falls along the 14-kilometre circular Loerie Nature Walk, beginning at the Ceylon Forest Station. Trout-fishing in the adjacent Sabie River is another popular pastime. To the west, the plantations of the Ceylon and Tweefontein state forests ascend to a long range dominated by 2 277-metre-high Mount Anderson. The first leg of the Fanie Botha Hiking Trail (*see also* p. 182) leads through pine plantations on the way to Mount Anderson.

The Forestry Museum in the town centre shows the contribution made by forestry to the regional economy and displays, among other things, forestry implements and different wood types. A variety of arts and crafts shops specializing in locally made pottery, leather goods and curios are located on the main road.

MAC-MAC FALLS Some 20 kilometres from Sabie, a viewing platform overlooks the Mac-Mac Falls. When gold was discovered along the Mac-Mac River in 1873, a frenzied gold rush ensued. Many of the miners were Scottish, and President Burgers of the

The Blydepoort Dam is surrounded by the dramatic Blyde River Canyon.

ZAR christened the camp 'Mac-Mac'. In an attempt to divert the river, the miners placed dynamite on the crest of the Mac-Mac Falls. The explosion split the 64-metre-high waterfall into two splendid streams which plunge into the forested gorge below.

From the falls, visitors can walk for two kilometres along part of the Fanie Botha Hiking Trail to the Mac-Mac Pools for a refreshing swim.

GRASKOP The first state-owned timber plantations in the region were planted on the farm Graskop in 1905, and today the pretty town of Graskop is a major forestry centre. Of particular interest is the trail that leads from the municipal tourist park across a grassy plateau to the edge of the cool Escarpment. Here a marker indicates the site of Percy Fitzpatrick's Paradise Camp, as described in *Jock of the Bushveld*. Perched on the rim of the temperate highlands that survey the Lowveld, the camp was home to transport riders during the humid summer months. The stream, pool and rock formations are all described in the book. Little has changed in the immediate vicinity since Fitzpatrick last camped here in 1887.

THE PINNACLE AND GOD'S WINDOW About 4 kilometres north of Graskop, a signpost leads to the 30-metre-high Pinnacle, a weathered column of free-standing sandstone rising above the tangle of indigenous forest that crowds Driekopkloof. About 7 kilometres on, close to the Escarpment's edge, God's Window gives visitors one of the finest panoramas of the Lowveld. God's Window forms part of the Blyderivierspoort Nature Reserve, which contains several hiking trails and a museum, and protects one of South Africa's most outstanding natural features – the 1 000-metre-deep, 30-kilometre-long Blyde River Canyon.

God's Window is situated at an altitude of 1 730 metres, and the annual precipitation of around 3 000 millimetres results in lush, damp forest festooned in Old Man's Beard. Viewsites overlook precipitous wooded slopes and over a distance of 4 kilometres, the landscape drops a dramatic 900 metres before fading into the distant haze of the Lowveld. God's Window marks the end of the Fanie Botha Hiking Trail and the start of the Blyderivierspoort Hiking Trail (*see also* p. 182).

BERLIN AND LISBON FALLS In the Blyde State Forest, two spectacular waterfalls plunge over rock sills into the Lisbon River. At the 80-metre-high Berlin Falls, water is forced through a narrow gap before tumbling in a single feathery cascade into a pool. Several vantage points along the edge of the cliff provide excellent views of the waterfall.

The breathtaking Lisbon Falls tumble in four cascades down a 92-metre-high cliff into a large, beautiful and icy cold pool. Traders display their curios nearby.

PILGRIM'S REST The romantic town of Pilgrim's Rest holds many attractions. Beyond the monument to Alec Patterson lies the single row of charming red-and-white corrugated iron buildings of the village's Uptown. Among these are the Royal Hotel, an authentic memento from the past, complete with mining memorabilia and period furniture.

Near the information centre, a bank and post office still operate from historic premises, while downhill, Dredzen's Store is a carefully restored 19th-century general dealer. Visitors can also explore a miner's house museum, watch gold-panning demonstrations at the Diggings Museum, visit several arts and crafts shops, or relax at the village's pubs, coffee shops and restaurants.

At the end of the village a pleasant camp site has been established on the banks of the Blyde River.

The beautiful Lisbon Falls plunges down a 92-metre-high cliff into the Lisbon River.

MOUNT SHEBA A side road en route to Lydenburg leads to the secluded Mount Sheba hotel and nature reserve, known for its forest walks, protea garden and streams. Surrounded by the reserve, the lovely hotel is encircled by steep hills clothed in indigenous forest. The reserve is home to bushbuck, samango monkey, red duiker, and many birds, including purplecrested lourie, crowned eagle and trumpeter hornbill.

LYDENBURG About 10 kilometres north of Lydenburg, the entrance to an unusual wildlife attraction appears

An unusual and inspired man-made creation near Lydenburg.

on the right. The farm is home to elephant, buffalo, rhino, sable, giraffe and lion, and even the amateur game-spotter will be able to locate them in the surrounding thornveld. The animals – all life-size reproductions cast in concrete – are the brainchild of artist Dick Heysteck, and a sign at the entrance asks visitors to refrain from 'feeding the animals'.

At an altitude of 1 400 metres, the country town of Lydenburg – 'place of suffering' – was named in memory of its founders' hardships in 1850. Today it is the centre of a productive agricultural region, and minerals such as chrome and platinum are mined here. The town council

manages 22 kilometres of trout-stocked river available to fishermen. The town's 1853 Dutch Reformed Church is the oldest church north of the Cape. The Lydenburg Museum displays replicas of seven clay heads dating back to AD 500 and the originals are housed in the South African Museum in Cape Town. Six of these Lydenburg Heads, believed to have been used for ritual purposes, have human faces and the seventh that of an animal. The FC Braun Aquarium has indigenous fish in display tanks and picnic sites in the grounds.

SCHOEMANSKLOOF PASS The Schoemanskloof road follows a scenic route through a fertile valley flanked by rolling, wooded hills. The R359 drops 600 metres over 25 kilometres, from temperate grasslands to humid valleys buzzing with insect choruses. An amusing landmark along the way is the unusual boulder nicknamed 'Old Joe'. Painting 'Old Joe', which resembles a podgy gentleman, has become a creative pastime! Further on, at the junction of the N4, the Crocodile River tumbles over the Montrose Falls. The hotel above the falls is a convenient stopover point and provides a lovely view of the valley.

SUDWALA CAVES Three kilometres after the turn-off to the Montrose Falls and hotel, the Mankelekele Mountain protects the intriguing Sudwala Caves. In the early 19th century, the caves served as a shelter for Swazi refugees. They are regarded as one of the country's foremost geological wonders. Formed by rainwater percolating through cracks in the surrounding dolomite, the caves feature a host of fascinating stalactites and stalagmites, and a labyrinth of interleading passages and caverns. About 600 metres of the caves' passages are open to the public. Some of the outstanding formations include the 11-metre-tall 'Space Rocket' and the 'Screaming Monster'. Outside the caves, lifelike dinosaur replicas are scattered among ferns and swamps.

Historic Pilgrim's Rest, a replica of the old gold-mining town and a living museum.

THE ROLLING GRASSLANDS

Mpumalanga's soils are rich and productive, and vistas of golden, rolling wheatfields, such as these near Ermelo, are typical of the region.

This historical and diverse region covers a broad spectrum of South African landscape. In the north, where the altitude averages around 1 800 metres, it is flat and characterised by the rolling grasslands of the Highveld. Transecting the southern sector is the Escarpment edge, where the inland plateau suddenly gives way in serried steps to the upper reaches of the coastal lowlands. Here, at 600 to 800 metres above sea level, the grasslands are punctuated by dense copses of acacia trees in the valleys and kloofs of the surrounding mountains and hills. Changing dramatically in the south-west, the scenery is dominated by the majestic Drakensberg mountains and the Lesotho highlands that lie behind them.

SHAKA, KING OF THE ZULUS

Incongruous though it may seem, most of the country's bloodiest battles were fought in this predominantly open and tranquil region during conflicts that pitted Boers,

Zulus and British against one another. During the early 19th century, the Zulu empire was forged by Shaka, chief of the Zulus. This brilliant strategist used his military skills to amalgamate many clans and tribal groups into a single nation. Shaka's wars of conquest sent waves of refugees radiating outwards across the grasslands, up and beyond the Drakensberg Escarpment and into the present-day Free State, where they created further waves of violence as they clashed with resident tribes and with one another. This period of political and social turmoil, known as *Mfecane* in Zulu or *Difaqane* in Sotho, coincided with the arrival of the first white settlers in the region.

BATTLE OF BLOOD RIVER

In 1838 the Voortrekkers hauled their wagons across the Drakensberg in search of fertile land and a new home where they could be free from English control. But the new Zulu king Dingane, who gained the throne after

assassinating Shaka, regarded the coming of the whites as a threat. He put to death Voortrekker leader Piet Retief and 69 men who had come on a mission to Dingane's capital, umGungundhlovu, to acquire land. A few days later, the Zulus attacked a number of Voortrekker *laagers* ('camps') at Bloukrans

This map highlights the regional map opposite. Overlapping regions and their page numbers are supplied.

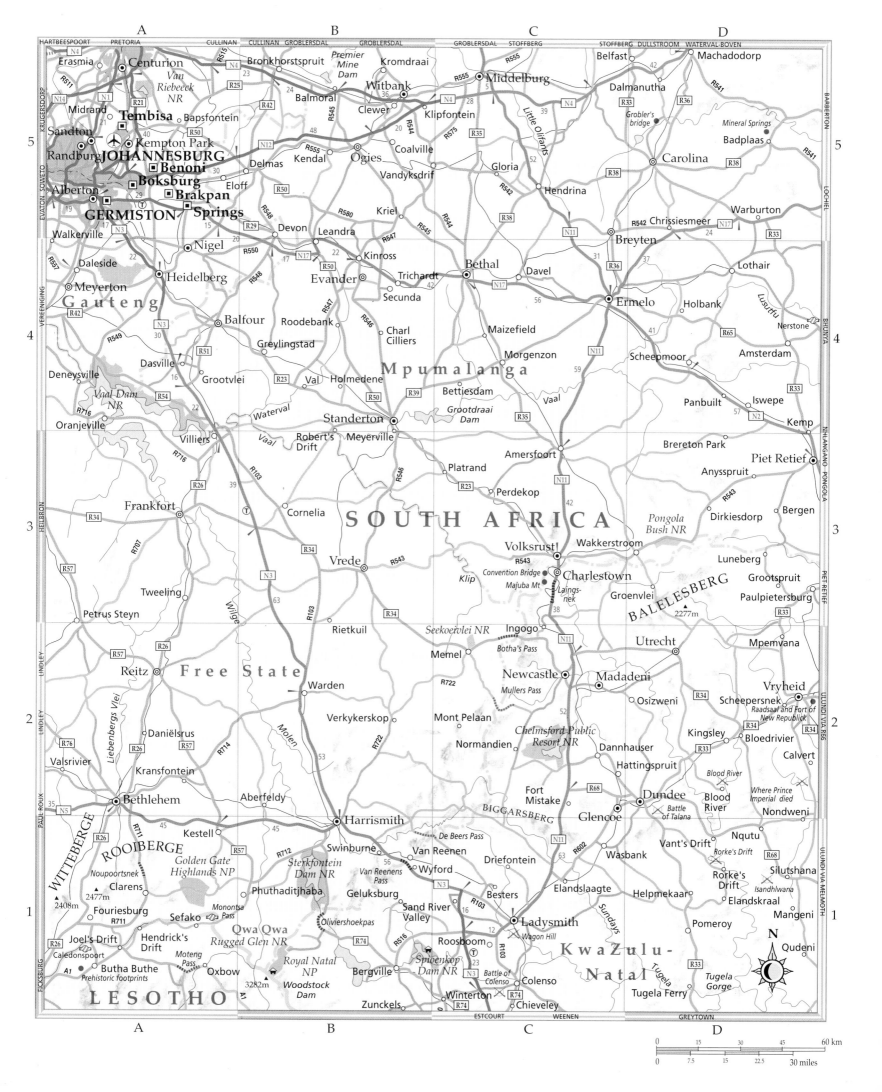

This vibrant Zulu tapestry forms part of the informative museum at Rorke's Drift.

near Ladysmith, killing 40 men, 56 women, 85 children and more than 200 servants. Exactly 10 months later, on 16 December 1838, the Voortrekkers met the Zulus in battle on the banks of the Ncome River, near present-day Dundee. Over 3 000 Zulu warriors died as they tried to prise open the Voortrekkers' tightly closed laager. So many were killed that the Ncome River turned red with blood, giving the river its new name, Blood River. Before the battle, the Voortrekkers vowed that if God granted them victory, they would build a church and each year commemorate that day as a sabbath. The anniversary – the Day of Reconciliation, as it has been renamed – has been marked ever since. The battle site is commemorated by the Blood River Monument, a laager of 64 ox-wagons, 48 kilometres from Dundee.

ANGLO-ZULU WAR

War clouds gathered again at the end of 1878 when the British colonial government, fearing that a powerful, independent Zulu kingdom could impede their policy of expansion in southern Africa, decided to go to war. Sir Bartle Frere, Governor of the Cape and British High Commissioner in southern Africa, saw no alternative but to subdue that

kingdom by military means. An impossible ultimatum was issued to Zulu king Cetshwayo on 11 December 1878 and when it expired one month later, the Anglo-Zulu War began. Three British columns marched on Cetshwayo's capital at Ulundi. The central column entered Zululand at Rorke's Drift and advanced to the foot of a sphinx-like hill the Zulus called Isandlwana ('like a little house'). It was there on 22 January 1879 that the British suffered the greatest defeat in their colonial history: 1 357 men were killed when 20 000 Zulu warriors overwhelmed their camp. The Zulu casualties are unknown, but are estimated to be well over 1 000 men. Only a handful of British soldiers

A laager of 64 bronze ox-wagons comprise the Blood River Monument near Dundee.

and Natal Volunteers managed to escape across the Buffalo River to the safety of Natal soil. Today white cairns placed along the fugitives' trail are a poignant reminder of those who died along the way.

Contrary to Cetshwayo's instructions, several Zulu regiments ran on to Rorke's Drift and attacked the small band of British soldiers holding the trading store. An epic battle between 110 defenders, some of them sick or wounded, and an estimated 3 000 to 4 000 Zulu attackers, lasted for 12 hours. It left 17 British and some 300 to 400 Zulus dead. No less than 11 of the defenders were decorated with the Victoria Cross, Britain's highest award for bravery – the biggest number ever awarded in a single battle. The museum at Rorke's Drift is noted for its visual information on the Anglo-Zulu War.

Some six months later, on 4 July 1879, Lord Chelmsford and a heavily reinforced column fought its way through to Ulundi, today one of the joint capitals of KwaZulu-Natal (*see also* p. 49). On the sparsely covered Mahlabathini plains, the British formed themselves into a tight square and used their superior firepower (including artillery) to vanquish the Zulu army. Chelmsford then razed Cetshwayo's kraal at nearby Ondini, and Cetshwayo fled to northern Zululand.

ANGLO-BOER WAR

Two years later war broke out once again, this time between the Boers and the British over the question of independence for the Zuid-Afrikaansche Republiek, annexed by the British in 1877. At the battle of Majuba ('hill of the doves') in February 1881, a small ZAR force inflicted a humiliating defeat on the British, who were forced to restore the republic's sovereignty. Visitors can follow a self-guided trail around the battle site, off the N11 between Volksrust and Newcastle.

Only 18 years were to pass before the British and Boers once more met in battle. In 1899 the second Anglo-Boer War erupted, again fought over the question of independence for the coveted Transvaal. When hostilities began, the Boers quickly invaded Natal, aiming to deny the British access to the port of Durban. The first engagement of the war took place on 20 October 1899 on Talana Hill just outside Dundee. Although

This monument is a poignant reminder of the Anglo-Boer War battle at Elandslaagte.

sustaining heavier losses, the British won the battle but were forced to withdraw to Ladysmith. The Boers besieged Ladysmith for 118 days, during which no less than five major battles, with considerable loss of life, were fought on the hills encircling the town.

Outside Dundee, the Talana Museum presents fascinating displays on the Anglo-Boer War and the region's early history. Visitors can gain insight into this war at the Ladysmith Siege Museum, and signposts point to the many siege sites around the town.

ECONOMIC DEVELOPMENT

The soils of the rolling grasslands are among the most productive in the country and it is considered to be South Africa's breadbasket. Most of the country's maize, a staple foodstuff, is grown here. Other important crops include sorghum, sunflower seed, potatoes, beans, groundnuts, rye, oats and barley. A dominant feature of many of the towns and surrounding countryside are the multistorey silos used to store agricultural produce. Beef, dairy and sheep farming are also extensively practised in the region. Locked below the surface of the land are South Africa's main coalfields. The northern sector of the region is dotted with the workings of the many coalfields that have been developed from Witbank in Mpumalanga to Newcastle in KwaZulu-Natal. The coal is used to feed enormous thermal power stations, which supply much of the country's electricity needs. The giant cooling towers of these power stations are as much a part of the landscape as are the farmers' silos. But a serious negative is the high levels of sulphur-based pollution emitted by these power stations.

Rich coalfields were the major reason for the establishment at Secunda of Sasol 2 and 3 – huge industrial plants that extract oil from coal. The first plant, Sasol 2, was born out of the oil crisis which occurred in 1973, when the Organization of Petroleum Exporting Countries (OPEC) virtually quadrupled the price of oil overnight.

The second plant, Sasol 3, was added when the Shah of Iran was overthrown in 1979 and oil supplies from South Africa's major supplier were shut off. Coal needed for these two plants is supplied by four nearby mines, which are collectively known as the Secunda Collieries.

WATER RESOURCES

Two of South Africa's principal rivers flow through this well-watered, fertile area. The Vaal River rises at Lake Chrissie, meanders westward until it is impounded by the Grootdraai and Vaal dams east of Vereeniging, and from there it flows on to join the Orange River. In the south, after cascading down the mighty Amphitheatre in the Drakensberg, the Tugela River flows eastwards through much of the region. The country's industrial heartland in Gauteng (*see also* p. 10) draws most of its vitally needed water from these two important rivers.

As the urban populations along the Witwatersrand have swelled over the years, so water has become an increasingly threatened resource. As a result, two highly imaginative water schemes have been developed in the Drakensberg and in the Lesotho highlands.

The first is the dual-purpose Drakensberg Pumped Storage Scheme (also known as the Tugela-Vaal or TUVA scheme), in which water is pumped from the Tugela River in KwaZulu-Natal over the rugged Drakensberg through a series of multi-level reservoirs to the especially created Sterkfontein Dam near Harrismith in the Free State. From there the water is released into the Wilge River, a tributary of the Vaal, in order to supplement the water supply in the Vaal Dam, especially during droughts. The scheme is also used to generate electricity for the national grid by utilising the flow of water between the Driekloof Reservoir, situated at the top of the Drakensberg Escarpment, and the Kilburn Reservoir at its foot.

The second scheme is the Lesotho Highlands Water Project, in which surplus water from the rivers in the Lesotho highlands is to be transferred through the Maluti Mountains to South Africa. Under an international agreement signed in 1986, the water resources of the Lesotho highlands will be developed in stages over a 20-year period. The first phase involves the construction of the ultra-high-wall Katse Dam, tunnelling 80 kilometres through the Maluti Mountains and the building of a 72-megawatt hydroelectric station as well as a regulation dam at Muela (near Butha Buthe in the Lesotho lowlands).

Much-needed oil is extracted from coal at the huge Sasol 2 industrial plant at Secunda.

SOUTHERN KWAZULU-NATAL

Dominating the Royal Natal National Park is the Drakensberg's magnificent Amphitheatre.

Colourfully garbed Zulu ricksha drivers enhance Durban's holiday atmosphere.

Embracing the lush, subtropical South Coast, the great grassland plains of the Midlands and the serried rampart of the Drakensberg, this fertile region is one of South Africa's prime tourist destinations. The South Coast's ample summer rainfall results in the abundant growth of plants, both endemic and exotic, while the temperate Midlands is an area of pastoral beauty. Providing an impressive backdrop to the Midlands are the Drakensberg, its soaring, often snowcapped peaks contrasting with its gently undulating foothills. These areas are easily explored from the region's two major centres, Durban and Pietermaritzburg.

RIO DE NATAL

Durban is the country's third-largest city. It had its beginnings on Christmas Day in 1497, when Portuguese seafarer Vasco da Gama, on his epoch-making voyage between Europe and the East, sighted the mouth of what he took to be a large lagoon lying behind a high bluff. Da Gama named it Rio de Natal ('Christmas river'), and from that time the name 'Natal' was used to describe the bay Da Gama saw and the land that lies beyond it. Today the name of the province fuses the name of the former Zulu homeland with Natal.

Over three centuries passed, however, before the first move was made to develop a port in the bay. In 1824 Lt. Francis Farewell obtained a grant from Shaka, the king of the Zulus, to establish a trading station on its shores. The new settlement was known as Port Natal until 1843, when the name was officially changed to Durban, in honour of Sir Benjamin D'Urban, then the British governor at the Cape.

TROUBLED TIMES

Durban's early years were far from peaceful. In 1838 the Zulu king Dingane ransacked the settlement after the murder of Piet Retief and the massacre of the Voortrekkers at Bloukrans. Durban's inhabitants took refuge aboard a ship anchored in the bay at the time. In 1843 the British annexed Natal to the Cape Colony, which resulted in a clash with the Boers who had settled in Natal during the late 1830s. The Boers laid siege to Durban, and the townspeople sheltered in a hastily built

This map highlights the regional map opposite. Overlapping regions and their page numbers are supplied.

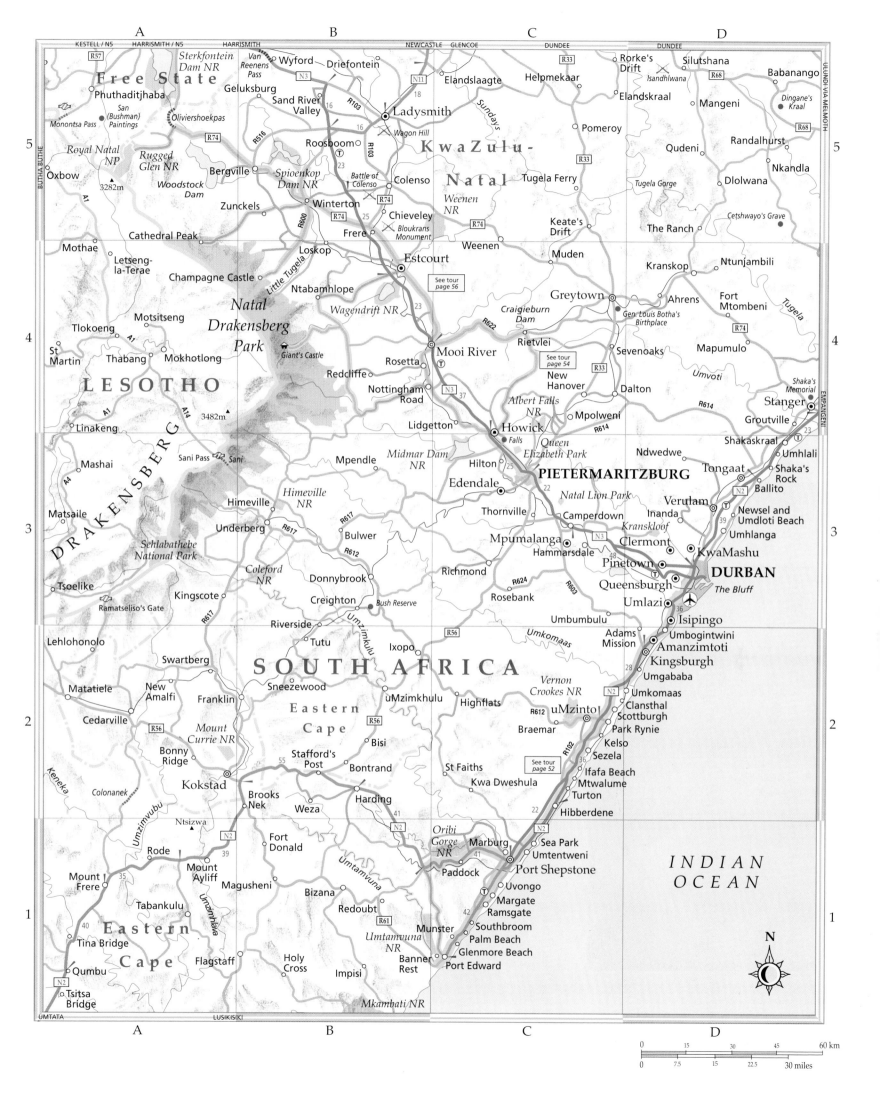

KESTELL / N5   HARRISMITH / N5   HARRISMITH   NEWCASTLE   GLENCOE   DUNDEE   DUNDEE

R57

Free State

Sterkfontein Dam NR

Wyford   Driefontein

Van Reenens Pass

N3

R103

Gelukburg

Sand River Valley

16

Phuthaditjhaba

San (Bushman) Paintings

Monontsa Pass

Oliviershoekpas

R74

R516

Ladysmith

N11

18

Elandslaagte

Helpmekaar

R33

Rorke's Drift

Silutshana

Isandhlwana

R68

Babanango

Dingane's Kraal

Mangeni

R68

5

Royal Natal NP

Rugged Glen NR

Roosboom

Wagon Hill

KwaZulu-

Qudeni

Randalhurst

Oxbow

3282m

Bergville

Spioenkop Dam NR

Colenso

Natal

Tugela Ferry

Nkandla

Woodstock Dam

Battle of Colenso

R33

Tugela Gorge

Dlolwana

Cathedral Peak

Zunckels

Winterton

R74

Chieveley

Weenen NR

Keate's Drift

The Ranch

Cetshwayo's Grave

Mothae

Loskop

Bloukrans Monument

Frere

R74

Weenen

Muden

Kranskop

Ntunjambili

4

Letseng-la-Terae

Champagne Castle

Ntabamhlope

23

Estcourt

See tour page 56

Greytown

Gen. Louis Botha's Birthplace

Ahrens

Fort Mtombeni

Tugela

St Martin

Motsitseng

Natal Drakensberg Park

Wagendrift NR

23

Craigieburn Dam

Sevenoaks

Mapumulo

Tlokoeng

Mokhotlong

Giant's Castle

Little Tugela

Rietvlei

See tour page 54

R33

Umvoti

Thabang

Redcliffe

Rosetta

Mooi River

New Hanover

Dalton

R614

Shaka's Memorial

3482m

Nottingham Road

N3

37

Albert Falls NR

Mpolweni

Stanger

EMPANGENI

Linakeng

Lidgetton

Howick

Groutville

LESOTHO

Sani Pass

Sani

Midmar Dam NR

Falls

Queen Elizabeth Park

PIETERMARITZBURG

Shakaskraal

3

Mashai

DRAKENSBERG

Himeville

Himeville NR

Mpendle

Hilton

25

Natal Lion Park

Ndwedwe

Umhlali

Tongaat

Shaka's Rock

Matsaile

Edendale

22

Verulam

Ballito

A1

Underberg

R617

Bulwer

Thornville

Camperdown

Inanda

Kranskloof

N2

Newsel and Umdloti Beach

Sehlabathebe National Park

R617

R612

Mpumalanga

N3

Clermont

Umhlanga

39

Tsoelike

Coleford NR

Donnybrook

Richmond

Hammarsdale

48

KwaMashu

R624

Pinetown

DURBAN

Kingscote

Creighton

Rosebank

R603

Queensburgh

The Bluff

Ramatseliso's Gate

Bush Reserve

Umlazi

36

Riverside

Umzimkulu

Umbumbulu

Isipingo

Lehlohonolo

Tutu

Ixopo

R56

Umkomaas

Adams Mission

Umbogintwini

Swartberg

Sneezewood

uMzimkhulu

Highflats

Vernon Crookes NR

28

Amanzimtoti

Kingsburgh

2

Matatiele

New Amalfi

Franklin

Eastern Cape

R56

N2

Umgabana

Cedarville

R56

Mount Currie NR

Bisi

Braemar

uMzinto

Umkomaas

Bonny Ridge

Stafford's Post

Bontrand

R612

Clansthal

Scottburgh

55

St Faiths

Park Rynie

Keneka

Kokstad

Brooks Nek

Weza

Harding

41

Kwa Dweshula

See tour page 52

R102

Kelso

Sezela

Colonanek

N2

36

Ifafa Beach

Mtwalume

Turton

1

Ntsizwa

Fort Donald

Oribi Gorge NR

Marburg

22

Hibberdene

Rode

N2

39

Umtamvuna

41

Paddock

N2

Sea Park

Umtentweni

Mount Frere

35

Mount Ayliff

Magusheni

Bizana

Umzimhlava

Redoubt

R61

Munster

Port Shepstone

Uvongo

INDIAN OCEAN

Tina Bridge

40

Tabankulu

Holy Cross

Umtamvuna NR

42

Margate

Ramsgate

Southbroom

N2

Eastern Cape

Flagstaff

Impisi

Banner Rest

Palm Beach

Glenmore Beach

Port Edward

N

Qumbu

N2

UMTATA

LUSIKISIKI

Tsitsa Bridge

Mkambati NR

0   15   30   45   60 km

0   7.5   15   22.5   30 miles

SOUTH AFRICA

fort – now a national monument known as the Old Fort. When their supplies ran low and the situation seemed hopeless, a trader named Dick King, together with his servant, Nongena, slipped through the Boer lines at night. They rode on to Grahamstown some 800 kilometres away through often hostile countryside to raise the alarm and bring relief, resulting in the Boers withdrawing. With peace restored, trade developed and the fledgling town expanded inland from the harbour. When Durban was declared a municipality in 1885, it had become a major port and trading centre. It attracted many settlers from Europe and Indian immigrants, the latter coming to Natal as indentured labourers to work on the sugar estates that were first established during the 1850s.

Durban is in fact the centre of South Africa's Indian community, and as a result, has become an exciting amalgam of East and West. A typically Oriental bazaar can be experienced at the sprawling Victoria Street Indian Market, an intoxicating mix of colourful stalls, enthusiastic merchants bartering their wares, and the exotic scents of incense, curries and spices. Mosques – such as the Grey Street Mosque, the largest in the southern hemisphere – and Hindu shrines are common features throughout the city.

Durban's beachfront paddling pools are ideally situated along the promenade known as the 'Golden Mile'.

DURBAN TODAY

Durban's harbour is the biggest and busiest in Africa. Its facilities include bulk storage and loading terminals for sugar, anthracite, coal and grain, a 102-hectare container terminal and a dry dock. Helped by a plentiful supply of labour and water, Durban has become one of South Africa's fastest growing industrial and manufacturing centres, second only in size to the Witwatersrand (*see also* p. 10), and is also the centre of the country's food-producing area.

Because of Durban's equable climate, its wide beaches and the warm Indian Ocean, the city is also a premier tourist destination. Multistorey hotels line its seaside

Beautiful saris and fabric for sale at one of Durban's many exotic Oriental shops and bazaars.

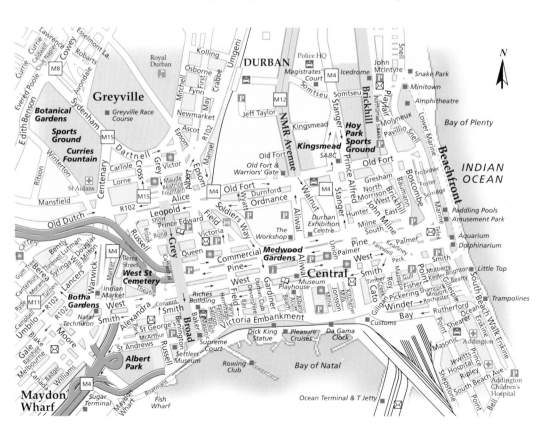

The small craft harbour at Durban's Victoria Embankment.

promenade, better known as the 'Golden Mile'; colourfully garbed Zulu ricksha drivers transport visitors along the beachfront; and a year-long tourist season gives the city a relaxed atmosphere.

Seaworld, in the heart of the Golden Mile, boasts an incredible array of marine life – ragged-tooth sharks, stingrays and turtles, to name a few – with the performing dolphins the main attraction. Close by is the Fitzsimons Snake Park, one of South Africa's most important snake research and education centres, and which also gives daily snake demonstrations.

One of Durban's many green 'lungs' is the Botanical Gardens (*see also* p. 181) which, besides its tropical vegetation, is famous for its Orchid House, Sunken Garden, Fragrant Garden for the blind, and its Herbarium. Other major drawcards include Minitown (a beautifully recreated miniature city incorporating Durban's well-known landmarks), sea cruises from Gardiner Street Jetty, the Bartle Arts Trust Centre (where local and international artists are exhibited) and the Hare Krishna Temple of Understanding.

THE SOUTH COAST

Washed by the temperate waters of the Indian Ocean and with sunshine all year round, the South Coast of KwaZulu-Natal is one of the country's favourite holiday areas. It extends for approximately 160 kilometres from Durban to Port Edward on the Umtamvuna River – the border between KwaZulu-Natal and the Eastern Cape. Virtually its entire length is fringed by a ribbon of golden beaches lined with dense, subtropical foliage that has steadily given way to a profusion of holiday retreats and small villages. Resorts such as Amanzimtoti, Port Shepstone and Margate offer a carefree world of warm ocean and lagoon swimming, lazing on the beach, fishing, golf, bowls and other sports. A notable feature along both the South and North coasts of KwaZulu-Natal are the sugar cane-covered hills. Sugar cane farming began in Natal in the 1850s, when Edmund Morewood successfully cultivated rootstock imported from Mauritius on his farm, Compensation, which lies between the iTongathi and umHlali rivers. Today the province's sugar industry enjoys an enviable international reputation for producing top-quality sugar, with exports exceeding a million tonnes annually.

PIETERMARITZBURG

Northeast of Durban lies Pietermaritzburg, the joint capital of Kwazulu-Natal with Ulundi (*see also* p. 44). The city was founded by the Voortrekkers, who decided to settle there and establish a republic after their victory over the Zulus at the Battle of Blood River in 1838 (*see also* p. 42). They chose a site that nestles in a fertile valley, where the Midlands rise some 1 200 metres above the coastal lowlands. The Voortrekkers wanted easy access to the port at Durban, but also longed to be far from English influence. They called the new capital Pietermaritzburg, in honour of their leaders Piet Retief and Gert Maritz.

The ornate City Hall, built in 1901, is a fine example of Pietermaritzburg's Victorian architecture.

The town was laid out with wide streets and drainage channels that could be led off the nearby Dorpspruit River to irrigate large gardens. One of Pietermaritzburg's first buildings was the Church of the Vow, completed in 1841 and built in terms of the covenant the Voortrekkers made with God before the Battle of Blood River. Today it is the oldest public building in South Africa outside of the Cape.

The Voortrekker republic was shortlived; after the British annexation of Natal in 1843, the Boers left Pietermaritzburg and trekked north. The town slowly developed as a commercial and farming centre which also served explorers, hunters and traders as they passed through on their way to the hinterland. In 1893 a grand Victorian assembly building was constructed to house the region's Legislative Assembly and Legislative Council, and the British established the colonial seat of government here. Pietermaritzburg soon developed into one of the most Victorian cities in Africa.

In 1893 Natal was granted responsible government by Britain and in the same year, the massive and elaborately ornamented redbrick City Hall was completed on the site of the old Voortrekker Raadzaal. This building,

A Victorian bandstand forms the centrepiece of the lovely Alexandra Park in Pietermaritzburg.

adorned with domes, a clock-tower and stained-glass windows, was destroyed by fire in 1895, but rebuilt in 1901. The City Hall once housed an art gallery, which has since been moved to the old Supreme Court building. The collection includes works by European artists of the 19th and 20th centuries, such as Pablo Picasso and Henry Moore. The Natal Museum in the city centre focuses on the province's natural and cultural history.

A CITY OF GARDENS

Pietermaritzburg's rich soil and relatively wet climate encourage luxuriant growth in the city's gardens and parks. It has no less than six major parks, as well as several smaller ones and indigenous forest reserves. The Natal National Botanical Garden (*see also* p. 181), founded in 1872, covers a 46-hectare site and contains a collection of exotic trees, including swamp cypress, camphor, fig and magnolia. It also has a bird sanctuary, ornamental ponds and interesting walks.

A popular picnic venue, Alexandra Park's main feature is the elegant pavilion and Victorian bandstand, with an orchid house, rose garden and rockery as added attractions. On Pietermaritzburg's outskirts lies Queen Elizabeth Park, a scenic 101-hectare nature reserve and headquarters of the Natal Parks Board. It conserves indigenous plants, trees, antelope and zebra.

Pietermaritzburg is a modern city with a busy central business district. A major aluminium manufacturing plant is located here and timber, wattle bark and dairy products are processed in the city's factories. Its population is growing as more people from surrounding rural areas seek employment here.

The construction of a number of Hindu temples and Muslim mosques, and the observance of such ceremonies as the annual fire-walking ceremony at the Hindu temple of Sri Siva Soobramonier and Marriamen, have imparted an Eastern flavour to parts of

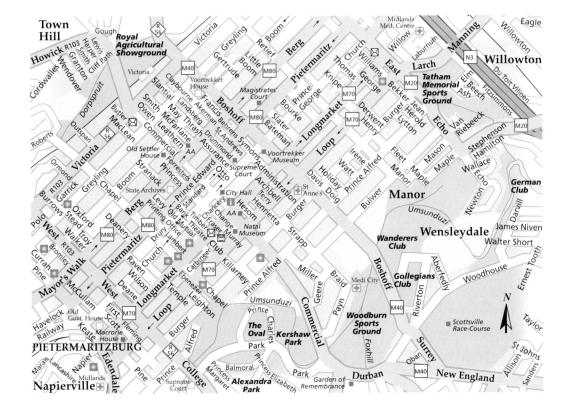

Pietermaritzburg. A famous visitor to the city was Mahatma Gandhi and a statue of him has been erected here. Because of his race, Gandhi was ejected from a train at Pietermaritzburg Station in 1893, and this laid the foundations of his philosophy of non-violent resistance to racism and oppression.

NATAL MIDLANDS AND DRAKENSBERG

Inland from Pietermaritzburg lie the Natal Midlands, an area of rolling hills and plains. It is a place of quiet beauty, with tumbling trout-filled streams and rich agricultural lands. Sadly evident, however, is the harsh contrast between prosperous Midlands farms and the former 'Native Reserves' established in the 19th century and perpetuated under apartheid. Here, population growth has outstripped the resources of the land, and severe erosion and environmental degradation has been the result.

The jagged peaks of the Drakensberg, carved by the erosive forces of wind, sun and rain, provide a dramatic backdrop to the Midlands. The Voortrekkers fancied they saw in the play of light on these rocks a gigantic dragon come to life, and so they called them the Drakensberg ('Dragon Mountains'). This escarpment ridge, which stretches from Mont-aux-Sources in the north to East Griqualand in the south, provides some of Africa's most impressive mountain scenery. Names like Cathedral Peak, Giant's Castle and Champagne Castle suggest the majesty

The statue of Mahatma Gandhi honours one of Pietermaritzburg's best-known visitors.

of this timeless landscape, and the Amphitheatre of Mont-aux-Sources in the Royal Natal National Park is probably the most oustanding of all these features. The Drakensberg is the remnant of a great outpouring of molten basalt and other igneous rocks that erupted from the earth's core, and spilled in huge contorted layers over its surface. These mountains divide the high inland plateau of southern Africa from the low-lying eastern seaboard. Within these mountain fastnesses lies the independent kingdom of Lesotho, settled in the 1820s by Sotho and other refugees from the wars and chaos engendered by Zulu expansion.

In the past, conservation of the Drakensberg was split between the Department of Water Affairs and Forestry and the Natal Parks Board. Control over the entire area was achieved with the consolidation of 15 wilderness areas, state forests and nature reserves into a single unit, now known as the Natal Drakensberg Park. The park stretches from the Umzimkulu River, south of Underberg, to Royal Natal in the north. The combined area of 235 000 hectares is the country's third largest conservation area. Today the Drakensberg, one of the country's foremost hiking areas, is a premier holiday destination.

Lush fields of sugar cane carpet the countryside along KwaZulu-Natal's subtropical South Coast.

THE SUBTROPICAL SOUTH COAST ❖ 400 km

AMANZIMTOTI Soon after leaving Durban, the traveller is rewarded with a lovely sweeping view of the coast stretching southwards, with the N2 passing within 400 metres of the surf-trimmed coast. Guarded by tall blocks of flats, the golden sands of Amanzimtoti's 8-kilometre beach unfurl into the distance.

The town's name means 'the sweet water', from Zulu king Shaka who drank from a particularly refreshing stream at the main beach and pronounced it *amanzi umtoti*. This riverside settlement has grown into a major holiday resort, with beach hotels, restaurants, shops and two golf courses. The main beaches, with shark-protected swimming areas, are Pipeline Beach and Inyoni Rocks. The latter stretches northwards from the Amanzimtoti lagoon. Picnic and braai sites, restaurants, a saltwater pool and excellent surfing are only some of its attractions.

Some 2 kilometres inland, the Ilanda Wilds Nature Reserve protects valuable coastal vegetation in the Amanzimtoti River flood plain. Here visitors can enjoy picnics or explore the reserve along several trails.

CROCWORLD One of the country's top five crocodile farms, Crocworld houses over 10 000 of these fascinating reptiles. A visit starts at an interpretative centre with its aquarium, tidal pool display and snake tunnel made of glass. A circular route winds around large landscaped ponds with hundreds of Nile crocodiles.

Crocworld also shelters American alligator, South American caiman and West African dwarf crocodile. Further attractions include a snake and reptile pit, a replica Zulu village, a children's playground and animal farm. The education centre and restaurant – noted for its croc steaks – border dense coastal forest, through which a 3-kilometre trail leads to a bird hide. Weaver, chorister robin and hamerkop are just some of the birds which may be seen here.

SCOTTBURGH The headland of the delightful town of Scottburgh overlooks the mouth of the Mpambanyoni River, beaches, caravan park and golf course. On a bank above the river is a large waterslide, and the adjacent

Scottburgh (below) *lies just before the start of the Hibiscus Coast, symbolized by a wealth of these vivid flowers* (left).

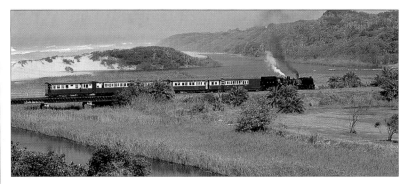

The vintage Banana Express *begins its scenic journey at Port Shepstone.*

sloping lawns are a favourite haunt of sunbathers. A restaurant and shopping complex, miniature railway and large tidal pool are added drawcards.

HIBBERDENE The start of the Lower South Coast, commonly known as the Hibiscus Coast for the profusion of these flowers in the area, begins at Hibberdene. A leading holiday resort, Hibberdene's main road hugs the coastline and is bounded by holiday flats, resorts, beach shops, restaurants and an entertainment complex. The attractive tree-edged beach at the mouth of the Mzimayi River is a favourite place for picnicking and swimming, and boating in the lagoon is popular.

PORT SHEPSTONE Occupying a headland overlooking the wide mouth of the Mzimkulu River, Port Shepstone was established in 1880, and the river is navigable by small boats for up to 8 kilometres inland. Port Shepstone is the terminal of the coastal railway line from Durban, and a branch line inland to Harding is travelled by the *Banana Express* (see also p. 53), one of the world's few narrow-gauge railways still operating. This vintage steam train departs from Port Shepstone's main beachfront. The railway hugs the shore before turning inland through lush sugar and banana plantations to Izotsha. On certain days the train continues to Paddock, where a braai is laid on for passengers.

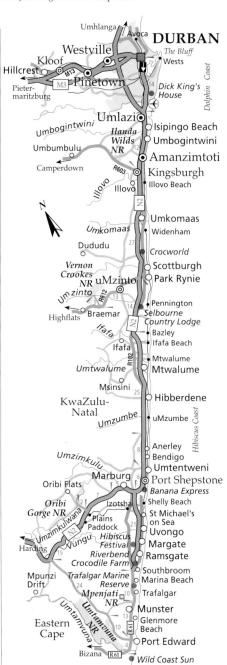

Uvongo's beach and lagoon are ideal for sunbathing, swimming and boating.

UVONGO Just before it reaches the sea, the Vungu River gives rise to a 23-metre-high waterfall which plunges into a sheltered lagoon bounded by cliffs. It is one of the most delightful lagoons on the South Coast and boating is popular here. The adjacent sheltered beach is an ideal playground for children, and a restaurant, store, and tidal and paddling pools are close by.

MARGATE The commercial and entertainment hub of the Hibiscus Coast, Margate is the South Coast's most popular resort. The town's broad expanse of beach is lined by the tall white towers of dozens of hotels and holiday complexes. The main approach to the beach is across palm-sheltered lawns that are a delight for sunbathers. On the beachfront, paddling pools, tidal pools, a freshwater Olympic-size pool, water slides, mini-golf, paddle boats, ice cream parlours and shopping centres are but some of the many attractions that compete for the visitor's attention. An annual event in July is the Hibiscus Festival which includes, among others, beach parties, floats and beauty competitions.

SOUTHBROOM Tucked between the Mbizane and Kaba lagoons, Southbroom's rocky shore encircles some of the South Coast's prime real estate. The beaches at the river mouths offer protected bathing, and the sheltered lagoons are popular venues for watersports. Other attractions include two tidal pools, an 18-hole golf course and the interesting Riverbend Crocodile Farm. Although motorized boats are not allowed on Imbizana lagoon (on Southbroom's northern boundary), boardsailing is permitted.

TRAFALGAR MARINE AND MPENJATI NATURE RESERVES Stretching from the mouth of the San Lameer lagoon south to the 51-hectare Mpenjati Nature Reserve, the Trafalgar Marine Reserve extends 500 metres seaward from the shoreline. It is the only marine sanctuary on the South Coast. Mpenjati protects fine examples of coastal grassland and forest, and small antelope such as blue duiker may be seen. The Mpenjati lagoon is the reserve's focal point, favoured by anglers and boardsailors. Facilities for picnicking and braaiing are located along the river bank.

PORT EDWARD The most southerly seaside resort in KwaZulu-Natal is Port Edward, and Silver Beach, north of the lighthouse, is popular for swimming and fishing. Lined by densely vegetated banks, the Mtamvuna River here is navigable for several kilometres upstream beyond the graceful steel arch of the bridge that links KwaZulu-Natal with the Eastern Cape. The Mtamvuna's estuary is ideal for ski-boats.

WILD COAST SUN The Wild Coast Sun (*see* p. 120), gateway to the legendary Wild Coast, occupies a landscaped site overlooking unspoilt coastline clothed in lush forest and grassland. Built as a gambling casino, it lured many South Africans over the border into the former Transkei. For sports enthusiasts, this extensive hotel complex has much to offer, from an 18-hole golf course, to fishing, jetskiing, sailing, boating, tennis and squash. Adjacent to the hotel, the Beachcomber Centre has a beachside bar, and the Mzamba Village Market, opposite the resort's main entrance, sells original curios.

UMTAMVUNA NATURE RESERVE Well worth visiting is the 3 257-hectare Umtamvuna Nature Reserve which extends up the Mtamvuna River for 30 kilometres and encompasses the river's impressive gorge. At the reserve's entrance, the Fish Eagle Trail leads up the forested gorge where many endemic trees and orchids are marked. Other trails begin from the office at the edge of the gorge. Rare Cape vultures breed on 200-metre-high sheer cliffs that tower above the river, and Umtamvuna's more than 200 bird species include crowned and fish eagles and the peregrine falcon.

ORIBI GORGE NATURE RESERVE Over many millennia, the Umzimkulwana River has eroded a gorge 24 kilometres long, 5 kilometres wide and 300 metres deep. Enclosed by sheer sandstone cliffs, the densely forested gorge is protected by the Oribi Gorge Nature Reserve which stretches for 7 kilometres on either side of the road descending into the gorge. A small rest camp, on the chasm's rim, can be accessed from the road before the descent. The 1 917-hectare reserve conserves a variety of forest-dwelling animals including bushbuck, blue duiker and monkey. The vegetation is particularly rich and 500 tree species have been identified. Three separate walking trails either follow the course of the Umzimkulwana River or descend into the valley from the rest camp. Twice a week the *Banana Express* (*see also* p. 52) visits the reserve. A ranger meets the train, accompanies visitors on a walk in the gorge and treats them to a braai in a boma.

VERNON CROOKES NATURE RESERVE From Park Rynie, the R612 runs inland through the coastal sugar cane belt to Vernon Crookes. The reserve encloses 2 189 hectares of undulating hills that rise to an altitude of 500 metres, and protects a valuable tract of forest and hillside grassland in a region where coastal development, population growth and sugar cane farming have destroyed much of the natural vegetation.

Visitors are encouraged to walk in the reserve and trails traverse much of the area. In the north a trail leads to a viewpoint overlooking the deep valley of the Mpambanyoni River, and about 13 kilometres of game-viewing road penetrates the eastern section of the reserve. Zebra, impala, reedbuck, bushbuck, eland and wildebeest can be see, as well as abundant birdlife, including martial eagle, narina trogon and cisticola. The small Nyengelezi camp consists of several rest huts and a bunkhouse.

The rare and dainty oribi antelope frequents short grasslands.

Midmar Historical Village's many attractions include the tugboat JB Eaglesham (above), and a fascinating cultural museum (left).

MIDMAR PUBLIC RESORT NATURE RESERVE

After the steep and often misty ascent from Pietermaritzburg, the N3 crosses prime agricultural land before reaching the turn-off to Midmar Dam, which stores some of the purest water in KwaZulu-Natal. It was built to impound the flow of the Umgeni River and was completed in 1965. The dam occupies an area of 1 600 hectares, and together with the surrounding lands, is conserved within the 2 857-hectare Midmar Public Resort Nature Reserve.

The reserve's entrance can be reached from the R617 to Bulwer and accommodation includes chalets, rustic cabins and many camping

sites. The R103 runs below the dam wall, and when the dam is full, a sheet of white water cascades down the spillway. Extensive picnic sites have been established along the northern shoreline and a grassy peninsula has been fenced off as a game park, safeguarding black wildebeest, eland, reedbuck, hartebeest, springbok, blesbok and zebra.

The road running along the northern shoreline provides splendid views across the lake backed by the rolling hills of the Midlands.

MIDMAR HISTORICAL VILLAGE

Opened in 1983, the Midmar Historical Village is situated 800 metres before the main entrance to Midmar Public Resort Nature Reserve. This carefully planned attraction includes a late 19th-century red-brick village, complete with village square and tree-lined streets, a farmyard, blacksmith's shop, village church and Hindu temple. Many of the buildings, such as the old library from the ghost town of York near Greytown, were relocated to the site.

Steam train rides depart from the meticulously restored railway station or visitors can tour the village in a carriage pulled by a large Shire horse. Adjacent buildings accommodate gift shops, coffee shops and restaurants, while several exhibition halls display vintage cars and farming implements. The tugboat *JB Eaglesham*, on the edge of the village overlooking the dam, is a popular attraction. Future expansion and development of the village is planned.

MIDLANDS MEANDER

The beauty and solitude of the Midlands region has always been an inspiration to artists, and in 1985 a handful of residents established an arts and crafts route called the Midlands Meander. Stretching between Mooi River and Hilton, the route grew in popularity and now includes over 65 participating members. Visitors can choose from three main routes that wind across the tranquil countryside.

This tour concentrates mainly on the attractions accessible from the R103 between Lidgetton and

Balgowan, and in the vicinity of Rosetta. Here, over a dozen enterprises specialize in commodities as diverse as herbs, pianos, leather goods, cheese, stained glass, antiques, furniture and mineral water. There is even a health hydro and a company that manufactures attractive decoupage wooden boxes. Ample accommodation is available en route in some of the finest country inns in the province, and tourists will delight in the quaint country pubs and coffee shops.

MOOI RIVER

At the western end of the Midlands Meander lies Mooi River, an important service centre for a productive agricultural region well-known for stock and dairy farming, and for its many stud farms. The Station Master's Arms, in the town's historic railway station building, is a popular country pub. Mooi River is famous for its arts and crafts, and several shops in and around town offer, among other things, silk embroidery, items made from hand-spun wool and woven garments.

CRAIGIEBURN DAM The R622 then follows the meandering course of the Mooi River as far as the Sierra Ranch Hotel, and crosses a landscape of grassland to the Craigieburn Dam on the Mnyamvubu River (a tributary of the Mooi). Completed in 1963 to provide water for citrus farmers downstream, the dam is popular with yachtsmen, windsurfers, canoeists and anglers. The 39-metre-high curved wall forms a narrow lake covering 220 hectares. A number of camping and picnic sites have been set out along the western shore.

KARKLOOF NATURE RESERVE After leaving Craigieburn Dam, the road crosses extensive wattle plantations before descending into the Karkloof Valley. At the beginning of the descent, a steep, 500-metre-high forested range curves away to the right. On the crest of this range is an extensive vlei, giving rise to several streams which plunge into the forests below. Mount Gilboa, the highest peak in the Karkloof at 1 768 metres, can be seen from the road.

A section of this beautiful indigenous forest, and the grassland and vlei on the summit, is protected by the 1 726-hectare Karkloof Nature Reserve. Forest-dwelling animals such as blue duiker, bushbuck, bushpig and samango monkey live in the forest, and rumours persist that leopards still roam in the range. Birders may see crowned and longcrested eagle, and rameron pigeon.

KARKLOOF FALLS After passing the Karkloof Nature Reserve, a signpost leads to the spectacular Karkloof Falls, which plunges 105 metres into a deep forested gorge. Upstream, visitors can relax at picnic sites along the river and while away the time swimming. Care should be exercised near the vertical drop of the falls as several people have lost their lives there. As they are situated on property owned by the timber giant SAPPI, much of the surrounding land has been planted with pine trees. For

this reason, the falls are normally closed to the public in winter during the fire hazard months.

Immediately below the falls, the tranquil beauty of the forested Karkloof Valley is complemented by Game Valley. This privately owned game reserve stretches for 6 kilometres down the valley and protects buffalo, white rhino, giraffe, roan, elephant and sable. Luxury accommodation is available at a lodge located on a lofty hillside overlooking the Karkloof River.

UMGENI VALLEY NATURE RESERVE Just outside Howick, the steep sides of the Umgeni gorge provide a perfect setting for the Umgeni Valley Nature Reserve. In a region where intensive commercial agriculture has produced a manicured landscape, the rugged boulder-strewn valley clothed in tall acacia trees and riverine forest within a short distance of town comes as a refreshing surprise. The 760-hectare reserve is managed by the Wildlife Society, and in keeping with the organization's philosophy, the four rest camps – some of which are only accessible on foot – blend into the surrounding forest.

An extensive network of hiking trails guides visitors through the valley and the plentiful wildlife which may be seen includes blesbok, zebra, bushbuck, impala, wildebeest, eland,

Distinctive blesbok are abundant at the Umgeni Valley Nature Reserve.

The beautiful Howick Falls plunges 94 metres over craggy, weather-beaten rocks.

nyala and giraffe. Crowned eagle, blackcollared barbet, forktailed drongo and white-eye are just some of the birds that occur here. A drive along the rough track which leads along the edge of the Umgeni gorge to a parking lot will reveal spectacular views of the deeply incised, forested Umgeni Valley and the distant Albert Falls Dam.

HOWICK In 1850 an important crossing over the Umgeni River was created and the services required by wagon drivers encouraged the development of a village. Thus the pretty town of Howick was established on the main wagon route into the interior from the coast. Although the Umgeni is now crossed by a modern bridge, Howick's main street still retains tangible signs from the

past. The Victorian-style museum, in the park adjacent to the river, preserves much of the town's history, and the Howick Falls Hotel, across the road, is another authentic reminder of the town's early years. In the centre of town, a magnificent stone mansion from the 1860s now houses a popular restaurant.

A short walk from the main street leads to a tree-lined park adjoining the lovely Howick Falls, and a restaurant here overlooks the falls' 94-metre-high plume. A platform allows for superb close-up views of these beautiful falls and of the deep gorge below. A two-hour circular trail leading down the steep bank enables visitors to reach the impressive base of the falls, which is especially spectacular when the Umgeni River is in flood.

KAMBERG From the village of Nottingham Road, the road traces the undulating folds of the Drakensberg's foothills. After 28 kilometres, it crosses a valley of irrigated pastures, cuts through the eastern end of the Natal Drakensberg Park and then follows the Mooi River through a scenic gap to Kamberg, one of five rest camps managed by the Natal Parks Board in the high 'Berg.

A pleasant 4-kilometre trail, with three 1-kilometre loops, leads along the Mooi River. Wildlife here includes blesbok, black wildebeest, reedbuck, duiker and eland, and birds, such as ground woodpecker, mocking chat, Drakensberg siskin and Gurney's sugarbird, are abundant. Just below the camp, a trout hatchery is open to the public, and fishermen have access to 13 kilometres of the Mooi River. Fishing is also permitted in several small dams located near the hatchery.

HIGHMOOR In a neighbouring valley to the north, a dirt road shares a narrow ravine with the course of the Klein Mooi River. Eventually the road reaches the upper end of the valley and a broad, grassland plain. At an altitude of 2 000 metres, this rolling grassland, appropriately named Highmoor, fades towards the distant peaks of Giant's Castle.

Highmoor's only accommodation is a camp site occupying a superb position on a hill crest overlooking the Klein Mooi's deeply-incised valley. Several lovely trails lead across the surrounding grasslands, and visitors can venture north into Giant's Castle, or south across the Mkhomazi Wilderness Area. Many raptors, such as black eagle, jackal buzzard and lammergeyer, are found in the area.

GIANT'S CASTLE The Zulus call the Drakensberg's jagged, magnificent basalt wall *Ukhahlamba*, a barrier of spears. Few places could provide better access to this spectacular scenery than the main camp at Giant's Castle, offering an awe-inspiring view of the deep Bushmans River valley, and in the distance, the serried rampart of the Drakensberg. Giant's Castle Hutted Camp is overshadowed by three of the four highest peaks on the South African side of the Escarpment – Giant's Castle (3 314 metres), Popple Peak (3 325 metres) and the 3 410-metre eNjasuthi dome. Hiking trails generally follow contour paths which lead to the base of these high peaks. In winter snow often covers these peaks and three mountain huts provide hikers with accommodation.

Game-viewing is a popular pastime, as is bird-watching, walking and trout-fishing in the Little Tugela and Bushmans rivers. Although harsh winter conditions limit the carrying capacity of the 'Berg's grasslands, a variety of animals such as grey rhebuck, mountain reedbuck, bushbuck, baboon and oribi can be seen. In 1903 a game reserve was established at Giant's Castle to safeguard some of the last free-ranging eland in South Africa. The eland flourished and the Drakensberg now maintains a population of 1 500, the second largest of its kind in the country. For birders, the camouflaged Lammergeyer Hide is open during winter. Although this endangered raptor is widely distributed, it is rare throughout its range. A recent survey recorded only 200 pairs in the Drakensberg.

Giant's Castle is particularly rich in San rock art, much of which depicts their great admiration for the eland. Although eland have survived, the San have not, and the 5 000 rock paintings that have been catalogued in Giant's Castle are the only impression they left on the landscape. From the camp, a short walk zigzags up the valley to a unique museum situated in a sandstone overhang that was once a San shelter. About 500 authentic paintings, some of which are thought to be about 800 years old, cover the cave walls. Artifacts and lifelike models depict the lifestyle of the Drakensberg's first people.

CHAMPAGNE CASTLE The second highest summit in South Africa, the 3 377-metre-high Champagne Castle juts out from the Escarpment wall and overshadows the Sterkspruit Valley. Other main peaks in the area include Cathkin Peak (3 149 metres), Sterkhorn (2 973 metres), Monk's Cowl (3 234 metres) and Intunja (2 408 metres), a conspicuous peak with a hole through its summit. As this lovely valley lies within 31 kilometres of the N3, it has become the 'Berg's most popular retreat. It boasts a cluster of hotels, cottages and timeshare resorts, and many walks lead into the State Forest area. Sterkspruit Valley is renowned for the Drakensberg Boys Choir School, and for Dragon Peaks and Monk's Cowl caravan parks.

The endangered lammergeyer is protected within the Drakensberg.

CATHEDRAL PEAK The Cathedral Peak Hotel high up in the lovely Mlambonja valley was built in 1937 and has been run by the Van der Riet family for two generations. It is surrounded by the Natal Drakensberg Park, and visitors can choose to ride horses, fish, play golf and tennis, or flit over the peaks in the hotel's helicopter. A labyrinth of paths explore the surrounding valleys and mountainous spurs.

From the conservation office near the hotel, Mike's Pass climbs 500 metres in under 5 kilometres along a route that includes four abrupt corners and several steep gradients. From the parking lot at the end of the road, motorists can enjoy a dramatic view of the high 'Berg.

Some of the most striking peaks are Cathedral Peak (3 004 metres), Mlambonja Buttress (3 007 metres), Cleft Peak (3 281 metres), Outer

A rewarding pastime: trout fishing on a lake in the Drakensberg's foothills.

The Injasuti Valley provides superb hiking opportunities in dramatic surroundings.

ROYAL NATAL NATIONAL PARK All roads to the northern 'Berg resorts lead, at some stage, through the centrally located village of Bergville, and from here, the road leads to the 8 856-hectare Royal Natal Park. The focal point is the awe-inspiring Amphitheatre, a crescent-shaped basalt ridge that is 6 kilometres wide and towers 1 500 metres above the lower valleys. The superb Tendele rest camp, situated on a hillside above the Tugela River, provides unparalleled views of the mountain.

In the lower-lying valleys, the Royal Natal Hotel and Mahai camp site occupy idyllic settings, and provide access to the walking trails that traverse the park. The Amphitheatre's summit can be reached by following the hiking trail that passes The Dome and joins the road on the Free State side of the mountain. The

The breathtaking Tugela Falls plunge down the wall of the Amphitheatre.

road ends at a parking lot at a lofty 2 550 metres. The trail continues for another 4 kilometres and, with the aid of two chain ladders, finally reaches the crest. Where the flat summit yields to the vertical rim of the escarpment, the Tugela Falls, second highest in the world, plummet 948 metres to the valley below.

Horn (3 005 metres), the Bell (2 930 metres) and Inner Horn (3 005 metres). Trails lead from the parking lot into Ndedema gorge, a delightful valley that protects the Drakensberg's largest indigenous forest and its greatest concentration of San rock art. Many hikers regard Ndedema as the most spectacular of the 'Berg's many valleys.

SPIOENKOP PUBLIC RESORT NATURE RESERVE The pretty 1 500-hectare Spioenkop Dam rests at the foot of an acacia-dotted hill where, during the Anglo-Boer War, British troops attempted to break through Boer lines and hundreds of British were pinned down by fire from Boer sharpshooters on the hilltop. Many graves and memorials are still scattered across Spioenkop's summit.

Today the 7 283-hectare nature reserve that protects the dam and surrounding land is perfect for fishing, boating, hiking and game-viewing. A camp site is located at the dam's edge and facilities include tennis courts, a swimming pool, children's playground, curio shop and battlefield museum.

Upstream from the camp site lies the secluded Ntenjwa rustic bush camp. It is only accessible by boat, and overlooks the upper reaches of the tranquil Spioenkop Dam.

Picnic sites are located along the southern shoreline, where fishing is permitted and two short walks have been laid out. Animals which may be seen here include hartebeest, waterbuck, impala, springbok and blesbok. Although boats can be launched from the southern shore, they are not allowed to berth on the northern shore which has been set aside as a reserve area. Here, buffalo, giraffe, white rhino and eland are common. Visitors staying at Iphika tented camp at the base of Spioenkop may only explore the surrounds on foot.

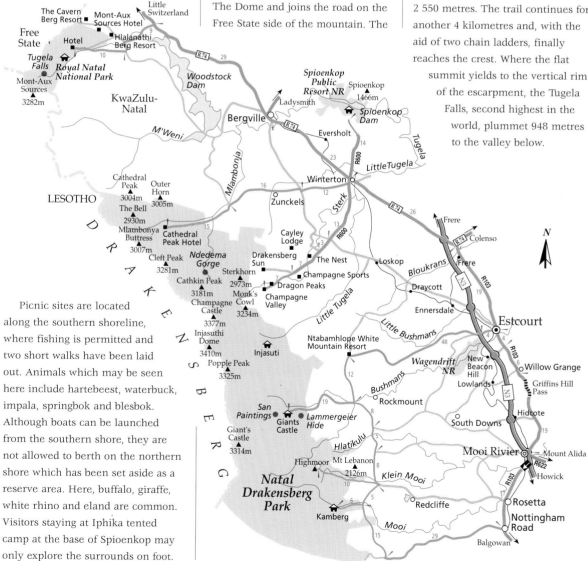

NORTHERN KWAZULU-NATAL

The Kosi estuary is one of the most pristine along the KwaZulu-Natal coastline.

A taste of the real Africa can still be savoured in some of the remote areas of northern KwaZulu-Natal. Here portions of King Shaka's royal hunting grounds have been kept aside as game parks and conservation areas, and here, some of Africa's oldest parks are located (*see also* p. 61). Pristine wetlands, sand forests and game-rich bushveld are just a few of the ecosystems that occur in this region.

ZULU SUPREMACY

The word Zulu – named from a small and insignificant Nguni vassal clan that once lived on the banks of the umHlatuze River, north of present-day Eshowe – is intimately associated with South Africa. In the late 1700s, Senzangakhona, a young Zulu chief, fathered a child out of formal wedlock. (Although he was betrothed to Nandi, the child's mother, she was not yet his wife.)

A Zulu woman inscribes a clay pot at Dumazulu Traditional Village, south of Hluhluwe village.

Nandi's pregnancy was scornfully dismissed by the Zulu elders, who said that she was not pregnant but merely swollen up because she had been afflicted by an *ishaka*, the Zulu word for an intestinal beetle. Custom required Senzangakhona to marry Nandi and she became his third and discredited wife, and Shaka his neglected child.

For a number of reasons, mother and child were eventually forced to leave Senzangakhona's household. Shaka was not accepted among his peers but his unhappy childhood gave rise to his resolve to one day control his own destiny. Through his prowess on the battlefield, Shaka became the chief of the Zulu clan when he was about 30. A combination of political skill and military genius brought him supremacy over an ever-widening circle of clans and tribes, creating the mighty Zulu empire.

Shaka remodelled the social and political system of the Zulu people. Young men and women were conscripted into age-based *amabutho* (regiments), some of which were garrisoned in the royal households (*Amakhanda*) where they provided domestic service to the king during peacetime. The *amabutho* also formed the structure of the Zulu army, ensuring that there were always regiments on stand-by while the others could be quickly assembled for war. This military preparedness and the discipline that was inherent in the *amabutho* system, combined with new fighting techniques and military strategies, made the Zulus a formidable and ferocious fighting machine (*see also* p. 42).

This map highlights the regional map opposite. Overlapping regions and their page numbers are supplied.

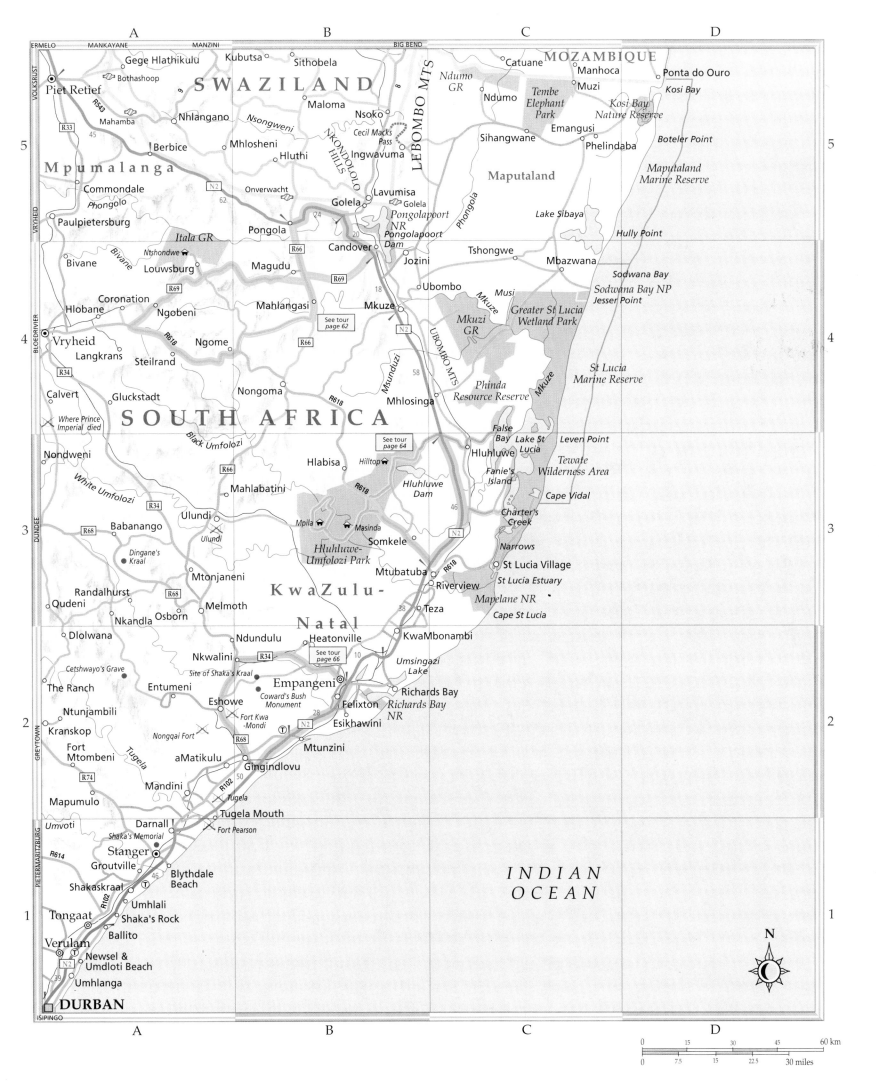

The delicate dune system at Cape Vidal, which lies about 60 kilometres from the St Lucia mouth.

During his reign, Shaka built three *Amakhanda*, his last being at Dukuza near present-day Stanger where he was assassinated. A memorial has been erected at the site where it is believed the killing took place, and an education centre has been built. After Shaka's assassination, his half-brother Dingane established the capital at umGungundhlovu, where Piet Retief and his companions were executed (*see also* p. 42). The site has been partially reconstructed and is now a national monument. It is situated in the Valley of Kings, *emaKhosini*, which is adjacent to the Melmoth-Vryheid road at the turn-off to Ulundi (*see also* p. 44).

GREATER ST LUCIA WETLAND PARK
One of the largest wildlife sanctuaries in South Africa, the Greater St Lucia Wetland Park protects a fragile and important environment, which ranges from tropical reef, wetland, swamp, beach, mangrove and ocean, to sandveld, mountain, thornveld, grassland and coastal forest. This remarkable park extends from Sodwana Bay in the north to Mapelane in the south. With its rich variety of scenery and abundance of animal, bird and plant life, the Greater St Lucia Wetland Park has become one of Africa's most exciting wildlife reserves.

The park comprises several protected areas: St Lucia Game Reserve, including the water and islands of Lake St Lucia; St Lucia Park, surrounding the village of St Lucia and a strip of land around most of the lake

Loggerhead turtles come to Sodwana Bay annually to lay their eggs.

shore; False Bay Park on the Western Shores of False Bay between the Hluhluwe and Mzinene rivers; the St Lucia and Maputaland marine reserves on the Eastern Shores; the Sodwana Bay National Park, adjacent to the St Lucia Marine Reserve; the Cape Vidal State Forest, about 60 kilometres from the St Lucia mouth; and when negotiations have been finalized, the Mkuzi Game Reserve, which protects sand forest.

LAKE ST LUCIA
Centrepiece of the park is the fascinating St Lucia estuary and lake system, a place of wild beauty that reflects many of Africa's poignant moods. Lake St Lucia, so named by the early Portuguese mariners, is the largest marine lake in Africa. The system is about 30 kilometres long, spreading northwards from the estuary mouth to the Mkuze River in Maputaland, the width varies from 100 metres to 15 kilometres, and its southern end is

linked to the ocean by a 20-kilometre-long channel known as the 'Narrows'. The average depth of this 368-square-kilometre expanse of water is only about one metre, with salinity levels varying from completely fresh to saltier than sea water. St Lucia is a vast natural workshop where the waters of the land meet the waters of the sea, and this leads to a fascinating interplay between marine life and freshwater life.

Along the Eastern Shores, which divide the lake from the sea, is a range of heavily wooded sand dunes believed to be among the highest in the world, and a flat plain of swampy ground in which there are a number of freshwater pans. These pans are home to hippo as well as crocodile, both of which also live in the lake where the salinity levels are moderate. The lake system supports over 345 different bird species in 11 major habitats – only a few places in Africa have a greater concentration of bird life. Comfortable rest camps are situated on the Western Shores at Charter's Creek and Fanie's Island, and at the mouth of the estuary, the burgeoning holiday resort of St Lucia has become a major destination for fishermen.

MKUZI GAME RESERVE
On the western perimeter of the Greater St Lucia Wetland Park, the Mkuzi Game Reserve covers 37 985 hectares and extends from Nsumu Pan to the top of the Lebombo Mountains. The vegetation is a varied mosaic of woodland and thicket, with patches of sand forest and small patches of riverine forest along the watercourses. Several seasonal pans are filled by floodwaters from the Mkuze River, providing a home for a wide variety of waterbirds. Both black and white rhino are found at Mkuzi, giraffe are fairly common and many species of antelope can be seen. A few elusive leopard are present and cheetah were reintroduced in 1966.

CORAL COAST
Between Kosi Bay in the north and St Lucia in the south lies South Africa's Coral Coast. Here, tropical corals have encrusted ancient coastal dunes formed during the Pleistocene period when the coastline lay further out to sea. As the sea level rose, water slowly reclaimed the land, submerging the dunes

which now lie between 5 and 25 metres beneath the surface. The coral reefs and their inhabitants provide a panorama of colour and endless fascination for scuba divers, and several scuba diving operators provide charter services at Sodwana Bay, at the northern end of this marine reserve.

HLUHLUWE-UMFOLOZI PARK

Across the Lebombo Mountains to the west lies the Hluhluwe-Umfolozi Park, the fifth largest and one of the oldest conservation areas in South Africa, extending across 96 453 hectares. Proclaimed in 1895, the Umfolozi Section – once Shaka's exclusive hunting territory (*see p. 58*) – lies between the *umFolozi emhlophe* ('White Umfolozi') River in the south and *umFolozi emnyama* ('Black Umfolozi') River in the north.

In 1989 the Corridor lands linking Umfolozi to Hluhluwe were incorporated into the park complex. This tongue of land is one of the most picturesque bush areas in southern Africa. Umfolozi's savanna and acacia grassland vegetation spreads out before a ridge of distant blue hills. It has rich grazing and plenty of water, and since time immemorial it has supported large numbers of wild animals, including the 'Big Five'. There are hutted camps, exclusive bush camps, game-viewing hides, a network of roads, 25 000 hectares of wilderness area and many wilderness trails.

To the north of Umfolozi, the Hluhluwe Section is also a place of great beauty and is 25 000 hectares in extent. Here the Hluhluwe River winds its way through bush-clad hills and open grasslands. As with the Umfolozi Section, Hluhluwe also boasts the 'Big Five' and a rich diversity of mammal and bird life. It has a hutted camp which includes the upmarket Hilltop Camp.

OPERATION RHINO

The unspoilt Umfolozi thornveld has been the arena for many conservation success stories. From the beginning the Umfolozi valley's abundant wildlife attracted many hunters and by the 1890s many species had become locally extinct. The shortsighted rhinoceros was particularly vulnerable, and was soon hunted to the brink of extinction. When the Umfolozi and Hluhluwe game reserves were proclaimed in April 1895 their thorny thickets sheltered southern Africa's last remaining population of white rhino – numbering about 35 – as well as a few black rhino. The area's recovery has been nothing short of miraculous. In 1953 renowned conservationist Ian Player counted 437 white rhino in Umfolozi; by 1960 the population had reached 700. The once-endangered white rhino was thriving and so they could be translocated to restock other reserves. In 1961 the highly successful Operation Rhino began. Using special techniques of capture,

white rhino were removed to game parks throughout Africa. To date over 4 000 white rhino have been successfully relocated and at Hluhluwe-Umfolozi the rhino populations have been stabilized at about 1 200 white rhino and 300 black rhino.

The once-endangered white rhino now thrives at the Hluhluwe-Umfolozi Park.

WILD KINGDOMS

Apart from the Greater St Lucia Wetland and Hluhluwe-Umfolozi parks, northern Kwa-Zulu-Natal boasts a number of smaller but no less important game reserves. At the northern end of the Phongolo River flood plain along the Mozambique border lies the Ndumo Game Reserve. Proclaimed in 1924, the reserve is only 10 000 hectares in extent, but is extremely rich in birdlife, with almost as many species (about 400 in total) as the Kruger National Park which is 190 times larger! Ndumo's main feature is the series of flood plain pans, fed by the Phongolo and Usutu rivers, which are rich in nutrients and provide a habitat for large numbers of hippo, fish, crocodile and aquatic birds.

Adjacent to the Ndumo Game Reserve is the Tembe Elephant Park, situated in the sand forest zone of Maputaland in an area known as Sihangwane. Opened to the public in 1993, the park provides sanctuary for what were the last of the free-ranging elephants in southern Africa and the now almost extinct and highly secretive suni antelope.

Higher up the Phongolo, near its confluence with the Bivane River, is the Itala Game Reserve. Proclaimed in 1973, the park is 29 653 hectares in extent and has three bush camps and a luxury camp. Itala's wide variety of animal species and special 'bush' ambience is hard to beat.

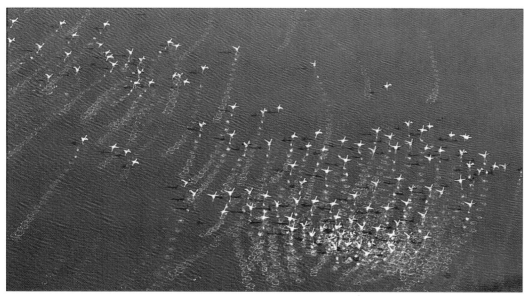

Flamingoes are just one of hundreds of bird species at the Greater St Lucia Wetland Park, a bird-watchers paradise.

WANDERINGS ALONG THE PHONGOLO ◆ 350 km

Itala Game Reserve boasts the splendid Ntshondwe Camp (above) *and is the only KwaZulu-Natal reserve which protects the rare tsessebe antelope* (below).

ITALA GAME RESERVE This beautiful reserve, with its open bushveld and grasslands, is made up of rugged terrain and 37 kilometres of frontage along the Phongolo River. Seven of the river's tributaries have carved the deep valleys that dissect Itala, and altitude varies from 1 446 metres on the Louwsberg Plateau to 335 metres in the east. Itala is the only reserve in the province where tsessebe, a rare antelope, occurs, and four of the 'Big Five' (excluding lion) are found here.

Flagship of the Natal Parks Board, Itala's magnificent Ntshondwe Camp is a good place from which to explore the reserve. Its setting at the foot of the imposing Louwsburg Plateau was carefully selected to provide panoramic views over the whole of Itala. One of Ntshondwe's most outstanding features is the design of its self-contained chalets, many of which are located between boulders and spreading fig trees.

As the camp is unfenced, animals such as warthog wander freely between the chalets. A pathway from

here leads to a superbly situated swimming pool tucked in a clearing at the foot of the mountain.

An elevated outdoor terrace adjoining the restaurant provides sweeping views of distant grassy summits dotted with game. Itala has over 300 bird species and an extensive wooden platform overlooking a reed-fringed waterhole is an ideal spot for bird-watching; a footpath leads through thickets and wild fig trees to Ntshondwe's hide where weaver, spurwing goose and egret may be seen. The grasslands area from the entrance to the reserve is known as Onverwacht and attracts tsessebe, as well as large herds of eland, wildebeest, zebra, red hartebeest and white rhino.

West of Ntshondwe, the 31-kilometre Ngubhu Loop along the base of the mountain encircles a broad basin and then hugs the cliff face on the return journey. The basin is home to giraffe, kudu, black rhino and elephant, and the drive provides superb views of the reserve's scenery.

Several self-guided nature trails and guided game walks are also offered from Ntshondwe. Apart from Ntshondwe Camp, visitors can stay at a camp site on the Mbizu River or in three rustic bush camps – Thalu, Mbizo or Mhlangeni – all of which have resident rangers who take guests on guided walks. Perched on a hilltop above deep valleys, the sumptuous Ntshondwe Lodge offers luxury accommodation, and its wooden deck and sunken swimming pool provide a view not easily surpassed.

PONGOLAPOORT DAM AND NATURE RESERVE Leaving Itala, the R69 meanders along a scenic ridge that forms the watershed between the Mkuze and Phongolo rivers. After the turn-off to the hilltop village of Magudu, the tar ends and a gravel road continues through untamed, hilly country clothed in dense woodland. From the crest of the Rooirante, visitors can enjoy a splendid view of the Pongolapoort Dam, set at the foot of the Lebombo

Mountains rising 600 metres above the water. The border with Swaziland crosses the northern part of the dam.

The 22 000-hectare Pongola Game Reserve encompasses the surface of the dam, the land between the dam and Swaziland, and the western shoreline. It was proclaimed on 13 June 1894, thus establishing Africa's first game reserve. But it was de-proclaimed in 1921 as it was

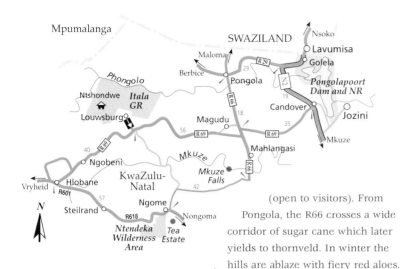

considered to be too small, and no rangers had been stationed there for many years. The re-establishment of the reserve was made possible by the completion of the Pongolapoort Dam in 1961. Water is now released from the dam to coincide with the natural flood cycle of the pans along the flood plain. Flanked by grassy plains dotted with acacia trees, the Pongolapoort Dam is a popular venue for fishermen, and affords catches of tigerfish and catfish. Picnic sites, a circular game drive and a boat launching area are added attractions.

A wide variety of game, such as blue wildebeest, impala, kudu, nyala, red duiker, reedbuck, giraffe, zebra, white rhino and leopard, live in the reserve's dense acacia thornveld and the Golela Forest, while hippo and crocodile inhabit the dam itself. The over 200 bird species include lilac-breasted roller and secretary bird. The reserve is open to day visitors but additional facilities, including overnight accommodation, are planned for the future.

PONGOLA This lovely corner of KwaZulu-Natal provides the traveller with a fine scenic drive. Located on the N2, Pongola is only 7 kilometres from Swaziland and 2 kilometres from the Phongolo River. The sweltering climate and fertile soils along the river make the area ideal for growing subtropical fruit and sugar cane. After it has been cut, the sugar cane is processed at a nearby mill

(open to visitors). From Pongola, the R66 crosses a wide corridor of sugar cane which later yields to thornveld. In winter the hills are ablaze with fiery red aloes.

MKUZE VALLEY After crossing the Mkuze River and the green irrigated fields that line its banks, a district road turning to the right heads to Ngome. The surrounding countryside is thickly vegetated in thornveld dotted with tall red aloes. Visible in the valley below is the Mkuze River, dominated by the Nhlavanne and Mathanga hills. Just before crossing the Mkuze at Mahlangasi, a turn-off leads to Mkuze Falls Safaris, a large ranch with its lodge overlooking the lovely Mkuze Falls. The ranch shelters some of the largest privately owned herds of kudu, nyala and

white rhino in the country, and offers game-viewing, bird-watching, walking trails and fishing.

Closer to Ngome, the thornveld yields with altitude to grassland. Soon the road reaches the cool highlands which are the source of the Black Umfolozi River. At an altitude of 1 200 metres, the air is refreshing, the forests tall and luxuriant. The road passes a tea estate and provides a panoramic view of the adjacent densely forested slopes.

NTENDEKA WILDERNESS AREA At Ngome, the 5 230-hectare Ntendeka Wilderness Area is one of the loveliest places in South Africa, and its most striking natural feature is the dolerite cliffs which tower above the forested valleys. Ntendeka preserves the upper catchment of the Black Umfolozi River and one of the largest inland forests in KwaZulu-Natal. This indigenous forest has been protected since 1903 and visitors will delight in its sylvan tranquillity. About 200 species of trees and shrubs have been identified here, the most common being the forest waterberry (many specimens grow to 30 metres in height), forest bushwillow, silver

oak, red currant and knobwood. The forest tree fern grows to record heights of up to 8 metres, and several trees found here occur nowhere else in KwaZulu-Natal. The forest is renowned for its orchids, often seen growing on tree trunks, and about 19 species have been identified, while the beautiful Ngome lily is endemic.

Equally prolific is Ntendeka's animals and birds (there are over 200 bird species in the forest). It is home to samango monkey, blue duiker, bushbuck and bushpig, and the patient bird-watcher will see such rarities as the bald ibis and blue swallow.

Ntendeka served as an important refuge for fugitives in the past. Mzilikazi, the founder of the Ndebele of Zimbabwe, hid in the forests after he refused to hand over cattle to Shaka, while after the battle of Isandlwana in 1879 (*see also* p. 44), Cetshwayo hid in the valley below the forest. Visitors are able to view the rock shelter, known as Cetshwayo's Refuge, reportedly the site of the king's hide-out. Guests can stay at a camp site in a clearing near the forest station. From here, a network of day trails penetrates the dense forest and the lower-lying grasslands.

Itala offers excellent game-viewing, nature trails, bird-watching and comfortable accommodation.

WILDERNESS, WILDLIFE AND WETLAND ◆ 250 km

UMFOLOZI SECTION Entering the Hluhluwe-Umfolozi Park via the Mambeni Gate, a 114-kilometre road network snakes through the northern half of the Umfolozi Section. Close to the gate is the Vulamehlo curio stall, where local communities sell their handicrafts. The road passes Masinda, smallest of the park's camps, crosses the Black Umfolozi River and climbs to Mpila Camp, which provides superb views over the surrounding wilderness. In the valley below, the Black Umfolozi meanders across the flood plain.

Near Masinda a self-guided walking trail gives a good view of the former Corridor section of the park, and a short trail from Mpila affords panoramic views of the wilderness. Both camps accommodate visitors in chalets and offer night drives. On the road west from Mpila, a lofty viewsite overlooking the White Umfolozi River captures the essence of Umfolozi: river valleys, sandbanks and rolling hills clothed in acacia woodland.

UMFOLOZI'S BUSH CAMPS The bush camps at Umfolozi provide visitors with a memorable experience. Guests are accommodated in remote corners of the park in reed-and-thatch huts, raised on stilts, designed to blend with the vegetation.

Nselweni Bush Camp lies on the bend of the Black Umfolozi River, and further west, Sontuli and Gqoyeni bush camps border the Black Umfolozi in the Sontuli region, the best game-viewing area in Umfolozi. Sontuli Loop – where cheetah, lion and white rhino are often seen – has one of the most popular picnic sites in the park. Gqoyeni lies on the summer migration route of elephant from Hluhluwe to Umfolozi and big herds are commonly seen. White and black rhino, buffalo and lion are often seen in the area and birds include greenspotted dove, yellowbilled kite and

Giraffe, browsing here at Umfolozi, feed on a wide range of trees and bushes.

blackcollared barbet. Each camp offers guided game-viewing walks. Mndindini base camp on the White Umfolozi is the starting point for Umfolozi's famous wilderness trails, the first created in the country. Mphafa hide in Umfolozi's wilderness area attracts many animals, including giraffe, zebra and blue wildebeest.

HLUHLUWE SECTION From Masinda camp a tarred road crosses the hills and links the Umfolozi Section with Hluhluwe's 95-kilometre road network. The journey northwards traverses a wide variety of habitats in a short distance, from lush forests to grasslands and woodlands. Several viewpoints along the way allow the visitor to stop and enjoy vistas of Hluhluwe's superb deep valleys, rolling hills and meandering rivers.

The average rainfall for the Hluhluwe Section is 985 millimetres – about 300 millimetres more than Umfolozi – which encourages the growth of dense woodland and forest. Forest-dwelling animals including red duiker, blue duiker and nyala inhabit Hluhluwe's thickets, as do many forest birds, such as tambourine dove,

trumpeter hornbill and purplecrested lourie. Buffalo, zebra and white rhino congregate on the open grasslands near Memorial Gate, and elephant often gather at Maphumulo picnic site on the Hluhluwe River.

The highest density of black rhino occurs in the Hluhluwe Section but they are sometimes difficult to detect in the thick vegetation. Thiyeni hide in Hluhluwe's southwestern area provides an opportunity to observe wildlife at close quarters.

Self-guided auto trails around Hluhluwe highlight rhino rubbing posts, tree species, and the interaction between plant and animal life.

HLUHLUWE'S BUSH LODGES Situated at the confluence of the Hluhluwe River and Munyawaneni stream, Munyawaneni Bush Lodge consists of four huts connected by walkways to a central lounge and kitchen complex. Munyawaneni is located close to a well-worn game path favoured by rhino and elephant.

Muntulu Bush Lodge has been expertly positioned on a rocky outcrop overlooking the palm-fringed banks of the Hluhluwe River. Its four units, each with their own viewing deck, are connected by covered boardwalks to the main dining area. A wooden platform in front of the lounge allows visitors to view game on the opposite bank, and the area is also known for its raptors. The luxury Mtwazi Lodge, set in a large garden, was the home of Hluhluwe's first Warden, Captain Potter.

Each lodge has a resident ranger who takes guests for game walks and where white and black rhino, bushbuck, nyala and even leopard have been recorded. Bird-watching along the rivers may reward the visitor with sightings of southern boubou and bush shrike, to name a few.

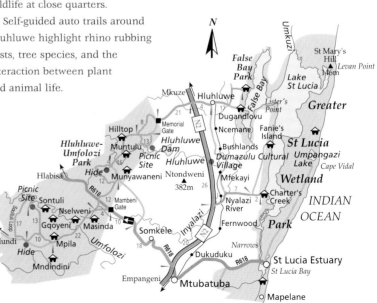

HILLTOP CAMP Situated at an altitude of 450 metres, Hilltop Camp offers sweeping views over Hluhluwe. It is the largest camp in the Hluhluwe-Umfolozi Park, and boasts a well-stocked store, and a superbly situated restaurant and lounge with lovely views over the valleys below. Guests are accommodated in attractive self-catering or non-catering units, most of which have viewing decks.

The well-organized, self-guided Mbhombe walking trail leads from the camp into the adjoining indigenous forest, providing an ideal opportunity for bird-watching and tree identification. Narina trogon, purple-crested lourie and tambourine dove are just some of the birds that visitors may see. An electric fence protects hikers from inquisitive lion or elephant. Hilltop conducts guided night drives, and early morning and late afternoon guided walks.

LAKE ST LUCIA Focal point of the Greater St Lucia Wetland Park, Lake St Lucia is a vital nursery for fish, prawns, crabs and other marine creatures, and many waterbirds thus depend on it as an important feeding ground. It protects breeding populations of birds such as the white and pinkbacked pelican, Caspian tern, spoonbill and fish eagle, and the combination of a shallow lake, grassland and forest is ideal for those interested in bird-watching.

The extensive lake also sustains an estimated 800 hippo and 1 200 crocodile, and the St Lucia Estuary is a premier fishing site for catches of kob, grunter, perch and yellowfin bream. No permits are needed.

FALSE BAY PARK Adjoining Lake St Lucia is False Bay Park, a 2 247-hectare corridor of woodland and sand forest. At Lister Point, where the lake is at its widest, a comfortable camp site and caravan park are set out under tall trees. The surrounding forest sustains nyala, suni, zebra, warthog and waterbuck, and the park is home to over 200 bird species, such as goliath heron, fish eagle and white pelican.

At Dugundlovu Rustic Camp, 7 kilometres south of Lister Point, quaint cottages are tucked into the sand forest on a high bluff above the lake. Visitors may drive to the camp or park at the main entrance gate and hike there on the 8-kilometre Dugundlovu Trail. The facilities are basic but a platform overlooking the lake provides superb views; a short walk from the camp leads through the forest to the shore.

One of the many attractions in False Bay Park is that the lake's waters can be explored in canoes. Fishing is popular, with catches of kob in winter, grunter in spring, and bream and perch throughout the year. Many walking trails traverse the area, allowing visitors to explore the fascinating sand forest. The Mphophomeni Trail in the northern section is a circular walk of either 7 or 10 kilometres through the sand forests and woodlands.

False Bay Park is unique for the abundance of marine fossils which are found along the lake's shores. Examples of these fossils include ammonites, the remnants of ocean life that flourished when the region was covered by a prehistoric sea.

A cattle egret perches on one of Lake St Lucia's resident hippos.

DUMAZULU TRADITIONAL VILLAGE The turn-off to Bushlands on the N2 south from Hluhluwe village leads to Dumazulu where visitors can gain insight into traditional Zulu culture. In two circular villages, connected by a raised boardwalk, members of the local communities make and sell crafts such as spears, baskets, bead-work and pottery, and Zulu dances are performed regularly.

Visitors can choose to stay at the village in thatched, traditionally decorated rondavels, or at the adjacent Bushlands Game Lodge where the wooden units are elevated on stilts above the surrounding sand forest. Some rooms look out over open country and dinner is often served in an open-air reed-walled boma. Guests can enjoy short walks where zebra, nyala, impala and wildebeest may be seen, and the resident rangers conduct game drives to Hluhluwe.

CHARTER'S CREEK AND FANIE'S ISLAND About 30 kilometres south of Hluhluwe village, a tarred road on the left leads to Lake St Lucia's Western Shores and the peaceful camps of Charter's Creek and Fanie's Island. Garnished with the bright red flowers of *Erythrina* (coral) trees, Charter's Creek is a charming, modest-sized camp overlooking a broad bay that is popular among fishermen. The camp consists of thatched rondavels and a communal kitchen (visitors bring their own food but meals are prepared by the camp staff), and it also has a swimming pool. Boats can be launched from both of these camps.

The rondavels, camp site and conference centre at Fanie's Island are delightfully situated. Visitors can enjoy first-class angling, good birding – including kingfisher, fish eagle and egret – and self-guided walks through the forest. Here the chances of spotting forest animals such as bushbuck and red duiker are excellent. Hippos can be seen in the lake, but a fence has been erected round the camp to keep them out.

Superb accommodation is provided at Hluhluwe's Hilltop Camp, the largest camp in the Hluhluwe-Umfolozi Park.

Skilfully crafted Zulu beadwork is for sale throughout KwaZulu-Natal.

GINGINDLOVU The village of Gingindlovu occupies a significant place in Zulu history. In December 1856 Zulu king Cetshwayo fought against five of his brothers over the right of succession to the throne of their father, Mpande. After Cetshwayo had successfully 'swallowed' his rivals he established a military encampment which he called Gingindlovu, meaning 'swallower of the elephant'.

At the Battle of Gingindlovu during the Anglo-Zulu War (*see also* p. 44), British troops defeated a Zulu regiment of 11 000 men here.

Today a monument and a cemetery, bordered by fields of sugar cane, mark the battle ground.

A petrol station marks the entrance to Gingindlovu village, which consists of a single row of busy shops along the main road. The town's cheerful ambience is reminiscent of a typically African marketplace: the bustling pavement is crowded with traders selling their wares, tailors work at their street-side sewing machines and shoppers load merchandise into heavily-laden minibuses.

ESHOWE Often judged the most beautiful town in KwaZulu-Natal, Eshowe was once home to the Zulu kings Mpande, Cetshwayo and Dinizulu. The town occupies a lofty hill crest 500 metres above sea level, and many a suburban garden has been enhanced by the gigantic tropical trees that flourish here. To the south lies the sweltering coastal plain; to the north the deep valley carved by the Mhlatuze River.

Eshowe surrounds the lush Dlinza Forest Nature Reserve, a 220-hectare stand of indigenous hardwoods to which there is free admission. Trails crisscross the forest and visitors may encounter bushbuck, duiker or monkey, and birds such as crowned eagle, trumpeter hornbill or golden-rumped tinker barbet. At the southern entrance of the town, the Ocean View Game Park is home to zebra, blesbok, wildebeest and impala.

In 1860 Cetshwayo established a village called Eziqwaqweni, about 2,5 kilometres east of what is now Eshowe's town centre. Later, a Norwegian missionary named Ommund Oftebro established a mission station at the site. The Zulus called the station KwaMondi, an adaptation of Oftebro's first name. In January 1879, KwaMondi was hurriedly converted into a fort by Col. Charles Pearson after word reached him of Lord Chelmsford's crushing defeat at Isandlwana (*see also* p. 44). Pearson's force was soon besieged by the Zulu army. In April 1879, after the battle of Gingindlovu, Chelmsford's force advanced to Eshowe and broke the 10-week siege of the fort. The graves of the heroic men who died during the siege mark the site.

After the Anglo-Zulu War, the British built the sturdy white-walled Fort Nongqai in what is today's Eshowe. This 1883 building has been declared a national monument and houses the fascinating Zululand Historical Museum. Among the artifacts in the museum's collection is a silver beer mug presented by Queen Victoria to Cetshwayo. A monument in Windham Street immortalises the site where Cetshwayo died on 8 February 1884, after his release from four years of confinement in Cape Town.

SHAKALAND In 1985 the producers of the epic TV series *Shaka Zulu* constructed several authentic Zulu villages, and in a dramatic finale,

Zulu men taking part in traditional stick fighting at Shakaland.

they were set ablaze. However, the village built to represent that of Shaka's father, Senzangakhona, was spared and later opened to the public as Shakaland.

Today this exciting village is home to several Zulu families who demonstrate traditional Zulu techniques of spear-making, hut-building, beer-brewing, pottery and weaving throughout the day, and visitors are encouraged to participate in these activities. Guides give fascinating talks on Zulu etiquette, traditional dress and the social structure of the village. This hands-on learning experience is complemented by the large open-air dining room which serves traditional Zulu food and affords lovely views over the hills and adjacent Goedertrouw Dam. Late in the afternoon, visitors can enjoy a sunset cruise across the tranquil waters of the dam. At night, vibrant Zulu dancing echoes across the hills, as it has done since the days of Shaka.

Within the village, Protea Hotels offers unusual accommodation in traditional beehive huts equipped with modern conveniences.

NKWALENI VALLEY The Nkwaleni Valley is particularly rich in Zulu history. Across the euphorbia-dotted valley from Shakaland, the towering stone cross of the 1934 Mandawe church surveys the countryside.

From a hilltop throne, 13 kilometres east of Mandawe, Shaka commanded an army that dominated much of southern Africa.

In 1823, Shaka began the construction of KwaBulawayo, a major military encampment overlooking the Nkwaleni Valley. While Cetshwayo's royal village Ondini, at Ulundi, and Dingane's umGungundlovu near Melmoth (see also p. 42), have both been partially reconstructed, nothing remains of Shaka's KwaBulawayo, except for a cairn marking the site and a few concrete steps.

The R34 follows the Mhlatuze River down the length of the Nkwaleni Valley and about 8 kilometres along the route, a dirt road crosses the river to Stewart's Farm. The farm's main attraction is a Zulu village which hosts regular demonstrations of Zulu traditional dances and lifestyles. Visitors are accommodated in beehive huts, and the restaurant serves Zulu cuisine. Wildlife which may be seen in the area includes nyala, cheetah and crocodile.

Although the floor of the Nkwaleni Valley is intensively cultivated, the dense bush of the hills still shelters a variety of game. Several farms have been stocked with animals such as zebra, nyala, kudu and wildebeest. The Mfuli and Nyala game ranches occupy hilly terrain on the valley's northern slopes, and

At Shakaland, visitors can experience Zulu culture first-hand.

their small secluded camps provide ideal bases from which to explore these sanctuaries. The larger Windy Ridge Game Park, on the road to the hamlet of Ntambanana, shelters waterbuck, giraffe and white rhino in addition to common antelope.

NGOYE FOREST To the right of the band of citrus and sugar cane bordering the Mhlatuze River, rolling hills rise to a height of 486 metres. The hills, within 15 kilometres of the Indian Ocean, are cloaked by moisture-laden ocean breezes, which encourages the growth of the 4 000-hectare Ngoye Forest, one of the most intriguing in KwaZulu-Natal. In 1916 a unique colony of male plants of the *Encephalartos woodii* cycad was discovered in the forest, but no female plants have ever been found. Ngoye is popular with birders as it is the only place in southern Africa where the green barbet occurs. The forest is also home to bronzenaped pigeon, red squirrel, forest green butterfly and the rare Ngoye centipede.

MTUNZINI AND UMLALAZI NATURE RESERVE From Empangeni, one of the largest towns on the North Coast, the gentle bends of the N2 are lined by tall timber plantations. Mtunzini ('in the shade') is a delightful subtropical town with its streets splashed with the red flowers of coral trees and an extensive wooded golf course

adjoining the central business district. The Raffia Palm Monument at the railway station is a botanical rarity in South Africa, the nearest known location of raffia palms being 260 kilometres to the north at Kosi Bay. The seeds were thought to have been obtained from Mozambique by Empangeni's district magistrate in 1910. A wooden boardwalk guides visitors through the palm grove, and bird-watchers should stay on the lookout for the rare palmnut vulture, a fruit-eating raptor. The town is sited on a hill above the coastal plain and offers magnificent views of the wave-trimmed ocean and the Umlalazi Nature Reserve. Dense dune forest clothes much of the Umlalazi Nature Reserve and secluded trails lead down to one of the most unspoilt, spacious beaches on the KwaZulu-Natal coast. The reserve's diversity of natural habitats – dune forest, vlei, mangrove, river, estuary and intertidal zones – is a magnet for nature enthusiasts.

The Mlalazi River is a popular venue for boating and fishing, picnic sites hug the river banks, and the adjacent mangrove swamp can be explored at low tide along muddy footpaths. The trails offer a glimpse of the complex, fascinating plants and animals that make their homes among the mangroves. Fiddler crabs scurry in and out of their mud tunnels, and mud-skippers dart along the river's edge. Umlalazi has two camp sites and enchanting forest log cabins.

A Shakaland sangoma (or diviner) uses herbs to clear his senses prior to divining.

SWAZILAND

The tiny kingdom of Swaziland covers only 17 000 square kilometres, making it the second smallest country in Africa. The greatest distance north to south is just 177 kilometres, and 132 kilometres east to west, but Swaziland's topography and geography have created many distinct natural regions with a rich and diverse scenic repertoire. In the mountainous north and west, mist and gentle rain often covers the summits, and the grassy mountain slopes are interlaced with streams that seldom run dry. The highest point in Swaziland is Bulembu, whose dome-like summit reaches 1 862 metres above sea level, and the country's largest river, the Great Usutu, flows across Swaziland from west to east.

Below the mountains of the Escarpment the topography gives way in stages to the bush-covered Lowveld, or *Hlanzeni* (meaning

Mlilwane Wildlife Sanctuary (top) *lies in the lovely Ezulwini Valley, where traditional beehive huts such as these* (above) *can be seen.*

'place of trees' in siSwati), which makes up the eastern half of the country. Along the eastern border, the Lebombo Mountains rise gently from the surrounding plains to an average height of 600 metres above sea

level, forming a natural as well as a political boundary that extends for 150 kilometres between Swaziland and its north-eastern neighbour, Mozambique.

This map highlights the regional map opposite. Overlapping regions and their page numbers are supplied.

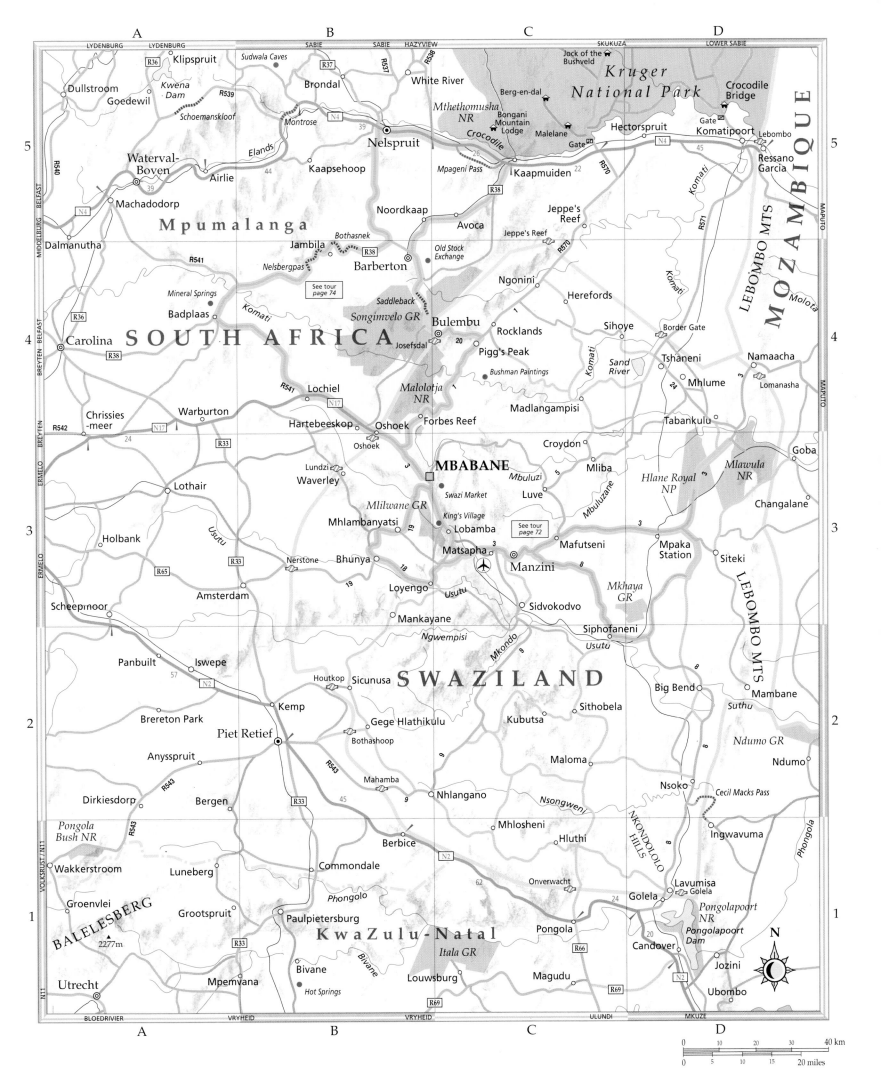

Swazi children prepare for the umhlanga, *or reed dance, where they pay their respects to the Queen Mother.*

HERITAGE

The Swazi people form part of the larger Nguni group, which includes their Zulu and Xhosa cousins further to the south. The Nguni belonged to a large migratory movement that came down the east coast of Africa in much earlier times. Under the leadership of a chief called Ngwane, one clan within the Nguni group settled on the lower slopes of the mountains and plains in what is now Swaziland. It is believed that the first families actually established their homes on the pointed hills and deep valleys that border the Phongolo River, an area which today lies beyond the kingdom's southern boundary.

Historians consider Sobhuza I, a direct descendant of Ngwane, to be the father of the Swazi nation. Sobhuza I lived at about the same time as Shaka and felt the effects of Zulu expansionism and the pressures engendered by the *Mfecane* (*see also* p. 42). In order to secure his kingdom Sobhuza began to absorb his weaker neighbours, building up an effective army that was able to back his programme of nation-building. Although he was frequently attacked by the Zulus he was able to avoid conquest through the combination of clever defensive action and skilful strategic retreat. On more than one occasion he called on the support of his Portuguese neighbours, who were prepared to assist the Swazis in order to form a buffer against the Zulus and the general turmoil created by the *Mfecane*.

In 1836 Sobhuza died and his son Mswati succeeded him. By this time increasing numbers of European traders and missionaries were passing through the territory. They called it Swaziland, and the people the Swazis. During the reign of King Mswati, Swazi influence and nationalism increased. Mswati imitated Zulu military strategy and relied on careful diplomacy to maintain peaceful relations with the powerful Zulu empire. To avoid any possible clashes with the Zulus, Mswati built his capital at Hhohho in northern Swaziland.

He was succeeded by Ludvonga, and in turn by Mbandzeni who came to the throne at a time when gold prospecting in southern Africa was starting to reach fever pitch. King Mbandzeni was approached by a wide range of concession-seekers who not only sought concessions to prospect and mine for gold and other minerals within the kingdom, but also to acquire land for farming and residential use. As the concession rush became more intense, concessions were sought for virtually everything, even the rights to establish and run refreshment rooms at future railway stations! The king was not versed in dealing with the opportunists, rogues and schemers who promised him the world, and his reign nearly crippled the Swazis.

When Mbandzeni died in 1889 he had granted some 500 concessions that gave away virtually the entire country. The Swazis had become squatters in their own land. Mbandzeni was succeeded by his son, Bhunu, who reigned for 10 years until his death, after which Sobhuza II, an infant at the time, became heir apparent to the Swazi throne. In 1921 he was installed as king and he ruled the country for the next 62 years, a period during which he fought for the release of the concessions which his grandfather had so blithely signed.

Sobhuza II created a national trust, the purpose of which was to raise funds from the Swazi people to buy back land as and when it became available from concessionaires and in this way to restore ownership to the Swazi people. Swaziland finally gained its independence from Britain in 1967, and under the legacy of stability left by Sobhuza II the country has prospered.

INDUSTRY

Each of the three geographic regions – the mountains (or Highveld), the Middleveld and the Lowveld – offer different economic opportunities. Gold was once mined in the mountains, especially around Pigg's Peak where the Devil's Reef yielded the precious metal for over 60 years, and at Jeppe's Reef further north. Today Pigg's Peak is a service centre for the enormous Peak timber plantation. Asbestos is still mined here today and dates back to 1886 when the Havelock Swaziland Prospecting Syndicate was formed (named after Sir Arthur Havelock, then governor of Natal). A cable car system was erected to transport the ore from the mine across the mountains and valleys to Barberton, some 20 kilometres away.

Iron ore is mined in the Ngwenya hills, where archaeologists have traced mining activities back to between 41 000 and 36 000 BC, making these among the oldest mines in the world. It is believed that the iron oxide extracted here was used as a pigment for personal adornment and for cosmetic purposes. Today the ore is transported by rail to Maputo harbour for export.

Timber growing is another important industry in Swaziland, and extensive plantations have been developed around Pigg's Peak and on the slopes of the mountains in the upper reaches of the Usutu River, where a pulp mill is sited.

CULTURE

Swazi traditional dress is very colourful and is frequently worn, especially at national annual ceremonies. Cloth with bold designs and bright colours, particularly in shades of ochre, pink and red, is favoured, and wearing brightly coloured feathers in the hair is another feature. The very important *Ncwala*, or 'First Fruits' ceremony, which aims at 'strengthening kingship', is performed as soon after the summer solstice (21 December) as possible and commences while the moon is still 'dark' (i.e. before the new moon). Feasting, dancing and singing form part of this stirring festival. The reed dance (*umhlanga*), when Swazi maidens pay their respects to the Queen Mother, is another important ceremony and national occasion, and culminates in the girls performing the beautiful, flowing reed dance.

MBABANE

The Middleveld is Swaziland's most densely populated region, and the country's capital, Mbabane, is situated there. Because of its location at the edge of the Highveld and the Lowveld, the area enjoys an agreeable climate. The origins of the city go back to 1888, when a former British Army gunner, Bombardier Michael Wells, opened a pub and general store at a ford over the Mbabane River. Wells' establishment served the many prospectors and travellers who scoured the country seeking their fortune, and gradually a hamlet was established.

When Mbabane became the seat of British administration after the Anglo-Boer War, the hamlet grew into a town and then into the capital of the Swazi kingdom.

EZULWINI VALLEY

The road from Mbabane descends into the beautiful Ezulwini (meaning in 'heaven') Valley, where a number of luxury hotels, golf courses and a casino have been developed around natural hot springs. Nearby is the attractive Mantenga Falls on the Little Usutu River and the Mlilwane Wildlife Sanctuary – Swaziland's first nature reserve – opened to the public in 1964.

The impetus to establish Mlilwane came from Ted Reilly, a local farmer and conservationist, who became concerned at the dismal state of wildlife conservation in Swaziland and its rapid disappearance at the hands of unscrupulous hunters. King Sobhuza II demonstrated his enthusiastic support for the project by becoming the sanctuary's patron. Subsequent grants of land by World Wide Fund for Nature-South Africa have enlarged the sanctuary to 4 545 hectares, more than 10 times its original size. Swaziland's largest wildlife sanctuary – the Hlane Royal National Park – was also established through King Sobhuza II's instigation and effort.

The Ezulwini Valley contains the Swazi royal residence at Lobamba, and the parliament and the national stadium are also situated here. Lobamba is made up of groups of beehive-shaped huts and forms the home of the Queen Mother and her attendants.

The valley's many handicraft centres and roadside stalls display the Swazis' skilful craftmanship – especially in grass-weaving – and colourful decorating techniques. Because of the good alluvial soils and the availability of water from rivers as well as through irrigation from the Lusutfu River, the Ezulwini Valley and the adjacent Malkerns district are important agricultural areas.

Further east, where the Middleveld gives way to the Lowveld, the important industrial and commercial centres of Matsapa and Manzini – where Swaziland's national airport is located – are situated. Manzini is Swaziland's second largest town and before the Anglo-Boer War was the capital of Swaziland. The town was first named Manzini, but this changed to Bremersdorp in about 1890. After independence in 1967 the name of the town reverted to Manzini. In the Lowveld that lies east of Manzini, cattle ranching and sugar production are the major economic activities.

The Swazis are known for their skilful craftmanship, especially in grass-weaving.

THE PICTURESQUE SWAZI KINGDOM ❖ 330 km

Game-viewing on horseback (above) *and a purplecrested loerie* (right) *at Mlilwane.*

MBABANE Swaziland's capital is a medium-sized town, and is a good starting point for tours of the country. The business district's main thoroughfare, Allister Miller Street – named after one of Swaziland's earliest European settlers – stretches uphill for a modest 400 metres from the Swazi Market. The market is a hive of activity and displays a wide variety of skilfully crafted wood carvings, colourful textiles and the superb basketwork for which the Swazis are renowned.

USUTU PLANTATION Heading southwest from Mbabane, the road enters 50 000 hectares of pine trees, a vast sea of conifers planted in 1949 by the Colonial Development Corporation in the upper catchment of the Lusutfu River. Approximately 75 million pines now grow in one of the largest pine plantations in the southern hemisphere.

About 18 kilometres from Mbabane, the Meikles Mount Farm is well worth a stopover. The terrain varies from outcrops of granite to eucalyptus plantations and grassy hillsides, and the farm offers a network of lovely walks and horse trails. The streams that run through the farm provide good fishing and swimming, and accommodation is available in picturesque cottages.

MALKERNS Leaving the pine forests behind, the road reaches the settlement of Malkerns. Along the Malkerns-Manzini road, Tishweshwe Crafts is housed in decorated cottages with thatched roofs, and exhibits local weaving, sculpture, sewing and pottery. A traditional Swazi homestead may be visited at the rear of the shop. The Malkerns Valley is renowned as a major production area for citrus, pineapples and avocados. From the valley, the

road rejoins the main Mbabane-Manzini road and passes through the Ezulwini Valley before crossing the Lusushwana River, a tributary of the Lusutfu. Matsapha, on the opposite bank, is home to several industries and is the site of Swaziland's national airport.

MANZINI Bustling with people and business activity, Manzini is Swaziland's leading industrial centre and hosts regular trade shows. It was founded in 1885 when a trader opened a store on the banks of the Mzimnene River. The store was later bought by Albert Bremer, and the settlement became known as Bremersdorp. In 1967, Manzini acquired its present name, which means 'at the water'.

Its central position and its location at the junction of major road routes has aided the town's rapid development, and today its attractions include a golf course and a country club. A busy market place is situated near the Mzimnene River, and statues outside the civic centre honour Sobhuza II, king of Swaziland from 1921 to 1983.

HLANE ROYAL NATIONAL PARK The main road from Manzini to Mozambique crosses Hlane Royal National Park, the largest wildlife sanctuary in Swaziland, which was

Hippo can be seen at close quarters at Mlilwane Wildlife Sanctuary.

proclaimed a reserve in 1967. Part of the park was originally set aside by King Sobhuza II as a royal hunting ground and today it is held in trust for the Swazi nation by King Mswati III. This 19 000-hectare park has the largest herds of game in the country and protects elephant, hippo, lion, wildebeest, zebra, white rhino and giraffe, among others.

Hlane is also a refuge for the world's most southerly colony of marabou stork, and the dense bush and shrubland attracts many other birds such as shrike, hornbills and lilacbreasted roller.

Self-guided game-viewing drives explore the park, and guided walks can be arranged. Two small self-contained camps – Ndlovu and Bhubesi – provide a rare retreat for those who seek peace and solitude.

MLAWULA NATURE RESERVE Close

to Hlane's southeastern boundary is the Mlawula Nature Reserve. Extensive fields of sugar cane, part of the Simunye Sugar Estate, occupy a triangle of land between the reserves. Stretching east to the Lebombo Mountains, Mlawula's 18 000 hectares encompass rugged bushveld, meandering rivers and ironwood forests, which shelter rare species of succulents, climbers and cycads, including the Umbuluzi cycad.

The reserve is a bird-watchers paradise with over 350 species of birds, such as narina trogon, African finfoot and vulture; the vulture restaurant, where animal carcasses are left for these birds to prey on, can be viewed from the Emangceni Hide. Mlawula's wildlife includes hippo, waterbuck, zebra, wildebeest and kudu, and several rare species such as the red duiker, samango monkey, mountain reedbuck and Sharpe's grysbok. A good network of game-viewing roads explore the reserve.

Archaeologists have unearthed artifacts dating back to the Early Stone Age and many of these sites are protected, but archaeological trails are being planned. A small tented camp and camping sites offer accommodation for overnight visitors.

MKHAYA GAME RESERVE Situated in

the lowveld, about 75 kilometres by road from Hlane, Mkhaya Game Reserve specializes in the breeding of endangered animals. The 6 200-hectare reserve was originally established by the respected conservationist, Ted Reilly, as a refuge for the indigenous Nguni cattle. The animals are still bred in a corner of the reserve and regular sales help to finance operations. In recent years, black rhino were reintroduced from

Zimbabwe, and further introductions include white rhino, elephant, roan, tsessebe, sable, buffalo, hippo and giraffe. Mkhaya's management strives to provide guests with an authentic bush experience, either on foot in the company of an experienced ranger, or from guided 4x4 tours. Accommodation is limited to a rustic stone cottage adjoining riverine bush, and a camp of furnished safari tents. Guests are met at the village of Phuzumoya on the main road and escorted to the reserve. Day visits can also be arranged.

EZULWINI VALLEY Bounded by ver-

dant rolling hills, the Ezulwini Valley is the most fertile and the most populous region of Swaziland. Within the valley lies Lobamba, the Swazi royal village and an ideal location for the Houses of Parliament, Swaziland National Museum and the Somhlolo Stadium – venue for soccer matches and the annual Independence Day celebrations. Examples of traditional dress, implements and weapons are on display at the museum, and visitors can explore a traditional Swazi beehive village in the grounds.

In December and January, Lobamba is the setting for the annual *Ncwala* (Festival of the First Fruits), which renews the strength of the king and his nation for the coming year. The Ezulwini Valley is

Exquisite hand-made candles are produced in the Ezulwini Valley.

home to many craft industries and a visit to the renowned Mantenga Handicrafts Centre is a must. Items produced include hand-made batiks, candles, tapestries, pottery, glass, jewellery, copper and leather goods, and baskets, for which Swaziland is renowned. In the upper reaches of the picturesque valley, close to Mbabane's luxury hotels, a casino, sporting facilities and a fine golf course have been developed around the Royal Swazi Sun Hotel.

MLILWANE WILDLIFE SANCTUARY

Lying on the border of the Highveld and Middleveld, this lovely sanctuary is an important transition zone for flora, fauna and birds. Since Mlilwane's inception, the reserve has been stocked with a wide variety of game and protects white rhino, hippo, giraffe, zebra, buffalo and 15 species of antelope. Over 200 bird species occur here, including the purple-crested lourie – Swaziland's national bird – blue crane and black eagle. The rest camp borders a hippo pool and heronry nesting colony, overlooked by the Hippo Haunt restaurant.

As there are no predators in Mlilwane, visitors can explore the sanctuary on foot (guided or self-guided walks), by mountain bike or on horseback. In the southern section, the self-guided Macobane Mountain Trail follows the course of an old aqueduct which carried water to a tin mine. En route there is a superb view of Mantenga Falls in the distance, and Nyonyane, a sheer granite outcrop.

Accommodation consists of comfortable thatched huts, traditional beehive huts, log cabins and cottages, and hippo, warthog and white rhino often wander unperturbed through the rest camp.

In Mlilwane's rugged northern section, the 1 437-metre Luphohlo peak towers over the sanctuary. For the energetic, guided walks lead to the summit of the mountain, where awe-inspiring views across Swaziland are afforded.

THE OLD GOLD MINERS' TRAIL ◆ 380 km

MALOLOTJA NATURE RESERVE

Named after Swaziland's highest waterfall – one of 27 in the reserve – Malolotja preserves 18 000 hectares of unspoilt mountain wilderness. The reserve is managed as a wilderness area and several tributaries of the Komati River flow through it, having carved deep gorges across the highlands. Ngwenya, at a lofty 1 829 metres, is the second highest peak in Swaziland and the reserve's 200 kilometres of trails make it a paradise for hikers.

Highveld antelope graze on Malolotja's rich grasslands, and zebra, wildebeest and hartebeest have been reintroduced. Bird-lovers will delight in the reserve's over 280 bird species which include bald ibis, Stanley's bustard and blue crane.

On the western side of Ngwenya is an attraction with a difference – a Stone Age mine named Lion Cavern where red oxides were extracted from 41 000 BC. It is possibly the oldest such mine in the world.

Malolotja provides accommodation in cabins, huts and camp sites.

PIGG'S PEAK TO BARBERTON From

the forestry town of Pigg's Peak, the route to Bulembu and the Havelock Swaziland Asbestos Mine meanders through an extensive pine plantation. Commencing at the Josefsdal border post, the dirt road zigzags across rolling mountain summits, while overhead, the 20-kilometre cableway that transports ore from Havelock mine to the railhead at Barberton (*see* below) charts a more direct course.

At the top of Saddleback Pass, the tarred road begins and drops 600 metres over only 9 kilometres. To the right exposed quartzite ridges form golden threads running across the landscape, and dense ribbons of forest hug the deep valleys below; to the left, Barberton nestles at the base of the folded mountains.

BARBERTON Although its mining days have ended (*see also* p. 29), the picturesque town of Barberton still retains many mementoes from its past, and several Victorian buildings can be seen in town. The white facade of the De Kaap Stock Exchange, established in 1886, is a prominent local landmark. The town's superb museum in Crown Street stands next to the site where the Barbers (cousins who found and worked Barber's Reef and gave their name to the place) made their strike, and three house museums – Fernlea, Belhaven and Stopforth – have been restored and furnished in the style of the late 19th century.

Visitors can also explore the surrounding mountains on three overnight hiking trails. The Barberton area is famous for two plants, widely propagated throughout the country: the shrub Pride of De Kaap, whose bright orange flowers adorn the roadside of the Saddleback Pass; and the Barberton daisy, which acquired its name in the 1880s when fortune-hunter Robert Jameson sent a sample of the beautiful scarlet flower to the Durban Botanical Garden. The curator sent samples to London's Kew Gardens in 1899, and before long the Barberton daisy was known throughout the world.

DE KAAP VALLEY The route from Barberton to Kaapmuiden is steeped in history. Early prospectors gazed down from the highlands over a broad valley interspersed with rugged ranges, and as the terrain resembled the Cape, they named the valley De Kaap. In 1886 Robert Pettigrew pioneered a new route through the tsetse-infested valley, giving transport riders a shorter trek between

Easily identifiable by its scarlet petals is the beautiful Barberton daisy.

Barberton and Lourenço Marques. Although the road forded the Kaap River eight times, it was still easier than the tortuous journey over the mountains of Swaziland.

Nowadays, it takes the traveller about 30 minutes to complete Pettigrew's route. After passing through a poort, the road passes tropical fruit orchards, and to the east, the hills rise to the highlands of Swaziland. Along the way, place names like Revolver Creek recall forgotten gold-rush-era adventures. Several mementoes from the transport riders' days can be seen. Jock's tree, a large umbrella thorn 10 kilometres from Barberton, was a popular resting place. At Sheba siding (*see* p. 75), a short track leads to a bridge across the Kaap River; the large fig tree on the river bank was once regarded as the largest in the country, but parts of it have since died.

In September 1887, legendary transport rider Percy Fitzpatrick, and author of *Jock of the Bushveld*, abandoned his last wagon under this tree after all his cattle had perished from tsetse-borne disease. The bankrupt Fitzpatrick completed the journey to Barberton on foot. The tragedy confined him to town life, ending his adventures and those of his dog, Jock.

The pretty town of Barberton, developed after gold was discovered in the region in 1884, retains many mementoes from its past.

SHEBA MINE AND EUREKA CITY The oldest operational gold mine in the world, Sheba Mine is sited on a side road leading from the Sheba siding. Three and half kilometres after the mine lies the old Sheba cemetery and the graves of early prospectors. Where the tar ends, a rough track continues through the hills to the ghost town of Eureka City.

Sheba Reef was discovered in 1885 by Edwin Bray, and soon the richness of the find spread throughout the world. Bray called the mine Golden Quarry, and in its first 10 years of operation it produced 18 200 kilograms of gold. Eureka City accommodated the mine's workers and, in its heyday, sustained three hotels, a race track, pubs and over 600 residents. When the gold ran out, the town was abandoned and only ruins remain.

The popular Badplaas Resort offers a wide range of leisure options.

CROCODILE GORGE At Kaapmuiden the N4 crosses the Crocodile River and enters the 15-kilometre-long Crocodile Gorge, carved by the river through a barrier of towering granite peaks. In the deep valley below, the Crocodile races over boulders on its way to the Kruger Park, where it forms the park's southern boundary. The rocky hills to the north of the Crocodile fall within the

8 000-hectare Mthethomusha Nature Reserve. Perched on a boulder-strewn mountainside near the south-western corner of the Kruger, the reserve's Bongani Mountain Lodge offers luxury accommodation.

As the terrain is steep and rugged, guests are driven from Mthethomusha's entrance along a precipitous mountain pass to the secluded lodge. Regular game-viewing drives take visitors through the reserve to see lion, buffalo, elephant, white rhino and wild dog.

HILLTOP PASS AND NELSHOOGTE On the return journey to Barbeton, the R40 negotiates the steep Hilltop Pass over the Krokodilpoort range and provides superb views across wild valleys and hills clothed in dense vegetation. The unspoilt beauty of the countryside contrasts with the conditions that prevailed here in the 1880s. Many of the gold prospectors who departed from Kaapsehoop, in the highlands to the west, hunted in vain for gold in the sweltering Noordkaap River valley. As many succumbed to malaria, the region soon became known as the Valley of Death.

From the intersection outside Barberton, the R38 climbs through tropical orchards and fertile farmland to the extensive timber plantations of the Nelshoogte State Forest. At the crest of the pass, at about 1 554 metres, splendid views can be enjoyed northwards across timber plantations and hot, bush-covered valleys. Fourteen kilometres further on, a picnic area on the right, bounded by tall aloes, provides a dramatic view of the grasslands and mountains stretching towards Badplaas. The road then drops steeply, descending 450 metres in just 5 kilometres, to the rolling grasslands of the Komati Valley.

At the bridge across the Komati River, the wall of the Vygeboom Dam spans the valley on the right. The 34-metre-high dam was built to provide water for power stations, and fishing is permitted here.

BADPLAAS RESORT Aventura's Badplaas resort has an idyllic setting with the grassy slopes and forested valleys of the 700-metre-high Hlumuhlumu Mountains forming a spectacular backdrop. Accommodation consists of comfortable hotel rooms, camp sites, rondavels and chalets. Aside from the hot mineral baths and immense swimming pools, other sporting interests include badminton, tennis, snooker, mini-golf and bowls.

Near the entrance gate there is a restaurant, takeaway and supermarket. A 1 000-hectare nature reserve, stocked with Highveld species such as hartebeest, blesbok and eland, embraces a portion of the mountain range. A network of game-viewing roads, and walking and horse-riding trails, allows visitors to savour the beauty of the undulating grasslands.

SONGIMVELO GAME RESERVE From Badplaas, the R541 to Lochiel passes the turn-off to the 53 000-hectare Songimvelo Game Reserve, the largest provincial reserve in Mpumalanga. Incorporating a

corridor of high mountain between Barberton and Swaziland, and a portion of the Komati River Valley, the reserve also encompasses several interesting Iron Age archaeological sites dating back 200 to 400 BC.

Straddling the Swaziland border, Mlembe Peak, at 1 862 metres, is the highest peak in the reserve. A thatched restaurant complex serves the luxury tented camp set in wooded valley overlooking a broad stretch of the Komati River.

Songimvelo is home to white rhino and elephant relocated from the Kruger Park, as well as to hippo, leopard, giraffe, red hartebeest, eland, zebra and tsessebe. The reserve is one of the few in the country where both black and blue wildebeest are present. Visitors can enjoy guided game drives and guided walks conducted by the resident rangers.

CAPE OF GOOD HOPE

Two of Cape Town's many faces: imposing Table Mountain (above), and the colourful Coon Carnival (below).

Cape Town, South Africa's Mother City, has one of the most dramatic natural settings in the world. The city's suburbs are spread out below a massive flat-topped mountain which is often covered by its famous tablecloth of swirling clouds. On each side, the sentinels of Lion's Head and Devil's Peak guard Table Mountain, while stretching away from Lion's Head is the 'lion's rump' of Signal Hill. Cradled in a bowl, the city has lying before it the sweep of Table Bay and Robben Island, where Nelson Mandela was once imprisoned.

North of Cape Town, the quiet West Coast towns of Langebaan and Saldanha Bay lure the visitor with their sandy beaches, clear waters, great number of seabirds, spring wild flowers and fine seafood restaurants.

Inland, the backbone of the Cape's famous wine industry is centred around Stellenbosch. Rich vineyards and large wine estates however reach into the Overberg, the Boland and the Little Karoo and even beyond. They also extend into the fertile valleys of the Berg, Eerste, Hex and Breede rivers.

TAVERN OF THE SEAS

Jan van Riebeeck came from Holland to establish a revictualling station for the Dutch East India Company, whose ships ploughed around the Cape on their way to trade in the Far East. He cast anchor in Table Bay on 6 April 1652, came ashore and soon constructed an earthen fort and laid out vegetable gardens. It was not long before a permanent settlement was established that not only supplied much-needed fresh vegetables, fruit and meat to passing Dutch ships, but also to those of friendly countries.

Over the years Van Riebeeck's settlement steadily developed into a 'tavern of the seas' as ships stopped, not only to pick up fresh food and water, but also for their sailors to come ashore and relax for a while. With expansion in trade, the outpost grew into a town as more and more settlers came to establish new homes. Van Riebeeck's settlement began to expand beyond the slopes of Table Mountain, Devil's Peak and Lion's Head, and many settlers moved out of Cape Town, seeking the soils and opportunities that lay across the mountains to the east.

In 1795 the British ended the Dutch occupation of the Cape in order to deny their enemy, France, the opportunity to establish a base there, and thus ensured British ships an unfettered passage to the East. In 1802 the British felt that the threat had passed and so they returned the Cape to the Dutch.

However, when France again began to flex its muscles the British invaded the Cape for a second time – in 1806 – and after a short but fierce battle at Blaauwberg, they took over the colony. This time they stayed, setting up a permanent administration which lasted until the latter half of the 19th century when responsible government was granted to the Cape and the Cape parliament was established, with its own elected representatives.

This map highlights the regional map opposite. Overlapping regions and their page numbers are supplied.

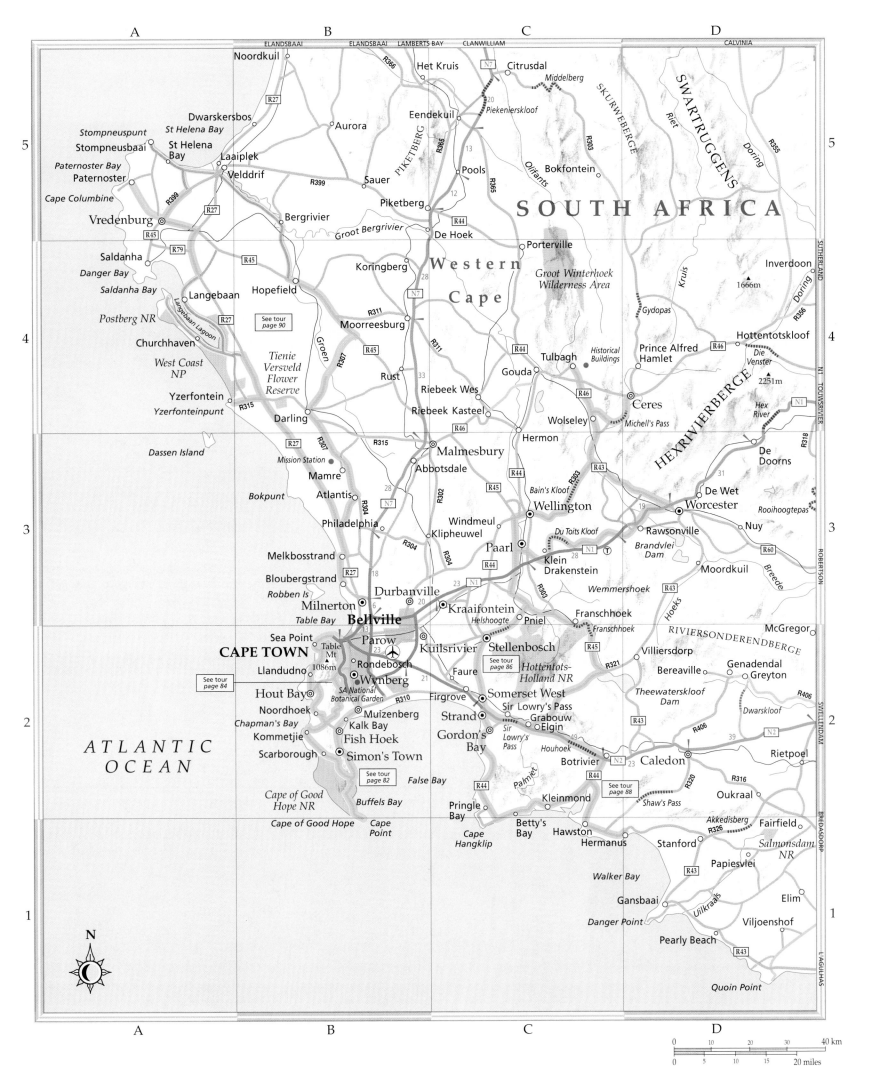

COSMOPOLITAN CAPE TOWN

Cape Town's unique cosmopolitan character derives from a blend of European, Asian and African influences. In its three and a half centuries of growth it has taken from Holland, reflected in a rich mix of Cape and Dutch architecture; it has taken from England, leaving the unmistakable stamp of Queen Victoria; and it has taken from Java and elsewhere in Indonesia, evident in its mosques, Malay Quarter and Cape Malay culture. And underlying it all is the unequivocal and tangible rhythm of Africa.

Onto this unique Cape rootstock has been grafted a modern city with a flourishing commercial, financial and industrial infrastructure. Skyscrapers, freeways, shopping malls and sprawling suburbs have radically altered the face of Cape Town, one of the fastest-growing urban sprawls in the world.

Its phenomenally successful Victoria and Alfred Waterfront is one of the country's foremost tourist attractions and with its working harbour, outdoor entertainment and buskers, hotels, waterside pubs and restaurants, museums and bustling shopping complexes, it is not hard to understand why.

TABLE MOUNTAIN

Cape Town's most famous landmark is the 1 086-metre-high Table Mountain. On clear days it is visible from as far as 200 kilometres out to sea, and it has provided a beacon of hope to countless sailors and an unforgettable sight to all who visit the city.

Although the sea is icy cold, Clifton's beautiful and sheltered beaches entice flocks of dedicated sun-worshippers.

Cape Town's unique character is enhanced by the cheerful flower-sellers in Adderley Street.

Application has been made for the mountain to be declared a World Heritage Site, not only because of the dramatic statement it makes within the urban context of Cape Town, but also because of its richly diverse flora. Many of its over 1 400 species are endemic and the red disa (*Disa uniflora*), known as the Pride of Table Mountain, is particularly well known. The big game that used to roam the mountain – such as Cape lion, leopard, hippo and buffalo – has long since been exterminated, and today only small mammals, such as baboon, dassie (rock hyrax), steenbok and the Cape grey mongoose, are found here.

Since 1929, two cable cars have ferried visitors to the summit of Table Mountain, a journey which rises from 366 metres to 1 067 metres above sea level in about 5 minutes. From the top, the magnificent views over Cape Town are unparalleled.

Table Mountain dominates the chain of mountains that form the prominent backbone of the Cape Peninsula, much of which is included in the Cape Peninsula National Park. The front of Table Mountain, which faces north, drops precipitously to the city below, but its back gives way gradually to Constantia Nek and then the Constantiaberg range takes over, continuing until it diminishes in a sharp point and disappears into the sea at Cape Point. The west face of Table Mountain is made up of the Twelve Apostles – a beautiful series of 12 sandstone mountain buttresses which overlook the magnificent beaches of Camps Bay and Clifton, and the southern Atlantic Ocean. The east face commands a view over False Bay, Kirstenbosch, the southern suburbs of Cape Town, the Cape Flats and the distant Hottentots-Holland Mountains.

Some 60 million years ago, the Cape Flats were covered by sea and when the water receded, a vast, sandy region of drifting dunes was revealed. Hardy shrubs and trees were planted to stablilize the sands, and today it is one of Cape Town's most densely populated areas.

KIRSTENBOSCH

Nestled in the lee of the southwestern slopes of Table Mountain, the South African National Botanical Garden at Kirstenbosch was a gift from Cecil John Rhodes to the nation. In 1895 Rhodes, mining magnate and Prime Minister of the Cape, purchased 560 hectares of virtually upsoilt land, and after his death in 1902, bequeathed this land to the state. In 1913 the whole area was proclaimed a national botanical garden.

Pincushion proteas attract sunbirds and sugarbirds at the world-famous Kirstenbosch gardens.

Kirstenbosch's fascination stems from two sources – the rich species diversity of the flora that is propagated, studied and preserved there, and its remarkable setting, with its hills, slopes, streams, forests and its beautiful mountain backdrop. At present no less than 6 000 of South Africa's 21 000 plant species are represented in the gardens.

Occupying a rocky promontory, Cape Point's lighthouse guides ships along this notorious coastline.

CAPE OF GOOD HOPE

The 7 675-hectare Cape of Good Hope Nature Reserve is situated at the southern tip of the Western Cape province, about 80 kilometres from Cape Town. Its attraction arises from a marriage of scenic beauty, a major display of Cape flora and fauna, and an absorbing history of maritime misadventure. Many vessels, wrecked by the turbulent seas, have found their final resting place along this rocky coastine.

The reserve is not only of great importance for the conservation of flora and fauna, but it also provides a variety of outdoor recreation facilities for Capetonians and is a major tourist attraction. Cape Point is washed by the waters of the Atlantic Ocean, with its own intertidal and marine life system. It will eventually form part of the Table Mountain National Park and application has been made for it too to be proclaimed a World Heritage Site.

GLORIOUS WINELANDS

The Western Cape is renowned for its wine and deciduous fruit industry. It was not long after Jan van Riebeeck's arrival that it became clear to the new settlers that the region had fertile soil, a temperate climate, access to perennial water and an abundance of sunshine – all the ingredients necessary for the cultivation of vines and deciduous fruit. Van Riebeeck planted the first vines shortly after he landed and in 1659 the maiden wine was tasted in the Cape. In 1685 the governor of the Cape, Simon van der Stel, was granted a shady valley with sunny slopes behind Table Mountain and he established Constantia, the genesis of the South African wine industry. Constantia's manor house, Groot Constantia, is now a museum, but its vineyards and cellars are still operative and together they make up one of Cape Town's most enticing drawcards. When Van der Stel died in 1712, the estate was subdivided and over the years, several well-known wine estates and superb examples of Cape Dutch architecture – including Klein Constantia, Buitenverwachting, Hope of Constantia, Nova Constantia and Constantia Uitsig – were built on the subdivisions.

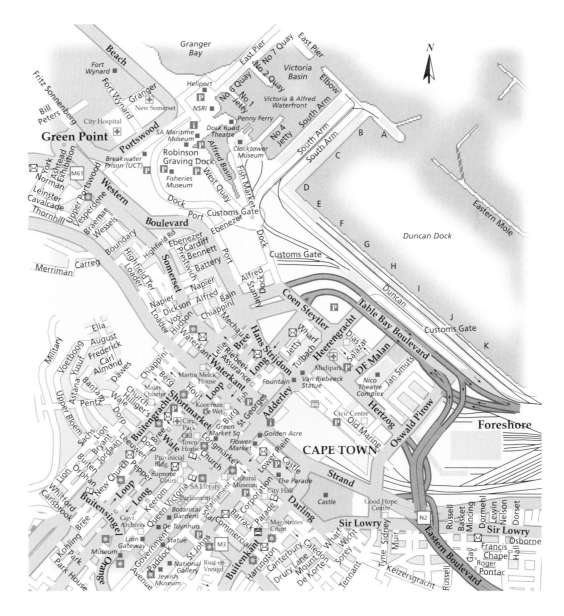

Autumn hues highlight the vineyards in the lovely Hex River Valley.

Today visitors can sample the fruits of the vine along a number of enticing wine routes – Paarl, Constantia, Stellenbosch and Franschhoek, for example (*see also* p. 184).

The heart of the wine industry lies in Stellenbosch, South Africa's second oldest town established shortly after 1679 when Simon van der Stel visited there. It has many fine examples of well-preserved Cape Dutch architecture, and Dorp Street has one of the longest rows of old buildings surviving in any southern African town. Another feature is its large number of oak trees, the first of which were planted by Van der Stel, giving Stellenbosch the apt title of Eikestad, 'city of oaks'. It initially served as an agricultural centre, but after the founding of Victoria College in 1881 – forerunner of Stellenbosch University – its character changed to that of a university town. Today it is a delightful mix of student jauntiness and historic charm.

Bright spring flowers add colour to the rocky Hermanus coastline. Southern right whales calve in these waters between July and November each year.

Not far from Stellenbosch is the beautiful Franschhoek Valley, where one of the Cape's oldest settlements was established by the French Huguenots, 200 refugees from France who were settled there between 1688 and 1690. Surrounded by mountains, Franschhoek ('the French corner') developed a proud tradition of making some of South Africa's most famous wines and for growing fruit. At the turn of the century Cecil Rhodes established a vast deciduous fruit-growing empire at Groot Drakenstein between Franschhoek and Stellenbosch.

Founded in 1720 as a farming and wagon-building settlement, the historic town of Paarl has lush gardens, long oak- and jacaranda-lined streets and extensive vineyards, and its many gracious buildings add to its charm. Paarl has a long history of viniculture and in 1918, the KWV wine co-operative, the world's largest, was founded.

On the southern slopes of the Paarl Mountains, the tall spires of the Language Monument commemorate the formation of the Afrikaans language movement in Paarl in 1875.

SOUTHWESTERN CAPE

Across the Hottentots-Holland Mountains lie a series of rugged, rolling hills, softened by vast orchards of apple trees. Nestled among these hills are the twin centres of Elgin and Grabouw, the Cape's famous apple-growing area which produces more than 50% of South Africa's export apple crop. During the apple-picking season (January to May), millions of apples are graded, washed and then sent to Cape Town harbour for export. The Elgin Valley, watered by the Palmiet River, also produces pears, peaches, wine and flowers such as chrysanthemums, roses and proteas.

Beyond Elgin and Grabouw and centred around an old harbour is Hermanus, once a fishing village, but today a popular holiday destination. Beyond the breakers that crash into the cliffs along much of Hermanus's beachfront, southern right whales can often be seen frolicking in the waves. Mating and calving whales frequent these waters each year between July and November.

A scenic route to Hermanus follows the coastal road from Gordon's Bay, hugging the shoreline in places and running through

The West Coast's quaint fishing village of Paternoster is renowned for its good catches of crayfish and perlemoen.

spectacular mountain scenery. It passes the seaside resorts of Koeëlbaai, Rooiels, Betty's Bay and Kleinmond, and is characterized by its abundant Cape coastal fynbos, especially lovely in spring.

At Danger Point, further up the coast, an important chapter was written into the annals of maritime history, for it was here on 26 February 1852 that the Birkenhead Drill – the practice of allowing women and children to evacuate a doomed ship first – was pioneered. It was in the early hours of the morning that a British troopship, HMS *Birkenhead*, foundered. All the soldiers stood to attention on the ship's deck while the ship's women and children passengers were allowed to climb aboard the few lifeboats available. A total of 445 soldiers' lives were lost.

WEST COAST SPLENDOUR

Langebaan Lagoon and Saldanha Bay are the West Coast's main attractions, and holiday-makers flock to their shores for the water-sports, seabirds and spring flowers. The tranquil lagoon, focal point of the West Coast National Park, is 16 kilometres long, 4,5 kilometres wide and on average about 6 metres deep, and it is connected to Saldanha Bay by a narrow channel. A variety of fish species occur in the lagoon and because of

its extensive mudbanks, which are exposed at low tide, it is a favourite feeding ground for a large number of birds, the most common being sandpiper, cormorant, flamingo, plover, gannet and gull. There was a time when Langebaan also had vast colonies of oysters, but by a quirk of nature they died out and the bed of the lagoon is now covered with an estimated 30 million tons of shells.

In 1985 a core national park consisting of Langebaan Lagoon, Sixteen Mile Beach and the islands of Marcus, Schaapen, Jutten and Malgas, was proclaimed. Land surrounding the lagoon remained privately owned. Over the years, the World Wide Fund for Nature-South Africa (WWF-SA), has allocated funds for the purchase of 16 500 hectares of land encircling the lagoon.

One of the finest natural harbours in the world, Saldanha Bay is virtually landlocked with only a narrow entrance open to the sea, but its depth allows deep-draught ships to enter. A bulk-loading facility has been established in the bay and a giant steelworks is to be developed a few kilometres from its shores from where finished product will be exported. Saldanha Bay is the centre of the West Coast's important fishing and crayfishing industry, which attracts huge populations of seals and birds.

THE UNRIVALLED PENINSULA ROUTE ◆ 160 km

The Two Oceans Aquarium (left), one of the Waterfront's attractions (above).

Orchestras, brass bands and folk musicians attract large crowds to the outdoor amphitheatre below the busy Victoria Wharf shopping complex, and buskers and mime artistes entertain the strolling crowds.

The University of Cape Town's Graduate School of Business, once occupied by a prison, and the Breakwater Lodge sit on a rocky promontory above the Waterfront.

VICTORIA & ALFRED WATERFRONT
The lively Waterfront complex, with its dramatic backdrop of Table Mountain, surrounds the Victoria Basin, where historic navy vessels can be viewed. Hotels, shops, boat trips (around the harbour and to Robben Island), movies, pubs, restaurants and takeaway outlets, historic buildings, museums and a working harbour all vie for the visitor's attention.

Some of the highlights include the BMW Pavilion, with its giant five-storey-high IMAX Cinema, and the acclaimed Two Oceans Aquarium, which has been judged the leading aquarium and marine education centre in the country. Apart from several hundred fishes, sharks, seals, penguins and waders, a Touch Pool allows visitors to feel tide pool animals such as sea urchins and starfish.

SEA POINT
The Western Boulevard follows the coast to the cosmopolitan suburb of Sea Point, one of Cape Town's most densely populated suburbs, tucked into a narrow, 1,5-kilometre-wide corridor between Signal Hill and the Atlantic Ocean. Apartment buildings, hotels, guest houses, restaurants and residential homes all compete for space along Sea Point's vibrant promenade which throngs with joggers, strollers, cyclists and roller-bladers. The largest seawater swimming pool in the southern hemisphere is on the promenade. Sea Point's Main Road, two blocks from the beachfront, is renowned for its high concentration of restaurants.

CLIFTON
Guarded by rocky headlands and sheltered by the sandstone summit of Lion's Head, Clifton's four famous beaches are well-protected from the Cape's notorious south-easter. Although parking is limited and the Atlantic Ocean icy cold, Clifton attracts flocks of dedicated sun-worshippers, surfers and 'beautiful people'. Picnickers and volleyball players enjoy the beaches in the long summer evenings.

CAMPS BAY
Often described as the most beautiful beach in South Africa, Camp's Bay is situated between the western slopes of Table Mountain and the sea, and offers uninterrupted views of the Twelve Apostles. Behind the wide sandy beach is a palm-fringed park and attractive boulevard (M6) lined with luxury hotels, timeshare units and sidewalk restaurants. The beach is a perfect venue for volleyball games, sun-tanning or simply for relaxing among the beautiful surroundings.

Gazing upwards to the summit of Table Mountain, the cable car can often be seen passing through the final jagged gap before reaching the crest, 1 040 metres above Camps Bay. Paragliders, making the jump from Lion's Head enjoy a novel way of getting to the beach. From Camp's Bay the M6 hugs the coast at the base of the lofty Twelve Apostles and passes curio and shell markets en route to the lovely resort of Llandudno, and Sandy Bay, a secluded nudist beach. This picturesque stretch of mountain fynbos, rugged coastline and sea eventually leads to Hout Bay.

HOUT BAY
A charming fishing village, Hout Bay is sheltered by two imposing peaks, the Karbonkelberg (653 metres) and Constantiaberg (928 metres). The Sentinel peak is a natural gateway to the fishing harbour, one of the town's main attractions. Here fishermen repair their boats or off-load catches of cray-fish and snoek, and screeching sea-gulls dive in search of titbits. From the pier a superb view stretches across the bay to the Constantiaberg where Chapman's Peak Drive cuts a course along the contour. Even better

views can be enjoyed from the boats which visit the seal colony on Duiker Island. The Mariner's Wharf emporium, adjoining the harbour, is a pirate's cove of nautical gifts, shells, a fresh fish market, a seafood bistro and restaurant. Hout Bay village is a quaint collection of craft shops, restaurants, museums and a flea market. Close by, the World of Birds is the largest bird park in the country, home to about 3 000 birds.

CHAPMAN'S PEAK DRIVE A statue of a leopard just outside Hout Bay marks the beginning of Chapman's Peak Drive, perhaps the most breathtaking route in South Africa. Built with great ingenuity in the 1920s, the 12-kilometre narrow road hugs the sheer cliffs that plunge down to the waters below. The winding route cuts through the folded red sandstones of the peninsula mountains, and at its highest point it climbs to 166 metres. Several viewsites along the road and an everchanging tableau of sea, rock and cliff encourage frequent stops.

NOORDHOEK AND LONG BEACHES
As the road descends Chapman's Peak Drive, a magnificent view of the peninsula's longest beach, Noordhoek, stretches away for 4 kilometres. Noordhoek's sandy beach, backed by a tidal lagoon, is a favourite surfing, walking and kite-flying venue. The road to the beach passes the Chapman's Bay Trading Centre, with its restaurants, craft shops and exhibitions by resident artists. Long Beach is popular for horse riding and surfing. The rusting remains of the ship *Kakapo*, wrecked in 1900, lie half-buried in the sand.

KOMMETJIE At the end of Long Beach, the seaside village of Kommetjie occupies the rocky Slangkoppunt promontory guarded by a lighthouse. Pathways lead along the coastline to spots favoured by surfers, fishermen and sunbathers, and several caravan and camp sites are in the village.

CAPE OF GOOD HOPE NATURE
RESERVE One of the Western Cape's top tourist attractions, this reserve conserves unspoilt mountain fynbos, 40 kilometres of pristine coastline and over 1 200 plant species.

Wildlife typical of fynbos vegetation includes bontebok, grey rhebok, Cape grysbok, eland, baboon, Cape fox and Cape mountain zebra. From the car park a steep walk, or a ride

Visitors can observe a colony of protected jackass penguins at Boulders Beach.

on the funicular railway, leads to the 1857 lighthouse. From this narrow, rugged viewsite, perched 209 metres above the pounding surf, the scene to the north across the mountain-framed shoreline of False Bay is spectacular, and Cape Hangklip and the Kogelberg are visible 30 kilometres to the east.

Most visitors head straight for Cape Point, but there are several roads off the main route, and a trip to Olifantsbosbaai or Buffelsbaai, with their picnic and braai spots, is recommended. At Olifantsbosbaai ostriches and bontebok often feed along the shore, while large numbers of waterbirds, such as Hartlaub's gull, swift tern and sooty shearwater, gather along the rocky shore. At Buffelsbaai there is a monument to Bartholomeu Dias, and a large cross commemorates Vasco da Gama's later voyage. On calm days the sea is ideal for scuba-diving and snorkelling.

SIMON'S TOWN Leaving the reserve, the M4 follows the eastern side of the peninsula to Simon's Town. Baboons are often seen along this road near Miller's Point. Five kilometres north, one of the few land-based colonies of jackass penguins can be seen nesting on the secluded Boulders Beach.

In Simon's Town, the main road passes the high walls of South Africa's principal navy base (photographs are not permitted) and then enters the 'Historical Mile', a row of attractive Victorian buildings lining the road. Jubilee Square is a good place to park, with several museums and souvenir shops within walking distance. A statue of the World War II navy mascot, Just Nuisance, stands in the square. This endearing Great Dane, friend of British sailors during the war, was buried with full military honours on a hill above the town. The square offers fine views of naval ships moored in the harbour.

FISH HOEK The seaside town of Fish Hoek spreads across the bay formed by the Kalkbaaiberg and Elsie's Peak headlands. The bay offers safe swimming in warm waters and the beach is popular for launching sailboards and catamarans. Jager Walk, a favourite with walkers and sunbathers, runs along one arm of the beach and offers lovely views across the bay where, in spring, southern right whales come to calve.

A novel way to visit Fish Hoek is to catch a train from Muizenberg, and this unforgettable journey follows the coast just above the high tide mark to Simon's Town.

Twisting Chapman's Peak drive (top) *affords splendid views over Hout Bay* (above).

RHODES MEMORIAL From central Cape Town, De Waal Drive (M3) runs along the lower slopes of Devil's Peak where eland, zebra and black wildebeest can often be seen grazing; to the left there are sweeping views over the city and Table Bay. Near Groote Schuur Hospital, where Chris Barnard performed the world's first heart transplant in 1967, the right branch of the M3 soon passes the ivy-draped buildings of the University of Cape Town before approaching the turn-off to Rhodes Memorial.

The enormous stone edifice, guarded by eight huge lion statues, was modelled after the Greek temple at Segesta. Shaded by tall conifers on the eastern slopes of Devil's Peak, the site, chosen by writer Rudyard Kipling and architect Sir Herbert Baker, was much favoured by Cecil John Rhodes. In the centre of the temple is a large bronze bust of Rhodes (1853-1902) with a tribute by Kipling to his 'immense and brooding spirit'. Rhodes's imperialis aspirations did much to shape southern Africa in the late 19th century.

The steps below the temple provide superb views across the southern suburbs and the Cape Flats, and there is a cosy tearoom right behind the monument. A walk from here leads up Devil's Peak to an old blockhouse, affording a fine panorama of the sea, city and suburbs.

KIRSTENBOSCH NATIONAL BOTANICAL GARDEN The botanical masterpiece of South Africa and one of the most famous gardens in the world, Kirstenbosch's setting is magnificent, with Table Mountain's imposing Junction and Fernwood peaks towering 800 metres above the entrance. Densely forested slopes cloak the mountain and four streams, fringed by trees and tall tree ferns, course through the verdant garden.

Many short strolls and forest walks crisscross Kirstenbosch, and three circular walking trails – ranging from 1,2 kilometres to 6 kilometres – explore the garden and the eastern forested slopes of Table Mountain. Hikers could climb the mountain from here via Skeleton Gorge or Nursery Ravine.

To discover the garden's splendour a full day is recommended. Aside from the formal beds, there are succulents, proteas, water features edged by dense vegetation, a cycad garden, a Fragrance Garden and a Braille Trail. Along one stream a sunken brick-lined pool shaped like a bird honours Lady Anne Barnard, a famous 19th-century letter-writer who lived in the Cape.

Tree enthusiasts will be delighted by fine examples of red mahogany, Clanwilliam cedar, yellowwood and keurboom trees, to name but a few. The renowned Compton Herbarium maintains a collection of 250 000 plant specimens and is a centre for botanical research.

Near the entrance is a restaurant – a favourite breakfast and cream tea venue – and a shop where seeds, books and souvenirs can be bought. In summer, sunset concerts are held and visitors are welcome to bring a picnic and enjoy the music in the beautiful surroundings.

CECILIA STATE FOREST From Kirstenbosch, Rhodes Drive (M63) winds its way to Constantianek. On the left lies the affluent suburb of Constantia, with its densely-wooded gardens and palatial homes cradled by the Constantiaberg. The Cecilia State Forest, on the right of the road,

Kirstenbosch garden's floral splendour is particularly beautiful in spring.

Rhodes Memorial on Devil's Peak honours mining magnate Cecil John Rhodes.

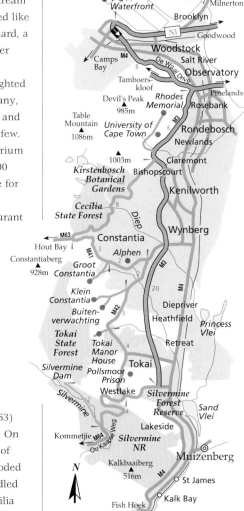

is crisscrossed by many contour paths and trails that lead to the crest of Constantia Ridge and to the Cecilia Waterfall. The forest is a restful place, ideal for picnics, walking dogs or strolling in the lovely surroundings.

GROOT CONSTANTIA

In 1778 Hendrik Cloete bought Groot Constantia, extended the main house and added on additional farm buildings. An alteration to the homestead made it necessary for the architects to raise its roof and consequently it has the highest and steepest roof of any existing Cape Dutch house. After years of careful restoration and preservation, Groot Constantia today is a stately homestead that is considered to be the finest hallmark of Cape Dutch architecture.

The exquisite manor house is open to the public as a cultural museum decorated with period furniture. Part of the old cellar houses a fascinating wine museum, and wine-tasting is offered at the modern cellar near the entrance to the estate. The Jonkerhuis, traditionally built for the oldest son, houses a restaurant serving traditional Cape cuisine. A tavern lies behind the homestead.

KLEIN CONSTANTIA

The lovely manor house, with its unpretentious gables and delightful setting, is not open to the public but the cellar can be viewed by appointment. Klein Constantia has won many awards for its excellent wines, and the estate is open for wine-tasting and wine sales on weekdays and Saturday mornings. Klein Constantia's vineyards, which fall under the shadow of the Constantiaberg and Vlakkenberg peaks, extend up the steep slopes bordering the plantations and mountain peaks of the adjoining Tokai State Forest.

BUITENVERWACHTING

Retracing the route along the Klein Constantia Road for one kilometre, a turn to the

right leads to Buitenverwachting ('beyond expectations') estate. Built in 1796, the historic homestead has been refurbished and includes gabled houses, slave quarters, stables and cellars. For connoisseurs of fine food, the restaurant at Buitenverwachting is regarded as one of the finest in the Western Cape and offers lunch and dinner menus. Famous also for its fine wines, the elegant estate is open for wine-tasting and sales, and tours of the cellars are conducted.

TOKAI MANOR HOUSE

Built in 1795, the Tokai Manor House is nestled beneath the Constantiaberg near the entrance to the Tokai State Forest. The privately owned house has a high veranda, graced by six white pillars, and a square gable above the main doorway. It is one of the finest surviving examples of Cape Dutch architecture. Researchers believe that Tokai was designed by the architect Louis Thibault and named after Tokaj in Hungary where the famous Tokaji wines are produced.

TOKAI STATE FOREST

The early Dutch settlers rapidly depleted the forest patches that grew in the

Peninsula and in the 1880s, the first experimental forestry plantations in the country were established at Tokai. Much of the eastern slopes of the Constantiaberg are now clothed in pine forests. The forest's arboretum at the end of Tokai Road was established by Joseph Lister in 1885 and is famous for its large variety of exotic and indigenous trees.

From the arboretum, the walk to Elephant's Eye Cave zigzags through the pine forests to a lookout on the crest. At an altitude of 560 metres, the lookout provides a panoramic view over the Cape Flats, Muizenberg mountains and False Bay. Aside from this trail, which requires a climb of 480 metres over 4 kilometres, there are also easier walks through the forest. The forestry tracks are popular among joggers, and horse riding and mountain biking are permitted.

SILVERMINE NATURE RESERVE

After leaving the Tokai forest, the M42 passes Pollsmoor Prison – where Nelson Mandela was imprisoned – and at Westlake joins Ou Kaapseweg (M64) which winds up the Steenberg to the two entrances of the Silvermine Nature Reserve; Ou Kaapseweg ('old Cape road') divides the 2 150-hectare reserve in two sections.

The viewsite on the right of the road provides a superb panorama over the Tokai and Constantia valleys, and a road leads to the western section's parking area below Silvermine Dam. The 7-kilometre Noordhoek Peak Trail leads up the amphitheatre surrounding the dam, and several trails branch off this route and explore the adjacent Tokai State Forest. The forest surrounding the dam is a popular venue for weekend braais and picnics.

The eastern section of the reserve extends over the mountains to Kalk Bay. Several walking trails crisscross the mountains, which are also used by mountain bikers, and shady picnic spots under pine trees are located near the entrance.

A popular restaurant (above) *and an excellent example of Cape Dutch architecture* (top) *at the historic Groot Constantia estate.*

SEVEN PASSES THROUGH THE BOLAND ❖ 370 km

STELLENBOSCH The oak-lined streets, water canals and white-washed Cape Dutch buildings of Stellenbosch combine to fashion a town of almost unrivalled charm. Die Braak, Stellenbosch's village green, was laid out in 1703 as a parade ground and is flanked by historic monuments open to the public. The Kruithuis, built as a powder magazine in 1777, houses antique weapons; the 1797 Burgerhuis, once an elegant home, is now a cultural museum; and the Rhenish Mission complex – a spacious church and parsonage – occupies the southwestern corner of the square.

In Dorp Street lies the Rembrandt van Rijn Art Museum – a treasure trove of South African art – the Stellenryck Wine Museum and Oom Samie se Winkel, a historic trading store which sells everything from wine to dried fish and candles. The Village Museum contains several houses representing different architectural styles, one of which, the 1710 Schreuderhuis, is believed to be the oldest house in Stellenbosch.

The University of Stellenbosch's extensive campus is one of the most beautiful in South Africa and its Botanical Garden is a perfect place to spend a few quiet hours. Visitors can also stroll along the tree-lined banks of the Eerste River or visit the Jan Marais Nature Reserve, a delightful fynbos sanctuary. In summer, open-air concerts are held at the Oude Libertas Amphitheatre while visitors eat their picnic suppers on the lawns.

The Stellenbosch Wine Route (*see also* p. 184) was the first to be established in South Africa and includes many excellent estates and co-operative wineries. Wine-tasting is offered at all the farms and many cater for lunches. Blaauwklippen, Simonsig and Delheim, Bergkelder and Spier are just a few of the estates worth visiting in the area, while insight into the history of brandy-making is given at the Oude Meester Brandy Museum in Old Strand Road.

In the nearby Jonkershoek Valley, the Assegaaibosch Nature Reserve protects rare proteas and fynbos, and is ideal for a picnic, braai or ramble.

HELSHOOGTE PASS The link between Stellenbosch and the Drakenstein Valley is the Helshoogte Pass ('hell's heights'). This scenic pass crosses the saddle separating Simonsberg from the Jonkershoekberge, and at its summit are the Delaire and Thelema wineries. The road winds through a landscape adorned with fruit farms, Cape Dutch houses and vineyards before reaching Boschendal (*see also* p. 184), a wine estate at the foot of the Groot Drakenstein Mountains.

PAARL Huge granite outcrops, the largest of which is Paarl Rock, dwarf the attractive town of Paarl which lies between the mountain and the Berg River. Many of its beautiful historic monuments can be seen along the oak-shaded Main Street, and the 1787 Oude Pastorie, now housing a cultural museum, and Strooidak Church, completed in 1805, are among the more notable national monuments.

About a dozen wine and brandy cellars are found in the district, many of which are on the Paarl Wine Route (*see also* p. 184). On top of the Paarl Mountains lies the 1 900-hectare Paarlberg Nature Reserve dominated by the granite outcrops of Paarl Rock, Gordon's Rock and Bretagne Rock. The reserve protects fynbos, proteas, wild olives, aloes and silver trees. Two dams afford anglers with catches of trout or black bass, and walks lead through the reserve, which has picnic and braai sites. The Language Monument is only a short walk away from here.

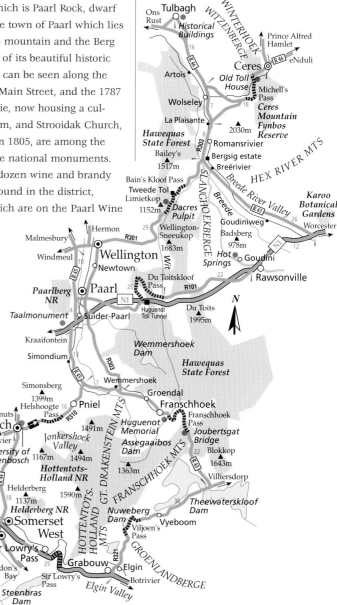

Scenes of Stellenbosch: lovely Lanzerac Hotel (above) and a quaint farm stall (top).

The huge granite outcrop of Paarl Rock dominates Paarlberg Nature Reserve.

DU TOITSKLOOF PASS Linking Paarl and Worcester, Du Toitskloof is the highest pass within a 100-kilometre radius of Cape Town. When the new 4-kilometre Huguenot Tunnel was completed in 1988, the route was shortened by 11 kilometres. But the most scenic section of the journey is on the old route where the road climbs to 823 metres before descending to a 222-metre-long tunnel. After completing the passage through the mountains, the N1 crosses the upper Breede River Valley which sustains extensive winelands.

BREEDE RIVER VALLEY Near Worcester, the popular Goudini Spa resort and caravan park surrounds the therapeutic 40 ˚C waters of the spring that feeds the resort's swimming pools. Continuing through the fertile Breede River Valley, the R43 passes the 400-hectare Bergsig wine estate, one of the country's largest. Just outside Wolseley, the 30-hectare Romansrivier Reserve protects a small population of the endangered geometric tortoise.

MICHELL'S PASS This 9-kilometre pass was named after Colonel Charles Michell, superintendent of works for the Cape in the 1830s, and he commissioned road-builder Andrew Geddes Bain to construct the road in 1846. Today the Old Tollhouse near the end of the pass is a national monument with a shop and tearoom. About 1,5 kilometres after the tollhouse lies a picnic site at Koffiegat, a pool fed by a pretty waterfall. The surrounding mountain slopes are preserved within the 6 800-hectare Ceres

Mountain Fynbos Reserve which protects birds such as the protea canary and orangebreasted sunbird.

CERES Named after the Roman goddess of agriculture, Ceres is an apt name for one of the country's top fruit-growing regions. Pears, apricots, apples, peaches, nectarines and cherries are grown here, and the Ceres Fruit Growers is the largest deciduous fruit co-operative in the southern hemisphere. During the fruit-picking season (December to April), visitors can tour the orchards and fruit-packing houses on the Ceres Fruit Route. The Dwars River runs through town and trout-fishing is popular in the streams of the Matroosberg.

TULBAGH The 20-kilometre diversion to Tulbagh is well worthwhile. In 1969 the picturesque town was nearly destroyed by an earthquake, but was carefully restored. Today Church Street preserves one of South Africa's finest historic precincts with many beautiful Cape Dutch homes dating as far back as 1754.

BAIN'S KLOOF PASS En route to Wellington, the R303 traverses what is often regarded as the most beautiful pass in the Western Cape. The narrow, winding road hugs the deep valley carved by the Wit River and negotiates several tight bends between huge boulders. The pass was completed by Andrew Geddes Bain and his workforce of 350 convicts in 1853.

After crossing the Breede and Wit rivers, the road passes Tweede Tol, with its pleasant camping and picnic sites, and enters the 64 600-hectare Hawequas State Forest. The 9-kilometre stretch to the crest of the pass – a narrow saddle between Wellington Sneeukop (1 683 metres) and Limietkop (1 152 metres) – is the most spectacular part of the journey, and several hikes can be enjoyed in the area. A famous landmark on Bain's Kloof Pass is Dacres Pulpit – a massive rock protruding

over the road – named after Reverend Dacres who delivered a sermon at the pass's opening. On the saddle of the pass, a small inn and a plaque commemorates Bain. Further on, a viewsite overlooks the Berg River Valley, Wellington and Paarl.

FRANSCHHOEK The R45 passes the renowned L'Ormarins, Bellingham, La Motte, La Provence, Dieu Donné and Haute Provence wineries before reaching Franschhoek. The names of these vineyards reflect the rich cultural heritage and tradition of viniculture left by the French Huguenots. Franschhoek is renowned for its classic Cape architecture, leafy avenues and superb restaurants.

The three graceful arches of the Huguenot Memorial, at the foot of the Franschhoek Mountains, commemorate the French Huguenot influence, and the adjacent museum displays antique Cape furniture and farm implements.

FRANSCHHOEK PASS This winding pass zigzags up the mountains, offering splendid views over vineyards, plantations and the rugged peaks protected by the 24 500-hectare Hottentots-Holland Nature Reserve. En route, the oldest road bridge in the country – the 1823 Jan Joubertsgat Bridge – spans the Du Toit's River.

VILJOEN'S PASS After crossing Theewaterskloof Dam, the R321 runs along its shoreline and then ascends Viljoen's Pass. After mounting the pass' crest at 524 metres, the road enters the Elgin Valley, skirts the Nuweberg Dam and provides lovely views over fruit orchards.

SIR LOWRY'S PASS The view from the summit of Sir Lowry's Pass affords superb vistas over Somerset West, False Bay and Table Mountain. A short walk into the mountains reveals the ruts worn by old wagons on the original Gantouw Pass.

Opened in 1825, the winding Franschhoek Pass is one of the country's most scenic.

THE FAIREST CAPE ◆ 180 km

SOMERSET WEST Founded in 1817, Somerset West lies between the foot of the Hottentots-Holland Mountains and False Bay. This attractive residential town has a delightful village atmosphere, and during the festive season, visitors come from afar to see the display of Christmas lights in Main Street. The Country Craft Market is open during the spring and summer months.

The Helderberg Nature Reserve, on the northern edge of town, conserves 245 hectares of fynbos on the slopes of the 1 137-metre-high Helderberg. The reserve is renowned for its proteas and abundant birdlife, and several ponds, a picnic area under tall oaks and a herbarium are added drawcards. Four trails lead up the mountain to Disa Gorge, but there are gentle rambles too.

Not to be missed is a visit to the beautiful Vergelegen Wine Estate. Just 4 kilometres from the centre of Somerset West, this historic Cape

Helderberg Nature Reserve, Somerset West, is famous for its rich floral and bird life.

Dutch estate is set at the foot of the Helderberg on the banks of the Lourens River. Vergelegen was established in 1700 by Governor Wilhelm van der Stel who planted 500 000 vines here. Its historic core – including extensive gardens, the Lady Phillips Tea Garden, the library and five stately 300-year-old camphor trees – is complemented by a fine museum, restaurant, gift shop, wine-tasting and winery tours.

GORDON'S BAY AND STEENBRAS DAM Nestling at the foot of the Hottentots-Holland Mountains, Gordon's Bay is a pretty holiday resort where fishing, swimming and sunbathing are the main pastimes. The small harbour, with its fishing boats and pleasure craft, is enclosed by two sheltering piers. Easily seen from a distance is the anchor of white painted stones, framed by the letters 'GB', which adorn the mountain slopes above the town. Gordon's Bay honours Captain Robert Gordon,

the last commander of the Dutch East India garrison. It has several camping sites and many holiday homes for hire.

At the nearby Steenbras Dam, picnic sites and bungalows have been laid out in the huge pine plantations around the dam, and a choice of recreational facilities are available. Anglers stand a chance of catching brown and rainbow trout, while birders should look out for Egyptian goose, Cape shoveller and grey heron, among others. The dam, completed in 1921, lies in a secluded mountain valley 340 metres above the town, but the spillway is a mere 3 kilometres from the sea. Permits must be obtained beforehand.

THE ROAD TO BETTY'S BAY The drive from Gordon's Bay to Betty's Bay is one of the country's most spectacular. From Gordon's Bay the road ascends the lower slopes of the Kogelberg from where Table Mountain and the Peninsula mountains can be seen across False Bay. Further along, Koeëlbaai's spacious beach is popular with surfers but swimming can be dangerous because of the strong backwash. Baboons are often seen along the road and, where

Gordon's Bay harbour is sheltered by the rugged Hottentots-Holland Mountains.

the sea surges against the cliffs below, Cape fur seals, seabirds and even whales are sometimes spotted.

After 20 kilometres of breathtaking scenery, the road skirts the quiet village of Rooiels, and then cuts inland between Hangklip peak and the Kogelberg before reaching Betty's Bay. Cape Hangklip, False Bay's most easterly point, is a lonely place with only a lighthouse and a hotel.

BETTY'S BAY This peaceful resort area occupies a narrow corridor between the coast and the Kogelberg, and several houses in Betty's Bay front onto mountain fynbos slopes. Over 1 600 species of plants, more than the total for Great Britain, have been identified in the Kogelberg, and leopards still roam the mountains. Betty's Bay has managed to remain relatively undeveloped (electricity was only connected in 1993) and nature-lovers cherish its solitude.

Just outside Betty's Bay, the Harold Porter Botanic Garden lies in a narrow valley dominated by the 916-metre-high Platberg. The garden is renowned for its fynbos displays and boasts proteas, ericas, watsonias and red disas. These attract many sugarbirds and sunbirds, and small mammals such as baboon, spotted genet and mongoose also occur here. Possibly the garden's most scenic spot is Leopard Kloof, and a trail of

the same name leads through a riverine forest to a waterfall. A marine reserve, for the protection of perlemoen and crayfish in Betty's Bay, extends eastwards from Stoney Point where a whaling station once stood. Here a colony of protected jackass penguins can be seen nesting among the rocks, and whales are often sighted in the vicinity.

KLEINMOND Two kilometres after Betty's Bay, the road reaches Kleinmond, a small coastal village overlooking the Kleinmond Lagoon. The magnificent stretch of beach here is ideal for a walk and swimming is popular in the Palmiet River estuary. On the main road just after the Palmiet, Kleinmond's Coastal and Mountain Nature Reserve, which occupies both banks of the Palmiet estuary, is noted for its fine indigenous flora. The reserve's picnic site is at Fairy Glen and the circular 37-kilometre Highlands Trail follows a splendid route along the coastline before climbing the Perdeberg.

BOTRIVIER LAGOON From the Kleinmond caravan park, the R44 hugs the base of the Kogelberg for 11 kilometres before reaching the intersection of the R43. On the right the broad Botrivier Lagoon, extending 7,2 kilometres inland from the sea, is one of the largest in the South

Africa. The lagoon and surrounding marshes are home to thousands of waterbirds, including spurwing goose, Cape teal, yellowbilled duck and Cape shoveller.

The Khoikhoi who lived here called this river *Gouga*, or butter, a commodity that they produced in abundance. The Dutch settlers in Cape Town bartered a variety of goods in exchange for the butter, and from 1672 onwards referred to this river as the 'Botter', which was eventually shortened to 'Bot'. Sailing and fishing are allowed on the lagoon but a license is required.

ONRUS VALLEY After passing the seaside hamlets of Hawston and Vermont, the R43 crosses the Onrus River outside Hermanus. Cooled by sea breezes, the Onrus Valley – also known as Hemel-en-Aarde ('heaven and earth') – would seem an unlikely setting for a wine route, but the Whale Haven, Hamilton-Russell and Bouchard-Findlayson estates produce fine Chardonnay and Pinot Noir wines. Onrus, a quaint coastal village inhabited by many artists, has a small beach, a lagoon and several camping grounds, and is popular for surfing, fishing and diving.

HERMANUS One of the Western Cape's premier coastal resorts, Hermanus enjoys some of the best whale-watching in the world from the 12-kilometre coastal path that weaves along its cliffs. From July to November, Walker Bay is visited by hundreds of southern right whales who come to mate and calve. An official 'whale crier' strides the streets sounding his horn to announce the arrival of these gigantic mammals.

Hermanus, especially busy during summer, has much else to attract the visitor. It is well-known as a fishing resort and has many fine seafood restaurants, while the Old Harbour has been preserved as a fishing museum. The town's best beaches – Langbaai, Voëlklip and Grotto – stretch along the eastern

The Hermanus whale crier announces the arrival of southern right whales.

side of Walker Bay, providing wide, sandy beaches and safe swimming, as do its two tidal pools. Surfing, golf and tennis are also popular pastimes.

Outside town, the 1 400-hectare Fernkloof Nature Reserve preserves a lovely tract of unspoilt fynbos where day walks can be enjoyed along the many footpaths. Klein River Lagoon, east of Hermanus, is the venue for the local yacht club and the lagoon is popular for sailing and birding. A superb view of Hermanus and the sweeping coastline can be seen from Rotary Drive, just outside town.

ELGIN VALLEY Retracing your steps to the junction of the R44, the road continues for 9 kilometres to the N2. From Botrivier the N2 climbs the fynbos-clothed slopes of the Houhoek Pass and then enters the fertile Elgin Valley. Dating back to 1779 the Houhoek Inn, at the crest of the pass, is the oldest in the country and is a favourite afternoon tea venue. A little off the track, the Eikenhof Dam, high up the Palmiet Valley, is surrounded by steep wooded slopes towering 1 000 metres above the valley. The Elgin Apple Museum, one of two in the world, traces the history of the Cape's apple industry. This scenic drive is lovely in spring when the apple blossoms are out.

From Gordon's Bay a spectacular drive curves along the coast to Betty's Bay.

Centrepiece of the West Coast National Park, Langebaan Lagoon is enhanced by a spectacular display of flowers each spring.

BLOUBERGSTRAND In recent years Bloubergstrand has seen rapid development and its beachfront is lined with modern holiday and housing complexes. Its extensive beach is favoured by surfers, walkers, joggers and kite-flyers. Bloubergstrand is famous for its superb views across Table Bay: to the south Table Mountain, framed by the twin sentinels of Devil's Peak and Lion's Head, is visible across 16 kilometres of ocean; to the west Robben Island lies 7 kilometres offshore. Ons Huisie, a national monument and well-known restaurant on the beach, is one of the oldest Cape fisherfolk cottages.

MELKBOSSTRAND From Bloubergstrand, the M14 hugs the coast and gives access to wide, sandy beaches, favoured among fishermen. The seaside town of Melkbosstrand is named after the many coastal milkwood trees found here. Lawns with picnic and braai sites have been laid out on the beachfront, and angling and diving are popular pursuits.

WEST COAST NATIONAL PARK The entrance to the West Coast National Park lies 10 kilometres after the turn-off to Yzerfontein, a fishing village with easy access to the beach. The park conserves one of the most important wetlands and waterbird habitats in South Africa.

The road curves through the low bushes of the West Coast strandveld, a dry form of coastal fynbos particularly suited to the diet of black rhino, and the Parks Board plans to reintroduce them here in the near future.

After 6 kilometres the road approaches an intersection. Keeping left, the road skirts Langebaan Lagoon, and heads for Kraalbaai. To the west is a splendid view of the sand dunes fringing Sixteen Mile Beach. After passing the hamlet of Churchhaven, which is surrounded by the park, the road reaches Kraalbaai, named after the remains of a Dutch fort that was mistaken for an old sheep kraal. Protected from the cold Atlantic currents, the bay's shallow waters are lukewarm and

shelter houseboats. The beach is popular for picnics, swimming and yachting. The rocky Postberg peninsula, north of Kraalbaai, falls within a 2 700-hectare privately owned nature reserve which forms part of the West Coast National Park. Postberg (open only in August and September) is renowned for its spectacular spring flower displays, and a two-day 25-kilometre trail is the best way to explore the peninsula. Apart from wild flowers and excellent views of the Atlantic Ocean and Langebaan Lagoon, Postberg protects fascinating rock formations as well as herds of eland, wildebeest and bontebok.

The 15-kilometre-long Langebaan Lagoon is unique as no river flows into it. Water levels are therefore influenced solely by high and low tides. At low tide extensive salt marshes and mud flats are exposed and these attract an estimated 30 000 wading birds. Langebaan is the largest wetland on the West Coast, the biggest salt marsh in South Africa

and the terminus for birds on the migration route from Europe and Siberia to Africa. Between April and August, up to 8 000 greater flamingoes gather on Langebaan Lagoon.

Apart from protecting waders, the islands in Saldanha Bay provide essential habitats for significant colonies of birds. A quarter of the Cape gannet population, about 60 000 birds, nest on Malgas Island. Marcus Island shelters the country's largest jackass penguin colony, and Jutten Island shelters about 25 000 breeding pairs of Cape cormorants. Schaapen Island is famous for its colonies of crowned cormorants. Birds such as Hartlaub's gull, swift tern and black oystercatcher also find a haven on these islands.

Retracing the route along the lagoon, the road to the left leads to the Geelbek Environmental Centre, based in an 1860 Cape Dutch farmhouse. Three bird hides are nearby and the centre offers environmental education programmes, guided excursions and weekend courses in marine ecology. The northern gate to the West Coast National Park is 15 kilometres from Geelbek.

LANGEBAAN The holiday village of Langebaan is conveniently close to the West Coast National Park. Angling and watersports are popular on Langebaan Lagoon, which has been divided into three zones to cater for the dissimilar needs of conservation and recreation. Catamaran excursions to the Cape gannet colony on Malgas Island, and boat trips during the flower season to Postberg depart from the park offices at Langebaan. The National Parks Board plans to open a restaurant, information centre and chalets on the site of the old Langebaan Lodge.

A famous alfresco restaurant, Die Strandloper, is situated north of Langebaan on the road to Club

Mykonos, a Greek-style hotel and timeshare resort with a yacht basin. Die Strandloper specializes in authentic West Coast cuisine: smoked angelfish, *bokkoms* (salted Cape herring), mussels, waterblommetjiebredie, braaied snoek and crayfish.

Authentic West Coast cuisine: crayfish (top) and snoek (above).

PATERNOSTER The R399 passes through Vredenburg, the commercial and educational centre of the West Coast, and leads to the quaint fishing hamlet of Paternoster. This village is known for its whitewashed cottages and for its good catches of crayfish and perlemoen. Many seabirds occur here, such as sacred ibis, cormorant and seagull. The Paternoster Hotel is famous for its Sunday lunches, and many gather here for the relaxed atmosphere and good food.

Close by is the Columbine Nature Reserve which protects coastal fynbos and succulents. It is especially worth visiting in the flower season when the reserve is a riot of colour. The Titiesbaai camp site provides basic accommodation here.

ST HELENA BAY Towards the end of 1497 the Portuguese mariner Vasco da Gama approached a headland on the West Coast and on 7 November (St Helena's Day), he dropped anchor in the bay and named it St Helena.

Today the town is a major fish-processing centre. During the fishing season (January to August) boats loaded with anchovies and other fish dock at the quays. A monument to Da Gama stands on the shores of the nearby Stompneus Bay.

VELDDRIF AND LAAIPLEK On the estuary of the Berg River lie the 'West Coast Twins', Velddrif and Laaiplek. Fisheries and fishermen's cottages line the river banks, fishing boats tug at their moorings and racks of *bokkoms* (salted Cape herrings) dry in the sun. The annual 280-kilometre Berg River Canoe Marathon, which begins in Paarl, ends at the bridge across the river. Large numbers of birds are attracted here, including pelican, flamingo and spoonbill, and a bird hide is situated on the river bank, upstream of the bridge. Downstream, Port Owen Marina is a luxury residential and timeshare development located on 3 kilometres of waterways.

From Velddrif the road follows the Berg River to Hopefield, which throngs with visitors during the flower season. Here the Bloemendal and Langrietvlei farms attract large numbers of water birds, such as sacred and glossy ibis, greenshank, blacksmith plover and Cape teal, and up to 2 000 flamingoes have also been counted at Hopefield.

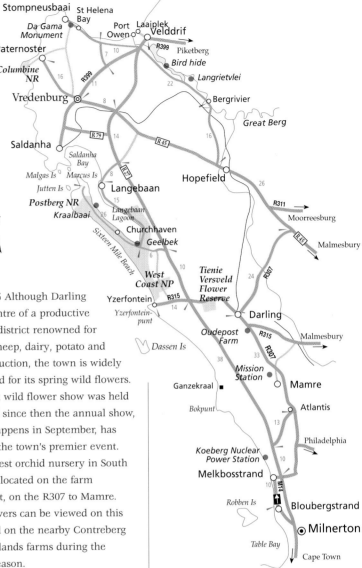

DARLING Although Darling is the centre of a productive farming district renowned for wheat, sheep, dairy, potato and pea production, the town is widely acclaimed for its spring wild flowers. In 1917 a wild flower show was held here and since then the annual show, which happens in September, has become the town's premier event. The biggest orchid nursery in South Africa is located on the farm Oudepost, on the R307 to Mamre. Wild flowers can be viewed on this farm and on the nearby Contreberg and Waylands farms during the flower season.

Darling's long association with the dairy industry resulted in the establishment of a butter museum, housed in the Darling Museum and Art Gallery, where a variety of old butter-making utensils are on display.

MAMRE In 1808, at the request of the Cape Governor, the Earl of Caledon, Moravian missionaries established a mission station in a region where many Khoikhoi lived under appalling conditions. The station prospered and neat rows of whitewashed, thatched cottages were built. The missionaries taught the Khoikhoi many skills including tanning, carpentry, bricklaying and farming. The mission became a haven for them and in 1854 it was given the name of Mamre, a reference to Genesis 13:18. The church, built in 1818, and a water mill are national monuments.

Approximately 60 000 Cape gannets nest on Malgas Island in Saldanha Bay.

THE OVERBERG AND LITTLE KAROO

The fertile farmlands of the Overberg are a changing tapestry of colour, from the golden hues of wheat fields to the deep green of oats and barley before they seed.

The Overberg, meaning 'the other side of the mountain', is the name originally used by the Dutch colonists at the Cape to describe the lands that lay to the east, stretching from beyond the Hottentots-

Hardy aloes, seen here in the Swartberg, thrive in the semi-arid Klein Karoo.

Holland mountain range to the Breede River at Infanta and Witsand on the coast in the east. The dramatic Riviersonderend and Langeberg mountains form the northern boundary of the region, and the towns of Riviersonderend and Swellendam nestle in their foothills. In the south, along the rolling coastal plains, wheat is the dominant crop. As the wheat ripens, it turns the landscape into a rich, golden-brown carpet that seems to extend uninterruptedly to the distant mountains. Oats and barley are also important crops, and before they seed, they add a patchwork of deep green to nature's changing tapestry. The town of Bredasdorp serves this lowland agricultural area.

The southern border of the Overberg is washed by the waters of two oceans – the cold Atlantic and the warm Indian – which meet at Cape Agulhas, the southernmost tip of the African continent.

The Overberg experiences a typical Mediterranean climate. Winters are mild and wet and summers are hot and dry. Winds blow mainly from the southeast in summer and the northwest in winter, and

This map highlights the regional map opposite. Overlapping regions and their page numbers are supplied.

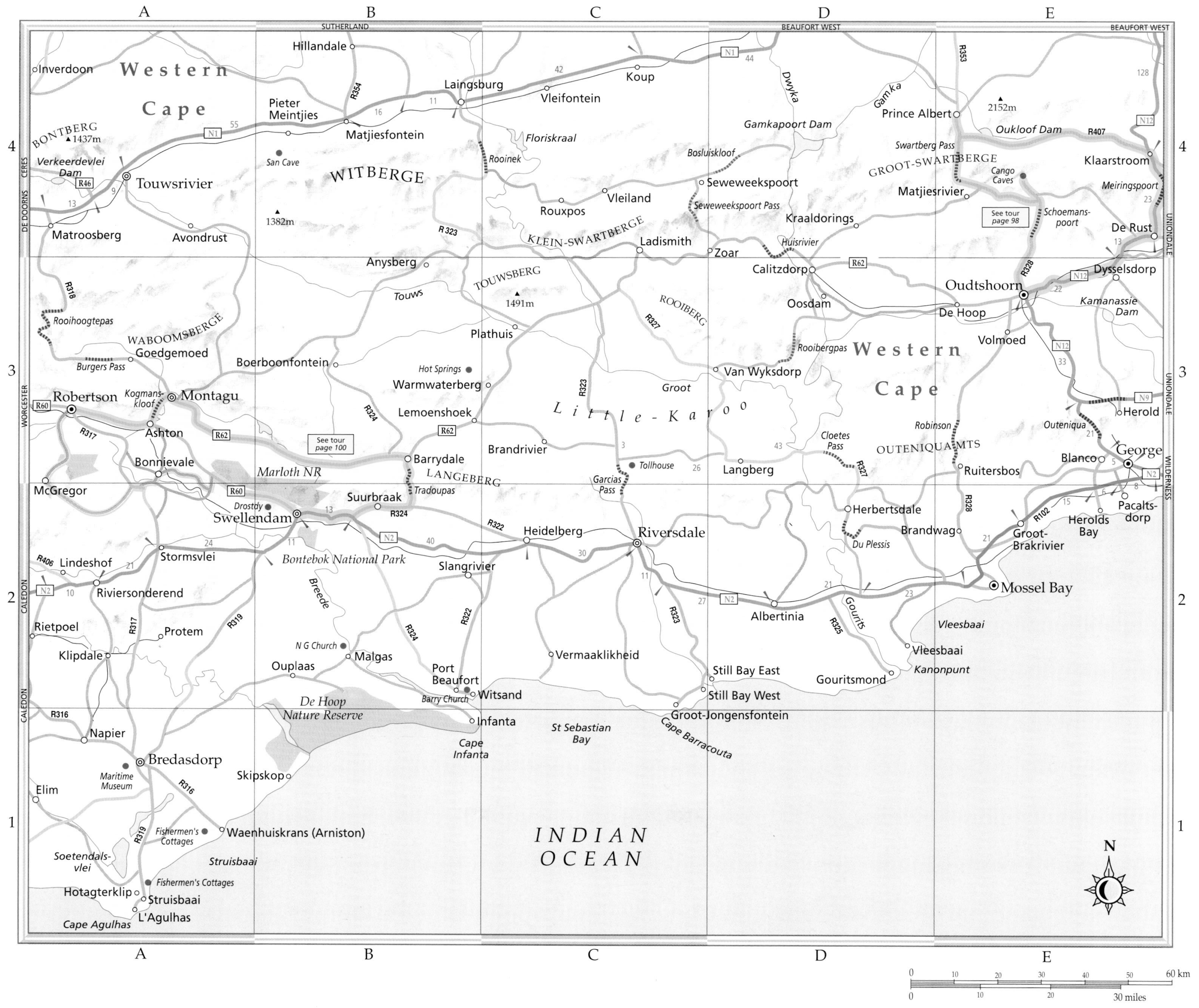

BEAUFORT WEST

N

60 km
30 miles

E

Western Cape

4

128

Klaarstroom
De Rust
Meiringspoort 23
N12
R407
Schoemans-poort
Prince Albert
Swartberg Pass
GROOT-SWARTBERGE
Matjiesrivier
2152m
Oukloof Dam
Cango Caves
See tour page 98

Dysselsdorp
Kamanassie Dam
N9
Herold
George
Pacaltsdorp
Blanco
Outeniqua 21
N2
Herolds Bay
Groot-Brakrivier
Mossel Bay

R353

Gamka
R62
Kraaldorings
Huisrivier
Calitzdorp
Oosdam
Rooibergpas
Van Wyksdorp
Langberg

Western Cape

OUTENIQUA MTS
Robinson
Ruitersbos
R328
Herbertsdale
Brandwag
Du Plessis
Cloetes Pass
R327
Gourits
R325
Gouritsmond
Vleesbaai
Kanonpunt
Vleesbaai
21

BEAUFORT WEST

D

Dwyka
Gamkapoort Dam
Seweweekspoort
Seweweekspoort Pass
Bosluiskloof
Zoar
Ladismith
ROOIBERG
R327
Groot
Tollhouse
Garcia's Pass
Riversdale
R323
Albertinia
N2
Still Bay East
Still Bay West
Groot-Jongensfontein
Cape Barracouta

INDIAN OCEAN

C

Koup
42
Vleifontein
Floriskraal
Vleiland
Rouxpos
KLEIN-SWARTBERGE
TOUWSBERG
1491m
Plathuis
Brandrivier
LANGEBERG
Heidelberg
R322
Vermaaklikheid
St Sebastian Bay

Laingsburg
11
R323
Touws
Hot Springs
Warmwaterberg
Lemoenshoek
R62
Barrydale
Tradoupas
Suurbraak
R324
R322
Slangrivier
Witsand
Infanta
Cape Infanta
Port Beaufort
Barry Church

N1
44
KLEIN-SWARTBERGE
Little-Karoo
3
26
27

B

Hillandale
Matjiesfontein
WITBERGE
San Cave
1382m
Boerboonfontein
Anysberg
WABOOMSBERGE
Goedgemoed
See tour page 100
Marloth NR
Bontebok National Park
Breede
N G Church
Ouplaas
Malgas
De Hoop Nature Reserve
Waenhuiskrans (Arniston)
Struisbaai
Skipskop

SUTHERLAND
R354
R354
16
Pieter Meintjies

A

Western Cape

Inverdoon
Touwsrivier
Avondrust
Matroosberg
BONTBERG 1437m
Verkeerdevlei Dam
R46
13
9

Montagu
Ashton
Bonnievale
R62
R60
Goedgemoed
Kogmanskloof
Burgers Pass
Rooihoogtepas
R318
Robertson
R317
McGregor
R406
Drostdy
Swellendam
13
11
Stormsvlei
24
Riviersonderend
Lindeshof
Rietpoel
Klipdale
R317
Protem
R319
Ouplaas
Napier
R316
Bredasdorp
Maritime Museum
Soetendals-vlei
Elim
Hotagterklip
Struisbaai
L'Agulhas
Cape Agulhas
Fishermen's Cottages

CALEDON
N2
10
R316

WORCESTER
N1
55
DE DOORNS
CRES

Northeast of Cape Agulhas lies the charming fishing village and holiday resort of Waenhuiskrans, or Arniston.

WHERE TWO OCEANS MEET

Cape Agulhas takes its name from the Portuguese word for needle, as Portuguese seafarers found that their compass needles pointed due north without any magnetic deviation when they sailed past this rocky coastline. Offshore, the continental shelf extends below the waves for another 250 kilometres, reaching a maximum depth of only 60 fathoms (110 metres). On this extensive bank are found some of the finest fishing grounds in the southern hemisphere. But these are dangerous waters for shipping, and many vessels have become victims of the deadly combination of strong winds, treacherous currents and rough seas. In order to warn ships of these hazards a lighthouse was built at Cape Agulhas in 1848; in 1962 a modern 18-million-candlepower light replaced the original, which is displayed in the Shipwreck Museum in nearby Bredasdorp.

To the northeast of Cape Agulhas lies the old fishing village of Waenhuiskrans, or Arniston, as it is more commonly known. The latter name comes from the wreck of

can reach gale force at times. The higher mountain peaks are often covered in snow in winter, adding to the beauty of the region.

The Overberg is the heart of the rich Cape Floral Kingdom. Although geographically it is the smallest plant kingdom in the world, it has the largest number of plant species. The predominant vegetation type is fynbos, the name of which is derived from the bushy structure and fine-leafed form of many of the shrubs (*see also* p. 183).

To the north of the Overberg, the broad valley of the Little Karoo is enclosed by the Langeberg and Outeniqua mountains in the south and the Swartberg in the north. The Little Karoo, an area about 250 kilometres long and 60 kilometres wide, is sometimes referred to as Kannaland, from a Khoi word for the root of an edible mesembryanthemum. The region is hotter than the Overberg, and its dry, aloe-covered scrublands contrast with the lush wheatlands of the coastal lowlands. Although the Little Karoo does not receive much rainfall, it is surprisingly well-watered in places by the streams and rivers that flow from the mountains.

Cape Agulhas – the southernmost tip of Africa – is guarded by the second oldest lighthouse in the country.

the *Arniston*, a British troopship that ran aground here during a storm in May 1815 with a loss of 372 lives. Many of the village's lime-washed fishermen's cottages have been restored, thus retaining much of its charming 18th-century character. Today it is a popular holiday resort. The village's official name of Waenhuiskrans (meaning 'wagon house cliff') refers to a huge cavern about 1,5 kilometres south of the village. Created through the pounding of the waves, the cave is so large that wagons can easily be parked inside it. Visitors can explore the cavern at low tide.

Some 15 kilometres northeast of Arniston, the De Hoop Nature Reserve incorporates about 50 kilometres of coastline and extends up to 10 kilometres inland. This important reserve still preserves its pristine dunes, extensive fynbos and wetlands. De Hoop has seven distinct ecosystems and supports some 1 400 plant, 67 mammal, 200 bird, 15 reptile and 6 amphibian species. The adjacent offshore marine reserve stretches 5 kilometres out into the Agulhas Bank, and from

April to January visitors can count on seeing southern right whales, which migrate in their hundreds to mate and calve here.

HEART OF THE OVERBERG

Lying on the southern slopes of the Langeberg range is the town of Swellendam, named after Governor Hendrik Swellengrebel and his wife Helena ten Damme. Swellendam is South Africa's third oldest town after Cape Town and Stellenbosch, and contains a number of beautiful historical buildings. Often described as the heart of the Overberg, the town grew up around the Drostdy (magistracy) which was established in 1747 on the banks of the Korenlands ('wheatlands') River.

Before European settlement, this area was the haunt of elephants and large herds of game. It offered abundant grazing and water and many Khoi tribes were attracted to the area. For many years settlers considered Swellendam to be the 'last outpost of civilisation' for beyond the settlement lay uncharted territory. But as more and more

adventurers, traders and settlers made use of the old 'Kaapse wapad' – the wagon route that led into the interior through Swellendam – merchants, wainwrights and blacksmiths set themselves up in business and the town's commercial base began to develop. Today Swellendam is an important commercial and agricultural centre for the surrounding wheatlands, and is the hub of South Africa's principal merino sheep region.

Southeast of the town is the 3 236-hectare Bontebok National Park, created to provide a home for the highly endangered bontebok, as well as for other species of antelope indigenous to the area such as duiker, grey rhebok, grysbok and steenbok. By the 1850s the bontebok – a subspecies of the more-abundant blesbok – was threatened with extinction and farmers in the Bredasdorp district began protecting the herds on their properties. Their numbers continued to drop until, in 1931, a national park was established near Bredasdorp with a nucleus of only 17 bontebok. Unfortunately the land was badly situated and susceptible to flooding, and so in 1960

The tranquil Breede River, in the heart of the Overberg, is a popular venue for canoeing.

the present site outside Swellendam was established, and 61 bontebok were moved there. Tucked between the Breede River and the Langeberg, the site was well chosen. The bontebok soon increased to about 300, and surplus animals have been relocated to reserves in the southwestern Cape.

OVER THE LANGEBERG

Dividing the coastal terrace from the dry interior, the Langeberg lies roughly parallel to the Swartberg range farther north. Together the two ranges enclose the long valley of the Little Karoo. Both the Langeberg and the Swartberg consist of layers of sandstone, deeply folded and contorted by movements in the earth's crust over many millions of years. The region's amazing mountain scenery is at its most spectacular along the Swartberg Pass, which connects Oudtshoorn with Prince Albert.

OUDTSHOORN

Founded in 1847 on the banks of the Grobbelaars River and named after Dutch nobleman Baron Pieter van Rheede van Oudtshoorn, the town of Oudtshoorn is the principal centre of the Little Karoo, and has become world-renowned for ostrich farming. The area around Oudtshoorn is ideal for raising the birds, because of the widespread availability of the various plants, berries and seeds that they feed on, and the suitability of the dry climate and arid terrain. Even the small stones ostriches swallow in order to

A typical Klein Karoo scene: an isolated farmhouse near Oudtshoorn framed by rugged mountain scenery.

facilitate digestion are present here. In the late 1800s, it became the height of European fashion to wear the splendid tail feathers of the ostrich. When measured weight for weight, the feathers acquired a value greater even than gold.

Feathers plucked from wild birds were first exported in 1826 but commercial farming with tamed birds began in 1867. Enormous wealth was generated as ostrich farms mushroomed in the Oudtshoorn district, and elaborate houses described as 'feather palaces' were built by ostrich feather tycoons eager to display their new-found wealth. Demand for ostrich feathers reached its peak just before the First World War, which reduced the demand for this luxury commodity to virtually nothing. The market revived somewhat at the end of the Second World War and relatively mild demand has been maintained ever since.

Today, however, ostrich farming has once again become a viable proposition; ostrich leather is used for high-quality handbags and shoes, and ostrich meat, biltong and bone meal are also much in demand. The crash of 1913-1914 forced the farmers in the district to diversify their activities, and today wheat, lucerne, honey, tobacco, wool and

mohair are also important crops. The Oudtshoorn area produces about 80% of the country's white honey and lucerne seed.

The Little Karoo is a major centre for the production of grapes and deciduous fruit, with some of the southern Cape's most intensive plantings of wine and table grapes situated west of Oudtshoorn around Ladismith. The town was named after Lady Juana Smith, the beautiful wife of Cape Governor Sir Harry Smith, but the spelling was changed to distinguish it from Ladysmith (also named after Lady Juana) in KwaZulu-Natal. Thanks to the area's hot climate, apricots, peaches, plums and nectarines are also grown here, and the greatest proportion of apricots exported from South Africa are packed in the Ladismith district.

THE CANGO CAVES

Just outside Oudtshoorn, in the foothills of the Swartberg, lies an intricate and fascinating network of limestone caverns known as the Cango Caves, one of the natural wonders of the world. The caves were formed over millions of years by the action of groundwater seeping through and enlarging cracks in the layers of limestone rock that make up the Kango Group.

Ostriches flourish in the Oudtshoorn region's dry climate and arid terrain.

The acidic groundwater dissolved the limestone, hollowing out chambers and passages. When the water table was lowered about one million years ago, nature began the slow process of adorning these caves. Rainwater seeping down from the surface picked up carbon dioxide from plants and soil to form carbonic acid. The acid reacted with the limestone to form a bicarbonate that dripped through the roof of the caves and accumulated to form the fascinating dripstone formations that so delight visitors.

In 1780 a herdsman stumbled upon the entrance to one of these caves. He reported his finding to the farmer, Jacobus van Zyl, who went into the cave with a lantern and gazed with wonderment at the stalactites and stalagmites, which ranged from gigantic shafts to delicate gossamer tendrils. From that day, word of the subterranean wonder spread, and the caves soon suffered the attentions of careless souvenir-hunters.

In 1828 the caves were reserved by the state and the local field-cornet (district magistrate) became responsible for charging viewing fees and imposing fines on any

One of the world's natural wonders: the intriguing Cango Caves just outside Oudtshoorn.

trespassers. In 1891 the first guide was appointed and control of the caves was passed to the Oudtshoorn municipality. Over the years the caves have been intensively studied and today they are one of South Africa's major tourist attractions and an important source of revenue to the Oudtshoorn district.

THE SWARTBERG'S UNIQUE VALLEY

In the heart of the Swartberg range is a deep gorge – approximately 20 kilometres long and 600 metres wide – that is almost completely enclosed by mountains. Some call it a paradise, others call it Die Hel. This is the name that has stuck, given to the valley by a stock inspector who had to negotiate its gruelling access path every two months. Its official name, however, is Gamkaskloof.

Initially the only way into Gamkaskloof was along the precipitous course of the Gamka (the Khoisan word for lion) River, which breaches the imposing rampart of the Swartberg and flows at right angles across the valley. Die Hel is watered by two tributary streams which flow into the Gamka River – one from the east and the other from the west. The mountain slopes are covered by a profusion of aloes, which in winter set the valley aflame with their orange and red flowers.

Die Hel is extremely fertile; long before the white man discovered the valley, San and Khoi people were drawn here, as Die Hel's perennial water and lush vegetation ensured an abundance of game. The first farmer to settle there was Petrus Swanepoel, who arrived with his family in 1830.

Another six families followed and eventually the population grew to around 120. For over a century these self-reliant people lived in splendid isolation, producing their own meat, vegetables, dairy products and fruit. Just one path, negotiable only on foot or by donkey, provided access to the outside world. It was only in 1962 that a road was completed to Die Hel. Inevitably, the younger generation began to leave, and the population of the valley dropped as parents either followed their children or death reduced their numbers. In 1991 the last active farmer sold his farm to the Cape conservation authorities and left the valley.

The road to the peaceful valley of Die Hel descends via a dramatic series of sharp, zigzag bends.

OUDTSHOORN The many roses and bougainvilleas that line Oudtshoorn's streets provide splashes of colour amid the somewhat drab Little Karoo scenery. As the hub of the ostrich feather industry from 1870 onwards, Oudtshoorn was also the scene of a building boom. The wealth generated by ostrich farming was often invested in ostentatious homes known as 'feather palaces', some of which are open to the public. One such residence is the Tuinhuis, in High Street, which preserves the interior and furnishings typical of the late 19th century. The development of the ostrich industry is explored at the CP Nel Museum, with many of the exhibits drawn from the private collection of local businessman Colonel CP Nel. The museum is housed in the former Boys' High School, one of the finest examples of stone masonry in the country.

Oudtshoorn was the home of poet Cornelius Langenhoven, author of *Die Stem van Suid Afrika*, one of South Africa's dual national anthems. Langenhoven's house, Arbeidsgenot, is now a museum and contains many of his belongings, as well as carvings of Herrie the Elephant, one of the author's creations (*see also* p. 99).

The Klein Karoo National Arts Festival is held annually from the end of March to early April. The increasingly popular festival offers music, drama, crafts and many other events, and attracts overseas as well as home-grown artists.

OSTRICH FARMS No visit to the Little Karoo would be complete without a stop at an ostrich farm. These offer the chance to see the ostriches from tiny hatchlings to enormous adults, as well as ostrich races and displays of the birds' enormous eggs. Two popular ostrich farms are situated within 10 kilometres of Oudtshoorn. The Safari Ostrich Show Farm, home to over 2 500 ostriches, offers guided tours, and the farm's stately Welgeluk 'feather palace' is a national monument. Highgate Ostrich Show Farm has been owned by the Hooper family for over a century. Tours of the estate take two hours, and ostrich meals can be arranged in advance.

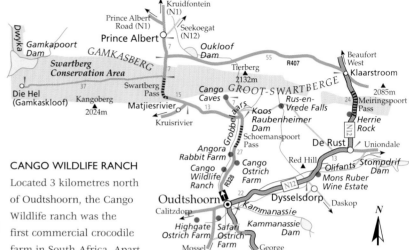

Pinehurst 'feather palace' (above), *and ostrich chicks* (top) *in Oudtshoorn.*

CANGO WILDLIFE RANCH

Located 3 kilometres north of Oudtshoorn, the Cango Wildlife ranch was the first commercial crocodile farm in South Africa. Apart from viewing several hundred crocodiles and alligators, visitors can stroll along an elevated walkway to see cheetahs, lions, pumas, pygmy hippos and otters. A farmyard provides entertainment for children, and a motorized train takes tours through a deer park. The thatched Zindago restaurant overlooks a water hole inhabited by flamingoes and ducks.

EN ROUTE TO CANGO CAVES Ten

kilometres on, the road passes the Cango Ostrich Farm where a short tour covers all aspects of ostrich farming. Ten species of butterfly are also raised on the farm; some are released into the wild for monitoring. The farm sells a selection of Little Karoo sweet wines and ports, and wine-tastings take place daily. The Angora Rabbit Show Farm, across the road, offers tours, pony rides and wool-spinning demonstrations.

After passing through Schoemanspoort, a dirt road to the right leads to the popular Cango Mountain Resort, bordering the Koos Raubenheimer Dam. Fishing in the dam is allowed, and permits are obtainable from the resort. The dam is set in a natural amphitheatre and is dominated by 2 132-metre-high Tierberg. The Rus-en-Vrede ('rest and peace') Waterfall, a few kilometres further on, cascades down a 61-metre-high

forested gorge. The falls are located within the Swartberg Conservation Area (*see also* p. 177), and picnicking and camping are permitted at the Rus-en-Vrede homestead.

CANGO CAVES Although not the largest in the world, the Cango Caves are renowned for their variety and beauty. Cango's exquisite dripstones include curtain-like formations hanging from cavern roofs, calcite flowers, stalactites and stalagmites. Visitors venture 800 metres into the mountainside on a one-hour guided tour. The first chamber, named after Jacobus van Zyl, on whose farm the caves were discovered, is 98 metres long and 18 metres high. Other chambers include Botha's Hall, with its petrified 'waterfall', the Rainbow Room, the Bridal Chamber, and the 107-metre-long Grand Hall.

Adventurous visitors can follow a longer, more strenuous route through the narrow passages of the Devil's Workshop, the Chimney and the Postbox. In the 1970s the discovery of additional chambers extended the caves 1 600 metres further into the mountain. These extensions – Cango 2, 3, 4 and 5 – are not yet open to the public. At the entrance to the caves is a restaurant, curio shop and crèche.

The Swartberg Pass, with its hair-raising bends, yields fine views of the Great Karoo.

SWARTBERG PASS After the caves, the road passes the De Hoek Mountain Resort on the right-hand side, after which the tar ends and the spectacular Swartberg Pass commences. The pass climbs 785 metres over 10 kilometres of sharp curves, and marks the entrance to the Great Karoo.The route was constructed in the 1870s by the celebrated road engineer Thomas Bain. As it was impractical to tunnel through the Swartberg, Bain decided to take the road right over the crest of the range. It took his workforce of convict labourers four years to complete the pass.

The area's mountain fynbos vegetation, which includes proteas and ericas, is most attractive between August and October. During winter, heavy snow can force the closure of the route. Just beyond the summit, the Ou Tol hiking hut is shaded by tall pine trees. The hut is one of five starting points along the five-day Swartberg Hiking Trail.

DIE HEL Some 3 kilometres beyond the summit of the Swartberg Pass, a 35-kilometre dirt road ventures westward through dramatic mountain scenery. The road then descends 580 metres over 3 kilometres of zigzag bends and ends in the peaceful valley of Die Hel, or Gamkaskloof, less than 400 metres above sea level. The valley is undoubtedly one of the most remote spots in the Western Cape. Over the years most of it has been acquired for conservation and now forms part of the 90 000-hectare Swartberg Conservation Area, which includes the Gamkapoort Dam. Some of the old farm buildings have been restored and are now national monuments. At the end of the 20-kilometre-long valley there is a camp site, and cottages are available for hire. Walking and mountain biking can be enjoyed on unmarked trails.

PRINCE ALBERT After the turn-off to Die Hel, the road plunges down a 4-kilometre section of tight bends and switchback curves and then passes between towering walls of folded sandstone to reach the enchanting village of Prince Albert. With its irrigated plots, water furrows and unique architecture, Prince Albert preserves the atmosphere of a bygone era. The old watermill on the Swartberg Pass road was built in 1850 and was used for over 120 years.

A walk down Church and De Beer streets reveals many attractive Cape Dutch houses, as well as fine examples of Victorian architecture and typical flat-roofed 'Karoo' houses. The characteristic 'Prince Albert gable' is best displayed at No. 5 Church Street, once the residence of the Dutch Reformed parson. The handsome Swartberg Country House Hotel in Church Street is a national monument, and boasts a charming pub. The town's Fransie Pienaar Cultural History Museum occupies a large Victorian house and preserves mementos from Prince Albert's short-lived gold rush of 1890. But history takes a back seat during Prince Albert's week-long Olive Festival, held annually in April or May.

MEIRINGSPOORT The road east from Prince Albert skirts the northern slopes of the Swartberg. At Klaarstroom, the route joins the N12 and heads south through the mountains via Meiringspoort, a pass discovered in 1854 by Petrus Meiring when he followed the Groot River through a *poort* (narrow gap). Thomas Bain completed the route in 1858 but it had to be rebuilt in 1886 after being frequently washed away by the Groot River. From Klaarstroom, visitors enter a wonderland of contorted sandstone layers. Flanked by cliffs, the road follows the Groot River for 17 kilometres, crossing it 25 times and passing a superb 55-metre-high waterfall, which can be reached after a short walk. About 3 kilometres after the waterfall the word 'Herrie' is carved into a rock, an inscription made in 1929 by the author CJ Langenhoven, in reference to his fictional creation, Herrie the Elephant, who hauled a tramcar from Oudtshoorn to Meiringspoort (*see also* p. 98).

DE RUST In the hamlet of De Rust, founded in 1900 on the farm owned by Petrus Meiring, canals and numerous trees provide a pleasant contrast to the surrounding Karoo scenery. De Rust's picturesque setting, Victorian houses and craft shops make it a tempting place to stop. The Stompdrif Dam, 5 kilometres to the east, offers waterskiing and fishing, and stores water for irrigation along the valley of the Olifants River. Below the dam and 11 kilometres from De Rust is Tante Maria's Stable on the Domein Doornkraal wine estate. Here, local wines can be sampled while enjoying excellent cuisine.

From De Rust the N12 follows the Olifants River to Oudtshoorn. Halfway along the route the prominent Red Hill dominates the Mons Ruber wine estate, which specializes in muscadel and hanepoot wines. A two-hour trail leads along the base of Red Hill and provides a superb view over the valley of the Olifants.

A Victorian cottage in the charming village of De Rust.

LANGEBERG AND THE BREEDE VALLEY ◆ 260 km

SWELLENDAM With its near-perfect setting at the foot of the Langeberg, its oak-lined streets and Cape Dutch buildings, Swellendam is one of the most beautiful towns in the country. The town's original structures include the Drostdy, built in 1747, and the centrepiece of the cluster of buildings that makes up Swellendam's Drostdy Museum. The museum complex also comprises the neighbouring Old Gaol, Secretary's House and Zanddrift – a reconstructed Cape Dutch farmhouse now used as a restaurant.

With its long level stretches and occasional rapids, the nearby Breede River is ideal for river canoeing excursions. Swellendam is the starting point for the annual 280-kilometre Berg River Canoe Marathon.

THE LANGEBERG From Swellendam the R60 follows the base of the Langeberg through the orchards and vineyards of the Breede River Valley. The famous Langeberg 'clock peaks' overlook Swellendam from east to west. The mountains bear the nicknames of Ten O'Clock, Eleven O'Clock, Twelve O'Clock and One O'Clock, because the time can be told from their shadows. The highest is Twelve O'Clock, which towers 1 428 metres above the valley. The mountains are protected within the scenic 11 269-hectare Marloth Nature Reserve, well known for its varieties of flowering trees, colourful fynbos

The historic Drostdy in Swellendam was once the landdrost's court and residence.

and protea. Wildlife includes leopard, Cape grysbok, klipspringer and grey rhebok, with black eagles among the abundant bird population. The six-day, 74-kilometre Swellendam Hiking Trail (*see also* p. 185) traces a circular route over the mountains and is regarded as one of the loveliest trails in the Western Cape.

BONNIEVALE Twenty-seven kilometres west of Swellendam, a turn-off to the left leads to Bonnievale. Situated on the banks of the Breede River, the town is a centre for wine, fruit and dairy production. Bonnievale's cheese factory is the largest in the country and produces fine varieties of Cheddar and Gouda. Visitors can tour the factory on weekdays. An attractive Cape Dutch building at the intersection of the R317 houses the Bonnievale Co-op; wine-tastings and sales take place on weekdays.

MCGREGOR Cradled by the northern slopes of the Riviersonderend Mountains, McGregor is renowned for its historic ambience. With its blend of Cape Dutch and Victorian architecture, McGregor has been described as the country's best-preserved and most complete example of a mid-19th-century town. In recent years the village has become a popular weekend retreat. Fourteen kilometres southwest of the town, the popular 16-kilometre Boesmanskloof Traverse begins at Die Galg ('the gallows'). The trail links McGregor to Greyton, on the southern slopes of the Riviersonderend.

ROBERTSON Renowned for its magnificent roses, peaches, superb wines, thoroughbred race horses and historic buildings, the town of Robertson was founded in 1853 at the foot of Arangieskop, the tallest peak in the Langeberg.

The 'Robertson Walkabout' showcases the town's varied architectural heritage, which ranges from modest gabled houses to Victorian villas. The Robertson Art and Craft route, formed by 16 artists, potters and craftsmen in and around the town, is open on the first weekend of each month and is well worth visiting.

The KWV brandy distillery and the Clairvaux, Roodezandt and Robertson Co-op wineries lie on the western edge of Robertson, and are open Monday to Saturday. North of the town, the 38-kilometre Dassiehoek and the 21-kilometre Arangieskop hiking trails traverse the Dassiehoek Nature Reserve. The trails ascend the Langeberg and offer splendid views over Robertson and the fertile valley below. The reserve is covered with mountain renosterveld and fynbos, the latter rich in proteas and ericas. Wildlife includes baboon, dassie, grysbok and leopard. Horse trails through the reserve depart from a neighbouring fruit farm.

Protected by Marloth Nature Reserve, the Langeberg offers excellent hikes and trails.

ASHTON AND COGMAN'S KLOOF

On the N15 between Robertson and Ashton, the Sheilam Cactus Garden is an unusual commercial enterprise which produces more than 1 000 cactus varieties. From here, it is a short drive to Ashton, the canning and processing centre for much of the region's fruit. The Zandvliet Estate Winery and Ashton Co-op offer wine-tasting and cellar tours.

Beyond Ashton, the R62 enters Cogman's Kloof, the most westerly of the Langeberg's passes. The road follows a narrow *poort* (pass) over-shadowed by folded sandstone mountains. Before the 7-kilometre pass could be completed in 1877, Thomas Bain's workers had to bore a 16-metre tunnel through the rock. A picnic site and a memorial plaque to Bain are located after the tunnel. The remains of Fort Sidney, built during the Anglo-Boer War, can be seen on the ridge above the tunnel.

MONTAGU
The pretty town of Montagu occupies a basin surrounded by the Langeberg and Waboomsberg ranges. Founded in 1851, the town derives much of its appeal from a number of historic buildings – there are 14 national monuments in Long Street alone. The Centenary Nature Reserve, in Van Riebeeck Street, is a well-known wild flower garden, and is noted for its vygies in spring. Montagu's flavoured muscadel and fortified wines can be sampled Monday to Saturday at the Cogman's, Drie Berge and Montagu Co-op cellars on the eastern edge of town.

The popular Montagu Springs resort surrounds the town's famous 43 °C mineral springs, the alleged healing properties of which have attracted visitors for over 200 years. The pure water is pumped into five outdoor and two indoor pools. The resort's facilities also include tennis courts, pedal cars, a children's play park, tractor trips to surrounding farms and a conference centre. The adjacent three-star Avalon Springs Hotel offers similar facilities, as well

Apricots drying at Ashton, the fruit-processing centre for the area's produce.

as a gym and indoor pools. Because of its lovely scenery, Montagu is a magnet for outdoor enthusiasts. Mountain biking and 4x4 routes have been opened a few kilometres north and northwest of the town, and the 16-kilometre Bloupunt and 12-kilometre Cogman's Kloof hiking trails begin at Die Ou Meul, north of the town. A shorter 2-kilometre trail starts just north of the town centre and follows the Badkloof watercourse to the mineral baths.

BARRYDALE
From Montagu, the R62 follows the Langeberg to Barrydale. A neat village of whitewashed houses, Barrydale guards the northern entrance to the Tradouw Pass, and is situated in a district renowned for its deciduous fruit, as well as for dried fruit and wine. The Country Pumpkin farm stall and restaurant is a good place to shop for fynbos honey, export grapes and fresh produce – especially pumpkins! Wine is produced by the Barrydale Co-op under the Tradouw label; many of the district's wine farms offer tastings.

East of the village lies the Boesmansbos Wilderness Area (*see also* p. 177), which can be explored along 65 kilometres of trails. At the southern boundary of this 14 200-hectare wilderness area, Grootvadersbosch is the largest indigenous forest remnant in the Langeberg.

The 10-kilometre Bushbuck Trail offers glimpses of stinkwood, yellow-wood, red alder and beech trees.

The lovely Knysna woodpecker has been recorded here, and other avian visitors include the emerald cuckoo, sombre bulbul, chorister robin, Cape robin, olive bush shrike and grey cuckooshrike.

TRADOUW PASS
From Barrydale, the route crosses the Langeberg via the Tradouw Pass. Thomas Bain began construction of the pass in 1869, choosing a route that follows the narrow valley carved by the Tradouw River through the Langeberg.

Although the surrounding mountains rise to 1 500 metres, at no point along the 17-kilometre route does the road climb to more than 351 metres. The first half of the pass is the most beautiful and it is worth stopping at the many parking areas to admire the exquisite scenery and the sheer sandstone cliffs. The original wooden bridge built by Bain can still be seen from the Andries Uys Bridge, about 3 kilometres after the crest of the pass.

At the end of the pass the R324 turns right to the village of Suurbraak, founded in 1812 as a mission station. The junction with the N2 is 8 kilometres further on, and the road then enters the fertile valley of the Buffelsjagrivier.

BONTEBOK NATIONAL PARK
Although the 3 236-hectare Bontebok National Park is the smallest national park in South Africa, a visit there is highly recommended. Apart from its role in saving the bontebok from extinction, the park preserves a valuable relic of South Coast renosterveld (shrubland fynbos), which supports 470 plant species. Apart from bontebok, the park is home to Cape mountain zebra, grey rhebok and Cape grysbok, and its extensive birdlife includes Cape weaver, olive woodpecker, Stanley's bustard and black korhaan. Early spring, when the fynbos blooms, is the most beautiful time of year, and in September the first bontebok lambs are born.

From the park entrance, a 25-kilometre circular route crosses the renosterveld and then follows the banks of the Breede River – where fishing and swimming are permitted – before reaching the caravan park, situated in a riverine thicket of Cape beech, acacia, false olive and Breede River yellowwood. Downstream, the 2-kilometre Aloe Hill Trail is superb in winter when the aloes flower. The 2-kilometre Acacia Walk heads upstream through riverine thickets.

The Bontebok National Park shelters the distinctive bontebok, as well as smaller creatures, like this tortoise.

THE GARDEN ROUTE

Along 227 kilometres of southern Cape coastline lies a string of white beaches, steep cliffs, gentle bays and prominent sandstone headlands, interspersed with lakes, lagoons and wetlands. Here nature has created a spectacular garden, and the route that passes through it is one of the most scenic in South Africa. Bordered by lush mountains and forests, the Garden Route offers the visitor superb scenery, a temperate climate and a wide range of leisure activities.

FORESTED BEAUTY

Between the town of George and the Tsitsikamma forests, the ruggedly beautiful Outeniqua and Langkloof mountains step down from the interior plateau to the coastal plain. The mountains capture the rain clouds that rise from the sea, and these fill the many streams and rivers, providing lifegiving water to large tracts of forest.

The name Outeniqua comes from the Khoi word meaning 'people with honey', as the Khoi collected the honey made by bees from the wild flowers that adorn the hills and valleys. The flowers of the Outeniqua Mountains form part of the fynbos community,

Scenes along the picturesque Garden Route: sunset gilding the tranquil Keurbooms beach close to Plettenberg Bay (above), with the fynbos-bedecked Outeniqua Mountains (below) lying further inland.

which makes up 80% of the Cape Floral Kingdom (*see* p. 183). The forests that carpet much of the Outeniquas form part of the remaining 20% of that kingdom. Some of South Africa's largest trees are found in these forests, including the massive Outeniqua yellowwoods (*Podocarpus falcatus*) which reach heights of up to 50 metres. (A tree of this size would probably be over 800 years old, with a trunk at least 3 metres in diameter.) The ironwood (*Olea capensis* subsp. *macrocarpa*) is another huge tree, with some specimens reaching 35 metres in height. Smaller in size, but of great commercial value is the stinkwood (*Ocotea bullata*), famed for the fine furniture made from it. In both the Tsitsikamma and Knysna forests, pathways have been cut through the forest to allow visitors to see some of these majestic 'Big Trees'.

Sadly, the great forests of indigenous hardwood trees have lost much of their former splendour due to ruthless exploitation during the 18th and 19th centuries. In areas where the indigenous forest cover has been cleared, plantations of exotic trees have been established to supply the demands of paper mills and other industries. Nevertheless, the Garden Route's 65 000 hectares of surviving natural forest, including 43 000 hectares of state land, makes up the largest indigenous forest reserve in South Africa.

This map highlights the regional map opposite. Overlapping regions and their page numbers are supplied.

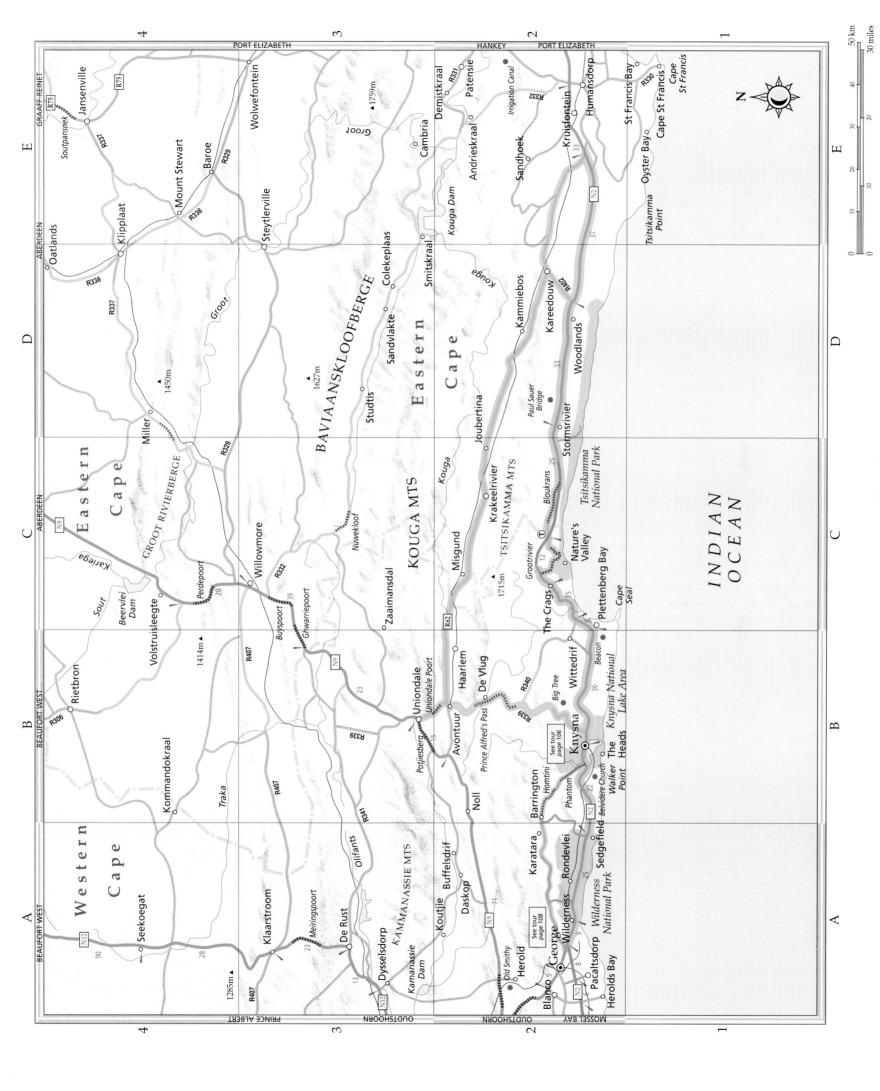

ELUSIVE FOREST ELEPHANTS

For centuries herds of elephant roamed the plains and wetlands of the southern Cape. By the beginning of the 20th century, however, they had all but lost access to the coastal plain due to increasing settlement. The elephants sought sanctuary in the depths of the Knysna forests, even though these woodlands are not well suited to their habits. The elephants have been officially protected since 1908, when only 20 animals remained, but their numbers have steadily declined since then, and today only one cow remains of the original herd. The decline in numbers is not attributed to poaching or hunting, but rather to a reduction in the elephants' reproductive capacity due to deficiencies in their forest-based diet.

In 1994, three juvenile females were translocated from Kruger National Park (one subsequently died) to bolster the numbers of the Knysna elephants, and if the remaining new arrivals adapt to their surroundings others will be brought in to join them.

UNDERWATER EDEN

Offshore, nature has carefully created carpets of marine life which correspond to an intricate species and marine life zonation dictated by depth. This shoreline zonation, which is typical of all coastlines, is of special significance along the Garden Route because the region is situated at the point of transition between the warm waters of the east coast of South Africa (influenced by the Agulhas Current emanating from the tropical reaches of the Indian Ocean) and the cold waters of the West Coast (where the Benguela Current sweeps freezing waters northward from Antarctica). As a result, remnants of a tropical fauna and flora, although diminished in both size and number, mingle with examples of the cold water fauna and flora which dominate South Africa's West Coast.

GARDEN ROUTE GATEWAY

George, the principal town on the Garden Route, is set against the magnificent backdrop of the rugged Outeniqua Mountains. Described in 1877 by English novelist, Anthony Trollope, as the 'prettiest village on earth', it still retains much of its early charm and beauty.

Founded in 1811, George was named after the English king George III. During the 19th century, the town was the centre for the burgeoning timber industry, and today mixed farming, including dairy, sheep, vegetables, wheat and hops, represents the major economic activity in the region. Most of the vegetables produced on the farms around George are processed in the town's large canneries, and virtually all of the country's hops – the dried flowers of which are used as a flavouring in beer – are grown in the Blanco area west of George.

WILDERNESS TO KNYSNA

Some 10 kilometres east of George lies Wilderness, one of South Africa's most sought-after holiday locations. Idyllically situated between mountains and beaches, with a chain of tranquil lakes locked in between, Wilderness has a unique beauty. The lakes, surrounding forests and 28 kilometres of coastline are protected within the 2 612-hectare Wilderness National Park, which stretches from the town of Wilderness to the Goukamma Nature Reserve at Buffels Bay. The park is a paradise for birders, with as many as 79 of South Africa's 95 waterbird species recorded here.

Further along the coast lies the attractive town of Knysna, a rapidly expanding commercial, retirement and holiday centre which began as a port for exporting timber cut from the surrounding forests. The port is situated on the northern shore of a huge tidal lagoon that opens to the sea through a narrow, treacherous inlet, and is guarded by steep sandstone cliffs on either side, known as The Heads.

The history of Knysna is intricately linked with the enigmatic George Rex, supposed illegitimate son of King George III and father of 13 children. Rex bought a farm in Knysna in 1804, and in 1817 persuaded the Admiralty to establish a harbour in the lagoon. A flourishing economy based on

Wilderness (above) *is known for its abundant birdlife, such as the lovely malachite kingfisher* (top).

Rustic wooden cottages at Storms River provide comfortable accommodation in the Tsitsikamma National Park.

timber processing, furniture-making and shipbuilding (spearheaded by the Thesen family, immigrants from Norway) developed in Knysna. The town has retained its reputation for fine furniture manufacture and boat-building, and today, items made from wood constitute the core of its industrial base. The town offers many leisure options, and has drawn a wide variety of craft industries to serve the tourist trade.

BEAUTIFUL BAY

Shipwrecked Portuguese sailors gave Plettenberg Bay the name of Bahia Formosa ('the Bay Beautiful') in 1630. In 1778, the Dutch East India Company's governor at the Cape, Joachim van Plettenberg, visited the area and named it after himself. A timber warehouse was established here in 1788 and timber was shipped directly from Plettenberg Bay to Cape Town. When the British occupied the Cape they decided to use Knysna as the point of shipment, because its harbour was safer. From 1912-1916 a Norwegian whaling station operated on a small rocky island situated on the main beachfront, a site now occupied by the Beacon Island, a modern, eight-storey hotel.

Today Plettenberg Bay, with its unspoilt, sandy beaches, warm waters and equable climate, is one of South Africa's premier holiday destinations, offering a wide range of tourist drawcards. The nearby Robberg and Keurbooms River nature reserves are a delight for ramblers and bird-watchers.

TSITSIKAMMA

Extending for 80 kilometres from just west of Nature's Valley to Oubosstrand in the east, the thin ribbon of the Tsitsikamma National Park encompasses some of the most exquisite coastal scenery in South Africa.

Throughout the park's length, the clear streams that cascade down from the mountains have cut deep kloofs through the sandstone cliffs that buttress the sea – such as at Storms River – or they tumble over cliffs to form waterfalls. In other places the rivers slowly meander along forested valleys and through pristine estuaries. Some of these rivers and estuaries are navigable by small boat for a considerable distance, such as at the charming village of Nature's Valley, and provide some of the finest bird-watching and nature experiences in the country.

Much of the fascination of the Tsitsikamma National Park lies in its wealth of both terrestrial and aquatic animals and plants, and in their interaction. The valleys and the mountain slopes are clothed in a rich variety of forest trees and shrubs, and on the narrow coastal plain the evergreen forests give way to fields of fynbos dominated by ericas, proteas, restios, agapanthus and watsonias. Terrestrial fauna found in the park includes the diminutive blue duiker, chacma baboon, vervet monkey, bushbuck, bushpig and the elusive Cape clawless otter (*Aonyx capensis*), as well as some 220 bird species which are associated with both sea and shore.

Tsitsikamma's rich and varied aquatic world is enhanced by the meeting of warm and cold waters along the Garden Route coastline, and dolphins and whales can often be seen in the breakers offshore. To explore the park's fascinating underwater world, a snorkelling trail has been laid out in the bay at Goudgate, situated just west of the camp at Storms River, and qualified divers can follow a diving route around Mooi Bay and Sand Bay at the Storms River Rest Camp complex.

Two of South Africa's most popular hiking trails traverse the park: the world-famous Otter Trail, which starts at Storms River and runs along 41 kilometres of spectacular coastline, ending at Nature's Valley five days later; and the 61-kilometre Tsitsikamma Hiking Trail, which follows an inland route from Nature's Valley through indigenous forest and ends at the suspension bridge over the Storms River (see also pp. 182 and 183).

The shy Cape clawless otter, after which the world-renowned Otter Trail is named.

GARDEN ROUTE AND LANGKLOOF ◆ 420 km

PLETTENBERG BAY Encompassing white, sandy beaches, an extensive lagoon formed by the Bietou and Keurbooms rivers and the prominent Robberg Peninsula, Plettenberg Bay is one of the Garden Route's most alluring coastal resorts. Affectionately known as 'Plett', its unofficial emblem is the pansy shell. Plettenberg Bay's business district adjoins the three most popular beaches and accommodation ranges from luxury

Cathedral Rock, Keurbooms beach, the Garden Route's 'Hole in the Wall'.

hotels to guesthouses and camp sites. Swimming is safest at Lookout and Central beaches, while surfers congregate mainly at Lookout Beach. August and September are the best months for spotting southern right whales coming into the bay to calf. Just outside of town, three circular trails explore the unspoilt coastal fynbos, the caves and rich intertidal zone and bird life of the Robberg Nature Reserve. Bird species found here include Cape sugarbird, great shearwater and greyheaded gull.

KEURBOOMS RIVER NATURE RESERVE

Extending up the Keurbooms River for several kilometres, the 800-hectare Keurbooms River Nature Reserve protects the steep forested cliffs along the pristine river. Waterskiing is permitted in the river's lower reaches, and fishing and birdwatching are also popular. The Keurbooms can be navigated by canoe upstream as far as Whiskey Creek. Aventura's Keurbooms resort, on the banks of the river, has chalets and camp sites, and activities include canoeing and riverside walks. Dense forest borders the Keurbooms, and kingfisher, fish eagle, lourie, blue duiker, vervet monkey and bushbuck are among the forest's wild creatures.

The Beacon Island Hotel overlooks one of Plettenberg Bay's famous sandy beaches.

NATURE'S VALLEY AND DE VASSELOT

After leaving Keurbooms River, the road climbs steeply and heads inland offering fine views over Plettenberg Bay and lagoon. In 1983 the opening of the new section of the N2 eliminated two winding passes, cutting out 9 kilometres, but the alternative route on the old R102 offers the best scenery. Dropping from 220 metres to sea level over 4 kilometres, this road follows the lush, forested Kalanderkloof to the edge of the Groot River Lagoon. Much of the route passes through the De Vasselot section of the Tsitsikamma National Park, where visitors can overnight in

delightful forest huts or in the caravan park. Six walking trails explore the surrounding indigenous forest and the river is ideal for canoeing. Close by, the unspoilt and enchanting village of Nature's Valley is entirely surrounded by the national park. After crossing the Groot River, the road climbs steeply

Plettenberg Bay's unofficial emblem is the fragile pansy shell.

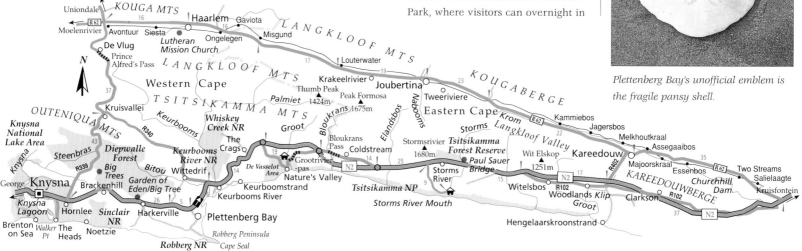

out of the valley, providing a superb view of the coastline, and then crosses timber plantations before re-entering indigenous forest. At the intersection with the N2, the most scenic route is again to follow the narrow R102 down the Bloukrans Pass. The road twists through dense forest before crossing the Bloukrans River.

One kilometre downriver is the impressive 450-metre-long Bloukrans Bridge, the longest concrete arch bridge in Africa, towering 216 metres above the riverbed.

STORMS RIVER MOUTH Roughly in the middle of the Tsitsikamma National Park is the mouth of the Storms River. From the entrance gate off the N2, the road descends a steep forested bluff, passes caravan sites and log cabins, and ends at the restaurant and shop overlooking a rocky cove. A short walk leads to a suspension bridge across the Storms River, affording superb views of the sea. Five short trails explore the rugged shore and the forest surrounding Storms River Mouth. Tsitsikamma's main attraction is the Otter Trail, widely regarded as the country's foremost coastal hike (*see also* p. 183).

Storms River has much else to offer. A beach is situated below the restaurant, fishing is permitted in a zone near the caravan park, and an underwater trail has been developed for scuba divers. The national park extends 5,6 kilometres out to sea, and dolphins, southern right whales, otters and seabirds are commonly seen. Besides these energetic pastimes, many visitors are content just to watch the untamed surf pounding against the rocky shore.

PAUL SAUER BRIDGE Rejoining the N2, the road enters the Plaatbos Forest about 3 kilometres before the Paul Sauer Bridge. From either of the two parking areas before the bridge, a short walk leads through lush forest to a 37-metre-high Outeniqua yellowwood tree. The impressive 192-metre-long Paul Sauer Bridge,

opened in 1956, spans the Storms River Gorge and replaced Thomas Bain's original route down Storms River Pass. A petrol station, restaurant and shop are at the bridge.

LANGKLOOF VALLEY From the junction of the R62, the 143-kilometre journey through the Langkloof Valley takes the visitor through one of the country's most important fruit-growing regions. Tucked between the Tsitsikamma and Kouga mountains, the temperate climate and fertile soils of this narrow valley produce top-quality apples, pears, peaches and plums which are exported overseas. The route passes through towns such as Kareedou, Joubertina and Haarlem. The most notable of these is Haarlem, laid out in 1856 and later acquired by the Berlin Missionary Society. Haarlem's Lutheran Church, completed in 1880, is a national monument and one of South Africa's few thatched-roof churches.

PRINCE ALFRED'S PASS South of Avontuur, the gravel R339 twists over Prince Alfred's Pass between Langkloof and Knysna. The idea of a road over the mountains was first proposed in 1856 by Andrew Geddes Bain. In 1863 his son, Thomas Bain, began construction, and it took his workforce of 270 convicts four years to clear the dense forest and push

Diepwalle Forest is home to many giant Outeniqua yellowwood trees.

the route over the mountains. The pass is often regarded as Bain's greatest feat of engineering.

At Diep River Bridge there is a picnic site and a plaque commemorating Bain. After passing through mountain fynbos vegetation for 40 kilometres, the road crosses the spine of the Outeniqua Mountains and descends through lush forest to the coastal plain and Knysna.

DIEPWALLE FOREST After crossing the Outeniquas, the R339 reaches the Valley of Ferns picnic site. A path leads through a moist forest renowned for its tree ferns, some of which reach heights of 4 metres. Soon the road is enveloped by the vast and splendid Diepwalle Forest.

The Elephant Walk is an easy 18-kilometre ramble that takes about seven hours to complete, but there are two shorter circuits of three and five hours each. The walk passes eight 'Big Trees' – colossal Outeniqua yellowwoods, some of which tower more than 40 metres above the forest floor. The King Edward VII tree is estimated to be over 600 years old. The Elephant Walk is named after the forest's most famous inhabitants, but the elephants are seldom seen in the thick vegetation. Although birds can be difficult to detect in the dense foliage, a quiet stroll will reveal animals such as bushbuck and duiker.

Noetzie's whimsical castles overlook the sand and sea.

NOETZIE AND BRACKENHILL WATERFALL At Hornlee the route rejoins the N2, and heads east toward Plettenberg Bay. An interesting detour is to continue south along a gravel track to the Noetzie River mouth, where there is a lovely sandy beach and a lagoon that is safe for swimming. Noetzie is famous for its imposing 'castles' built on the surrounding hillsides by wealthy families early in the 20th century. After returning to the N2, the route soon passes a turn-off to the right that leads to Brackenhill Waterfall, where a forest stream tumbles over a series of rocky ledges into a thickly wooded gorge. Viewsites overlook the falls and a picnic site is located nearby.

GARDEN OF EDEN Just off the N2 between Brackenhill and Harkerville lies a superb example of wet, high forest, aptly named the Garden of Eden. Several short walks explore the luxuriant forest and a route has been laid out for wheelchairs. South of the road, the Harkerville State Forest includes a 20-kilometre stretch of coastline and the Sinclair Nature Reserve, protecting indigenous forest and a section of coast. The two-day Harkerville Trail crosses dense yellowwood forest and hugs the rocky coastline.

LAKES AND LAGOONS ◆ 230 km

Guarded by the Heads, the Knysna Lagoon is a popular venue for watersports.

KNYSNA Situated on the edge of an extensive 18 000-hectare lagoon framed by the Heads, Knysna has developed from a timber-exporting port into a fashionable coastal retreat. The town's superb natural setting has attracted artists and entrepreneurs from around the country, and a stroll down the main road reveals art galleries, coffee shops, restaurants, furniture shops, and outlets trading in wool, shells, leather and carved wooden birds.

Not only has the town lent its name to the exquisite Knysna lourie and the endemic Knysna seahorse, but it has become synonymous with several unique enterprises. The Knysna Oyster Company raises 300 tons of oysters annually on 13 hectares of the lagoon and visitors

can sample these delicacies here. Mitchell's Brewery is renowned for its fine draught ale, and is open for tours.

Of historic interest are Millwood House and Parkes Cottage, both from the old Millwood gold-mining village west of Knysna (*see* this page). On the western shores of the lagoon is the beautiful Belvidere Church, built in 1855 and modelled on an 11th-century Norman design.

The lagoon is popular for bird-watching, fishing and diving, and several ferry companies offer cruises. One ferry conveys visitors from the edge of the lagoon near the town centre across to the unspoilt western head, which forms part of the Featherbed Nature Reserve. Visitors can explore the reserve on a drive up the mountain or on the 2,5-kilometre

Bushbuck Trail, where bushbuck, Cape grysbok and blue duiker can be observed. From several points along the trail there are magnificent views over the lagoon. More than 100 bird species have been recorded here, including the Knysna lourie, cinnamon dove, sombre bulbul and the Natal and chorister robin. On the water, kingfisher, cormorant, heron and gull are commonly seen.

MILLWOOD RUINS Two kilometres after the N2 crosses the Knysna Lagoon, the gravel road to Rheenendal follows the Seven Passes Road (*see below*), laid out by Thomas Bain in 1868. Before reaching Rheenendal, the traveller first crosses Phantom Pass, a twisting road that follows the valley slopes and affords lovely views over the Knysna River valley. Soon after the pass, a dirt road to the right passes the Goudveld Forest Station and a picnic site at a 'Big Tree'. From here, a left fork leads through the Millwood Forest to Jubilee Creek,

The distinctive Knysna lourie, often seen along the Garden Route.

where there is a lovely picnic site, while the road to the right continues on for 4 kilometres until it reaches the ruins of Millwood.

Gold was discovered here in 1876, and before long a village of corrugated-iron buildings had sprung up. Millwood soon boasted several banks and stores, a post office, six hotels, three newspapers and over 40 mining syndicates. But the gold reef was thin and difficult to work. By 1900 only a handful of miners remained. The only reminders of this short-lived town are a cemetery, a few fruit trees, an old steam boiler and the Bendigo Mine Shaft, which extends 200 metres into the hillside.

THE SEVEN PASSES ROAD In 1868, Thomas Bain embarked on the task of building a road from George to Knysna. Although Bain and his workforce of convicts laboured more than 10 years to finish the 90-kilometre road, today's traveller can complete the route in under two hours. From east to west, the seven passes are Phantom, Homtini, Karatara, Hoogekraal, Touw River, Silver River and Kaaimans River. The road winds through dense forests, down deep gorges, crosses numerous rivers over narrow bridges, and passes small settlements and forestry stations.

The original bridges have been replaced and sections of the route have been tarred, but even so the Seven Passes Road is one of the few in South Africa that has been declared a national monument. Where signposts are unclear, keep to the right to continue on this road.

After negotiating Karatara and Hoogekraal passes, the route runs along the boundary of Woodville State Forest. The strenuous, five-day Outeniqua Hiking Trail (*see also* p. 183) begins at the Beervlei Forest Station in Woodville Forest. At Woodville, a track to the right ends at a picnic site and the Woodville 'Big Tree', a 33-metre-high Outeniqua yellowwood. The last three passes – Touw River, Silver River and Kaaimans River – take the road through the Silver and Kaaimans river valleys. The stone bridge over the Kaaimans, built in 1903 to replace Bain's original wooden structure, is a national monument. Two kilometres on, the road passes the respected Saasveld College of Forestry, which has produced forestry graduates since its foundation in 1932.

GEORGE Set at the foot of the Outeniqua Mountains, George is a thriving commercial centre. It was founded as a timber-cutting outpost in 1785 and wood still plays an important role in the town's economy. The George Museum, housed in the old Drostdy built in 1812, focuses on indigenous wood and the history of forestry in the area. In front of the Old Library stands the Slave Tree, one of the original oak trees planted when the town was laid out in 1811. The name comes from the old chain and lock embedded in the trunk, rather than any association with slavery. St Mark's Cathedral, the smallest cathedral in the southern hemisphere, gives George its city status. Consecrated in 1850, St Mark's was modelled on a church

at Littleworth, near Oxford in England, and is renowned for its large array of stained-glass windows.

George is also the western terminus for the Outeniqua Choo-Tjoe, a narrow-gauge steam train that runs daily between George and Knysna, except on Sundays and certain holidays. The trip along the coast to Knysna takes two-and-a-half hours, and the scenic route offers magnificent views of river mouths, lakes, wooded valleys and the sea.

The Bado Kidogo Parrot Farm and Farmlands Animal Farm are added attractions in town. On the eastern side of George, eight hiking trails traverse the mountains and the attractive shores of the Garden Route Dam. To the west, the world-renowned 36-hole Fancourt golf course and hotel occupies a 140-hectare country estate.

WILDERNESS From the junction of the N9, the N2 passes the turn-off to Victoria Bay, a small, secluded beach much favoured by surfers, and then descends rapidly to the Kaaimans River. This is a favourite venue for photographers and rail enthusiasts who come to see the Outeniqua Choo-Tjoe cross the bridge at the river's mouth. At the crest of the pass out of the Kaaimans valley, Dolphin's Point lookout affords a lovely view of Wilderness's extensive

The vintage Outeniqua Choo-Tjoe crosses the Kaaimans River en route to Knysna.

beach stretching away to the east. Wilderness occupies a narrow spit overlooking the sea and the chain of lakes formed by the estuaries of the Touw, Diep and Karatara rivers. With its splendid views, dense coastal vegetation and proximity to the lakes, it is an enchanting resort.

The 2 600-hectare Wilderness National Park embraces four lakes – Island Lake, Langvlei, Rondevlei and Swartvlei – 28 kilometres of coastline and the Touw and Swartvlei estuaries. Pedal boats and canoes can be hired and a boardwalk leads for one kilometre along the banks of the Touw River. There are various nature trails in the park, four of which are named after the different species of kingfisher found at Wilderness.

The scenic lakes drive is a must. Beginning at the Wilderness Hotel, the drive passes the Fairy Knowe Hotel and winds through the national park's rest camps, Ebb and Flow North and Ebb and Flow South. The gravel road then skirts the northern bank of the Serpentine River, linking the three western lakes (Island, Langvlei and Rondevlei) with the Touw River. Island Lake, the first lake on the drive, is a favourite watersports venue and derives its name from the forested Drommedaris Island, in the centre of the lake. Before the road joins the N2, visitors will see the tranquil Langvlei and Rondevlei lakes, both of which

have bird hides. Among the birds to be seen here are osprey, crested grebe, purple gallinule, kingfisher and thousands of ducks.

Seventeen kilometres after the Touw bridge, the N2 crosses the northern end of Swartvlei estuary, linking Swartvlei, the largest of the five lakes, to the sea. The resort town of Sedgefield lies on the eastern shores of Swartvlei estuary. Groenvlei, the only freshwater lake in the system, is part of 2 200-hectare Goukamma Nature Reserve (*see* below).

BUFFELS BAY The road to Buffels Bay follows the Goukamma River for 10 kilometres, the last 4 kilometres of which passes through the Goukamma Nature Reserve. This reserve protects 14 kilometres of unspoilt sandy coastline to the west of Buffels Bay village. Mammals in the reserve include bushbuck, grysbok, and blue duiker, but the 150 species of birds found here – the secretarybird, fish eagle and Knysna lourie among them – are more frequently sighted.

Buffels Bay, a favourite place for swimmers, surfers and anglers, is situated on the narrow Walker Point, which separates it from the larger sweep of Walker's Bay. From the picnic site on the Goukamma River, a 13-kilometre walking trail explores fynbos-covered dunes and provides superb views of the white, sandy beach and wave-trimmed shore.

George's Dutch Reformed Church at the foot of the imposing Outeniqua Mountains.

SETTLER COUNTRY

Fort Frederick in Port Elizabeth is one of many reminders of Settler Country's turbulent early years.

Settler Country embraces a landscape that varies from lush coastal grasslands to the southern edge of the semi-arid Great Karoo. As the setting for the nine Frontier Wars fought between white settlers and the Xhosa, the region endured a turbulent coming of age. Beginning in 1781, and ending only in 1878, these often-brutal conflicts raged back and forth across the Great Fish River – the frontier of the Cape Colony – with great loss of life. Settler Country takes

Typical of the Eastern Cape is the striking crane flower, here with a lesser doublecollared sunbird.

its name from 4 000 English settlers brought here in 1820, after the Fifth Frontier War, as a way of increasing the numbers of white farmers along the frontier. The authorities hoped that they would cultivate the land as well as provide a buffer against incursions by the Xhosa. The settlers brought with them the skills they had acquired in England as well as an unshakeable faith and a tradition of learning, all of which they bequeathed to their adopted land.

The vegetation varies from typical Cape fynbos in the south of the region to savanna and dryland savanna in the north, interspersed with valley bushveld – a tangle of acacia, spekboom, guarri, boerbean and a variety of other thorn trees and shrubs. Climatically Settler Country is a region of transition, from the eastern extremes of the winter rainfall area of the Western Cape to the southern limits of the summer rainfall areas of the remainder of the subcontinent. The region thus receives rain throughout the year, although it is inclined to be erratic.

MOUNTAIN HEIGHTS

Running laterally across the region, from Graaff-Reinet in the west to Stutterheim in the east, is a continuous range of mountains which roughly divides the better-watered coastal lowlands from the dry, higher-lying Great Karoo. In the west the stark, angular mountains that rise from the Karoo's barren plains are known as the Sneeuberg. The road between Graaff-Reinet and Middelburg cuts through these mountains in three separate and often spectacular passes – Naudesberg, Wapadsberg and Lootsberg.

Between Graaff-Reinet and Somerset East the mountains are known as the Coetzeesberg, and formed the eastern boundary of the Cape Colony at the end of the 18th century. East of Somerset East the mountains continue as the Winterberge, and give way in the east to the beautiful Amatola range. Rising in places to an altitude of 2 000 metres above sea level, the Amatolas form an impressive escarpment, which falls away to the broad, green Tyume valley lying at its feet.

During the Frontier Wars, the Amatola Mountains were a Xhosa stronghold, and a place of great conflict. An important feature of the Amatola escarpment is a mountainous spur which has been eroded away to create three separate flat-topped mountains, each resembling a hog's back. The attractive

This map highlights the regional map opposite. Overlapping regions and their page numbers are supplied.

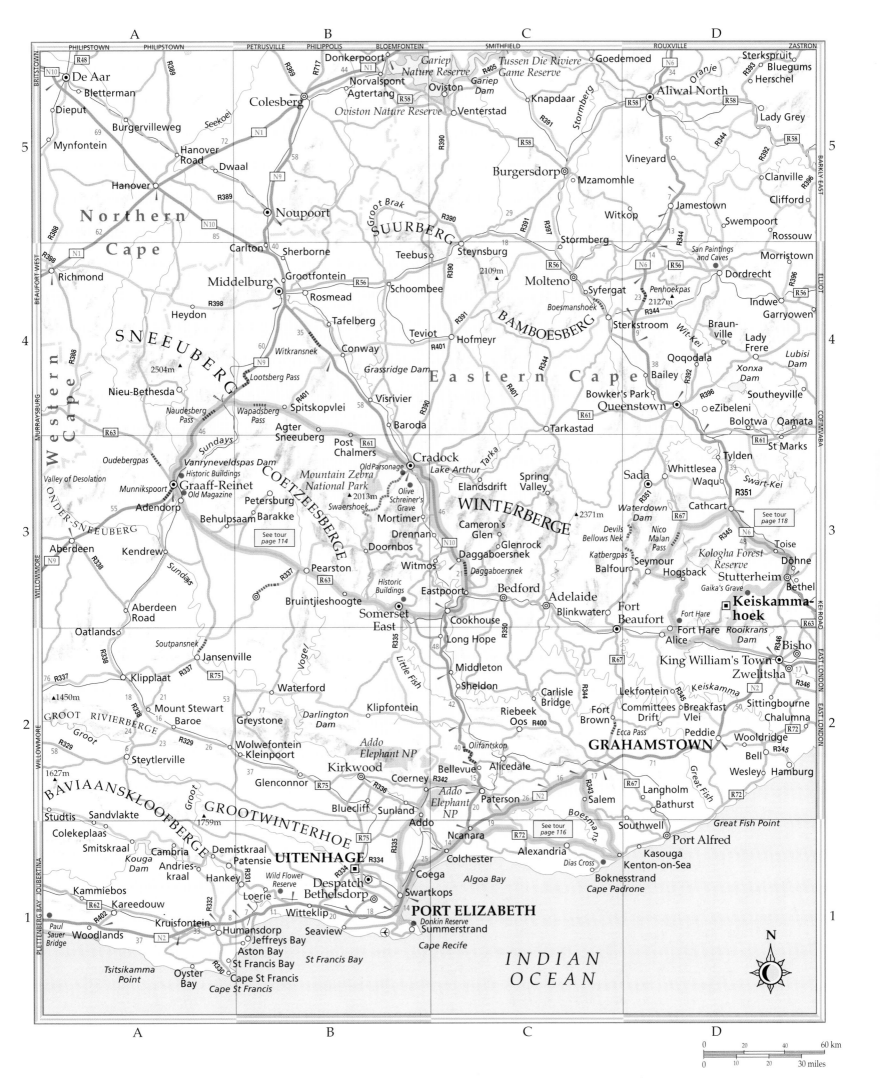

resort village of Hogsback, in a valley in the mountains, takes its name from these mountains. Rainfall in the Hogsback region is plentiful, averaging about 1 200 millimetres annually. As a result natural hardwood forests cover the mountain slopes and gather thickly in the intervening kloofs. Enormous yellowwoods, often draped with bearded monkey-rope, tower above a variety of other indigenous trees, including the red-berry forest currant, the white ironwood, cabbage trees, wild lemon and many, many others. The king of all the trees in the Eastern Cape is the ancient Eastern Monarch. With a circumference of 9 metres and a height of more than 30 metres, this magnificent yellowwood reigns supreme in the Amatola forests.

PORT ELIZABETH

Despite its violent beginnings, Settler Country is an area in which culture and learning have enjoyed a high priority, together with progressive agriculture, technical innovation and industry. One of the main centres in the region is the bustling industrial city of Port Elizabeth, the third largest port and the fifth largest city in South Africa. Located on the shores of Algoa Bay – called Bahia de Lagoa ('bay of the lagoon') by the Portuguese because of the small lagoon situated at the mouth of the Swartkops River – Port Elizabeth was founded in 1799 when the British built Fort Frederick on a low rise overlooking the bay. The 1820 Settlers came ashore under the protection and surveillance of this fort. Sir Rufane Donkin, acting governor at the Cape at the time, visited Fort Frederick to welcome the settlers and named the growing settlement Port Elizabeth in memory of his wife, who had died in India two years previously.

Port Elizabeth prospered and the city became the principal port for the Eastern Cape. The lack of a natural harbour, however, meant that ships had to anchor offshore and load and off-load by means of lighters. Because of its unprotected anchorage, Port Elizabeth became known among mariners as one of the most dangerous harbours in the world. It was only in 1928 that the harbour was developed to provide quayage and a partly sheltered roadstead.

Port Elizabeth's pastimes include sailing regattas (above), *and performing dolphin shows* (below).

Notable among the traditional exports from the region were ostrich feathers from the Oudtshoorn district (*see also* pp. 96 and 98); this industry grew so fast that by 1883 it became necessary to erect a massive stone structure in Port Elizabeth, today known as the Feather Market Hall, to store the feathers before shipment to Europe. Hides and skins, wool and mohair were other important exports from Port Elizabeth and the concentration of the city's expertise in these fields has led to its dominance in the leather industry in South Africa, as well as to the establishment of knitting mills and allied garment industries.

In the early 1920s Port Elizabeth became the Detroit of South Africa, when General Motors and Ford opened motor vehicle assembly plants in the city. With the establishment of these factories a host of smaller industries developed, producing motor car parts. Volkswagen later followed the lead given by the American makers when the company set up an assembly plant in nearby Uitenhage, a town originally founded by the Dutch in 1804 as a military outpost.

SAILORS' BAY

From Port Elizabeth's southern limits at Cape Recife, a huge bay stretches approximately 100 kilometres to the southwest, which the Portuguese navigator Manuel Perestrello named in honour of St Francis, the patron saint of sailors. The bay's gentle sweep culminates at Cape St Francis. Nearby, the little fishing village of Sea Vista has developed into the attractive and fashionable holiday resort of St Francis Bay, noted for its thatched, white-washed houses. Also situated within the sweep of the bay is Jeffreys Bay, an international surfer's mecca renowned for its giant curling waves and for the large variety of beautiful shells washed up on its shores.

THE ELEPHANTS OF ADDO

Elephants occurred historically throughout the Cape Colony, but as the land was apportioned into farms, their numbers declined rapidly. A relic population survived in the impenetrable Addo bush, a tangle of thornbush thicket to the northeast of Port Elizabeth. But even these elephants were soon threatened by the establishment of citrus estates in the nearby Sundays River Valley, and in 1919 Major Philip Pretorius was appointed to exterminate them. He succeeded in shooting 120 over 11 months. Only 15 traumatised elephants survived and as public opinion favoured their protection, the survivors were spared.

In 1931 a 6 852-hectare tract of bush was set aside as the Addo Elephant National Park, but the elephants continued to venture onto the surrounding farms at night. A fence made from railway tracks and elevator cables was specially designed to contain the elephants within the park; by 1954 some 2 270 hectares of Addo had been fenced and all the elephants were safely confined. As the elephant population responded to protection – rising to 108 in 1981 and 220 in 1996 – it became necessary to allow them access to the entire park. Additional land was purchased and Addo has now been linked with the Zuurberg National Park. The consolidated park now covers over 50 000 hectares and the National Parks Board has ambitious plans for its future development.

THE CULTURAL CITY

While the Port Elizabeth-Uitenhage axis is the industrial centre of Settler Country, Grahamstown is its cultural heart. This city is sometimes called the the 'City of Saints and Scholars' because of its more than 50 places of worship, and because of the many fine schools that have been established there. Grahamstown is also the seat of Rhodes University, established in the early 1900s. However, the foundations of the city do not rest upon the noble pursuits of worship and education, but rather on the spectre of war and bloodshed.

During the Fourth Frontier War in 1812, most of the farms and settlements sparsely spread along the Cape Colony's eastern frontier had been ransacked by the Xhosa. To secure the frontier and drive the Xhosa out of the coveted Zuurveld (coastal grassland), Governor Sir John Cradock decided to build a line of forts along the Fish River, and Colonel John Graham was assigned the task of finding suitable locations for these forts. Graham selected a burnt-out farm called Rietfontein to serve as headquarters, as it could be easily defended in the event of attack and was accessible to the outlying forts to be built along the Fish River.

The Addo Elephant National Park supports more than 200 of these gigantic beasts.

The name of this outpost was changed to Grahamstown, and it soon attracted many of the 1820 Settlers, who had become disillusioned by the vagaries of farming in the Albany district, where the weather was unpredictable and the soils poor. It was not long before Grahamstown had the largest concentration of wheelwrights, carpenters, blacksmiths, gunsmiths and millers outside of Cape Town, and it became a significant trading centre.

The importance of Grahamstown as a commercial centre was steadily challenged, however, by the growth of Port Elizabeth. As a result, the character of Grahamstown changed and it became an educational centre of national importance as well as the judicial centre of the Eastern Cape. Every year in July, the city hosts the renowned Standard Bank National Arts Festival, a 10-day extravaganza of theatre, music and fine art. For many English-speaking South Africans, Grahamstown – with its Georgian buildings, its stone churches and its 1820 Settlers Monument and Cultural Centre overlooking the city from Gunfire Hill – is their spiritual home.

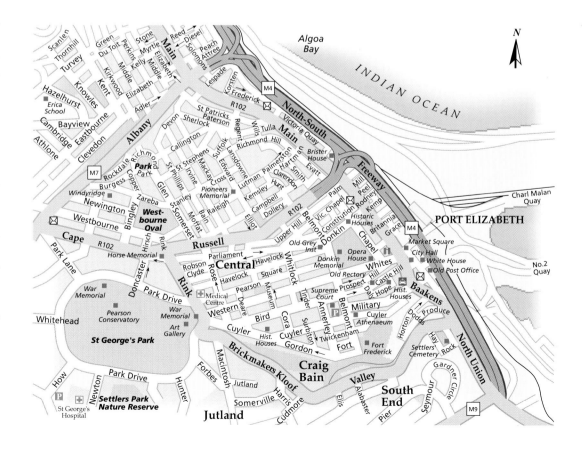

AN OASIS IN THE KAROO ❖ 500 km

GRAAFF-REINET Established in 1786 as the seat of a Dutch East India Company *landdrost* (magistrate), Graaff-Reinet is the country's fourth oldest town and well deserves the title of 'Gem of the Karoo'. This lovely town lies within a broad horseshoe of the Sundays River and its lush gardens, parks and tree-lined avenues are in sharp contrast to the semi-arid vastness of the surrounding Great Karoo. Graaff-Reinet's neat grid-pattern layout consists of rows of white, flat-roofed Karoo cottages, Cape Dutch masterpieces and ornate Victorian mansions.

Over the years many of Graaff-Reinet's historic buildings have been restored. The most important of these are located on either side of Church Street, which is dominated by the towering Grootkerk, an 1887 copy of England's Salisbury Cathedral. Parsonage Street has virtually been restored in its entirety and the adjacent Drostdy Hotel – built on the site of the original residence of the landdrost – dates from 1806. Behind the hotel is the restored Stretch's Court, a lane of Cape Dutch cottages that housed labourers in the 1850s and now accommodate hotel guests.

Stretch's Court, an historic lane of Cape Dutch houses in Graaff-Reinet.

In Murray Street, Reinet House and the Residency are fine examples of Cape Dutch architecture and form part of the town's museum complex. The Residency displays an impressive collection of old weapons. The grape vine at Reinet House was planted in 1879 by Charles Murray, son of the Scottish-born Dutch Reformed reverend, Andrew Murray.

Aside from these well-known landmarks, over 200 private homes have been declared national monuments. Many of the houses offer accommodation and a chance to sample appetizing local dishes such as Karoo lamb and springbok fillet.

KAROO NATURE RESERVE Graaff-Reinet is the only town in South Africa that is virtually surrounded by a nature reserve. The 16 000-hectare Karoo Nature Reserve was established in 1975 to protect striking examples of Karoo landforms such as the Valley of Desolation, Spandaukop and Drie Koppe. Wildlife typical of the Karoo, such as kudu, mountain zebra, black wildebeest, hartebeest, springbok and blesbok, occur here. Game-viewing roads explore the section of the reserve around Van Ryneveld's Pass Dam.

North of Graaff-Reinet, a 14-kilometre road leads to the popular Valley of Desolation viewsite. Here a short walking trail hugs the edge of the cliff and offers breathtaking views of the eroded dolerite columns and the sweeping plains of the Great Karoo.

NIEU-BETHESDA Located at the foot of the 2 500-metre-high Kompasberg – highest peak of the Sneeuberg range – the remote village of Nieu-Bethesda dates back to 1875. Pear trees line the village's main streets and many properties are surrounded by quince hedges. But Nieu-Bethesda is best known for Owl House, the home of visionary artist Helen

Martins. Born in Nieu-Bethesda at the end of the 19th century, Martins devoted 25 years to the creation of the Owl House's intriguing garden of concrete and glass statues. With the help of an assistant, she fashioned owls, camels, people, sphinxes and religious symbols. Inside the house, Martins continued her 'search for light and brightness' by decorating the walls, ceilings and doors with finely ground coloured glass.

After Martins died in 1976, interest in her art increased, and her life and work were portrayed in Athol Fugard's play *The Road to Mecca*. The internationally-acclaimed playwright, also known for playing the part of Jan Smuts in the movie *Gandhi*, has now made his home in the village.

MOUNTAIN ZEBRA NATIONAL PARK Despite being the second smallest national park in the country, the Mountain Zebra National Park has much to offer. It was established in 1937 to save the Cape mountain zebra from extinction. Today over 200 mountain zebra inhabit the park, which is also home to wildlife such as caracal, black-footed springbok, Cape fox and black wildebeest, and more than 200 bird species.

Nieu-Bethesda's Owl House, created by visionary artist Helen Martins.

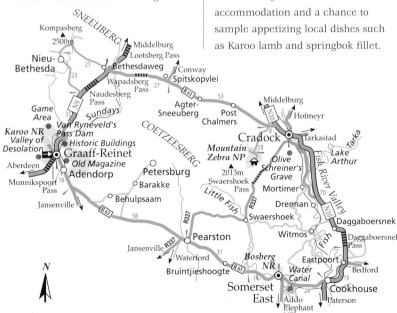

The 12-kilometre dirt road that runs from the R61 to the park entrance follows the course of the Wilgeboom River in the direction of the imposing Bankberg, and then leads to the rest camp tucked into a secluded valley. Facilities at the rest camp include a restaurant, store, swimming pool and information centre, and accommodation consists of cottages and a caravan park.

Two drives traverse the park. The first is a 28-kilometre circular route which explores the wooded Wilgeboom Valley, noted for the rugged granite mountains which overlook it. Due to the steep terrain, the higher sections of this route can only be travelled in an anti-clockwise direction. The lower loop bypasses Doornhoek cottage (where the film version of Olive Schreiner's novel, *The Story of an African Farm*, was shot; *see* below), which overlooks a large dam, and leads to an attractive picnic site in Weltevreden Kloof. Here a pleasant water hole attracts many birds, including palewinged starling, redheaded finch and Karoo prinia.

The second route follows a steep ascent from the Wilgeboom Valley to the Rooiplaat Plateau. The majority of the park's wildlife, especially the mountain zebra, congregates on the fertile grassland plateau. Early morning or late afternoon are ideal times for making this journey, and the

Over 200 Cape mountain zebra are protected at the Mountain Zebra Park.

route affords unparalleled views across the Great Karoo. The three-day Mountain Zebra Hiking Trail explores the park and offers the chance to see the Cape mountain zebra at close quarters.

CRADOCK At the end of the Fourth Frontier War in 1812, Sir John Cradock established two military outposts to secure the eastern frontier: one was Grahamstown, the other Cradock, strategically situated on the bank of the Great Fish River. Cradock soon became the centre of a prosperous sheep-farming district. The impressive stone Dutch Reformed Church, with its pillared portico, commands the town's central square. The church was modelled on St Martin's-in-the-Fields in London and was completed in 1867.

Despite the march of progress, Cradock still retains the distinctive characteristics of a Karoo town: there are many fine sandstone buildings, verandas enclose the steep-roofed houses, and many dwellings are painted in bright pastel shades. Several banks and commercial buildings are housed in historic sandstone structures. In Market Street, Die Tuishuise is an ingenious project that has seen the careful restoration of 14 mid-19th-century houses which now serve as cosy bed-and-breakfast venues. Each house represents a different architectural style, complete with period furniture.

The house in Cross Street where Olive Schreiner – author and women's activist – lived for three years from the age of 12, has been preserved as a museum of literature. In the 1870s Schreiner worked for six years as a governess on farms in the Cradock district, and her epic novel, *The Story of an African Farm*, was written during this period and published in 1883. On a return visit in 1892 she met and later married local farmer Samuel Cronwright. After climbing Buffelskop, 24 kilometres south of Cradock, the newlyweds were overwhelmed by the view of

Cleverly crafted miniature windmills for sale on the outskirts of Cradock.

the surrounding countryside, and Schreiner expressed the wish that they should one day be buried together on the summit. In 1920 she died alone in a boarding house in Cape Town. Cronwright buried her on the summit of Buffelskop with her dog, Nita, alongside the remains of their only child who died just 16 hours after birth. Half a day is needed to visit the tomb and, as a courtesy, permission must first be obtained from the owner of the farm.

FISH RIVER VALLEY On the outskirts of Cradock, miniature windmills made from wire can be seen turning in the breeze. These skilfully crafted replicas of the 'lifeblood of the Karoo' are the work of township residents who enthusiastically market their products to passing travellers.

After leaving Cradock, the N10 runs parallel to the fertile Fish River Valley. On either side of the valley, the typical flat-topped mountains (*koppies*) of the Karoo descend to a patchwork of green pastures and crops, but where the road veers away from the river, the countryside is clothed in characteristic Karoo scrub and acacia thickets. Ostriches, goats and sheep thrive in this arid terrain.

After Cookhouse, the road crosses the Sundays-Fish canal, linking the Fish River to the important citrus-

producing Sundays River Valley (*see also* p. 116). The canal is part of the Orange River Project, the country's largest water development project.

SOMERSET EAST Set at the foot of the wooded Bosberg range, Somerset East is known for its well-tended gardens, profusion of flowering plants and many waterfalls. The town was named after Governor Lord Charles Somerset who, in 1815, chose this site as its deep soils were ideal for growing fodder for the British cavalry units stationed on the eastern frontier. A town was laid out in 1825.

The Beaufort Street Museum is a fine example of a Georgian manor house, and served as the residence for ministers of the Dutch Reformed Church from 1832. In the same street, the Walter Battis Art Gallery occupies a building that the famous landscape artist lived in as a child and houses the largest collection of his paintings in South Africa.

The 2 000-hectare Bosberg Nature Reserve occupies the scenic mountain slopes west of the town. There are several vegetation types within the reserve, and animals present include the rare mountain zebra, baboon, mountain reedbuck and steenbok It is also the haunt of birds such as the black eagle, jackal and steppe buzzard, and lesser kestrel.

INLAND FROM PORT ELIZABETH ◆ 450 km

SUNDAYS RIVER VALLEY After leaving Port Elizabeth, the R335 passes through dry scrub before crossing into the Sundays River Valley near the village of Addo. In 1877, local farmer James Kirkwood identified the potential of the region and began to use the river for irrigation. Water from the Sundays River has transformed the arid valley into one of the country's principal citrus-growing regions. In the 1920s Percy Fitzpatrick, author of *Jock of the Bushveld*, bought a farm in the Sundays River Valley and invested large sums of money in irrigation development – his political influence brought about the construction of Lake Mentz upstream in 1922. Fitzpatrick, his wife and two sons are buried at 'The Lookout', which gives a superb view of his beloved valley.

The flightless dung beetle, one of the Addo's most industrious residents.

ADDO ELEPHANT NATIONAL PARK
Set up to protect the Cape's last remaining viable elephant population, the Addo Elephant National Park's thick bush supports the highest concentration of large mammals in the country. Besides the more than 200 elephants, wildlife includes black rhino, kudu, eland, bushbuck, duiker and grysbok. It is also home to the country's first Corridor disease -free population of Cape buffalo. (A second group has been established by De Beers Consolidated Mines near Kimberley in the Northern Cape.)

Visitors often overlook one of Addo's most fascinating creatures – the flightless dung beetle. As this insect is virtually restricted to the park, signs along the road appeal to visitors to take care not to drive over any beetles. The main focus of the park is the Addo rest camp, which provides accommodation in Cape Dutch-style chalets and in an excellent caravan park. An extensive network of roads allows visitors to explore the park's dense spekboom (*Portulacaria afra*) vegetation, best seen from the Kadouw lookout.

To help monitor the effects that elephant, buffalo and black rhino have on the vegetation, a botanical reserve has been set aside in the south. The 6-kilometre Spekboom Trail explores the reserve and allows visitors the opportunity to learn more about this intriguing succulent vegetation type.

If time allows, it is worth exploring the Zuurberg section of the park by continuing along the gravel R335 for 15 kilometres to the Zuurberg Inn. From the pass there are fine views over the Sundays River Valley and the Addo bush. Two circular walks, from which the folded quartzites, sandstones and shales of the Zuurberg are clearly visible, depart from the National Parks Board office located opposite the inn. The longer 12-kilometre trail enters the forest and climbs a fynbos-covered ridge. The shorter route leads to a superb viewsite overlooking grassy slopes and forest-filled valleys.

SHAMWARI GAME RESERVE The largest private reserve in the Eastern Cape, 8 000-hectare Shamwari is one of a handful in the country where black rhino can be seen. Shamwari was the brainchild of Adrian Gardiner who originally bought a farm in the hills near Paterson as a family retreat. Over the years he acquired four neighbouring farms and began

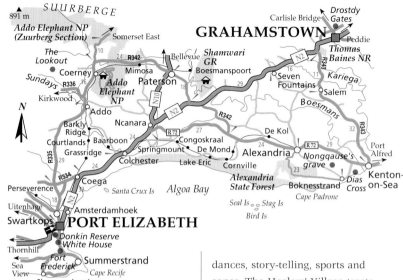

reintroducing wildlife: elephant, hippo, black and white rhino, giraffe, eland, wildebeest and zebra. Today overnight visitors can stay in luxurious lodges or self-catering farmsteads. Shamwari's pride and joy is the Long Lee Manor, a two-storey mansion built by William Fowlds in the 1860s and decorated with trophies, animal skins and chandeliers.

Shamwari's cultural village Kayalendaba (the 'house of stories') aims at promoting and preserving African culture through traditional dances, story-telling, sports and songs. The Healers' Village treats patients and trains traditional healers but is closed to the general public.

A novel way to visit Shamwari is to take the overnight *Algoa Express* train between Johannesburg and Port Elizabeth. On the trip from Johannesburg, guests sleep in wood-panelled compartments and are collected at Paterson station after breakfast the next morning. Hitched onto the regularly scheduled train is the antique Elephant Carriage, which once served as a private saloon for the Attorney-General and is virtually a travelling museum.

Guests on a game drive at Shamwari view white rhino at close quarters.

Rhodes University in Grahamstown, one of many seats of learning in the 'City of Saints and Scholars'.

GRAHAMSTOWN The historic town is renowned for its museums, many schools and for the more than 50 churches, some of which were built before 1845. Many of Grahamstown's early settler houses have been restored, and fine examples of Georgian and Victorian architecture can be seen. Dominating the business district is Grahamstown's Cathedral, situated on its own block in the High Street; the church contains many monuments and memorial tablets. The Drostdy Gateway, the distinctive entrance to Rhodes University, is all that remains of the original 1842 Drostdy (magistrate's residence). One of Grahamstown's noted museums is the Observatory Museum – originally the home of jeweller Henry Carter Galpin. It was in this house that South Africa's first diamond was identified in 1867, and where Galpin constructed a *camera obscura* – still in perfect working order and the only one in the southern hemisphere.

The Settler's Monument on Gunfire Hill is the principal venue for the annual Standard Bank National Arts Festival, attended by close to 100 000 people. The festival draws participants from throughout the country and, increasingly, from overseas. The slopes of the hill have been transformed into a botanical garden specialising in flora indigenous to the Eastern Cape. Outside Grahamstown, the road to Salem passes the 1 000-hectare Thomas Baines Nature Reserve, where bontebok, eland, Cape buffalo and white rhino can be seen.

SALEM The village of Salem (meaning 'peace'), was founded in 1820 by Hezekiah Sephton and his party of 344 English settlers. Because of the constant threat of Xhosa raiding along the troubled eastern frontier, it was necessary to construct robust houses, and many of these original structures still stand. The neat, unpretentious Methodist Church,

completed in 1832, often served as a refuge in times of strife. During the Sixth Frontier War of 1834, Richard Gush, a Quaker who opposed violence, left the safety of the church unarmed to negotiate with the Xhosa raiders. The Xhosa chief explained that his warriors were hungry, so Gush strode back to the church and returned with 15 loaves of bread and some rolls of tobacco. One by one, the warriors shook hands with Gush and disappeared, leaving Salem unscathed.

KENTON-ON-SEA An attractive seaside resort situated between the Boesmans and Kariega rivers, Kenton-on-Sea offers fishing, yachting and water-skiing in the Kariega estuary. The beach is ideal for swimming and sea fishing, and its many shallow pools offer safe bathing for children. Along the coast between the two rivers can be seen fascinating examples of rocks carved into unusual shapes by the sea.

ALEXANDRIA In the heart of some of the Eastern Cape's most beautiful country, Alexandria is the centre of an important chicory-producing district. Dense patches of forest clothe the higher slopes of the hills; green pastures, dotted with dairy cattle, spread across the valleys. Close to Alexandria, the 24 000-hectare Alexandria State Forest protects 60 kilometres of the coastline adjoining Algoa Bay and extensive tracts of dune forest. The 2-day circular Alexandria Hiking Trail begins at the forest station, leads to to the coast and follows the largest active dune system in the country. The 34-kilometre dirt road from Alexandria to the coastal resort of Boknesstrand passes through a large section of state forest land with some of the country's finest indigenous forest.

On the farm Glen Shaw, southeast of Alexandria, lies the grave of Nongqause, one of the most tragic figures in South African history. One day in March 1856, the 14-year-old girl gazed into a pool in the Gxara River, which flows into the Kei near Kei Mouth, and saw the faces of her ancestors. Returning to her village, she reported that the spirits were planning to return and would expel all whites from the country. But the people would first have to demonstrate their faith by killing all their cattle and destroying their crops. Those who refused to would be turned into frogs and mice, and would be blown into the sea.

For 10 months the people obeyed Nongqause's command, and on 18 February 1857, the day finally dawned. The people watched expectantly, but the sun did not depart from its usual course. Nongqause's people were ruined and over 25 000 died of starvation. The deluded mystic escaped to King William's Town and appealed to the British authorities for protection. She was sent to prison on Robben Island for a while, and after being released spent the rest of her life on Glen Shaw until her death in 1898.

The Katberg range forms an impressive barrier north of Seymour.

STUTTERHEIM The picturesque town of Stutterheim rests at the foot of the forested Xolora Mountains, a spur of the Amatola range. The Kubusi River, a tributary of the Kei, rises in the mountains above the town and is a favourite haunt of fly-fishermen. Among the town's craft enterprises are establishments producing pottery and woven goods, as well as Old Cape and cottage furniture from indigenous wood; these are included on the Amatola Craft Amble.

Stutterheim's settlement history can be traced to 1837 when the Reverend Jacob Döhne, of the Berlin Missionary Society, founded the Bethel Mission on a ridge above the present-day town. The dominant vegetation type of the Amatola region, Döhne Sourveld, was named after this German pioneer. The old mission church and parsonage are located 2 kilometres outside Stutterheim.

After the end of the Crimean War over 2 000 German veterans of the King's German Legion accepted the offer to settle in the troubled Eastern Cape. One group established a village near the Bethel Mission in 1857 and named it after their leader, Baron Richard von Stutterheim.

CATHCART The road to Cathcart skirts the eastern flank of the Xolora Mountains and passes through attractive grassland dotted with trees. Cathcart stands at the foot of the 1 652-metre-high Windvogelberg ('weather vane mountain'), named after a Khoikhoi resident who neither supported nor opposed the arrival of white settlers. The village, founded in 1876 on the site of the old Windvogelberg Fort, is named after Sir George Cathcart, governor of the Cape from 1852 to 1854. Cathcart preserves many fine buildings, such as the public library, housed in an extravagant Edwardian Art Nouveau building. The sandstone-walled St Alban's Anglican Church has an unusual roofed outside balcony to which there is no access. Locals believe that it was intended as a belfry, but no bell has ever rung there. A row of wood-and-iron cottages, built in the 1870s, has been declared a national monument.

SEYMOUR Elands Post fort was established in 1846 at the foot of the 2 016-metre-high Elandsberg, the region's highest peak. A village was founded a few years later and named

after Lieutenant-Colonel Charles Seymour, military secretary to Governor Cathcart. Part of the fort's walls and its powder magazine have been preserved, and the Seymour Hotel was once the officers' mess.

Leaving Seymour gravel Mitchell's Pass road climbs 700 metres over 19 kilometres to the junction of the R345 to Hogsback. Mitchell's Pass follows a broad valley that has been formed by the Elands River along the southern slopes of the Elandsberg. At the crest of the pass, Gaika's Kop and the Hogsback peaks dominate the scene to the east.

HOGSBACK The charming village of Hogsback perches on the edge of the Tyume Valley, and is overlooked by the three highest peaks of the Amatola Mountains, which resemble the bristles on the back of a bushpig. Much of the village lies above 1 200 metres and receives a high annual rainfall. Early English

settlers cherished the cool summers that result from the high altitude and planted berries, hazelnuts and other floral reminders of their native land. Over a century later, Hogsback's lanes and gardens still retain much of their English atmosphere, and its three hotels – Hogsback Inn, Hogsback Mountain Lodge and King's Lodge – accentuate this old-world ambience. One of the smallest chapels in the country, St Patrick's-on-the-Hill, is a thatched stone rondavel built in 1935 as a private chapel. It is a popular wedding venue, only seating about 30 people.

Much of Hogsback's appeal is found in the many short walks – known as 'piggy walks' and indicated by pig emblems – that crisscross the surrounding forests and pine plantations. The indigenous Auckland Forest, at the southern end of the village, encompasses the lovely Bridal

Hogsback's Madonna-and-Child falls (left) *and 'piggy walk' marker* (above).

Veil, Swallowtail and Madonna-and-Child waterfalls, and Californian redwoods are among the trees that can be seen in the Arboretum. A four-hour walk enters the forest near King's Lodge and then descends to the Big Tree, a 36-metre-high Outeniqua yellowwood believed to be 800 years old, before continuing to the Madonna-and-Child Falls. A picnic and camping site is situated in the pine plantation near the centre of the village where the nearby 39 Steps Waterfall cascading down the rocks forms a feathery veil.

Tor Doone, at 1 565 metres, is the highest point in the village. From the summit there is a panoramic view of the village and surrounding forests.

ALICE Situated 4 kilometres west of the junction of the R345 and R63, Alice is a modest country town which serves as a market place for the surrounding district. Traders, craftsmen, shoppers and minibus taxis crowd the town's central square and main streets. Founded in 1847, Alice's origins can be traced to the establishment in 1824 of the Lovedale Mission by the Glasgow Mission Society. Although it was twice destroyed during the Frontier Wars, Lovedale grew to become the foremost mission in South Africa and the leading education centre in the Cape during the 19th century. Outside Alice lies the University of Fort Hare, originally founded in 1916

as the South African Native College and for 44 years the only university that was open to black South Africans. The university takes its name from a British military post set up in 1847 at the end of the Seventh Frontier War. Over the years Fort Hare developed into one of the finest universities in the country, and its distinguished former students include Nelson Mandela, Albert Luthuli, Oliver Tambo, Thabo Mbeki, Bishop Desmond Tutu, Robert Mugabe and Sir Seretse Khama. The university houses the largest collection of contemporary black South African art in the country.

KEISKAMMAHOEK Four kilometres after turning onto the R352, a turn-off on the left leads to the twin curved concrete spires of Ntaba Ka Ndoda, the national shrine of the former Ciskei homeland. The monument was erected by former president Lennox Sebe and is situated in a forest clearing at the foot of the 921-metre-high Ntaba Ka Ndoda ('mountain of men'), a significant peak in Xhosa folklore. Located nearby is the grave of Chief Jonga-msobomvu Maqoma, who led the Xhosa during the Frontier Wars and died a prisoner on Robben Island in 1873. After Ciskei was declared independent in 1981, Maqoma's remains were transported by naval ship from Cape Town to East London and re-interred at the national shrine.

Keiskammahoek is situated in a curve formed by the Keiskamma River as it flows across a basin encircled by the Amatola range. It was established as a military outpost and

the remains of Fort Eyre, built in 1852, are a reminder of the turbulent era of the Frontier Wars. It was here that the Xhosa chiefs Sandile and Anta surrendered to the British in 1847, ending the Seventh Frontier War, also known as the War of the Axe. This war resulted from Sandile's refusal to hand over to the colonial authorities a tribesman who was accused of stealing an axe from a Fort Beaufort store. Sandile was killed in 1878 during the Ninth Frontier War, and his gravesite lies in the Amatolas, 15 kilometres east.

AMATOLA MOUNTAINS Extending in an arc between Stutterheim and the Katberg, the Amatola Mountains partially enclose the Keiskamma basin. One of the best ways to enjoy their scenic beauty is to follow the Amatola Hiking Trail (see also p. 182), considered by some to be the most beautiful inland trail in the country. The demanding 105-kilometre hike begins at Maden Dam, 23 kilometres north of King William's Town, and takes six days to complete, but as there are five departure points, it is possible to do shorter sections. From Keiskammahoek, visitors can join the second section of the trail by following the road winding up the Dontsa Pass to a forest station. From here, a

particularly scenic section of the trail crosses forest and pine plantations, and passes numerous waterfalls before reaching an overnight cabin.

XOLORA MOUNTAINS From Keiskammahoek, the R352 passes between the Isidenge and Kubusi state forests. To the north of the road run the Xolora Mountains, the western spur of the Amatolas, and the two-day Kologha Hiking Trail traces a scenic route through them. The trail starts south of the R352, at the Isidenge Forest Station. The giant oak tree at the picnic site near the forest station was planted in 1858 in honour of Baron de Fin, an Austrian forester who did much to conserve the Eastern Cape's indigenous forests. Hikers spend the night in a log cabin overlooking Gubu Dam, a popular venue for trout fishermen.

Four popular day walks explore the enchanting Kologha Forest, renowned for its massive yellow-wood trees, and begin from Kologha Forest Station, which is about 6 kilometres northwest of Stutterheim. The Eagle's Ridge Country Hotel and the new Manderson Hotel, 1 kilometre apart, are on the edge of the forest and are good bases for walking, horse riding (from Manderson), trout-fishing and picnicking.

Tranquil Gubu Dam against the backdrop of Mount Thomas, part of the Amatolas.

THE WILD COAST

To the east of the Great Fish River lies the land of the Xhosa, an area which stretches almost unbroken up to the Mtamvuna River, the boundary between the Eastern Cape province and KwaZulu-Natal. During the apartheid era, this region was divided into three sub-regions, two of which – the Ciskei and Transkei, now incorporated into the Eastern Cape province – were considered independent countries intended for the Xhosa people, with the third region, a tongue of white-controlled Republic of South Africa, sandwiched between them. This corridor of land carried the railway line and main road networks to the harbour city of East London, the region's principal industrial and commercial centre.

The portion of the Eastern Cape that incorporates the Wild Coast is an area of comparatively high average rainfall, with the coastal and mountain regions receiving over 1 000 millimetres per annum, except in the south where the rainfall is less. Snow is not uncommon at high altitudes in winter, but the remainder of the region is temperate, with high subtropical temperatures in summer. But it is the magnificent, rugged coastline, the dense coastal forests and the lush coastal grasslands for which the region is best known.

TREACHEROUS SHORES

This verdant coastline, running like a jewelled necklace for its entire length, has a wild beauty that excites all who visit it. Undulating green hills descend in a series of steps from the high peaks of the Drakensberg to the sea. When the land eventually meets the Indian Ocean, it either does so gently, with grass-covered slopes ending in beautiful bays and long white beaches, or it does so abruptly, particularly in the north where Table Mountain Sandstone cliffs are battered by the sea. Waves, wind and rain have steadily eroded the rock formations of the Wild Coast to create a rugged and changing beauty. One of the most spectacular of

One of the Wild Coast's famous landmarks is the spectacular Hole in the Wall.

Fishermen cast their lines at the mouth of the Nahoon River, East London.

these creations is the prominent Hole in the Wall, near Coffee Bay, where the sea has hammered an archway through a large rock massif just offshore. The arch is tall enough for a large fishing boat to pass through, and as the waves rush in and out of the opening, they create a great pounding noise which echoes through the archway. The Xhosa call this magnificent landmark *esiKhaleni* ('the place of calling').

It is with good reason that mariners call this the Wild Coast. Over the years, numerous ships have met with disaster along this

treacherous shoreline, which must rank as one of the world's largest shipping graveyards. One of the most famous wrecks took place off what is now Port Grosvenor, when the celebrated British treasure ship, the *Grosvenor*, was lost in 1782. Although most of the *Grosvenor's* passengers survived – and were succoured by the local Mpondo people – it is believed that the vast wealth carried by this vessel is still waiting to be claimed.

This map highlights the regional map opposite. Overlapping regions and their page numbers are supplied.

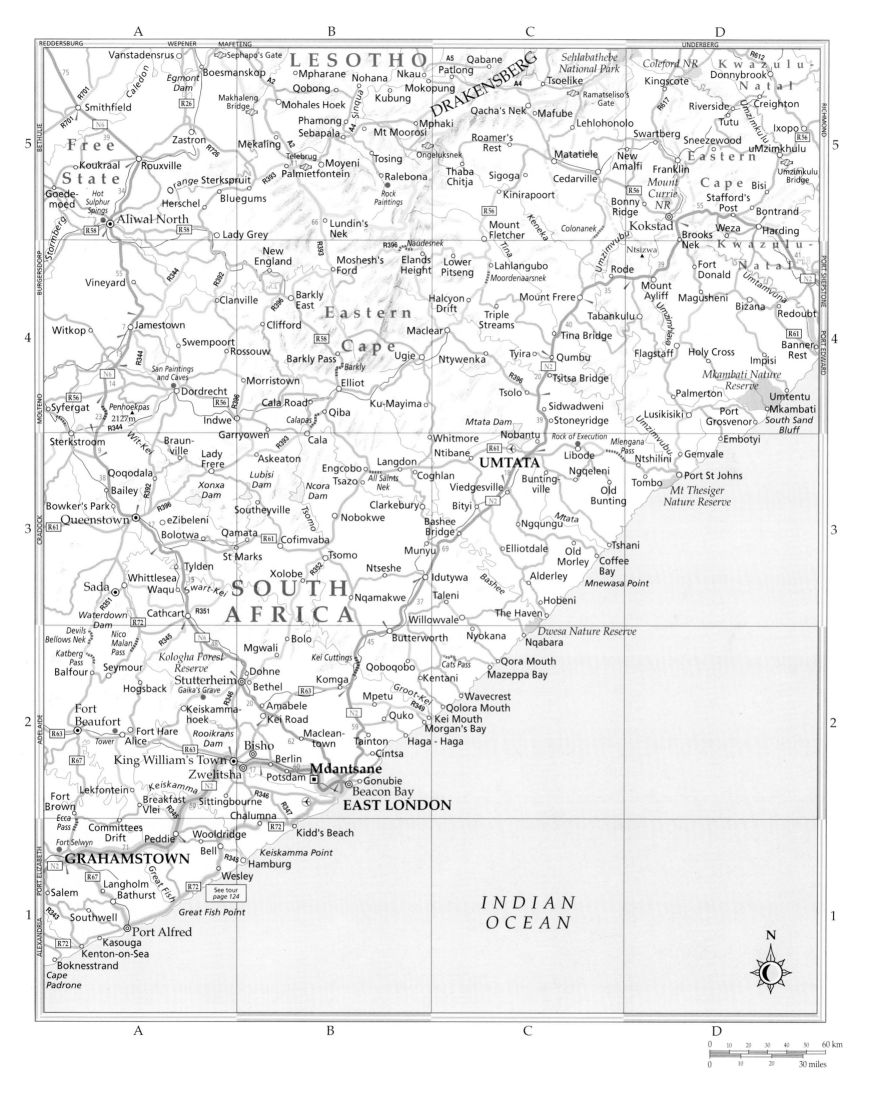

MARINE TREASURES

The waters that wash the shores of the Wild Coast support a wide variety of organisms, due to the mixing of warm waters brought down by the Agulhas Current from the north, and the cold waters that are swept closer to the shore by the counter-current from the south. Subtropical fish abound, and in winter the Cape sardines migrate northward, bringing with them an entourage of game fish that make the waters about the shoals boil as they pursue the little silver fish in a feeding frenzy. Bottlenose dolphins are often seen playing in the waves, and during the breeding season – July to November – southern right whales are common, with minke and humpback whales also seen.

The Wild Coast is celebrated for its excellent fishing. Species include bronze bream, garrett, yellowbellied rockcod, shad (elf), galjoen, kob (kabeljou), spotted grunter, red roman and a number of others. Watching seabirds such as petrel, albatross and tern in search of fish offshore is not only a rewarding pastime, but these birds also provide fishermen with some indication of where shoals of fish can be found.

The countless rock pools, gullies and inlets along the coast are lined with a rich array of marine life. Here many fascinating hours can be spent simply observing the occasional octopus, colourful anemones, sponges, starfish, well-camouflaged cushion stars, armoured chitons clinging to the rocks and little fish – usually blennies and gobies. In deeper gullies rock lobsters were once plentiful and still are occasionally seen. In the numerous small protected bays, the sea piles up beautiful shells on the beaches.

A number of small, secluded coastal resorts – Gonubie, Haga Haga, Kob Inn, Morgan's Bay, Kei Mouth, Mazeppa Bay, Coffee Bay, Trennery's and Port St Johns among them – are scattered along the Wild Coast. These sheltered resorts offer good accommodation, excellent fishing and a variety of watersports.

REMOTE AND RUGGED BEAUTY

Several distinct vegetation zones are found in this region. In the high-lying areas along the lower Drakensberg Escarpment hardy alpine veld dominates. Most of the central interior is covered in highland sourveld, and where the larger rivers – such as the Tina, Mzimvubu, Keneka, Umtata and Mbashe – cut through this landscape they are flanked in their lower reaches with valley bushveld, dominated by acacia and euphorbia.

Along the coast the vegetation varies from coastal grasslands to coastal forests, with the most common species being dune allophylus, coastal red milkwood, pioneer canthium and large-leaved guarri. These hardy species are well adapted to tolerate the sea's salty spray and the sometimes fierce winds which lash the shore. Large stands of mangrove are located around the Mgazana River estuary, southeast of Port St Johns – the southernmost limit of their distribution. Recognisable by their complex branching root systems which jut above the surface of the mudflats in which they grow, these salt-tolerant trees are a vital nursery for snails, crabs and fish.

A common resident along the fringes of both coastal and riverine forests is the banana-like Natal strelitzia, with its cousin, the striking crane flower, usually found hidden along the banks of protected streams or in the understory of the dune forests that grow all along the coast. Another plant that is characteristic of the coastal grasslands and the coastal forest fringes is the beautiful flame lily which, together with the flowering strelitzias, attract colourful sunbirds. In the forests the fruiting trees attract birds such as the trumpeter hornbill, the sonorous black-collared barbet and the green pigeon.

At several places along the coast of the former Transkei, coastal dune forests have broadened into larger evergreen coastal forests which constitute an area of almost 40 000 hectares and represent the largest and least disturbed area of coastal forest in South Africa. These forests are protected in separate nature reserves, of which Dwesa, Hluleka and Silaka are the most important. The forests, with species from both the temperate southern Cape and subtropical KwaZulu-Natal, include yellowwood, forest mahogany, stinkwood and red beech.

Traditional Xhosa huts dot the Wild Coast (above), *and Xhosa youths prepare for a coming-of-age ceremony* (top).

DISCOVERING THE WILD COAST

One of the best ways to savour the superb meeting of land and sea along the Wild Coast is to follow the famed 280-kilometre Wild Coast Hiking Trail, which winds over green hills, along deserted beaches and across tidal estuaries from Port Edward in KwaZulu-Natal to Kei Mouth in the Eastern Cape. The whole trail takes about 25 days, but is split into shorter 3- to 6-day sections. Accommodation is in traditional Xhosa-style rondavels. Between Gonubie and Kei Mouth, the 60-kilometre Strandloper Trail gives visitors the chance to experience the beauty of intertidal zones, beaches, cliffs, coastal forest, surrounding farmland and river estuaries along the southern portion of the Wild Coast.

East London, the country's only river port and its sixth largest harbour.

Inland from the Wild Coast lies a rich agricultural area, including the sheep farming district of Elliot.

HARSH REALITY

The scenic splendour of the Wild Coast presents a sharp contrast to the poverty of the interior. Here the Xhosa live in the constantly expanding villages that dot the overgrazed and steadily eroding hillsides. With virtually no industry of note in either the former Transkei or Ciskei, the increasing population inevitably exploit the resources of the land and coast. Further into the interior, the people rely on cattle breeding and dryland crop farming, but because of overcrowding, poor agricultural techniques and lack of capital, the land is unable to provide for their needs. Many have little option but to migrate to the cities in order to survive.

EAST LONDON

Occupying the headlands above the deep Buffalo River Valley, East London is the country's sixth largest harbour, as well as its only river port. The foundations of the city were laid in the late 1840s, when the mouth of the Buffalo River was used as a harbour to land supplies for British troops fighting against the Xhosa during the Seventh Frontier War (1846-1847). In 1856 the first quays were built on the west bank of the Buffalo River and in 1857 the first lighthouse was finished. In the mid-1850s German veterans of the King's German Legion who had fought in the Crimean War settled on the eastern bank of the Buffalo River, and a little village began to take shape. The British government then arranged for 157 Irish women to be brought out to correct the settlement's marked imbalance between the sexes. Since then East London has developed steadily into a major industrial centre, and today its factories produce items as diverse as confectionery, pharmaceuticals and motor cars.

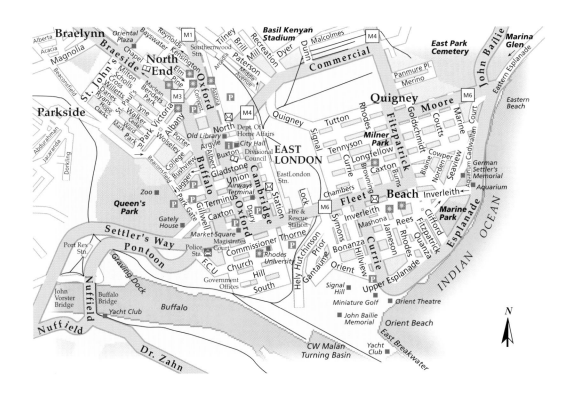

EAST LONDON'S ROMANTIC COAST ❖ 380 km

EAST LONDON From the central business district, the Esplanade skirts East London's popular Orient and Eastern beaches. The Aquarium between the two beaches displays over 400 fascinating species of marine life. Performing seal shows take place there twice a day, and the aquarium also houses a breeding colony of the rare jackass penguin. Orient Beach has a children's pool, swimming pool and takeaway outlets, and Eastern Beach, backed by a high forested dune and a rugged headland, has several popular pubs and restaurants overlooking this picturesque shore. Further north, Nahoon Beach is the city's most popular surfing and swimming beach.

The East London Museum in Oxford Street is world-famous for its coelacanth, a bony fish thought to have been extinct for millions of years until a specimen was netted off East London in 1938. The museum also houses the only known egg of the extinct dodo from Mauritius.

One of South Africa's most intriguing shopping centres is the Lock Street Gaol in Fleet Street.

The cells and gallows are an eerie reminder of the building's past as South Africa's first women's prison, but the courtyards within the high stone walls are crowded with gift shops, boutiques and restaurants.

From the business centre, Settler's Way passes the densely wooded Queen's Park Zoo. Extending across a hillside above the harbour, the zoo acquired a group of chimpanzees from the United States a few years back and specialises in breeding these rare primates. Children will delight in the farmyard and pony rides, and a kiosk serves light meals.

Latimer's Landing, East London's waterfront development, is a lively meeting place, with several pubs, sports bars and restaurants in a cosy precinct overlooking the river. Yachts moor at the wooden pier leading along the waterfront, and there are regular yacht cruises around the harbour. Sunset cruises operate over weekends and public holidays.

East London's Nahoon Beach is popular for swimming and surfing.

Upriver from Latimer's Landing, the 560-hectare Umtiza Nature Reserve protects a dense forest that is home to the rare and endemic umtiza tree, *Umtiza listeriana*. The tranquil forest should be avoided on hot days, when it becomes humid

inhabit the forest, and the many birds include chorister robin, sombre bulbul and cinnamon dove.

WINTERSTRAND AND IGODA The peaceful village of Winterstrand surveys a rocky coastline. From here, a dirt track runs parallel to the coast in the direction of the Igoda River mouth, while a walk along the beach to Cove Rock is especially beautiful. A corridor of land bordering the coast forms part of the East London Coastal Forest Reserve, which protects much of the coastline. A few patches of coastal forest occur along this stretch, and in summer, the grasslands that tumble down to the shore are ablaze with yellow flowers.

Igoda's vast, white, sandy beach is a perfect retreat for swimming and sunbathing, and the lagoon is ideal for windsurfing and canoeing. On either bank of the placid Igoda River, the tall dunes are cloaked in dense coastal forest. Where the river curves inland, a popular holiday resort occupies a splendid grassy site.

KIDD'S BEACH About 30 kilometres from East London, Kidd's Beach is a lovely holiday village on a beautiful

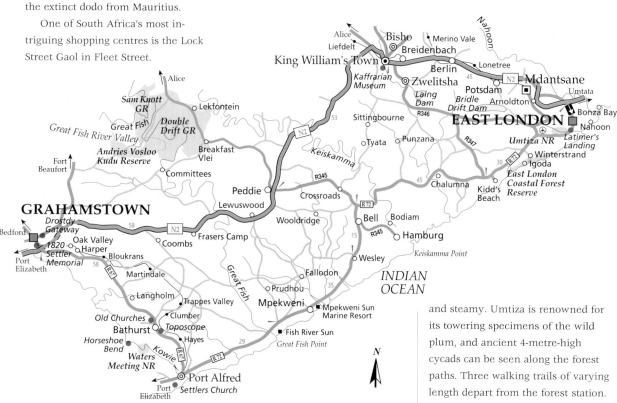

and steamy. Umtiza is renowned for its towering specimens of the wild plum, and ancient 4-metre-high cycads can be seen along the forest paths. Three walking trails of varying length depart from the forest station. Bushbuck, monkey and duiker

stretch of coast. Several hotels and holiday resorts provide accommodation, and the rocky coast is known for its excellent fishing. The safest bathing beach is at Mcantsi River mouth, and a parking area near the tidal pool provides access to a broad expanse of unspoilt beach.

MPEKWENI SUN MARINE RESORT

After the turn-off to Kidd's Beach, the R72 turns inland and winds down the pass through the Keiskamma Valley. At Mpekweni, the Mpekweni Sun Marine Resort overlooks a picturesque lagoon. The hotel caters for the outdoor enthusiast and offers good fishing, swimming, tennis, golf, horse riding and a variety of watersports.

FISH RIVER ESTUARY The Fish River

Sun, a casino hotel 12 kilometres further along the coast from Mpekweni, is set on a hillside overlooking the seashore and the Great Fish River Valley. An 18-hole golf course extends from the hotel down to the forested coastal dunes, and the nearby Great Fish River estuary is an important waterbird refuge. At low tide extensive mud flats are exposed and thousands of geese, ducks, stilts

The famed Kowie Canoe Trail begins at the Royal Alfred Marina in Port Alfred.

and greenshanks congregate here. For the adventurous, the four-day Shipwreck Trail hugs the coastline for 64 kilometres, from the Great Fish River Mouth to the Chalumna River near Kidd's Beach, and several wrecks can be seen along the way.

PORT ALFRED Renowned for its

superb beaches, dunes and marina, Port Alfred is the Eastern Cape's most popular coastal resort. Little Beach, on the Kowie River's west bank, provides safe bathing for children, and the coast from West Beach to beyond Kelly's Beach is perfect for swimming and surfing. Port Alfred is a favourite spot for fishermen, and is known for its catches of kob. The Kowie Museum depicts the town's history, and the centrepiece is a figurehead from an old sailing ship.

The concrete arch bridge across the Kowie River is a conspicuous landmark in Port Alfred. The river, navigable for 21 kilometres upstream, is the site of the canoe trail up the Kowie River to the Waters Meeting Nature Reserve. Canoeists should paddle the 21 kilometres upriver on an incoming tide and return on an outgoing tide. An overnight stop at the Horseshoe camp site in

the reserve allows visitors to explore the trail through the forest. The dense stands of euphorbia and thorn trees conceal bushbuck, blue duiker, rock and tree dassie, bushpig, caracal and Cape clawless otter, while fish eagle and several kingfisher species are among the birds found here.

BATHURST The charming town of

Bathurst is the centre of South Africa's pineapple-growing region. On the way into Bathurst from Port Alfred, Summerhill farm boasts a giant, man-made pineapple, as well as a traditional Xhosa village, pub, mini-farm and tractor rides.

Bathurst's St John's Anglican Church, built in 1838, is the oldest unaltered Anglican church in South Africa, while the Pig & Whistle Pub, established in 1821, still refreshes the thirsty traveller. Bradshaw's Mill, the country's first wool mill and erected in 1821, is on the road to the lookout over the Kowie River's Horseshoe Bend. East of the town is the 1820 Settlers Toposcope on Thornridge, an elevated site where places of interest in the district are indicated, and which affords panoramic views over the surrounding countryside, dotted with acacia and fields of pineapple.

GREAT FISH RIVER VALLEY From

Bathurst, the route passes through the university city of Grahamstown (*see also* pp. 113 and 117), where it joins the N2 and heads east through scattered acacia trees and grassland toward the Great Fish River. The hot, dry river valley is characterised by dense stands of *Euphorbia bothae*.

About 14 kilometres north of the bridge across the Great Fish, the Double Drift/Sam Knott Game Reserve and adjacent Andries Vosloo Kudu Reserve together embrace 44 500 hectares of rugged hills and thorn-crowded valley. The dense scrub is an ideal habitat for the reserve's abundant kudu population. Other animals present include warthog, hippo, buffalo, black rhino, zebra and giraffe, as well as more

Summerhill farm's giant pineapple near the pineapple centre of Bathurst.

than 180 bird species, among them secretarybird, brownhooded kingfisher and cardinal woodpecker.

KING WILLIAM'S TOWN Founded in

1835 on the site of Reverend John Brownlee's mission station, King William's Town was the birthplace of black consciousness leader Steve Biko, who is buried here. The renowned Kaffrarian Museum, established in 1884, is a good place to begin an investigation into King William's Town's history. As well as exhibits on 19th-century frontier life, the museum displays more than 25 000 African mammal specimens. Pride of place goes to Huberta the Hippo who, from 1928 to 1931, wandered more than 1 500 kilometres through South Africa and became a local hero and household name.

An adjacent building displays the Kaffrarian Museum's noted ethnographic collection, devoted to the history, traditions and mythology of the Xhosa and Khoisan peoples. Some of King William's Town's more important historic buildings include Grey's Hospital (1859), Sutton House (1877), the Town Hall (1867), the Holy Trinity Anglican Church (1850), and the Old Residency, site of John Brownlee's original mission house.

NAMAQUALAND AND THE CLANWILLIAM REGION

In spring Namaqualand's arid landscape is transformed into a radiant display of bright wild flowers.

The name Namaqualand conjures up images of a vast, arid and uninhabited land, but also of the glorious carpets of brightly coloured flowers that cover these great spaces in the springtime. This hot, dry region is relentless in summer, but soft, beautiful and infinitely appealing in winter and spring when the previously harsh landscape is transformed by nature.

The traditional Nama matjieshuis *is a dome-shaped hut usually made of skins or reed mats.*

Namaqualand – an area of approximately 48 000 square kilometres stretching from the Orange River in the north to the Olifants River mouth, Vredendal and Vanrhynsdorp in the south – is made up of four geographically diverse subregions, namely the Richtersveld, the Namaqualand Klipkoppe, the Sandveld and the Knersvlakte.

South of the Knersvlakte lies the Clanwilliam region, a fertile area of citrus trees, rooibos (*Aspalathus linearis*) bushes and vineyards, superbly framed by imposing, craggy mountains, and roughly divided into the Olifants River Valley, the Cedarberg range and the Biedouw Valley.

A FLOWERING WILDERNESS

The flora of Namaqualand is unique. Here the visitor will find not only the bright spring flowers which appear after reasonable rains, but also a wide variety of geophytes, dwarf shrubs and succulents. These vary from the creeping rank-t'nouroe

(*Cephalophyllum namaquanum*), a succulent with delicate, daisy-like flowers, to the tree-like kokerboom (*Aloe dichotoma*) and the stubby botterboom (*Tylecodon paniculatus*).

As the region has a very low, sporadic winter rainfall, the plants here are equipped with ingenious strategies for survival. Miracle grass (*Enneapogon desvauxii*) germinates, flowers and runs to seed within eight days after the rains have fallen. Annuals evade the hot, dry summers by quickly germinating, growing, flowering and setting their seed during the moist winter and spring months after which they die off, in this way ensuring the species' survival. The geophytes survive underground in the form of bulbs, corms and tubers, while the succulents live off the water they stored in their stems and leaves during the rainy season. Evergreen dwarf shrubs either have succulent leaves, as in the case of the rank-t'nouroe, or they have small leaves which limit the area from which transpiration can occur. Dwarf shrubs with larger leaves shed them in the dry summer for the same reason. Some plants have no leaves but rather green stems in which photosynthesis occurs, which helps to reduce transpiration.

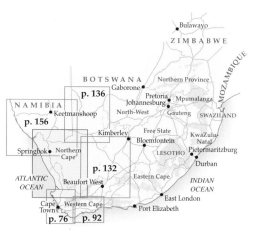

This map highlights the regional map opposite. Overlapping regions and their page numbers are supplied.

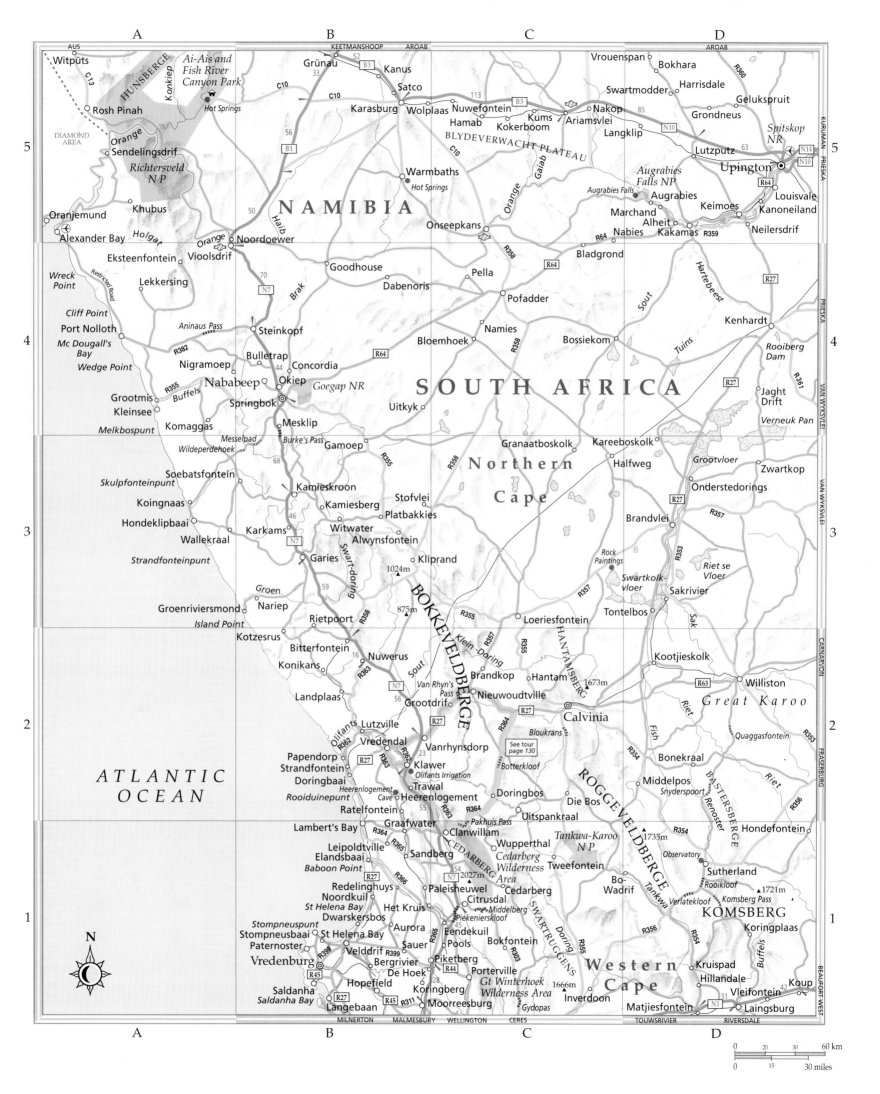

THE RICHTERSVELD

Early explorers referred to the Richtersveld as the 'land that God created in a fury' and on first sight it is easy to understand why. This mountainous desert appears to be stark and inhospitable, but within the Richtersveld lies a rich variety of plant life, with the greatest number of endemic succulent plants in the world.

The Richtersveld was originally inhabited by the San (Bushmen) who were hunter-gatherers. Later the Nama (circa AD 500) moved into the area and as they were pastoralists, a form of mutual co-existence prevailed with the San. The latter hunted wild animals in the hills and the Nama grazed their livestock in the valleys. When game became scarce the San moved on but the Nama stayed, becoming the forebears of the region's present inhabitants and giving their name to today's Namaqualand.

Small Nama settlements have been established at Leliefontein, Eksteenfontein and Kuboes (where their traditional dome-shaped huts, or *matjieshuise*, can be seen) and as their populations have grown, pressure on the Richtersveld's delicate ecological fabric mounted. For 18 years a protracted debate raged on between the development and the conservation of the region, but eventually in 1991 the 162 445-hectare Richtersveld National Park was proclaimed. It is South Africa's first contractual park, in terms of which traditional land use (domestic livestock grazing) has been integrated into the management of the park, and close co-operation is maintained with the local communities in all aspects of the park's further development and control. Due to the rugged terrain, only 4x4 vehicles can traverse most of the region. The mighty Orange River, where canoeing is popular, forms its northern boundary.

The Richtersveld, the only true mountainous desert region in South Africa, receives less than 100 millimetres of rain per annum. It is the home of several species of quiver tree (or kokerboom), the bark of which the San used to make quivers for their poison arrows, and the fascinating 'halfmens' (*Pachypodium namaquanum*), given this name because of its half-human, half-plant appearance. Legend has it that these succulents were descended from the early Nama people who were driven

The Richtersveld's mighty Orange River (above), *and curious 'halfmens'* (below).

from Namibia by the Bondelswarts, a rogue element of the Nama. The fact that these elongated succulents lean to the north is believed to indicate their longing to return to the land of their birth.

Minerals such as copper, lead, silver, tin, asbestos, uranium, limestone and gypsum, as well as semi-precious stones, are found in the Richtersveld, while offshore and along the Atlantic Ocean beaches to the west lies one of the richest diamond fields in the world. From a purely geological and particularly a stratigraphic point of view, the Richtersveld is of considerable importance since locked in its sedimentary formations is the key to the structure of the entire Atlantic seaboard of southern Africa. Almost every geological process in nature has created this extraordinary region and fashioned the Richtersveld's unique character.

NAMAQUALAND KLIPKOPPE

Considered by many local inhabitants to be the true Namaqualand, the Klipkoppe is distinguishable by its round, granite hills separated by sandy plains. An escarpment about 50 kilometres wide, it stretches from the Richtersveld in the northwest to the Knersvlakte in the southeast. It is famous for its spectacular display of spring wild flowers – among them beetle daisies, gousblomme, vygies and gazanias – and these are best viewed at the Skilpad Wild Flower Reserve near Kamieskroon. Rainfall varies between 100 and 200 millimetres per annum, but at some places in the Kamiesberg, up to 400 millimetres has been recorded.

Sheep and goat farming is the most important economic activity in the region, and wheat is grown in the Kamiesberg. This part of Namaqualand has many minerals of which copper is the most important. The oldest mine in South Africa, Simon van der Stel's Copper Mine, is situated near Springbok, the 'capital of Namaqualand' (*see also* p. 156) and the service centre for copper and diamond mining operations in northern Namaqualand.

THE SANDVELD

Small-stock farming is practised extensively in the Sandveld, which stretches for some 30 kilometres along the coast from the Orange River in the north to Lamberts Bay in the south, but the main income-earning industries are the fish and crayfish industries centred at Lamberts Bay and Saldanha (*see also* p. 81) and the diamond industry at Alexander Bay in the north. Lamberts Bay is also renowned for its abundant birdlife, and nearby Bird Island provides sanctuary to large numbers of gannets and cormorants.

Lamberts Bay's Bird Island shelters huge populations of Cape cormorants.

The Sandveld is made up of loose, white sand at the coast which gradually changes to red in the interior. With an average rainfall of between 50 millimetres at the Orange River to 150 millimetres at Lamberts Bay, vegetation seldom reaches more than a metre in height. The predominant species are vygie bushes, with t'arra t'kooi (*Ruschia frutescens*) the most common along the coast and the skildpadbos (*Zygophyllum morgsana*) frequently found inland.

THE KNERSVLAKTE

Lying between Bitterfontein in the north to Vanrhynsdorp in the south, and bordered by the Sandveld to the west, the Knersvlakte is

an area of saline hills covered in small, white quartz pebbles and giving way in places to large patches of red sand. Rain-fall ranges between 100 to 200 millimetres. The vegetation is dominated by a rich species diversity of the vygie family (*Mesembryanthemaceae*), varying in height from 10 to 50 centimetres . Small-stock farming is practised extensively and gypsum-mining is widespread.

OLIFANTS RIVER VALLEY

The Olifants River Valley stretches from Citrusdal, through Clanwilliam, Klawer, Vredendal and Lutzville and sometimes along the Olifants River to the sea. The Clanwilliam-Citrusdal region receives higher rainfall than the Vredendal area, and has massive flower displays in spring. Extensive small-stock farming is practised throughout the subregion. Along the river irrigated cultivation takes place, with tobacco, citrus, wheat, grapes and vegetables being important crops. In the 18th century the Khoikhoi discovered a green bush that grew on the mountains. They found that by cutting off the leaves, bruising them and leaving them in the sun to cure, a refreshing herbal tea could be made – the forerunner of the present-day rooibos tea industry, which is centred at Clanwilliam.

Although Vredendal was founded as recently as 1933, the town is the major commercial centre of the district. Its rapid growth was made possible by the extension of the Olifants River Irrigation Scheme, built between 1912 and 1922. In 1935 the Clanwilliam Dam was completed to increase the supply of water available to farmers. Canals carry water along both banks of the river and about 10 000 hectares is under irrigation, the principal crops being wheat, grapes and fruit.

THE CEDARBERG

The Olifants River Valley is flanked by two mountain chains: to the east the impressive Cedarberg range, and to the west the chain formed by the Achenbach, Kransvlei, Elands, Kleinpoort, Lang and Heerenlogement mountains. The Cedarberg extends for nearly 100 kilometres and comprises a gigantic mass of sandstone, richly coloured by iron oxides and eroded into a variety of weird

and often surrealistic shapes, giving the Cedarberg a distinctive character. In the cracks and crevices of the contorted rocks and in the open spaces between the outcrops a rich plant life flourishes, including a number of very rare species, such as the snow protea (*Protea cryophila*).

The Clanwilliam cedar (*Widdringtonia cedarbergensis*), after which the mountains have been named, grows at an altitude of between 1 000 and 1 500 metres, and the age of some trees has been put at over 1 000 years. Overexploitation in the 19th century and indiscriminate fires have taken their toll, and conservation officials are currently re-establishing the trees by germinating seeds in nurseries and planting several thousand seedlings in the mountains each year.

BIEDOUW VALLEY

Southeast of Clanwilliam, the Biedouw Valley lies along the Biedouw River, a tributary of the Doring River. With an average rainfall of between 200 and 400 millimetres per annum, it is a particularly rich area for wild flowers – mainly of members of the vygie family – during the spring season.

Wupperthal, a quaint Moravian mission village in the valley, was established in 1830 on the banks of the Tra-Tra River by German missionaries. Two years after the station was founded an agriculturist was sent out from Germany and fruit trees were planted, and a tannery and mill were built. The tradition of shoe-making, particularly *veldskoen*, still lives on today.

One of the Cedarberg's striking and unusual sandstone formations is the towering Maltese Cross.

Famed for rugged rock formations like the Wolfberg Arch (above), the Cedarberg also preserves many San paintings (below).

CLANWILLIAM One of South Africa's ten oldest towns, Clanwilliam is the centre of the rooibos tea industry. The town's library is dedicated to Dr Nortier, who innovated new methods for propagating the rooibos bush, and Dr Louis Leipoldt, grandson of the founder of the Wupperthal mission station and well-known South African writer and poet who lived here for several years. Visitors can tour the rooibos packing sheds or pay a visit to the town's *veldskoen* factory. The Clanwilliam Wild Flower Show, held at the end of August in the old Dutch Reformed Church, attracts many visitors.

The 54-hectare Ramskop Nature Reserve, one kilometre south of the town, overlooks the Clanwilliam Dam. Ramskop preserves a sample of the region's floral splendour and a cultivated section displays many indigenous species which attract sugarbirds and sunbirds. Clanwilliam Dam west

of town stretches up the narrow Olifants River Valley for 17 kilometres and is popular for fishing and water sports, especially water-skiing.

PAKHUIS PASS The 39-kilometre gravel road over the Pakhuis Pass was built by Thomas Bain in 1887 and winds through rugged country between fascinating weathered sandstone sculptures before reaching the crest at 905 metres. Coming from Clanwilliam, the grave of Dr Louis Leipoldt can be seen 9 kilometres from the beginning of the pass.

Leipoldt loved the Cedarberg's craggy landscape, and when he died in 1947 his ashes were buried in a cave that was once home to San hunters. Traces of their rock paintings can still be seen here. Beyond Leipoldt's grave the Kliphuis camp site is a convenient base to set out on several hiking trails which explore the Cedarberg Wilderness Area.

CEDARBERG WILDERNESS AREA
The Pakhuis Pass road crosses through the northern corner of the 72 000-hectare Cedarberg Wilderness Area, the Western Cape's largest wilderness, whose mountains shelter an important population of the Cape leopard. An uncharted tract of hidden valleys and extraordinary rock formations, the wilderness area is traversed by a network of 250 kilometres of trails, and access is restricted to hikers. Facilities are limited to rudimentary huts, a few jeep tracks and footpaths.

During winter, snow sometimes falls on the Cedarberg's high peaks and sub-zero temperatures are common. Erosion of the rugged landscape has produced spectacular rock formations, including the Maltese Cross, a 20-metre-high sandstone block at the foot of the 2 028-metre-high Sneeuberg, the highest peak in the range; the Wolfberg Cracks, a 30-metre-high narrow cleft; and the Wolfberg Arch, a 14-metre-high gap in a sandstone wall.

WUPPERTHAL At the foot of the Pakhuis Pass a road to the right crosses mountainous terrain for 31 kilometres en route to Wupperthal. After 8 kilometres the road descends the Uitkyk Pass and at its bottom it crosses the Biedouw River. A worthwhile detour is to turn off here to the left and follow the road along the narrow Biedouw Valley. In spring this lovely valley is transformed into a riot of bright wild flowers such as the mauve *Senecio*, orange *Gazania*, golden *Ursinia* and blue *Heliophila*. Within this rugged wilderness is Bushman's Kloof, a private reserve conserving the only wild dog population in the Western Cape. Bontebok, springbok and gemsbok are also found here. To retrace the route back to Wupperthal, turn around after 29 kilometres at the drift across the Doring River.

The road climbs to 914 metres before the final descent down the Kleinhoog Pass above Wupperthal. This charming old-world oasis is hidden in a narrow valley surrounded by sandstone mountains, with craggy peaks rising 1 400 metres above the hamlet to the west.

Wupperthal's picturesque white-washed, thatched cottages occupy terraced ground above the main road. Many cottages have low white walls, crowned with flower gardens, and steep steps lead up to patios shaded

The fine tradition of shoe making lives on in the quaint village of Wupperthal.

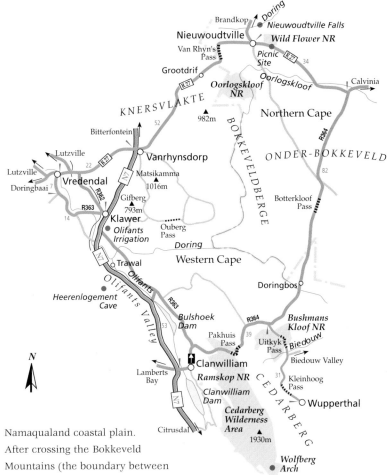

by grapevines. The attractive gabled Rhenish Church, built in 1834, is the focal point of the village, but Wupperthal is best known for its hand-crafted *veldskoen* ('field shoes', comfortable walking shoes), made here since 1836. Visitors can camp in Khaki Park which is managed by the church.

BOTTERKLOOF PASS AND THE ONDER-BOKKEVELD

Retracing the route up Uitkyk Pass, the dirt R364 to the right crosses the Botterkloof Pass and the Onder-Bokkeveld (an arid Karoo plain) en route to Nieuwoudtville. Extensive sheep farms thrive in this arid landscape which is transformed into a colourful celebration of flowers in spring.

NIEUWOUDTVILLE

A small town noted for its sandstone buildings and fantastic display of spring flowers, Nieuwoudtville occupies a 700-metre-high plateau. As a result the region receives more than twice the rainfall of surrounding areas and is often called 'the Boland of the northwest'.

The 66-hectare Nieuwoudtville Wild Flower Nature Reserve, just outside the town, is well worth visiting. The 3-kilometre Klipkoppies Trail explores the dolerite *koppies* in the north of the reserve, which is home to the richest concentration of geophytes in the world, with over 300 plant species. A small council-owned camp site caters for visitors.

The lovely Nieuwoudtville Falls on the Doring River (6 kilometres north of town) plunges 100 metres over a sandstone cliff into a deep pool. Picnic and braai sites are available.

OORLOGSKLOOF NATURE RESERVE

The 5 070-hectare Oorlogskloof Nature Reserve, 12 kilometres south of Nieuwoudtville, preserves a rugged plateau of dry mountain fynbos in the Bokkeveld Mountains, and the Oorlogskloof River carves a gorge along its eastern boundary. The reserve is home to baboons, small antelope and jackal, and to birds such as black eagle and olive thrush. Access is restricted to hikers, and two four-day trails explore the deep ravines and sandstone formations, with nine San rock art sites concentrated on the Geelbekbosduif Trail.

VAN RHYN'S PASS

The viewsite on the crest of Van Rhyn's Pass, built by master road builder Thomas Bain, provides sweeping views across the

Nieuwoudtville is famed for its annual display of dazzling spring flowers.

Namaqualand coastal plain. After crossing the Bokkeveld Mountains (the boundary between the Western and Northern Cape), the road drops 500 metres to the Knersvlakte, an arid plain of Karoo scrub. From the foot of the pass, Vanrhynsdorp and the N7 are 36 kilometres distant, and in spring wild flowers are abundant along the roadside.

VANRHYNSDORP

Established in 1887, Vanrhynsdorp is the gateway to southern Namaqualand and is a convenient base from which to explore the Gifberg and the 1 016-metre-high Matsikamma Mountains. The Kern Succulent Nursery, one of the town's main attractions, is the country's largest nursery of indigenous succulents.

VREDENDAL AND THE OLIFANTS RIVER VALLEY

Vredendal is mainly a service centre for the irrigated farms along the Olifants River, but it is also home to several artists and potters. The largest wine cellar in South Africa, the Vredendal Co-op is located here and is open for wine-tasting

and sales. In March, the annual Agriculture, Wine and Food Festival takes place. From Vredendal the R363 runs for 23 kilometres along the Olifants River Valley to Klawer. The Spruitdrift Co-op winery is 6 kilometres beyond Vredendal, and the Klawer Co-op, on the N7 south of Klawer, is open for wine-tasting and sales. The 793-metre-high sandstone Gifberg, towering above the valley, has mountain streams, pools, fynbos, proteas and San art to attract visitors.

At Trawal, a dirt road to the right leads for 23 kilometres to the Heerenlogement Cave ('gentlemen's lodgings'). In the past the cave was used by travellers as a stopover on the route north. Some of the guests engraved their names on the cave, and the earliest graffiti artist was Kaje Slotsbo (1712), of the Dutch East India Company's Policy Council. Among the cave's other guests were Simon van der Stel (1685) and Andrew Geddes Bain (1854).

THE GREAT KAROO

Covering the southwestern reaches of South Africa's high interior plateau is the Great Karoo, a region which takes its name from a Khoi word meaning 'land of great thirst'. What struck the Khoi most about this arid land was its total lack of surface water, its space and its silence. Here there are few villages and even fewer towns. From the summits of the many flat-topped hills (*koppies*), expansive plains spread out in all directions.

The Great Karoo loses its harshness after the infrequent rains and becomes cloaked with a mantle of tiny, brilliantly coloured wild flowers, its sparse bushes suddenly turn green, and tall, swaying grasses cover the hard bare earth.

The main economic activity of this semi-arid region is sheep farming and the farms are large, often many thousands of hectares in extent. The dryness of the land is deceptive, however, for water is relatively plentiful deep underground. To bring the water to the surface, farmers have for decades made use of windmills, and the turning sails and skeletal outlines of these have become a Karoo landmark.

THE RECORD OF THE ROCKS

The Karoo forms part of the Karoo System, the geological base for the interior plateau covering two-thirds of southern Africa. Between 150 and 200 million years ago, vast

The Karoo National Park, with its comfortable restcamp, protects a portion of the Great Karoo's flora and fauna.

sediments were laid down in a series of three distinct layers. At the bottom was the Dwyka Series, a layer about 900 metres thick consisting of rocks encased in a matrix of mudstone and moraine and believed to be the debris of a previous ice age. After its deposition came a period of climatic change when much of the earth was covered in forests, thick swamps, huge lakes and densely vegetated wetlands.

From this steamy world of mud, jungles and water the Ecca Series, a 3 000-metre-thick layer of shales and sandstone, was formed. Locked into the rocks of this series is a wealth of fossils ranging from small reptiles to huge tree stumps, some still upright.

Above the Ecca Series is the Beaufort Series, a layer of sedimentary deposition about 5 600 metres thick that created the face of the Karoo that we know today. The Beaufort Series is rich in fossils, including reptiles, dinosaurs and a variety of amphibious creatures with mammalian features. The Karoo National Park just outside Beaufort West is one of the best places to see some of these fossils.

Over time igneous material from the centre of the earth forced its way through vertical and horizontal cracks in the Karoo's sedimentary depositions, forming dolerite dykes (vertical) and dolerite sills (horizontal). As the soft sedimentary rocks weathered away, the harder and more resistant dolerite dykes and sills remained, forming the flat-topped or 'table' mountains and bell-like buttes which characterise the Karoo.

Fascinating examples of fossils can be seen along the Fossil Trail at the Karoo National Park.

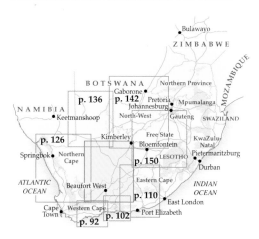

This map highlights the regional map opposite. Overlapping regions and their page numbers are supplied.

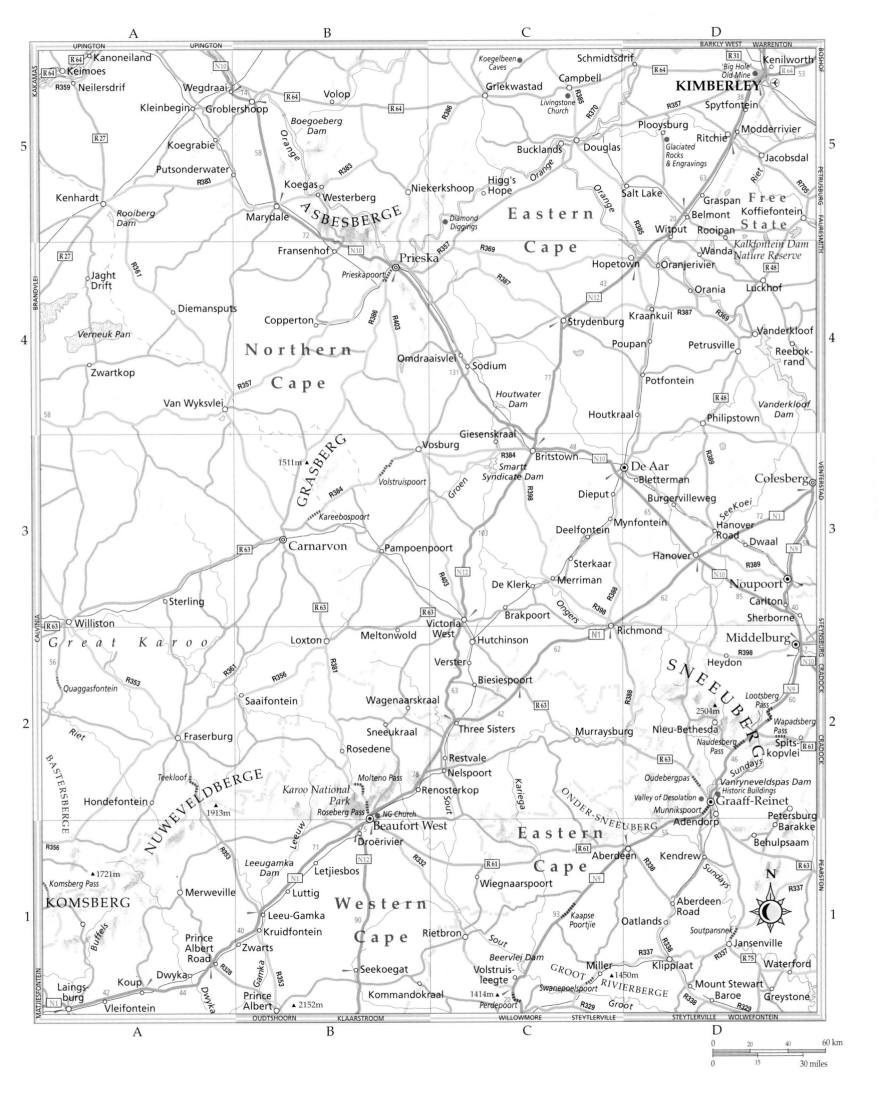

After the Great Karoo's infrequent rains, the region is transformed into a brilliant kaleidoscope of colour.

WILD KINGDOM

While the Karoo may appear a barren land, for those who are patient and who have the ability to observe the fullness of nature, an interesting world will open up before them. Underfoot you may see termites scurrying about looking for food and bits of grass to build their nests. If you are lucky you may also see the region's unusual trapdoor spider dig its neat, round hole with its powerful mandibles and build the intricate trapdoor that lets in its prey. In the distance you may see a herd of springbok grazing, or maybe even pronking – in which the graceful, prancing animals reach extraordinary heights, their bodies bent into U-shapes with their legs absolutely straight.

You may see the inquisitive ground squirrel sitting on its hind legs with its back ramrod-straight surveying the surrounding countryside. If your eyes are good you may pick out a black-backed jackal carefully going about its business. It may flush out a pair of bustards which suddenly take off, flying obliquely to the ground while croaking out their unusual call. And when your ears become attuned to the initial blanket of silence, you will become aware of its subtle sounds – the gentle whistling of the Karoo lark, the distant bleating of sheep, the metallic ring of the blacksmith plover and the different, often shrill, calls of the region's desert and scrubland birds.

IN THE HEART OF THE KAROO

Beaufort West is the Karoo's largest town. It was established in 1818 on the banks of the Gamka River, which only flows after rain, at the foot of the Nuweveld Mountains. The town was named after the fifth Duke of Beaufort, the father of the Cape governor Lord Charles Somerset. The town prospered after the introduction of merino sheep into the area and one of its citizens, John (later Sir) Charles Molteno built up a substantial sheep and wool trading empire.

One of Beaufort West's unusual features is that it is probably the only town in South Africa where pear trees, the ancestors of which were originally planted in the 1830s, grace its sidewalks.

KAROO NATIONAL PARK

Situated some 11 kilometres outside Beaufort West is the 43 261-hectare Karoo National Park, established in 1979 to preserve the flora and fauna of the south-central Great Karoo, where the average annual rainfall seldom exceeds 250 millimetres. When the park was established kudu, klipspringer, grey rhebuck, duiker and steenbok were already resident there. A number of other species that were indigenous to the area have subsequently been reintroduced, including black rhino, springbok, mountain zebra, black wildebeest, red hartebeest, gemsbok and the endangered riverine rabbit. Over 190 bird species have been recorded here, such as the black eagle, rock pipit and Karoo korhaan. The vegetation – consisting of hardy shrubs and herbs, and annual grasses that come with the rain – is typical of the Great Karoo.

The park has a number of hiking trails and a 4x4 trail, which allows visitors to explore its remotest corners. The very comfortable rest camp has excellent accommodation in Cape Dutch-style cottages, as well as a restaurant and swimming pool. Along the park's Fossil Trail, visitors can see typical Karoo fossils as well as a model explaining the region's fascinating geological history. The information on this trail is also supplied on Braille plaques.

VANDERKLOOF AND ROLFONTEIN

The Vanderkloof Dam is situated 130 kilometres downstream from the Gariep Dam and was completed in 1977. The dam wall rises 107 metres – the highest in South Africa – and the surface area of the dam covers 13 875 hectares. Adjacent to the dam is the Rolfontein Nature Reserve, which contains most of the common antelope species, but is particularly noted for the large numbers of eland resident there. It is also rich in bird life, with over 200 species recorded in the reserve, among them Egyptian goose, black duck, martial eagle, fish eagle and hoopoe.

Pear trees adorn the streets of Beaufort West, the Karoo's largest town, established as far back as 1818.

Situated in the southeast corner of the Vanderkloof Dam is the Doornkloof Nature Reserve. It incorporates a 10-kilometre stretch of the Seekoei River, the banks of which are lined with dense riverine and valley forest. The combination of forest habitats, the muddy and marshy margins of the dam and the surrounding semi-arid countryside provide home to many species of waterbirds, as well as to fish eagle.

GEM OF THE KAROO

Some 150 kilometres east of Beaufort West, on the Sundays River, lies the historical town of Graaff-Reinet (*see also* p. 114), the fourth oldest town in South Africa. Established in 1786 as the seat of the *land-drost* (magistrate) appointed by the Dutch East India Company, the settlement was named after Governor Cornelis Jacob van de Graaff and his wife Reynet.

The town grew slowly at first but as the interior began to open up with the arrival of more and more *trekboere* (emigrant farmers), who had trekked to the surrounding plains and to the Sneeuberg Mountains to the north in search of new farming areas, Graaff-Reinet became an important commercial and service centre. Many English settlers who had become disillusioned with the farming potential of the Eastern Cape moved to the area and began farming with woolled sheep. By the 1850s Graaff-Reinet was producing more wool, and of a higher quality, than any other district in the Cape Colony. With the introduction of angora goats into the Graaff-Reinet area in 1857 the mohair industry began in South Africa. Today this interesting town is the centre of one of the finest farming areas in the Karoo.

Graaff-Reinet is often referred to as the 'Gem of the Karoo', or even as the the 'Athens of the Eastern Cape' – in reference to its rich architectural heritage. Today Graaff-Reinet has 220 national monuments – more than any other town in the country – and through this living association with its elegant past, the town has indeed become the shining 'Gem of the Karoo'.

Visitors can see fine examples of gabled thatched-roof residences and flat-roofed dwellings – both typical of the Great Karoo – as well as the Victorian homes introduced

by the English settlers. The latter features a steeply pitched corrugated-iron roof and a covered verandah supported by carved wooden posts and balustrades decorated with intricate latticework (known today as 'broekie-lace'). Public buildings were styled on the typical lines of Cape Dutch architecture, a notable example of which is Reinet House, which has been fully restored to its former pristine glory. The building, believed to have been designed by noted architect Louis Thibault and completed in 1812, is a six-gabled H-shaped structure. It was first used as a manse for the Dutch Reformed Church and today is a cultural history museum, displaying an unrivalled

Flat-topped hills, or koppies, *such as the Three Sisters* (above) *near Beaufort West, and springbok* (left) *are distinguishing features of the Karoo.*

collection of period stinkwood and yellow-wood furniture. Stretch's Court comprises a group of perfectly restored mid-19th-century Cape Dutch cottages which were once the homes of labourers but today form part of the luxury Drostdy Hotel.

KAROO NATURE RESERVE

Almost totally surrounding Graaff-Reinet is the 16 500-hectare Karoo Nature Reserve (*see also* p. 114), established in 1975 by the South African Nature Foundation on land that had become badly overgrazed and barren. The focal point of the reserve is the spectacular Valley of Desolation, whose weathered dolerite rocks have been sculpted into bizarre shapes and forms. Here jumbled dolerite pillars, which have resisted erosion longer than the sedimentary rocks that surrounded them, rise up to over 120 metres above the boulder-strewn valley floor. Across the valley is the fortress-like Spandau Kop, named by a Prussian settler because of the rocky column's resemblance to Spandau Castle near Berlin.

THE KALAHARI AND NORTHERN CAPE

Sociable weavers' huge nests in camelthorn trees dot the timeless Kalahari landscape.

Although the vast, unspoilt Kalahari is described as a desert, it has little in common with the conventional notion of desert: its gently rolling sandy plains are, for the most part, surprisingly thickly vegetated, particularly in spring when the first rains turn it into a flowering wilderness. Should reasonable midsummer rains follow,

The Kalahari Gemsbok Park boasts lion (above), leopard, hyena and cheetah among its predators.

this desert area is rapidly covered by tall grass and leafy shrubs. But without rain, it is a harsh, hot land of shimmering red sands and dry riverbeds. The name Kalahari specifically refers to the vast sandveld region of central and western Botswana, extending into eastern Namibia and the Northern Cape (of which the fertile parts along the Orange River are known as the Green Kalahari).

A TIMELESS LAND

The Kalahari's red sands, the colour of which comes from a thin film of red oxide covering each grain, constitute what is probably the largest continuous sand surface in the world. Varying in thickness from less than 3 metres to over 100-metre-high sand dunes, the Kalahari sands cover almost a third of the African subcontinent, an area of some 2,5 million square kilometres. The sands of the Kalahari accumulated in a huge depression which resulted from the

continent being raised to a higher level more than 60 million years ago, and with climatic changes over the eons, clay and limestone were added. But the desert was formed when sand was blown into the depression some three million years ago. The vegetation in this area embraces forest and swampland in the northeast, tree and bush savanna in the southeast, and arid scrub savanna and thornveld in the southwest. Across its plains great herds of game, that have long disappeared elsewhere in southern Africa, still range according to the seasons.

Ironically, the absence of surface water was once one of the Kalahari's greatest assets as it discouraged permanent settlement and protected the sensitive semi-desert ecosystem from being over-grazed by domestic animals. At the same time, the Kalahari enabled the San to preserve their traditional way of life long after they were driven away from all the better-watered parts of the subcontinent. But in time, ways of tapping underground water supplies were developed and as these improved, so pastoralists were able to penetrate ever deeper into this huge thirstland, thereby opening up bigger areas to domestic grazing and cattle ranching.

This map highlights the regional map opposite. Overlapping regions and their page numbers are supplied.

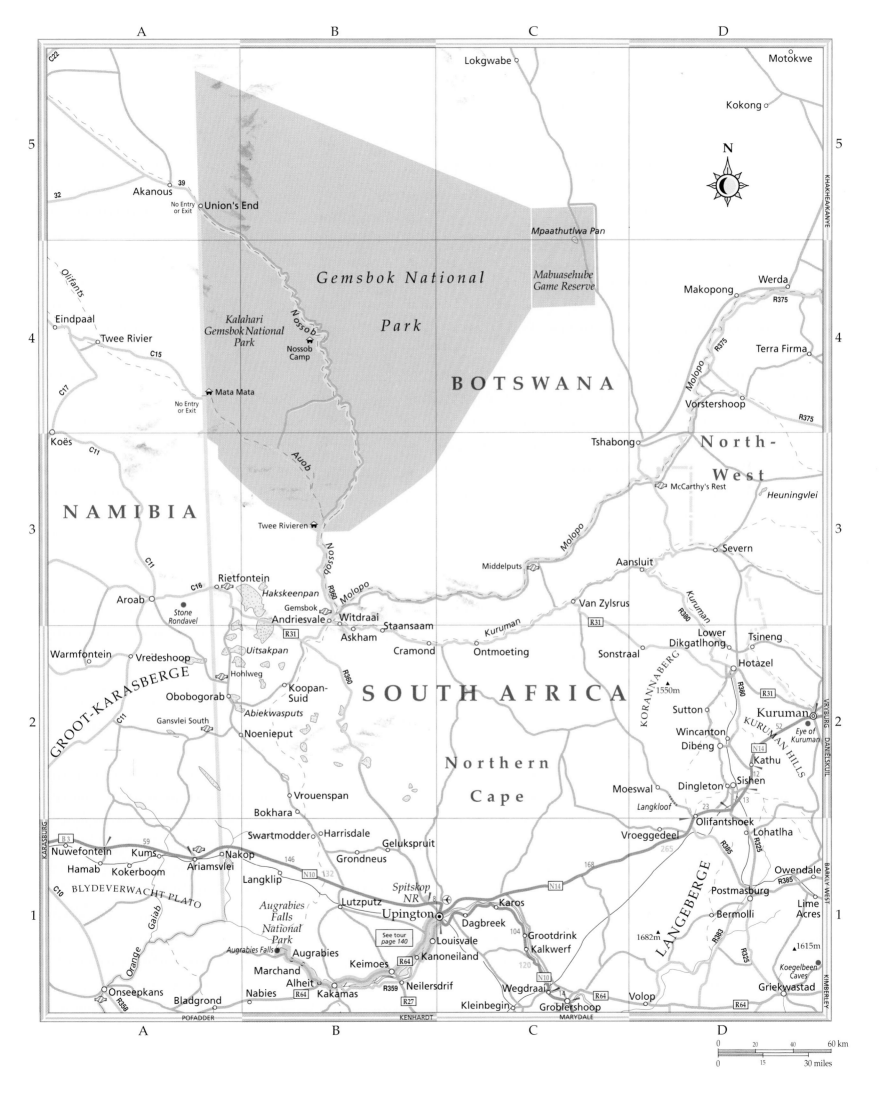

The Kalahari Gemsbok National Park was created to protect the graceful, once-endangered gemsbok.

KALAHARI GEMSBOK NATIONAL PARK

Proclaimed in 1931, the Kalahari Gemsbok National Park covers 36 200 square kilometres, of which 10 000 square kilometres lies in South Africa's Northern Cape and the remainder in neighbouring Botswana where it is known as the Gemsbok National Park. Together these two parks make up one of the largest national parks in the world.

As its name implies, the park was established to protect what many people consider to be the prince of all antelope, the gemsbok (*Oryx gazella*). These large, graceful desert animals had been ruthlessly hunted for a century or more and were on the brink of extinction, when a number of far-sighted people lobbied government to create a sanctuary where they could be left in peace and their numbers allowed to multiply.

Today the Kalahari Gemsbok National Park has 58 species of mammals (including the famous black-maned Kalahari lion, cheetah, leopard, jackal, springbok, eland, wildebeest and the rare brown hyena), 55 species of reptiles, more than 260 bird species (of which raptors and sociable weavers, with their distinctive nests, are most noticeable), and an almost infinite number of insects.

On the South African side of the border, the park is made up of wave after wave of red sand dunes of various heights. For many visitors, the epitome of the Kalahari is the sight of a herd of graceful gemsbok topping a dune, pausing awhile at its summit, before slowly disappearing down the other side. Prancing springbok, the deep-throated roar of a Kalahari lion on the hunt, or the chilling cry of the brown hyena in pursuit of its prey are all evocative symbols of this wild desert area.

PLACE OF GREAT NOISE

One of South Africa's most outstanding natural wonders and the sixth largest waterfall in the world, the Augrabies Falls lies about 160 kilometres south of the Kalahari Gemsbok National Park. Here the mighty Orange River, which has a combined width of some 3 kilometres immediately above the falls, is forced through a narrow channel, down a series of cataracts to a final plunge of some 65 metres into a 250-metre-deep ravine hewn out of solid granite. The 15-kilometre-long gorge is the world's largest eroded through granite. When the Orange River floods – an event which seldom happens – over 405 million litres of water tumble into the ravine every second over no fewer than 19 falls. In

the process a great noise is generated, hence the Khoi name of *aukurabis*, 'place of great noise'. Because of the pounding might of the river, the pool below the falls is inaccessible, even in the driest season, and this has led to a number of legends and myths. Perhaps the most wishful is that in the pool lies an absolute fortune in alluvial diamonds, washed there by the Orange River over the ages. Another is that the South African equivalent to the Loch Ness monster lurks there, ready to drag down to the water's murky depths any person who should perchance find themselves in the ravine.

The Augrabies Falls forms the centrepiece of the 14 745-hectare Augrabies Falls National Park, proclaimed in 1966. The scrubby vegetation, typical of semi-desert areas, includes the evocative quiver tree (*Aloe dichotoma*), Karoo boer-bean (*Schotia afra*), Cape willow (*Salix mucronata*), wild olive (*Olea europaea*), the hardy liliaceae (*Haworthia tessellata*), and for those who have the eye to find them, lithops – the fascinating plants that survive predation because of their resemblance to stones. In 1985 black rhino were introduced to the

The Augrabies Falls in full flood. Care must be taken when walking on the slippery rocks near the falls.

park, and other resident animals include klipspringer, springbok, rock dassie and chacma baboon, while over 180 species of bird have been recorded.

KAKAMAS AND KEIMOES

Some 36 kilometres east of Augrabies Falls lies Kakamas, established by the Dutch Reformed Church as an irrigation settlement scheme for 'poor white' farmers who had been rendered destitute by the rinderpest epidemic of 1896. The first settlers were given £12 by the Church as capital to clear the lands allotted to them, dig irrigation canals from the Orange River and commence their farming. Ownership of the land remained with the Church, but in 1964 the Church's interest in the land was finally liquidated.

In 1933 the now-famous Kakamas peach was discovered on the river banks. The golden peach was perfect for canning and it was distributed to farmers in the Western Cape. Within five years of its discovery, the Kakamas peach had transformed the South African canned fruit industry, and from this single tree species came 75% of the peach trees which supply the canning factories. Other important crops produced are sultanas, grapes and lucerne. Irrigation is supplied by *bakkiespompe* (Persian waterwheels), still in daily operation along some of the canals.

Between Kakamas and Upington lies the little village of Keimoes. Here the Orange River splits up into a number of channels forming islands in the river, the largest being Kanoneiland. This is a rich farming area because of the availability of water through irrigation and the area's rich alluvial soils. Sultanas and a variety of other grapes, lucerne and wheat are the principal crops.

UPINGTON

Situated on the banks of the Orange River and 40 kilometres east of Keimoes lies Upington, the second largest town in the Northern Cape. In the late 19th century this province was a wild frontier far from the reaches of colonial law emanating from distant Cape Town. It could therefore offer refuge and a place of residence to many roughnecks and outlaws on the run. Nomadic bands of Khoikhoi resented the

intrusion of white settlers into the area and often stole livestock from frontier farms, and the densely wooded islands along the river offered ideal bases from which they could mount their cattle-rustling activities.

In 1871, at the request of the Khoikhoi chief Klaas Lukas, the Reverend Christiaan Schröder established a mission station at Olyvenhoutsdrift, a ford across the Orange River (known to the Khoikhoi as the Gariep, 'the great river'). Schröder built a church and the first irrigation canals were dug. When the Prime Minster of the Cape, Thomas Upington, visited the settlement in 1884, it was named in his honour. Today Upington is an important agricultural, administrative

Ever-watchful suricates (left), *among the Kalahari Gemsbok Park's smaller residents, are often seen by guests at the park's Twee Rivieren camp* (above).

and commercial centre serving the Northern Cape. The main crops grown on the irrigated lands along the Orange River are sultanas and other grapes (there are several wineries in the district), deciduous fruit, vegetables, lucerne and cotton. Away from the river the major economic activities are sheep farming (merino and karakul), salt extraction from nearby pans, and the mining of pegmatite, tungsten and semi-precious stones.

THE ROARING SANDS

A strange and most remarkable natural phenomenon, called the 'roaring sands of the Kalahari', lies 75 kilometres southwest of Olifantshoek. On the western flank of the Langeberg is an unusual aggregation of fine white sand dunes, covering about 3 200 hectares and believed to have been blown there from the northwest some 500 000 years ago. When a person steps on the sands during hot, dry weather, when the wind is relatively light and the direction right, a loud rumbling is emitted, clearly audible up to 400 metres away. Scientists are not sure how to explain this unique occurrence, but believe that it could be due to the unusually symmetrical nature of the grains of sand rubbing against each other, thereby resonating the sound created through friction.

The quiver tree, or kokerboom, from whose bark the San made quivers for their poisoned arrows, thrives in desert conditions.

A short walk leads down to the sandy river bank, and fishing is permitted in the river.

Visitors can tour one of the five cellars of the Oranjerivier Wine Cellar Co-op, as well as the South African Dried Fruit Co-operative along the N10 just outside town. The co-op is the second largest in the world and can process up to 250 tons of dried fruit a day. Freshly packed dried fruit is sold at the co-operative.

The road from Upington to Keimoes passes through terrain described as Orange River broken veld, an arid landscape interspersed by rocky mountains. Where the road runs near the river, vineyards and irrigated fields flourish, and ostriches are often seen along the route. What appears initially to be broken glass reflecting the sun's rays on the road-side is in fact countless fragments of shiny rock

KEIMOES After 39 kilometres the N14 reaches Keimoes, and the town's name, emblazoned in white letters, can be seen on a distant hill. The hill falls within the 77-hectare Tierberg Nature Reserve, established to protect succulents and aloes, and the summit provides fine views over the Orange River Valley. Horse-drawn carts are still a major form of transport in the Northern Cape and can often be seen trotting along Keimoes' streets.

UPINGTON Situated on the north bank of the Orange River, Upington is a thriving town. In the grounds of the Kalahari-Oranje Museum in Schröder Street, the simple white gables of Reverend Schröder's mission church can be seen, and an unusual statue of a donkey harnessed to a water pump stands next to the church. The bronze statue, sculpted by Hennie Potgieter, honours the contribution made by donkeys to the development of the Orange River Valley.

In the same street is another interesting animal statue: the camel-and-rider statue outside the police station recalls the mounted police-men and their camel mounts who patrolled the Kalahari in the past. The grave of South Africa's Robin Hood, Scotty Smith, can be seen in

Upington's local cemetery. Smith, a soldier, settled on the edge of the Kalahari desert and became an accomplished horse and stock thief, smuggler, confidence trickster, gun-runner and illicit diamond buyer. He assembled a team of San trackers who kept him informed of police movements, and he often robbed the rich and distributed their valuables to the poor. Scotty Smith eventually settled in Upington and died during the flu epidemic of 1919.

Where the N10 crosses the Orange, an avenue of date palms, extending over one kilometre, leads to Die Eiland resort. Planted in 1935, it is the longest avenue of palms in the southern hemisphere and was declared a national monument in 1982. Delicious dates can be bought throughout the area.

Die Eiland is one of the finest municipal-owned resorts in South Africa, with an enormous swimming pool and comfortable chalets. Some of the largest buffalothorn and camelthorn trees in South Africa provide ample shade between the chalets, and lush lawns extend throughout the resort and camp site.

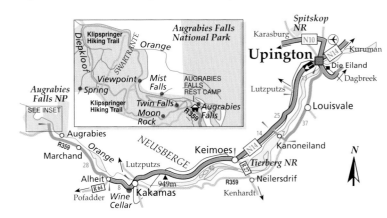

The majestic bateleur eagle favours semi-desert and open thornveld.

A long, narrow town situated on the northern bank of the Orange River, Keimoes has developed along the main road to the Augrabies Falls. Passing the old mission church, rows of vines, irrigated by a canal and a large waterwheel bearing the name 'Keimoes', stretch into the distance. On the rocky outcrop directly across the road several fine examples of the kokerboom aloe, which is endemic to this region and southern Namibia, can be seen.

KAKAMAS Leaving Keimoes, the road follows the vineyards for 27 kilometres before turning away from the Orange River. The N14 then crosses a picturesque plain of desert grass dominated on either side of the road by the black and reddish-brown peaks of the Neusberge. Near Kakamas – Khoikhoi for 'water for livestock' – the road passes through a gap in the range and crosses the Orange before reaching the town.

The five-cellar co-operative, owned by the Oranjerivier Wine Cellar Co-op, is open for wine-tasting and sales. It is the largest in South Africa and is noted for its hanepoot and dessert wines. Enormous stainless steel tanks, each one storing 44 000 litres of wine, line the passages in the main building.

AUGRABIES FALLS NATIONAL PARK

The magnificent Augrabies Falls is the highlight of the Augrabies Falls National Park. Here the Orange River squeezes through a narrow channel and plummets into a dramatic, sheer-sided gorge. Polished by eons of water erosion, the rocks near the falls are extremely slippery, and despite the safety fences which prevent visitors from falling into the gorge, great care should be exercised. The rough topography flanking the gorge is the favoured domain of the rock dassie and countless rainbow-hued Cape flat rock lizards.

The park's delightful rest camp consists of chalets, swimming pools and an extensive, grassy camp site, and this green oasis in the middle of a semi-desert area comes as a refreshing suprise. The main complex at the entrance to the park houses a shop, restaurant and bar, and its curved veranda overlooks the rugged granite terrain adjoining the falls. From the patio, with its educational displays, paths lead down to viewpoints overlooking the falls. The two-day, 39-kilometre Klipspringer Trail explores the southern section of the park and provides spectacular views of the gorge. The gorge can also be viewed from the road that leads to lookouts at Ararat, Oranjekom and Echo Corner, while a walk to the summit of Moon Rock provides splendid views over the surrounding broken landscape.

For something different, the 18-kilometre Gariep 3-in-1 Adventure, the first of its kind for a national park, is a one-day outdoor experience that combines canoeing, hiking and mountain biking. The exciting Black Rhino Adventure

The Augrabies Falls, named aukurabis *– the 'place of great noise' – by the Khoi.*

The sure-footed klipspringer thrives in the Augrabies Falls National Park.

includes a trip down the Orange River in an inflatable boat and a 4x4 drive tour of the northern section of the park. Here visitors can see black rhino, a small group which were relocated from Etosha in Namibia. Augrabies offers the best klipspringer-viewing in South Africa and these agile antelope are common throughout the park. Eland and springbok are also often seen along the road to Ararat.

KANONEILAND Some 25 kilometres from Upington, the road to the right leads to Kanoneiland, a 12-kilometre-long island that is the largest on the Orange River and the biggest populated inland island in the country. Fish are bred for sale and the island boasts a catfish farm where visitors can savour this fish, along with local wines, under camelthorn trees.

Kanoneiland's Afrikaans name originated from the Khoikhoi word, *keboes*, an onomatopoeic reference to the noise made by cannon shells during a war in 1878. The Cape Field Artillery fired a cannon – which can be seen in front of the old school building – at the Khoikhoi who replied with an improvised cannon fashioned from a hollowed aloe stem. The weapon exploded and killed six Khoikhoi soldiers.

THE GREAT NORTH WEST

The Kimberley Mine Museum (above) and its 'Diggers Rest' pub (below) recaptures the spirit of Kimberley's early mining days.

Straddling three of the country's provinces (the Northern Cape, North West and Free State), the Great North West region shares its northern boundary with that of southern Botswana. It is generally an area of low rainfall with the annual amount decreasing towards the west and northwest. As a result of variable precipitation, the vegetation ranges from typical desert scrub in the drier western areas, to bushveld in the north, and Highveld grasslands in the east. The relatively featureless nature of the region's predominant landscapes, however, belies the fabulous wealth that is locked beneath the surface of the land.

This map highlights the regional map opposite. Overlapping regions and their page numbers are supplied.

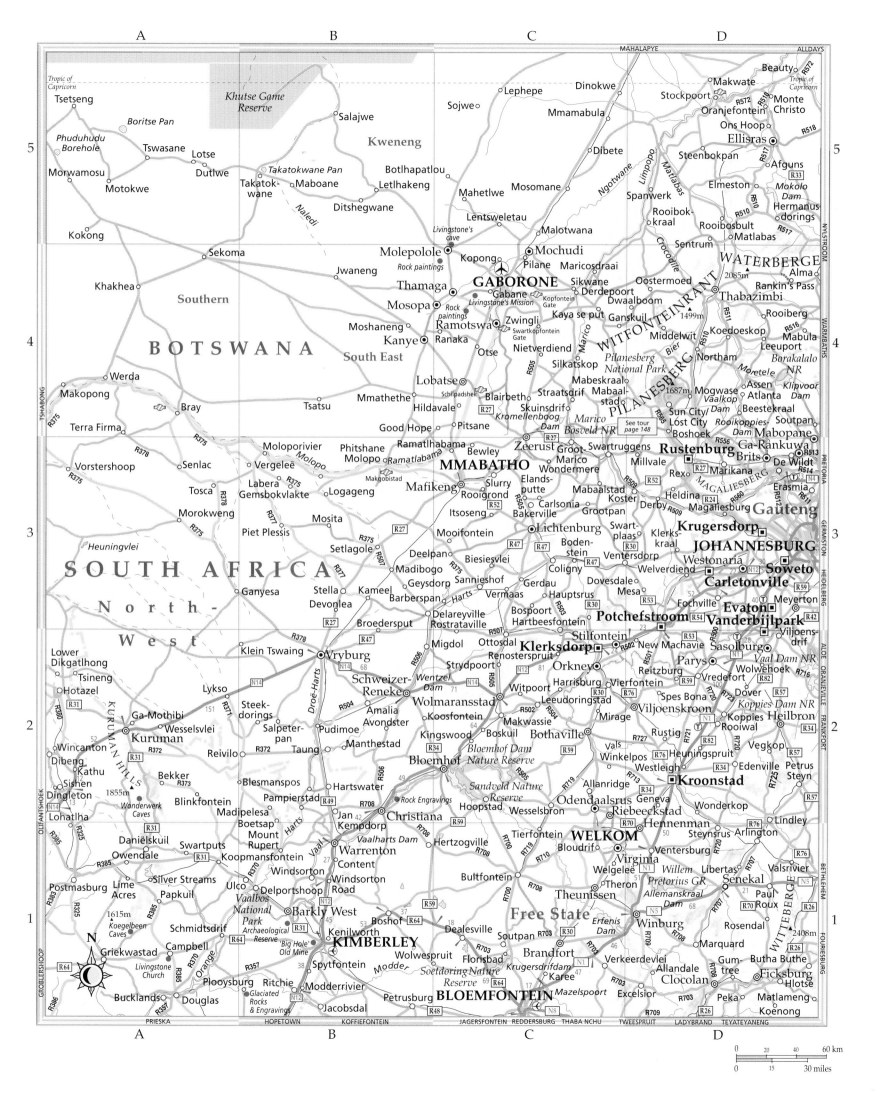

The Diggers Memorial commemorates the thousands of miners who toiled at Kimberley's diamond mines.

MINERAL WEALTH

In the west, near the village of Hotazel (a corruption of 'hot as hell'), is one of the world's richest deposits of manganese, while at Sishen, 60 kilometres south, colossal iron ore deposits were discovered in 1940. In the midst of the vast dolomite plain of the Northern Cape at Postmasburg, massive manganese deposits were found in 1922, while the road to Griquatown passes Asbestos Mountains, so named because of the massive quantities of this fibrous mineral they contain. But to the east and across these mountains was one of nature's most glamorous treasure troves: here, diamonds were discovered in the barren veld, and Kimberley rose up to become the diamond capital of the world.

However, the mineral wealth of this region does not end at Kimberley. In the late 1940s rich deposits of gold were found to the northeast in the reefs beneath the grasslands of the Free State, and the town of Welkom was built to serve these gold mines (*see* p. 152). North of the Free State goldfields, the deep reefs below Orkney and Klerksdorp yielded further deposits of gold, while to the northwest, around Rustenburg, lavish deposits of platinum – the precious metal more valuable than gold – were uncovered.

DIAMOND FEVER

Kimberlite pipes were created about 60 million years ago when there was volcanic activity in the region, and pipes or 'throats' were formed through which the earth pumped kimberlite, some of which was studded with diamonds. The puzzle that geologists still grapple with today is how the diamonds came to be in the kimberlite: diamonds are made from carbon that has been subjected to severe pressure and yet kimberlite contains no carbon. Furthermore, not all volcanic pipes contain diamonds in the kimberlite.

Once the pipes reached the earth's surface they formed low volcanic cones, but as kimberlite is soft, it was not long before these volcanic hillocks were eroded away and their overburden spread about the surrounding countryside. In time much of the overburden, including diamonds, was washed into the rivers and over the ages these diamonds and the gravel that accompanied them were carried to new resting places downstream.

In 1869 a traveller spent a night at a farm called Bultfontein some 25 kilometres southeast of Barkly West, when he noticed an unusual stone in the mud walls of the farmhouse. Suspecting that it might be a diamond he removed it and sent it to an apothecary in Grahamstown who confirmed his suspicions. This finding rapidly led to the greatest diamond rush in history. At first diggers concentrated on the Bultfontein area, and the farmer's house was demolished and claims were pegged out around the area of the homestead.

The diamonds which led, in January 1870, to the first diamond diggings in Africa, were alluvial diamonds washed into the Vaal River with the overburden from nearby kimberlite pipes. The diggings were at Klip Drift, a ford on the Vaal some 25 kilometres from present-day Kimberley.

Diggers rushed to peg out claims there and chaos shattered the tranquility of the mission station which was situated at Pniel nearby. The Republic of Klip Drift was established and a president elected, a certain Mr Stafford Parker, who tried to introduce a semblance of order and control over the unruly diggers as they swarmed about and vied with each other for the biggest and best claim. In December of the same year the British stepped in and in due course the present town of Barkly West was proclaimed.

But interest in Barkly West soon evaporated when fortune seekers discovered a rich and rare kimberlite pipe on Colesberg Koppie (at present-day Kimberley) the following year. The hillock was dug away but the trail of diamonds continued to lead the diggers onwards and downwards. A large hole began to appear in the barren veld, and a tin-town soon spread around the ever-deepening and widening hole which, when dug away, became the famous Big Hole (today the focal point of the fascinating open-air Kimberley Mine Museum).

THE BIG HOLE

The allure of the diamond industry reached its climax at Kimberley. While the diggers clambered over, under and around each other using spades, picks, shovels and primitive overhead cableways in order to dig out this fantastic wealth, other men wheeled and dealed in the smoke-filled boardrooms of their rapidly growing commercial empires.

Men such as Cecil John Rhodes, one of Africa's greatest magnates, began his career in Kimberley in partnership with a certain Mr C Rudd selling ice to the diamond diggers. Rhodes later became not only South Africa's richest man at the time, but also a politician of considerable prominence whose goal was to spread British influence from the Cape to Cairo.

Barney Barnato, another legendary figure and empire builder of that time, came to Kimberley when he was 20 years old and was a multimillionaire by the time he was 25. He eventually sold his mining company in 1888 for £5 338 650 to Cecil Rhodes, who paid him by cheque! Rhodes steadily amalgamated all the other mining companies operating in Kimberley into a single conglomerate called De Beers Consolidated Diamond Mines Ltd. He then had the power to finance the operation and equipment that was required to take mining operations from the initial 400-metre-deep hole that the 30 000 diggers had made, down another 800 metres in pursuit of the diamondiferous kimberlite pipe.

Kimberley's famous Big Hole, where over 14,5 million carats of diamonds were extracted.

KIMBERLEY TODAY

At the beginning of the First World War, Kimberley's fortunes as a diamond centre began to wane when the demand for diamonds slumped and mining became too expensive in relation to the returns received. By the time the mine was closed in 1914 over 25 million tonnes of kimberlite had been removed and 14 504 566 carats (equal to 3 tons) of diamonds recovered. However, the Kimberley Diamond Mine laid the foundations for a flourishing town which has continued to grow and has become the most important administrative, commercial and industrial centre in the Northern Cape, of which Kimberley is also the capital.

The infrastructure that was developed in the city has continued to serve the diamond industry in South Africa as a whole. Diamond mining still continues in the Northern Cape, with prospectors and small-scale operations centred on the alluvial deposits along the Vaal River and large-scale operations concentrated at the Finsch Diamond Mine near Postmasberg. Those interested can follow the Diamond Route which runs between Victoria West, Hopetown, Kimberley and Warrenton to Potchefstroom.

DIAMOND CITY

In its heyday Kimberley was a lively, thriving town in which many made money quickly and spent it almost as quickly. Horse racing, lotteries, rowdy bars and barmaids, boxing booths and dancing halls all became part of the town's social fabric. Opulent houses and grand buildings were built as wealth became more and more conspicuous. Steadily Kimberley lost its temporary tin-town nature, and, in 1882, the town electrified its streets, the first urban development in Africa to do so. In 1887 a tramway service began operations.

It was in Kimberley that the plans were made for the abortive Jameson Raid, which took place in 1896 and which laid the foundations for the Anglo-Boer War (*see also* pp. 12 and 44) three years later. The Boers besieged Kimberley from 4 November 1899 until 15 February 1900 during which they pumped shell after shell into it from their long-range artillery (known as Long Toms) strategically placed on the town's outskirts.

The defenders replied with 'Long Cecil', which was made in the De Beers mine workshops and which could fire 28-pound shells. Some of the more notable battles of this war were fought along the railway line that travelled to Kimberley from Cape Town as the British forces fought their way through the Boer lines to relieve the besieged mining town.

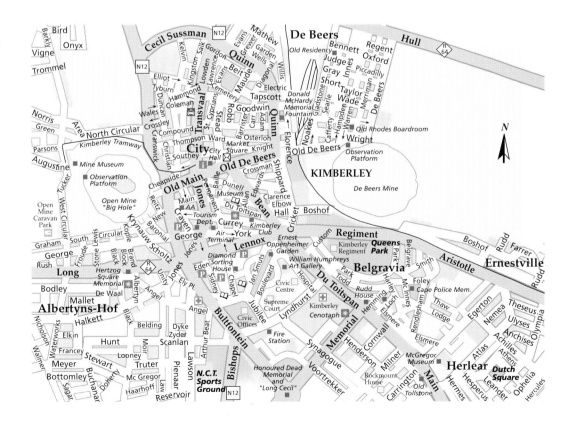

The Pilanesberg National Park, which encloses the remains of an ancient volcano, supports 17 species of antelope, including eland.

KURUMAN

Approximately 180 kilometres northwest of Kimberley lies the town of Kuruman which owes its origin to one of southern Africa's natural wonders – an 'eye' of crystal-clear cold water that emerges from the foot of a low range of hills. Each day about 20 million litres gushes out, irrespective of season, and feeds the Kuruman River. Because of this regular water supply people were attracted to the region and in 1801 a mission station was built to serve those who had settled there.

In 1824 Robert Moffat of the London Missionary Society arrived and formed what has probably become the best-known mission station in Africa. It was here that the intrepid explorer, adventurer and missionary, David Livingstone, met and married Robert Moffat's daughter, Mary, and it was

from Kuruman that Livingstone set out to explore the uncharted central African hinterland. The mission buildings are still in excellent condition and some are in daily use.

PILANESBERG NATIONAL PARK

The northern sector of this region incorporates the western edge of the Bushveld Igneous Complex (*see also* p. 18), which owes its origin to volcanic action and is immensely rich in minerals. In the Rustenburg district alone there are mines which produce asbestos, chrome, tin, lead, marble, granite, slate and notably platinum – with the two largest platinum mines in the world located here.

Adding to the geological fascination of this region are the remains of another form of volcanic action, the circular mountain

mass of Pilanesberg which has a diameter of 27 kilometres and rises to a height of over 500 metres above the surrounding bushveld. Situated some 40 kilometres north of Rustenburg, the jagged relics of this ancient volcano form six roughly concentric circles and contain some of the largest known outcrops of syenite – a rock similar to granite – in the world. The mountain mass has been proclaimed a national park of some 55 000 hectares and provides a spectacular setting for visitors, where they can see 56 species of mammals, including the 'Big Five', and some 300 species of birds. The Pilanesberg National Park is situated in a transitional zone and thus has seven different habitat categories, ranging from vegetation typical of moist savanna regions on the hills to scrubby thorn thickets on the valley floors.

PLEASURE CITIES

The Pilanesberg National Park is adjacent to the largest integrated casino and hotel complex in southern Africa – Sun City, with its adjoining Lost City and Gary Player Country Club, the venue for many major international golf tournaments.

Sun City consists of three luxury hotels clustered about a lake and set in magnificent gardens, each with its own character and each offering superb accommodation. The resort complex also contains a Superbowl, as well as gambling, recreation and diverse sporting facilities. The Lost City, an extravaganza built on a fantasy, covers 25 hectares of man-made jungles and cliff-tumbling gardens, waterfalls, swimming pools, alfresco entertainment areas, a man-made valley of waves and a water-adventure park. The Palace, a 338-bedroom hotel in which exotic design, opulence and consummate luxury are the essential features, forms the centrepiece of the Lost City.

THE MAGALIESBERG

Southeast of the Pilanesberg National Park lies the Magaliesberg range (*see also* p. 17), which runs from Pretoria to Rustenburg 120 kilometres away. Although they seldom reach more than 300 metres in height, the pointed slopes of the Magaliesberg make an impressive statement against the backdrop of the flat surrounding countryside. The mountains were formed 2 000 million years

ago when sedimentary rock layers warped under the weight of immense outpourings of volcanic magma. The saucer-shaped basin that resulted is bounded by the gradual tilt of the mountains' northern face, which differs markedly from the steep southern slopes.

Many parts are still wild and pristine and the Magaliesberg has become a popular weekend and holiday resort. The mountains also provide one of the last places of refuge for the endangered Cape vulture, which in nature lives on the bones of carcasses crushed by hyenas, but now has to rely on food provided by man at 'vulture restaurants' and on forays into the Pilanesberg National Park, some 70 kilometres away.

Nestling at the foot of the Magaliesberg is the 1 620-hectare Hartbeestpoort Dam (*see also* p. 17) which provides a wide variety of resort and recreation facilities. It also supplies water for an irrigation network that covers a total distance of 547 kilometres and provides water for 16 000 hectares of land.

Sun City's fantasy world includes the luxurious Palace of the Lost City (above)*, and its casino* (top) *attracts thousands of local and international visitors.*

SUN CITY AND THE PILANESBERG ❖ 400 km

MAGALIESBURG VILLAGE From Johannesburg, the M47 crosses a gentle landscape of smallholdings, and to the south, the protea-dotted slopes rise to the Witwatersrand. Before reaching Tarlton, the route skirts the northern boundary of the Krugersdorp Game Reserve (*see also* p. 16), crosses open country and descends to the village of Magaliesburg. Located in a scenic valley on the ecological border between the Highveld and bushveld, the village, with its restaurants and resorts set among riverine trees, has become a popular stopover and weekend destination. Other attractions in the vicinity include a farm where Koi fish are bred, art galleries and holiday camps.

As the road leaves the village it runs parallel to the Magaliesberg River as it carves a course through a narrow valley clothed in dense indigenous vegetation.

MAGALIESBERG RANGE The rounded peaks, steep cliffs and wooded slopes of the Magaliesberg rise above the surrounding countryside as the road veers away from the Magaliesberg River. An observant traveller will notice telltale white markings on some of the quartzite cliffs, an indication of some of the few remaining nesting colonies of the endangered Cape vulture. Other birds which occur here are pied crow, rock kestrel and black eagle.

On the mountains' isolated crest, mountain reedbuck, klipspringer and baboon are common, and nocturnal predators, such as leopard and brown hyena, still persist in this narrow band of wild country bordered by cultivated fields, towns and platinum mines. It was in the Magaliesberg that the satin-black sable antelope, or 'Harris buck' as it was once known, was first described by the hunter Cornwallis-Harris in 1836.

OLIFANTSNEK DAM The route to Rustenburg follows the Hex River through the mountains and passes through a poort on the western side of the valley. When the road reaches the crest of the Olifantsnek Pass, the

Paragliding is an unusual way to view the rugged beauty of the Magaliesberg.

view of the surrounding quartzite Magaliesberg range is reflected in the Olifantsnek Dam below. Built in 1928, the dam is used for irrigation in the Hex River Valley.

RUSTENBURG Sunny throughout the year, Rustenburg, with its historical, cultural and archaeological museum, is a pleasant stopover on the way to Sun City. On the first weekend of every month, an art ramble, which includes visits to various artists' studios, takes place.

A busy bushveld town, Rustenburg has changed much since it was founded by Afrikaner settlers in the 1850s. In 1842 Paul Kruger married Maria du Plessis and later settled on a farm called Boekenhoutfontein, named after the tree, *Faurea saligna*, about 15 kilometres north of town. The homestead has been preserved as a museum. Rustenburg is the major service centre for a region that produces tobacco, citrus, cotton, maize, groundnuts and cattle, and a tobacco research institute is located just outside the town.

RUSTENBURG KLOOF A popular resort at the foot of the Magaliesberg, Rustenburg Kloof, just south of town, takes its name from a dramatic, narrow kloof through which the Dorpspruit tumbles. A wide variety of indigenous trees grow along the banks of the stream, and the area is an ideal spot for bird-watchers who may see blackshouldered kite, steppe buzzard, grey lourie or crested barbet. The resort features a tea room and restaurant, caravan and camping sites and comfortable chalets, and its lovely swimming pool, bordered by a grove of tall trees, also attracts large numbers of day visitors. The kloof also offers a number of good walks.

RUSTENBURG NATURE RESERVE The farm Rietvallei, once the property of Paul Kruger, forms the core of the Rustenburg Nature Reserve which occupies the broad summit of the Magaliesberg above the Rustenburg Kloof and town. Subsequent land purchases increased the size of the reserve to 4 257 hectares. It occupies

a high grassy plateau and the grass-lands are dotted with trees such as acacia, karee, protea and wild syringa. A shady picnic site and a visitor centre are situated in the centre of the reserve, which affords panoramic views across the country-side south of the Magaliesberg.

This secluded mountain retreat is an ideal destination for hikers. A two-day hiking trail, and the shorter 2-hour Peglerae Nature Trail, offer visitors the chance to explore the reserve which shelters a variety of wild animals, including sable, eland, hartebeest, zebra, giraffe, leopard and brown hyena. A total of 230 bird species have been recorded here, among them martial eagle, jackal buzzard and marico sunbird.

SUN CITY AND LOST CITY Some 20 years ago the lovely bush-covered valley on the southern edge of the Pilanesberg hills would have been the most unlikely site for the devel-opment of an international entertain-ment resort. Today Sun City and the Lost City are known world-wide as venues for golfing championships, beauty competitions, gambling, box-ing tournaments, music concerts and

sun-saturated leisure. Sun City first opened in 1979 as a casino hotel in what was then the self-governing territory of Bophuthatswana. As South African laws prohibited gambling, the resort attracted large numbers of visitors from Johan-nesburg and Pretoria. Later expan-sion included the opening of the Cabanas, Cascades Hotel, Superbowl and the Lost City complex. The ostentatious Palace of the Lost City, and the sheer indulgence of its design and furnishings, has become a legend in itself.

Below the imposing Palace Hotel, with its life-size elephant statue guarding the entrance, paths lead through the magnificent tropical jungle (which includes indigenous trees, a swamp area, rainforest and baobab forest) to water slides – one of which is a thrilling water chute ride with a near-vertical drop into a pool – and the exciting Valley of the Waves where realistic breakers crash onto a tropical beach.

At the adjacent Cascades Hotel, waterfalls spill over caverns housing restaurants, before cascading through a forest of tropical trees and birds. In the Entertainment Centre, the

restaurants, amusement arcades and cocktail bars keep visitors amused for hours, and the centre's Superbowl hosts anything from rock concerts to boxing events. An 18-hole golf course, designed by Gary Player, cuts a green swathe alongside the Sun City Lake, and each December, the Million Dollar Golf Challenge entices professional golfers from around the world. Below the Sun City Hotel and Cabanas, visitors can engage in a variety of watersports, including jet-skiing, windsurfing and water-skiing. A farmyard and mini-golf are added attractions.

PILANESBERG NATIONAL PARK

Occupying the weathered remains of an ancient volcano, the Pilanesberg National Park is one of South Africa's foremost conservation showpieces. As recently as 1979, the park con-sisted of little more than a boundary fence and two dusty roads that crossed the crater floor. Wildlife was limited to a few baboons, mountain reedbuck, klipspringer and the occa-sional leopard. Once the boundary of the park had been secured, 6 000 animals representing 19 species – including hippo, elephant, and rhino – were reintroduced, and tourist camps, picnic sites, water holes, and game-viewing roads and hides were constructed.

The Pilanesberg now supports sizeable herds of hartebeest, zebra, wildebeest, kudu, eland and giraffe, and safeguards the world's third-largest population of white rhino. After game herds had reached sus-tainable levels, 14 lions from Namibia were released in 1993.

A wide choice of accommodation is available in the park, with three exclusive game lodges – Bakubung, Kwa Maritane and Tshukudu – situ-ated in its southern region. Although these lodges are all close to Sun City, it in no way detracts from the ambi-ence of these bush retreats. Hippos inhabit a pool below Bakubung, leopards have been sighted at the Kwa Maritane hide, and guests at

Tshukudu often awake to the sight of white rhino in the valley below. For the visitor who seeks an affordable and authentic bush experience, the tented Kololo and Mankwe camps are highly recommended. At Mankwe the safari tents have been carefully positioned around a rocky *koppie*, and at night hippos cavort in the lake below the camp.

At Manyane, the main entrance to the park, two spacious walk-in aviaries exhibit African birds – includ-ing crimsonbreasted shrike, white-fronted bee-eater and lilacbreasted roller – among indigenous trees, and they are within walking distance of the restaurant, supermarket and swimming pool. Accommodation at Manyane Camp consists of comfort-able, self-contained chalets and a superb caravan park.

The Pilanesberg National Park protects the endangered Cape vulture.

To explore the park thoroughly several days should be set aside. A hot-air balloon trip is an unusual way to see the Pilanesberg and its wildlife. If time is limited, it is best to concentrate on the central region in the vicinity of Mankwe Lake. From the hide situated at the west-ern end of the lake, hippos and waterbirds, such as whitefaced and yellowbilled duck, darter, malachite kingfisher and fish eagle – are usu-ally visible. Mankwe Way is a good road for seeing a variety of game, including white rhino, wildebeest, tsessebe and giraffe, particularly in late afternoon. The lookout at Tilodi Dam near Manyane is a perfect spot to savour the last few moments of daylight, when the chances of seeing animals coming to drink are good.

Lost City's Valley of the Waves, a tropical paradise in the middle of the Bushveld.

HIGHLANDS AND GOLDEN PLAINS

The Free State: home of the Basotho (above) *and the dramatic sandstone Brandwag Sentinel* (below).

Occupying a portion of South Africa's high-lying interior plateau, the Free State is a relatively sparsely populated region, characterized by lonely, wide-open spaces. For the most part it consists of grassland, punctuated by flat-topped dolerite *koppies* (hills), and dotted with the pastures and maize fields of the province's many farms. But in the eastern parts of this region the topography changes substantially as the plains rise up to the dramatic heights of the Maluti Mountains in neighbouring Lesotho.

With its source in the Maluti Mountains, the meandering Caledon River forms the northwestern boundary between the Free State and Lesotho. Much blood has been shed on the banks of the river as Boer and Basotho battled against each other at various times in the 19th century over land and cattle.

EASTERN HIGHLANDS

The northeastern corner of the Free State is notable for the weathered sandstone mountains and the intriguing shapes that nature has carved out of the golden rocks that cap them. When these are seen against the backdrop of the Rooiberge, an offshoot of the Drakensberg, the result is breathtaking.

It was this beauty that motivated the authorities to proclaim the Golden Gate Highlands National Park in 1963. The park is named for its red and yellow striated sandstone cliffs, which stand like giant sentinels above the grass-covered valleys and which turn golden in the rays of the setting sun.

The eastern Free State is a rich agricultural area, with the main products being maize, dairy, wool, wheat, vegetables and cattle ranching. Cherry farming is an important activity, and the Ficksburg district is particularly famous for its cherry and asparagus crops. In spring the pink cherry blossoms are complemented by vibrant displays of cosmos, and a cherry festival is held in the town every November.

FREE STATE GOLD

Although the Free State appears to be mainly agricultural, it owes much of its prosperity to the large-scale mining of coal, diamonds, platinum and especially gold. As geologists and prospectors learned more about the formation of the Witwatersrand's gold-bearing reefs, they began to wonder whether the reefs extended further afield. They postulated that sediments dumped by ancient rivers

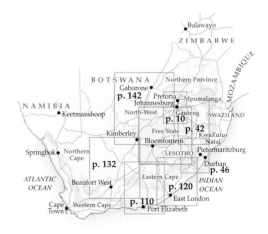

This map highlights the regional map opposite. Overlapping regions and their page numbers are supplied.

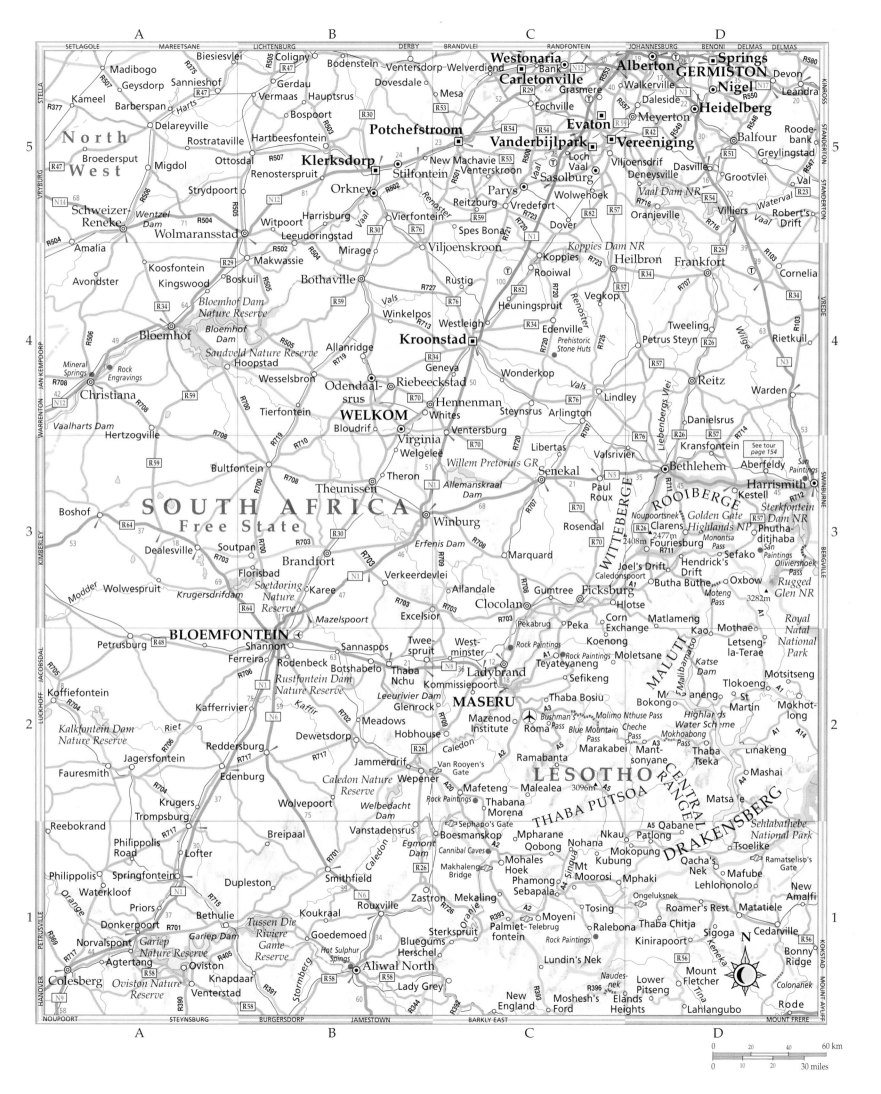

The lovely Clarens district lies between the high Rooiberge and the Maluti Mountains.

from Odendaalsrus, indicated a massive 62 ounces per ton of ore worked! The discovery triggered a new, but different, gold rush in South Africa, in that it was carried out by large mining corporations rather than individual fortune-seekers. Today the gold-fields of the Free State account for half of South Africa's total gold output and nearly 21% of world production.

WELKOM

To serve all the mines to be developed in the vicinity, the Anglo American Corporation of South Africa bought the farm Welkom, which lay some 11 kilometres south of Odendaalsrus, and commissioned town and regional planners to design a model garden city. The work of the planners is evident in Welkom's open layout, with its commercial centre built around a landscaped central square, its wide streets, open pavements and parks – in which well over one million trees have been planted. Building started in 1947, and for the first 14 years of its existence Welkom was administered by the Anglo

on the shores of a huge inland lake provided the geological basis for the formation of the Witwatersrand reefs. Geologists theorised and prospectors felt in their bones that gold reefs should also be found east, west and south of the Witwatersrand, along the perimeter of this long extinct and deeply buried lake. They were right, but it took half a century to prove it, because the gold-bearing reefs they sought lay at much greater depths than on the Witwatersrand and the technology to discover and reach these depths simply did not exist at the time.

In the Free State, the search had begun in 1890 when a trader found a quartz reef near his store, some 13 kilometres outside Odendaalsrus. Drilling revealed the presence of gold, but a lack of finance prevented development of the find. By the 1930s, however, new prospecting methods had been developed that revealed the existence of gold at great depths west of the Witwatersrand in the direction of Potchefstroom and Klerksdorp. In 1938, geologist Oscar Weiss, using new technology and equipment that he had designed himself, finally pointed to the place where gold could be found in payable quantities.

In April 1938, a borehole struck the reef 737 metres below the farm St Helena, near present-day Welkom. Further drilling took place over the next year, with virtually

every borehole revealing positive or at least encouraging results. The real breakthrough came on 16 April 1946 when a borehole drilled on the farm Geduld, 4 kilometres

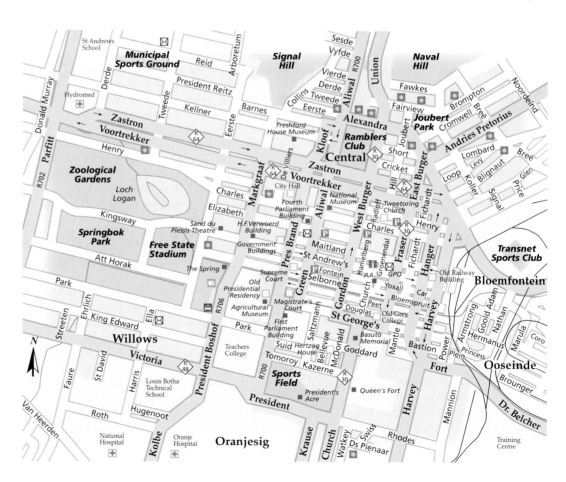

The Basotho Cultural Village outside Golden Gate is a major tourist attraction in the Free State.

American Corporation. Today it is the second biggest urban centre in the Free State. The neighbouring town of Virginia, laid out in 1954 on the banks of the Sand River, was also built to serve the burgeoning goldfields. The town takes its name from the word 'Virginia', carved on a rock in the vicinity allegedly by two homesick American engineers who were helping to lay out the railway line from Cape Town to Johannesburg in 1892.

Prolific birdlife, including Maccoa duck, Egyptian goose, flamingo, seagull, sacred ibis and marsh owl, is a feature of the pans that surround Welkom. The pans have been created with water pumped out from the gold mines to prevent flooding underground. One of these pans, Flamingo, has been developed into a recreational lake on which yachting, water-skiing and regattas take place over weekends.

Besides mining, Welkom and Virginia serve a productive mixed farming area, with maize production, dairying, cattle and sheep breeding being the major activities. In this region, as in much of the Free State, the land is dry for most of the year. Surface water is scarce, except where rivers have been impounded to form dams, and thus windmills are a frequent sight throughout the province. Winter nights are often bitterly

cold, while the summers are hot and dry, although frequent thunderstorms at this time help to nourish the rich soils.

CITY OF FLOWERS

Approximately 150 kilometres south of Welkom is Bloemfontein, capital of the Free State province. As the seat of the Appeal Court, it is the judicial capital of South Africa. The name of the city means 'flower fountain', and is believed to come from a *fontein* (spring) that was often surrounded by waterlilies and other flowers. The local Basotho people referred to the spring as *Mangaung* ('the place of leopards'), and it became a welcome oasis for travellers, explorers, hunters, transport riders and Voortrekkers crossing the arid plains. The settlement lay on the main route from the Cape to the gold mines in the Transvaal, and so it soon grew into a town. Bloemfontein was linked into the telegraph network in 1878 and the railway from the Cape reached here in May 1888.

Bloemfontein is known affectionately as the City of Roses, and the well-known Rose Garden in King's Park displays more than 4 000 rose trees. Bloemfontein's Rose Festival takes place in October and November – the best time to see the roses. The city is often selected as the venue for national conventions and conferences, as it is situated within 12 hours' drive from all major urban centres.

Fine sandstone buildings and a number of important monuments grace the centre of Bloemfontein. Perhaps the most poignant memorial is the National Women's Memorial, a 34-metre-high obelisk surrounded by a circular 'whispering wall' that conveys

The Free State is well-known for its beautiful fields of golden sunflowers.

Bloemfontein's National Women's Memorial honours the innocent victims of the Anglo-Boer War.

sound with little loss of volume around its entire inner circumference. The memorial was erected to commemorate the 26 000 Boer women and children who died in British concentration camps during the Anglo-Boer War (*see also* pp. 12 and 44). The Tweetoringkerk, which was modelled on the cathedral of Bamberg in Bavaria, was consecrated in May 1880 and is a major landmark in the city. Bloemfontein's most prominent natural feature is Naval Hill, named for the British naval battery stationed there during the Anglo-Boer War. An important feature of Naval Hill is the 198-hectare Franklin Nature Reserve, which protects springbok, blesbok, red hartebeest and eland, as well as numerous bird species.

Although Bloemfontein enjoys the reputation of being a quiet, peaceful if not somnolent place, it has not been bypassed by the pressures of rapid urbanisation and modernity. It has the largest railway repair workshops in the country, a number of industrial areas and a thriving central business district. It has also developed into an educational centre of considerable standing, with some of the country's leading tertiary institutions, including the University of the Orange Free State, the Free State Technikon and Glen Agricultural College, which is situated some 20 kilometres from the city.

HARRISMITH Founded in 1848 and named after Cape governor Sir Harry Smith, the town of Harrismith was relocated after a few years and was re-established 16 kilometres to the east on the banks of the Wilge River. The superb sandstone-topped landscape of the eastern Free State finds a perfect expression in the striking Platberg, which towers 800 metres above the town. The Harrismith Botanic Garden (*see also* p. 181), on the lower slopes of the Platberg, displays plants indigenous to the high grasslands of the eastern Free State.

Leaving Harrismith, the route leads across a landscape punctuated by fields of maize and bundled hay, and grasslands dotted with cattle and sheep. Where rivers meander across the land, weeping willows and poplars add splashes of green, which fade to gold in winter. In autumn, the dominant yellow-ochre hues of the high grassland is enlivened by bright displays of cosmos, which form a floral border along the roadside. Although cosmos is actually an alien plant, its abundant white, pink and purple flowers form one of the region's most striking features.

STERKFONTEIN DAM NATURE RESERVE At the junction of the R74 and R712, 11 kilometres from Harrismith, the short diversion to Sterkfontein Dam Nature Reserve

The Basotho Cultural Village, a living museum of Basotho customs and culture.

should not be missed. Continue along the R74 for about 10 kilometres to reach the entrance on the right.

The 11 000-hectare nature reserve that surrounds the dam is one of the largest grassland reserves in the country, and sustains antelope, sungazer lizard and many birds, including korhaan, lark and cisticola. Windsurfing, yachting and fishing are popular activities at Sterkfontein, and facilities for visitors include two-bedroom chalets, caravan sites, slipways, boathouses and a clubhouse.

From the resort, it is worth continuing along the R74 for 10 kilometres to the Driekloof Dam at the southern end of the reserve near the KwaZulu-Natal border. Further along

the road there is a fine viewsite overlooking the Sterkfontein Dam: grassy hillsides tumble down to its vast blue waters, and sandstone-crowned mountains provide a grand backdrop.

BASOTHO CULTURAL VILLAGE After crossing the boundary fence of the QwaQwa Park (formerly the QwaQwa Conservation Area), a road turns left across the grassland to the Basotho Cultural Village, a living museum of Basotho customs, culture and architecture. From the reception office, where visitors are met by a guide, the first stop is at the chief's village. After exchanging greetings, visitors can sample traditional beer. Nearby dwellings accommodate the traditional healer and the chief's wives.

A particularly interesting feature of the village is the circle of houses which depict the evolution of Basotho architecture, household articles and clay items from the 16th century to the modern age. A piano accordion player and other musicians play live music, and an outdoor restaurant is an added attraction at this well-managed and carefully planned attraction.

GOLDEN GATE HIGHLANDS NATIONAL PARK Together with the adjacent QwaQwa Park, the Golden Gate Highlands National Park comprises the country's largest Highveld reserve. On the intensively farmed Highveld, it is unusual to find a large area of uncultivated grassland dominated by spectacular sandstone mountains. From the boundary fence, the R712 winds for 30 kilometres through picturesque valleys carved by tributaries of the Caledon and Wilge rivers. The surrounding countryside was once the property of commercial farmers and was acquired over the years by the National Parks Board, or was expropriated under the former homeland policy. The initial core

The Basotho decorate their houses with detailed designs and bold colours.

national park – a 4 792 hectare area in the sandstone Rooiberge – was acquired in 1963 to protect outstanding examples of Clarens Sandstone, a layer of sedimentary rock laid down some 170 million years ago.

Golden Gate Highlands, some 11 500 hectares in extent, is well known for its prolific and unusual bird life. It is home to the rare lammergeyer, or bearded vulture, which has a wingspan of up to 3 metres. Some of Golden Gate's other birds of prey include black eagle, steppe buzzard and jackal buzzard. In the grasslands and valleys blue crane, lark and plover are common. Animals found in the park include blesbok – the most numerous – springbok, black wildebeest, eland,

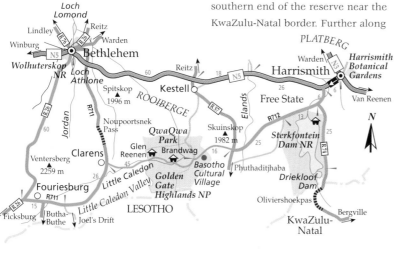

Golden's Gate's Brandwag Rest Camp, framed by the imposing Brandwag Sentinel.

mountain reedbuck, rhebok, oribi and zebra. Until the QwaQwa section has been fully developed, the Golden Gate valley (through which the main road runs) will remain the focus of outdoor recreation activities. After a scenic ascent to a high crest that provides views of the Drakensberg Amphitheatre, the road drops into a deep valley and reaches Glen Reenen camp with its attractive caravan park bordering the Little Caledon River. The chalets are on the opposite side of the road behind the sandstone reception office. Two circular game drives explore the high grasslands above Glen Reenen, where blesbok, zebra, black wildebeest and mountain reedbuck are commonly seen.

Close to Glen Reenen, Golden Gate's Brandwag Rest Camp overlooks the Brandwag Sentinel, a large, reddish-ochre sandstone cliff and the most famous and dominant rock formation in the valley. Accommodation is on a bed-and-breakfast basis, and although Brandwag offers tennis, snooker and bowls, many visitors prefer to ramble along the trails and short walks, go horse-riding or simply relax amid the scenic splendour.

CLARENS From Golden Gate, the R712 follows the Little Caledon River to the village of Clarens, where the road meets the R711. The R711 by-

passes the village, but a short distance north toward Bethlehem, visitors can turn up a steep approach to the main street. Clarens was founded in 1912 and named after the town in Switzerland where Paul Kruger, President of the Zuid-Afrikaansche Republiek (ZAR), died in exile in 1904. Clarens nestles in a natural amphitheatre at the foot of the Rooiberge which runs north of the Little Caledon valley. It has become a popular tourist destination, and its main street boasts coffee shops, a range of restaurants, art galleries, and gift and leather shops.

Much of Clarens's appeal stems from its relaxed atmosphere. The village's crisp Highveld air resounds with the soothing 'work harder' calls of Cape turtle doves, and the quiet lanes that lead off the main road encourage visitors to amble around Clarens' splendid sandstone houses and churches. In the autumn the golden leaves of the area's Lombardy poplar trees complement the surrounding sandstone formations.

LITTLE CALEDON VALLEY From Clarens the R711 follows the picturesque Little Caledon valley, and the 36-kilometre route to Fouriesburg hugs the Lesotho border, passing through some of the most scenic farming country in South Africa. The valley is bordered by spires and pinnacles of sandstone, sculpted into

fanciful forms by eons of erosion and weathering. Near the Linwood Gallery a turn-off leads to a viewsite of the aptly named Mushroom Rock.

Rejoining the R711, the route soon climbs up through dramatic rock formations before it crosses the Little Caledon River again on the way into Fouriesburg. On the right there is a turning to Surrender Hill, an Anglo-Boer War battle site where the Boers, trapped by the British, had to surrender all their weapons. From the high points on this route, sweeping panoramas are afforded across the lower-lying valleys, which are overshadowed by the jagged peaks of the Maluti Mountains in Lesotho.

FOURIESBURG The intersection of the R711 and the main R26 to Bethlehem skirts the unhurried town of Fouriesburg. Founded in 1892, this gateway to Lesotho is surrounded by flat-topped sandstone hills. There are a number of walking trails in the area. During the Anglo-Boer War the town – the last proclaimed seat of the Free State's mobile government – served as a stronghold for Republican (or Boer) forces. From a railway carriage that was kept just ahead of advancing British forces, the newspaper *De Brandwacht* was published. Three editions were printed in Fouriesburg before the carriage had to be moved.

After the retreat of the Republican army, the town was virtually destroyed by the British.

BETHLEHEM On the main road from Fouriesburg approaching Bethlehem, the popular Loch Athlone Holiday Resort is situated on the shores of Loch Athlone. A unique feature is the Athlone Castle restaurant, a concrete replica of the mailship *Athlone Castle*. The restaurant was 'launched' in 1952 and contains many items from the original ship. For hikers a two-day trail explores the adjacent Wolhuterskop Nature Reserve, which also offers horse trails and picnic sites. The Gerrands Dam is the focal point of the reserve and wildlife, including springbok, red hartebeest, zebra and eland, is abundant.

Established in 1864 on the banks of the Jordan River, Bethlehem's biblical name, meaning 'the house of bread', is fitting, as the surrounding district is a major producer of wheat. Visitors can follow the Sandstone Walking Trail, which passes many of Bethlehem's superb sandstone buildings, historic edifices and a fine cultural museum.

Surrounding the town are four major water bodies – Loch Lomond, Loch Athlone, Saulspoort and Gerrands – and watersports are permitted on all except Gerrands.

A typical rural scene near Harrismith, the gateway to the Malutis and Golden Gate.

SOUTHERN NAMIBIA

Windblown sand dunes, sun-baked landscapes and the remains of occasional hardy bushes are typical features of the southern Namibian countryside.

Along southern Africa's cold Atlantic seaboard a beckoning desert country lies sprawled between the Orange River in the south, the Kunene and Okavango rivers in the north, and the Kalahari Desert in the east. This is Namibia, a fascinating land which enchants all who visit.

From Springbok, the administrative centre of Namaqualand (*see* p. 126), the N7 highway runs through extensive plains of arid wilderness and crosses the Orange River into Namibia at Vioolsdrif. From here the route to Lüderitz on the Diamond Coast passes through immense stretches of flat, uninhabited terrain, with occasional patches of green provided by drought-resistant plants and succulents. The journey can be broken up with detours to the breathtaking Fish River Canyon, the warm mineral springs at Ai-Ais, or a visit to southern Namibia's main city, Keetmanshoop.

Southern Namibia is characterised by shifting desert sands and sun-baked landscapes. Although the desert can be exceedingly hot, air temperatures are generally moderate along the Namib coastline. The cold Benguela Current sweeping along its shores – the temperature of the water seldom reaches as much as 9 ˚C in winter and 18 ˚C in summer – causes the dry desert air

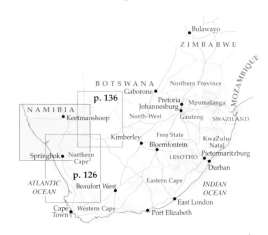

This map highlights the regional map opposite. Overlapping regions and their page numbers are supplied.

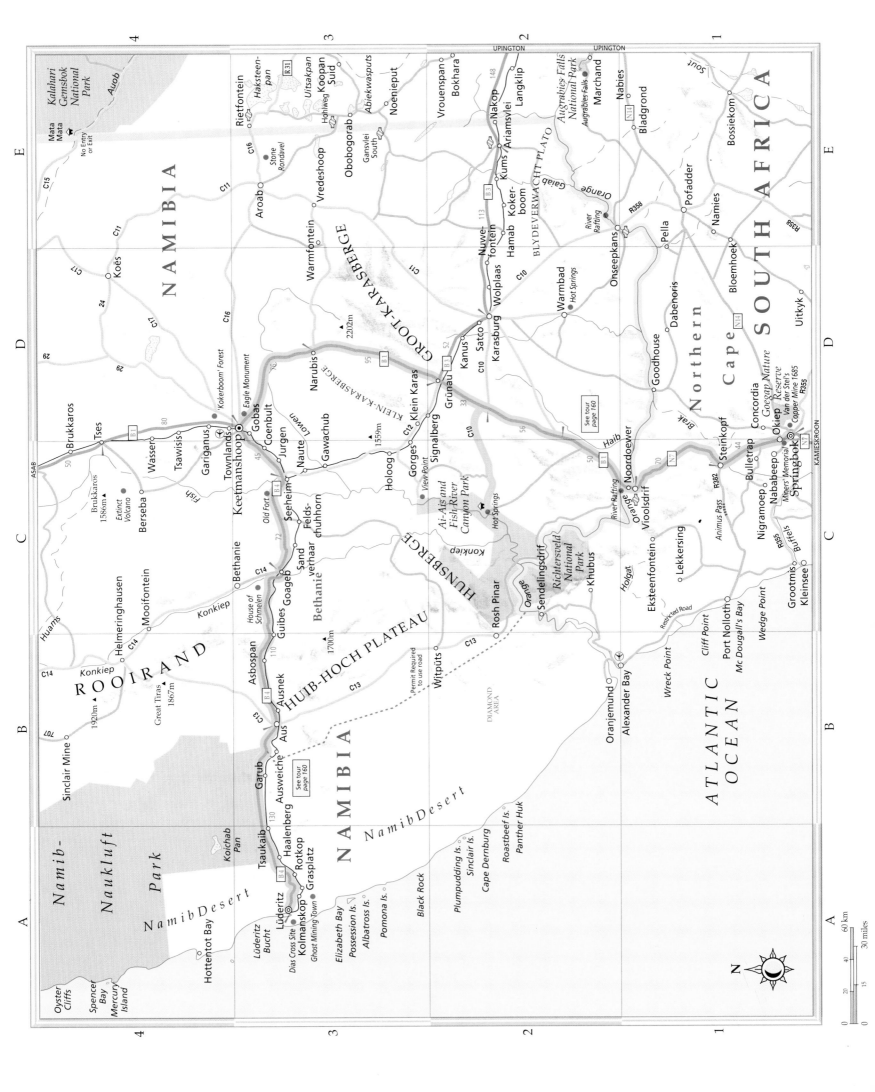

The 'ghost town' of Kolmanskop, now half-buried in sand, was once a thriving diamond-mining town.

to cool and form dense banks of mist when it comes into contact with the icy sea. The moisture-laden onshore winds – which often create weird and contorted shapes out of the Namib's massive dunes – do not bring any relief because as they pass over the hot desert sands, the moisture they contain simply evaporates. Perpetual drought is therefore a way of life.

A LAND OF HARDY PEOPLE

From the few artifacts, paintings and other traces that have been found at various places around the country, archaeologists believe that it was the nomadic San who first ventured into the deserts and wastelands of Namibia. Unhampered by a culture that valued material wealth, they roamed across the desert sands and broad plains hunting animals and gathering fruits and roots wherever these could be found. Between two and three centuries ago, the Nama, a migrant Khoi tribe, moved into the country from the south, bringing with them their cattle and fat-tailed sheep. As they migrated north in search of hospitable land, they

steadily pushed the San out into the more desolate corners of the country. From the lake districts of Central Africa came the Herero, who first settled in the Kaokoveld in the northwest. In the middle 1700s, as their numbers grew, they gradually migrated south. They clashed with the Nama and for more than 50 years numerous skirmishes and battles took place, principally over access to natural resources. The Herero triumphed over the Nama and remained in central Namibia, while the Nama settled largely in the southern parts of the country.

For over a century after the Dutch settled at the Cape, the harshness of the territory beyond the Orange River deterred any thoughts the Dutch settlers may have had of venturing deeper into the area. But gradually tales of abundant game on the plains of central and northern present-day Namibia and even rumours of large gold deposits started filtering south. Copper was discovered at Okiep south of the Orange and this discovery fanned an increasing interest and desire to explore the lands further north. A number of expeditions followed and in the late 1800s, traders and missionaries, principally of the German Rhenish Missionary Society, moved into the country.

In 1883, a Bremen-born tobacco dealer, Adolf Lüderitz, purchased an ostensibly barren coastal strip stretching from the Orange River to 26˚S from the Bethanien Khoi chief, Joseph Fredericks. Lüderitz was an ambitious man who dreamed of a German colony in southwest Africa, and he established a trading station in what is known today as Lüderitz. In 1885, in a deal with Britain, Prince Otto von Bismarck, the German Chancellor, took over the settlement which became German South West Africa. Adolf Lüderitz abandoned his dreams, went prospecting along the Orange River and eventually drowned at sea. The territory remained a colony of Germany until 1915 when the South African army defeated the German colonial forces during World War I. The South African government then administered the territory under a mandate from the League of Nations. In 1990 Namibia gained its independence from South Africa.

During the colonial period Namibia acquired an unmistakeable German character, and it is still very much in evidence. In Lüderitz, for example, the railway station, hospital, old post office, town hall, Lutheran church and old gaol represent the essence of German colonial architecture.

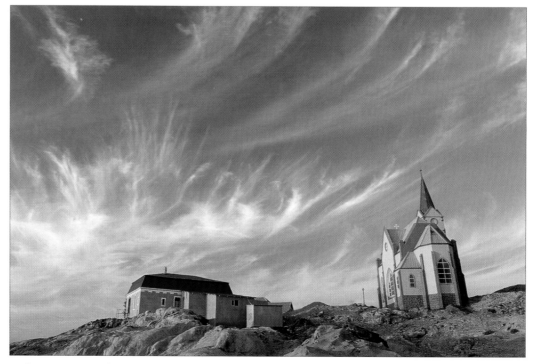

Lüderitz's German colonial past is evident in the architecture of its old gaol and Lutheran Church.

THE DESERT'S DIAMOND FIELDS

In 1907, a German railway engineer and amateur geologist named August Stauch was handed a stone by one of his workers as they built an embankment on the railway line between Lüderitz and Aus. He recognised it as a diamond and excitement mounted. Prospecting commenced along the coastline from Lüderitz to the mouth of the Orange River in the south. A mining company was launched and two mining towns created in the shifting sands of the desert: at Kolmanskop where over 700 families stayed in well-built, comfortable houses, and at Elizabeth Bay. But then World War I came, fortunes changed, and not only did the diamond industry slump but the diamond fields at Kolmanskop yielded fewer and fewer precious stones. Mining operations were abandoned and Kolmanskop was left to face the relentless and encroaching desert on its own. Many of the abandoned houses still stand, but their rooms steadily fill with the desert's fine sands.

In 1920 Consolidated Diamond Mines of South West Africa was formed and a concession for 50 years (which has been subsequently extended) was granted over an area that runs along the coast from the mouth of the Orange River to Hottentots Bay, north of Lüderitz. Because of the abundance of diamonds on the desert's surface, this is a restricted area (known as Diamond Area 1 or the Sperrgebiet) to which the public are denied access.

A MISSIONARY'S HOPE

Although not a missionary himself, a German industrialist, Johan Keetman, made funds available in 1866 for a mission station to be built in present-day Keetmanshoop ('Keetman's hope'). The mission was built on the banks of the Swartmodder ('black mud') River, and it was hoped that it would not only bring the word of God to an unbelieving people, but that it would also bring peace to an area that was marked by conflict and cattle rustling.

In 1895 a substantial stone church was built which dominates the town that slowly developed around it, and here too a strong German colonial influence is evident in the town's architecture. Today Keetmanshoop is

The magnificent 161-kilometre-long Fish River Canyon is one of the natural wonders of Africa.

the major road and rail centre for southern Namibia and it also serves the karakul sheep industry, with trade in karakul skins being its principal industry.

A NATURAL WONDER

The Fish River Canyon is one of the wonders of Africa and is second in size only to the Grand Canyon in Arizona. It is 161 kilometres long, its twisted gorges vary in width from a few hundred metres to 27 kilometres, and its depth reaches 549 metres at its deepest point. The canyon's rugged beauty and grandeur is enhanced by the fact that it is recessed into a flat plain of sand and stone, and the road from Holoog draws up unannounced at the canyon's edge, exposing the visitor to the immensity of this majestic natural wonder.

Hiking trails have been opened at various places for those who wish to venture into the canyon, but because of the oppressive heat of the desert, which is magnified during summer, hiking is restricted to the relatively cooler months of May to August. At the end of the canyon, Ai-Ais is a popular-

resort located on the banks of the Fish River. It surrounds a hot spring rich in fluoride, sulphate and chloride which provides relief for muscular aches and pains.

Lying northwest of Mariental on the road to Windhoek is the Hardap Dam and Nature Reserve. Here the Fish River is impounded by the 32,3-metre-high Hardap Dam, creating the largest dam in Namibia covering a total area of some 25 square kilometres. Fishing, boating and swimming are favoured recreational activities at the dam, and on the northwestern shores, a caravan park, comfortable bungalows and a restaurant have been developed. The dam contains a variety of freshwater fish, including carp, barbel, both large- and small-mouthed yellowfish, kurper, mudfish and mud mullet, and an aquarium exhibits the different fish species. A small game reserve has also been established with an amazingly wide range of animals, including springbok, kudu, hartebeest, eland, mountain zebra and gemsbok, while over 100 bird species, among them white pelican, Egyptian goose, goliath heron and kelp gull, have been sighted here.

SPRINGBOK The gateway to South Africa's northern districts, Springbok is known as the capital of Namaqualand. Just outside town, the traveller will come across Namastat, a fascinating place where visitors can experience Nama culture first-hand and overnight in traditional dome-shaped reed huts.

Fifteen kilometres east of Springbok, the Goegap Nature Reserve incorporates 15 000 hectares of flat plains and rugged granite hills. The reserve's Namaqualand Broken Veld, a desert vegetation type, is characterised by succulents and quiver tree aloes (or kokerbooms). Although rainfall is limited to an annual average of 160 millimetres, over 600 plant species have been identified, and many of the fascinating succulents and flowering plants of Namaqualand are raised in the reserve's nursery. The Hester Malan Wildflower Garden, near the main office, displays many species of indigenous plants.

Three walking trails of varying lengths explore the reserve and bird-watchers should look out for rock kestrel, Namaqua sandgrouse, red-eyed bulbul and Namaqua dove. The harsh desert environment does not support many mammal species, but gemsbok, springbok, klipspringer, Hartmann's mountain zebra, caracal and black-backed jackal occur. Although Hartmann's mountain zebra of Namibia has been introduced to a few South African reserves, Goegap is the only one in South Africa where they occur naturally.

As early as 1685, Simon van der Stel led a party of explorers north-wards from Cape Town in search of copper, and three shafts were sunk east of present-day Springbok. The largest has been preserved as a national monument, and Van der Stel's initials, engraved in a rock, are still visible at the shaft. At the

Springbok Lodge, a huge private collection of over 900 rocks, gem-stones and minerals can be seen. During the spring flower season Springbok is abuzz with visitors and the roads south to Kamieskroon, or west to Kleinsee and Port Nolloth, are popular flower routes (*see* p. 181).

VIOOLSDRIF AND THE ORANGE RIVER From Springbok the N7 heads north, crossing flat desert before descending to the Orange River at Vioolsdrif, less than 200 metres above sea level. Here the eroded reddish-brown slopes of the Nababieps Mountains, along the river's southern bank, are devoid of vegetation, but the river paints a verdant stripe through this desert environment. Vioolsdrif marks the halfway point on the 600-kilometre Namaqualand 4x4 trail (which starts at Pella mission to the east and ends near Alexander Bay). The route west, which traverses the 11 000-hectare Helskloof Nature Reserve, explores some of Namaqualand's most dramatic scenery. About 25 kilometres downriver from Vioolsdrif, the Peace of Paradise camp site is a comfortable

Ai-Ais resort is a refreshing oasis in an otherwise harsh environment.

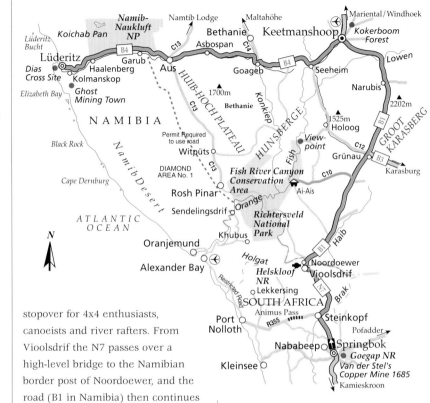

stopover for 4x4 enthusiasts, canoeists and river rafters. From Vioolsdrif the N7 passes over a high-level bridge to the Namibian border post of Noordoewer, and the road (B1 in Namibia) then continues over the flat desert plain punctuated by rocky outcrops for 143 kilometres en route to Grünau.

FISH RIVER CANYON AND AI-AIS The Fish River is the longest river in Namibia, but the present-day insignificant flow of water in the bottom of the chasm and the denuded slopes of the canyon are evidence that drastic changes in climate have occurred over the millennia. The canyon and an extensive tract of uncharted mountains and incised valleys, bordering the Orange River and the Richtersveld National Park in South Africa (*see* p. 128), is protected within the 350 000-hectare Fish River Canyon Conservation Area. Trees such as wild tamarisk, quiver tree and camelthorn grow in the canyon, and provide food for animals like the kudu, Hartmann's mountain zebra and klipspringer.

Just over 30 kilometres before Grünau, the dirt C10 to the left leads for 73 kilometres to the Ai-Ais resort. (There is also a secondary gravel

road branching off the B1 about 65 kilometres before the C10 turn-off.) Fourteen kilometres before reaching Ai-Ais, the road begins the 500-metre descent into the spectacular Fish River Canyon. With its extensive lawns, shady trees and palm trees contrasting vividly with the surrounding sun-scorched walls of the Fish River Canyon, Ai-Ais is a veritable oasis with a restaurant, store and petrol station. The 60 ˚C water is piped out of the bed of the canyon into indoor baths but there is also a cooler outdoor pool. As Ai-Ais is only 200 metres above sea level, mid-summer temperatures often reach 45 ˚C, and therefore the resort is only open from mid-March to the end of October. Visitors can stay in holiday flats or they can make use of the camp and caravan sites.

After retracing the route to Ai-Ais, a dirt road to the left leads along the canyon's eastern rim to four view-sites. From these elevated positions, the Fish River can be seen carving

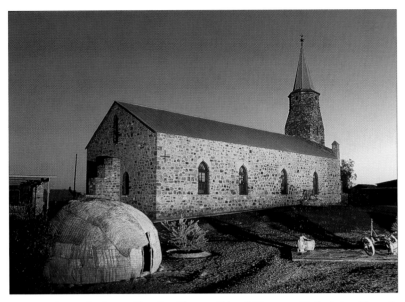

Keetmanshoop's Lutheran Church with a traditional Nama matjieshuis (reed house).

It offers overnight accommodation, guided walks, horse rides and game drives to view animals such as springbok, gemsbok, cheetah, spotted hyena and leopard. The remains of a First World War prison camp can be seen just outside Aus, where over 1 500 German prisoners of war were confined from 1915 to 1919.

After passing the Ausweiche rail siding, the road reaches Garub where a viewing platform has been erected above a water point (the region's only surface water) that is specially maintained for a herd of wild horses. Their origin is unclear but the horses have adapted to the harsh conditions and can be seen drinking here.

LÜDERITZ AND KOLMANSKOP

In 1487 the Portuguese mariner Batholomeu Dias sailed down the desolate coast of the Namib, which he termed 'the Sands of Hell'. He planted a stone cross on a rocky point overlooking a sheltered bay, and a replica of the cross still stands on what is known as Dias Point, at the entrance to present-day Lüderitz Bay. The road to the cross passes a lighthouse that was built in 1910.

Named after a German tobacco dealer, Lüderitz's German influences are still apparent. Some of its German buildings include Kreplin House (1909), Goerke House (1910) and Felsenkirche (1912), and the latter two are open to the public. On Shark Island, a rocky promontory connected to the town by a causeway, stands a monument to Adolf Lüderitz. A yacht cruise, which sets sail from the adjacent harbour each morning, provides a grand perspective of the entire bay. Weather permitting, the boat rounds Dias Point and passes Halifax Island, allowing visitors to view the resident jackass penguin colony. The ocean is rich in nutrients and supports a diverse marine life which includes lobster, crab, kabeljou, pilchard, steenbras and galjoen. The sea's bounty attracts thousands of Cape fur seals and a multitude of birds, including Cape gannet, jackass penguin, bank and whitebreasted cormorant, swift tern and Hartlaub's gull.

When diamonds were discovered in 1908, the mining village of Kolmanskop was established about 10 kilometres east of Lüderitz. Today it is an eerie ghost town and visitors are intrigued by its many houses lying half-buried in sand. In its heyday, Kolmanskop boasted a school, post office, shops, an ice-making machine and the two-storey 'kasino', which contained a theatre and skittle alley. But the discovery of diamonds at the mouth of the Orange River led to the town's demise as many of its inhabitants were transferred to the new mine. In 1956 the last resident left Kolmanskop and the desert slowly began to reclaim the site.

its route through the tight bends that the river has worn in the surrounding Precambrian sandstones over thousands of years. Near the Hot Springs viewpoint, in the extreme north of the canyon, lies the Hobas camp site with its grove of trees and refreshing swimming pool.

The challenging 85-kilometre Fish River Canyon Hiking Trail begins at this viewpoint, follows the course of the river and ends at Ai-Ais four to five days later. The trail is only open from the beginning of May to the end of September, and because of the harsh terrain, lack of facilities and boulder-strewn stretches, only fit and experienced hikers should undertake this demanding but rewarding trail.

KEETMANSHOOP

Situated on the main road to Windhoek, Keetmanshoop is an important gateway to southern Namibia. The Lutheran Church in Kaiser Street, completed in 1895, is a national monument now serving as a museum, and a traditional Nama *matjieshuis* (a house made of reed mats) can be viewed in the church grounds. Just north of the town, on the road to Windhoek, visitors can see over 200 quiver tree aloes at the Kokerboom Forest on the farm Gariganus. The trees grow among outcrops of black dolerite and some exceed 5 metres in height.

The dramatic Giant's Playground, where huge boulders are piled on top of one another, is nearby.

THE NAMIB DESERT

From Keetmanshoop the B4 runs to Lüderitz for 340 kilometres. As the road heads towards the sea, a change in the landscape is evident, and the sparse vegetation yields to the windswept sands of the Namib Desert. It is one of the driest deserts in the world, with Lüderitz receiving a paltry annual rainfall of only 20 millimetres. A few kilometres after Aus the road enters Diamond Area 1 and all land surrounding it is restricted.

The land to the north of the B4 forms the southern boundary of the immense Namib-Naukluft National Park. More than twice the size of the Kruger National Park (*see* p. 31), the park conserves 4 976 000 hectares of the Namib Desert. It extends for 450 kilometres up the Namibian coastline and is the third-largest conservation area in sub-Saharan Africa.

The Namtib Desert Lodge, about 90 kilometres north of Aus, borders the park at the foot of the rugged Tirasberg. The 16 400-hectare livestock- and game-ranch is renowned for its magnficent desert scenery of craggy granite mountains and outcrops of massive red boulders scattered across extensive desert plains.

A specially maintained water point sustains a herd of wild horses near Garub.

SOUTHWESTERN ZIMBABWE

about AD 500 the San were steadily pushed out by the Karanga people who came from the north. These Iron Age ancestors of today's Shona (Zimbabwe's dominant ethnic group) were pastoralists and agriculturalists, and made iron weapons and artifacts from the rich deposits of iron ore they found in the hills of Zimbabwe. Around AD 1000 a strong trade in copper and gold developed between the Karanga and Arab traders operating out of the port of Sofala on Africa's east coast and the little island of Mozambique (after which the present country of Mozambique was named). A great kingdom came into being in Zimbabwe, under the leadership of Mwene Mutapa, whose name the Portuguese explorers subsequently corrupted to Monomotapa and whose prowess has become one of Africa's great legends.

The Karanga mining industry flourished, and in order to protect themselves and their cattle, they built stone walls around their settlements, which they called *madzimbabwe*, meaning 'stone building'. The remains of these settlements are located throughout southern Zimbabwe and the greatest of these, where the Karanga *mambo* (king) lived, lies in the Mutirikwi Valley, and today is known as

B eyond the Soutpansberg and Louis Trichardt, South Africa's Great North Road (*see* p. 18) snakes through a heat-hazed landscape of bush-covered plains and baobab trees, before reaching Messina and the Limpopo River – the frontier between South Africa and Zimbabwe. From here it is an easy transition over the border into one of southern Africa's most spectacular countries, Zimbabwe. From Beitbridge, the Great North Road forks, with a left branch going west to Matabeleland and Bulawayo. The eastern branch stretches into the country's hot, dry Lowveld and heads north to Masvingo and the celebrated ruins of Great Zimbabwe.

Matabeleland to the west is a low-lying land and home of the biggest minority group in Zimbabwe, the Ndebele. Throughout southwestern Zimbabwe trees are pushed aside by huge outcrops of granite, the rocks of which rank among the oldest on earth. In the Matobo Hills near Bulawayo, these outcrops occur in many different shapes, some as massive domes, others like the ruins of a giant's castle or the smooth back of a whale.

Great Zimbabwe (above), *where carvings of the mythical Zimbabwe Bird* (below) *were discovered.*

EARLIEST INHABITANTS

The first people to inhabit Zimbabwe were the San who were hunter-gatherers, and who lived in the area from prehistoric times. From

This map highlights the regional map opposite. Overlapping regions and their page numbers are supplied.

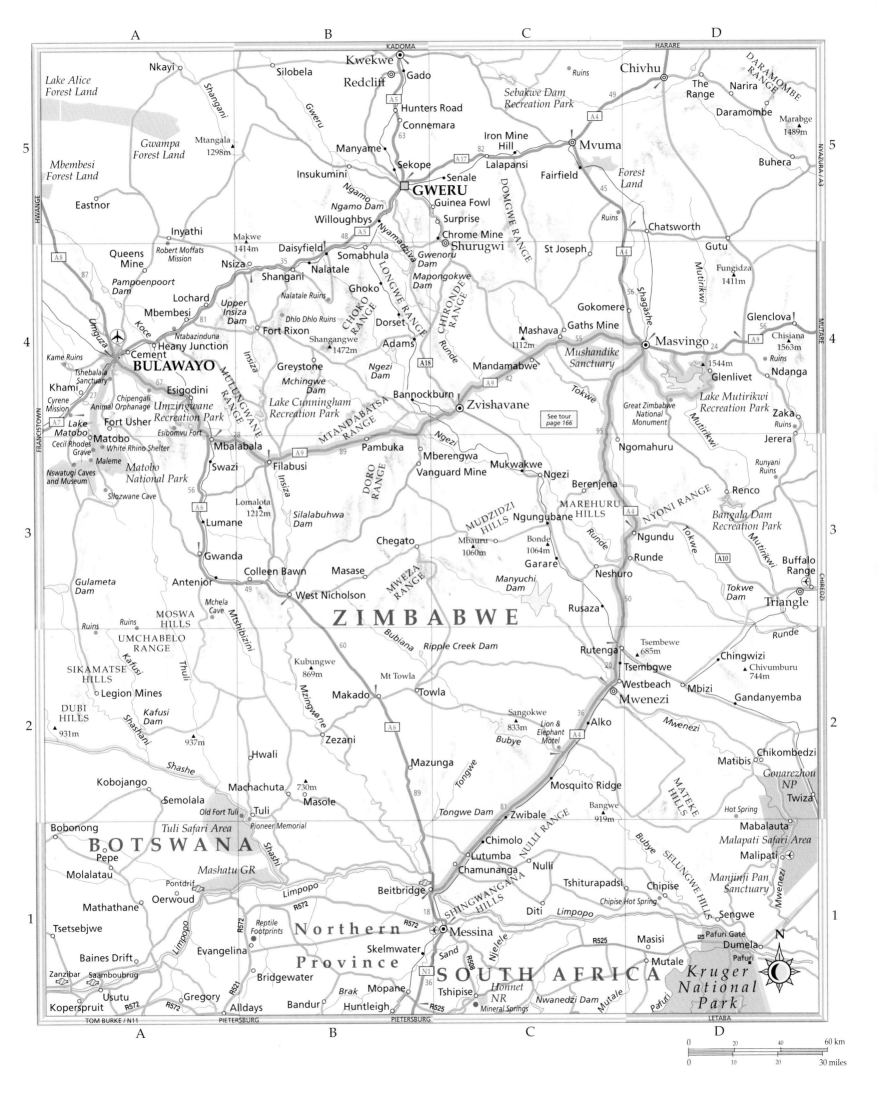

Great Zimbabwe. Early explorers speculated that Great Zimbabwe was a lost Phoenician or Egyptian city, but careful research revealed that it formed the heart of an indigenous Karanga empire that flourished until around AD 1500. Second only to Great Zimbabwe in size are the Khami Ruins, west of Bulawayo.

In the early 19th century invaders came from the south, first the Ndwandwe led by Zwangendaba who, after being defeated by Shaka, the Zulu king in South Africa (see pp. 42 and 58), fled north. The Ndwandwe stopped for a while to conquer the Karanga, before continuing their pillaging north to as far as present-day Tanzania. Later came the Matabele under the leadership of Mzilikazi, the renegade Zulu warrior who had broken with Shaka. He drove the Karanga-Rozvi (who had regrouped after Zwangendaba had passed by) out of the southwestern region of present-day Zimbabwe and established his own kingdom, which became known as Matabeleland.

Also from the south came Cecil Rhodes, the mining magnate who created his commercial empire on the fortunes he made out of Kimberley's diamond fields (see p. 144), and who saw the mineral-rich lands beyond the Limpopo as a new path for British expansion. He financed a Pioneer Column which trekked across the Limpopo River in 1890 and in today's Masvingo district established the first white settlement in Rhodesia – the territory that took its name from him, and which, after independence in 1980, became the Republic of Zimbabwe. The whites brought the expertise and capital necessary to open up vast tracts of land to commercial farming and to establish successful mining, commercial and industrial enterprises.

BUILDINGS OF STONE

Some 30 kilometres southeast of Masvingo, the ancient ruins complex known as Great Zimbabwe lies in a beautiful, fertile valley at the head of the Mutirikwi River. The circular stone walls, narrow passages, lofty hill citadel, mysterious conical tower and mythical bird sculptures of Great Zimbabwe represent one of southern Africa's foremost archaeological sites. The site was well chosen for the capital of an important Karanga *mambo* because of the fertility of the land, easy access to water and the cooling winds that blew up the valley. Furthermore, the hill that overlooks the Great Enclosure provided a stronghold for defence purposes and so it was secure against any possible attack. It is postulated that the Hill Complex, the oldest

The traditional game of tsoro – popular throughout Zimbabwe – being played at the Khami Ruins.

part of the ruins and noted for its intricate patterns of stonework, was home to Karanga nobles. It was here where most of the eight Zimbabwe birds, carved from stone, were unearthed. Today this bird has been adopted as Zimbabwe's national symbol and it adorns the country's flag. At the height of Great Zimbabwe's existence, some 18 000 people probably lived at this World Heritage Site.

Archaeologists have traced five eras of occupation here, with the first being dated around the 4th century AD. The richest period in the history of the ruins was around AD 1500 when trade with the Arabs was at its height. Glass beads and china have been found here, providing positive proof of trade also with the East. This period probably came to an end with unsustainable population growth, a decline in gold production and a split in the Karanga kingdom. The last era of occupation was by the Rozvi, remnants of the Karanga, who were eventually attacked and probably driven away by Zwangendaba and other invaders from the south.

THE MAJOR CENTRES

Bulawayo is Zimbabwe's second-largest city and owes its origin to Chief Lobengula, the son of Mzilikazi. In 1872, after Lobengula's accession to power upon his father's death, he established his capital, which he called *kwaBulawayo* ('at the place of the persecuted one') after Shaka's capital of the same name. Nothing remains of Lobengula's capital except for the thorn trees under which he held his council meetings and which today stand outside State House. The city is built on an elevated part of the country's rolling central plateau, covered in a savanna parkland dominated by acacias. Being some 1 356 metres

The Great Zimbabwe ruins, built from sandstone without using mortar, lies in the aloe-studded Mutirikwi Valley.

above sea level, the climate is equable, sunny to hot in summer and mild to cold in winter. Rain falls mainly in summer and is subject to sudden, often violent thunderstorms. Today Bulawayo is a modern city that mixes the sedateness of a colonial past with the vibrance of an African city.

Gweru, in the north of this region, is the administrative capital of the central province of Zimbabwe. Founded in 1894 and proclaimed a city in 1971, cattle ranching, as well as mixed farming and industrial development, have added to its prosperity. Mining has also been a major contributor to the development of the Gweru district since it is rich in gold, chrome, iron, asbestos, limestone, tungsten, lithium, barytes, coal and even diamonds. Mining has taken place here for centuries and traces of the ancient workings of the Karanga-Rozvi can be found in places. Gweru, which means 'dry' in Shona and refers to the river which still runs intermittently through the city, has streets shaded by many flowering trees: jacarandas display their purple flowers in September and October, crimson bougainvillea creepers hang from many buildings, and the red flowers of flamboyant trees bloom in November.

Masvingo lies on the eastern side of the region and within the district are the celebrated ruins of Great Zimbabwe, the Mutirikwi Recreational Park and the Mushandike National Park. Masvingo was first called Fort Victoria because of the fort which the Pioneer Column built here in 1890 and named after their queen, but after independence its name was changed. It serves as the commercial centre for a large district in which the main economic activities are mining, tourism, mixed farming and cattle ranching.

NATURE'S OUTPOSTS

Lying within the beauty of the granite domes which dominate the Matobo Hills south of Bulawayo is the Matobo National Park. Legend has it that when Mzilikazi saw these granite domes, he likened them to the bald heads of old men and so he named the area *amaTobo* ('bald heads'). The hills, extending for 80 kilometres, have changed little since their genesis some 3 000 million years ago. They have been permanently inhabited for about 14 000 years, first by the San (who left only their art as a legacy of their stay), then the Torwa, Rozvi and Zulu. Cecil Rhodes was enthralled by the beauty

Cecil Rhodes lies buried atop World's View (top) *in the Matobo National Park* (above).

of the Matobos and decreed that when he died he should be buried on the crown of one of the giant boulders, which, as he put it, was a place of peace which commanded a world view. Rhodes was buried there, but before he died he bequeathed to the country his land holdings along the margins of the Matobos and the Matobo National Park was proclaimed in order to conserve the area. It protects a wide variety of wild animals, of which white rhino are of special interest.

The Mutirikwi Recreational Park is a game reserve created on a peninsula that juts into the northern end of Lake Mutirikwi. The 63-metre-high dam wall, spanning a gorge of smooth granite that sandwiches the Mutirikwi River, was built in 1961 to provide water for the sugar and citrus estates in the Lowveld regions, particularly at Triangle. The 8 900-hectare park provides sanctuary for various antelope, giraffe, zebra and white rhino.

West of Masvingo lies the 12 900-hectare Mushandike Wildlife Sanctuary, opened in 1954. Mushandike Lake is popular with fishermen, and the park protects a wide range of animals and birds. It also houses the Natural Resources College which trains Zimbabwe's aspirant game rangers.

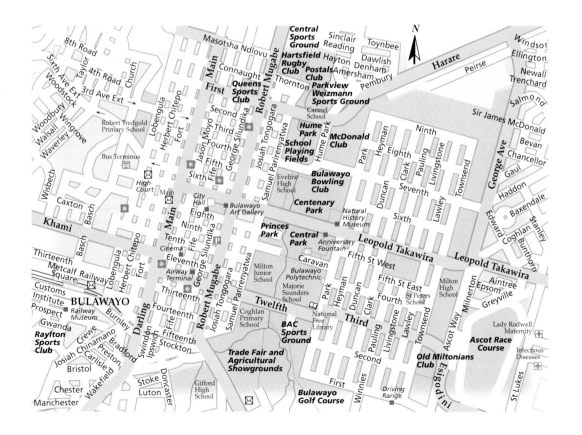

ANCIENT STONES AND CITADELS ❖ 950 km

SOUTHEASTERN LOWVELD From Louis Trichardt (*see* p. 21) in South Africa, the N1 ascends the Soutpansberg and runs through the sun-baked mining town of Messina before reaching the border between South Africa and Zimbabwe. After crossing the Limpopo River at Beitbridge, the A4 to the right leads to Masvingo and Harare. Thatch-roofed settlements dot the countryside and small herds of cattle, overshadowed by enormous baobab trees, feed on the sparse grasses. Apart from the communal lands near Beitbridge, enormous game and cattle ranches partition this wilderness, and wildlife such as giraffe, impala and kudu is often seen along the roadside.

The Chapel of St Francis' interior mosaic, made up of hand-painted tiles.

LION AND ELEPHANT MOTEL After a long, hot drive through arid mopane veld, a stop at the Lion and Elephant Motel for refreshments and a swim is a must. An isolated oasis in a vast wilderness, the motel has the ambience of a safari camp, and is superbly positioned on the banks of the Bubi River. Tall trees shade the thatched cottages, main buildings and tennis court, and the grounds are alive with bird song. A walk along the river reveals birds typical of dry bush, such as yellowbilled hornbill, glossy starling and lilacbreasted roller.

ROAD TO MASVINGO Where the A4 crosses the Runde River, the traveller enters a spectacular landscape of colossal granite whalebacks with villages and maize fields tucked at their feet. At a huge craft market along the way, visitors can choose from numerous clay creations, notably hundreds of painted clay guineafowl, a distinctive art form in this region. The road continues to climb to cooler heights and Masvingo, situated at an altitude of 1 100 metres.

Masvingo's history is evident in the main street where Fort Victoria's watch tower still stands, and the Craft Market near the Publicity Bureau is a good place to shop for the lovely soapstone sculptures that are so characteristic of Zimbabwean craftsmen. The tiny Chapel of St Francis, 4 kilometres from Masvingo, was built by Italian prisoners of war some 50 years ago. The interior of the 15-metre-long chapel is decorated with exquisite hand-painted mosaics.

GREAT ZIMBABWE Built by the ancestors of today's Shona, the ruins of Great Zimbabwe comprise the Great Enclosure in the aloe-studded Mutirikwi Valley, and the Hill Complex rising 80 metres above the valley. Dominated by the 11-metre-high

Lake Mutirikwi, the third largest in the country, is a popular watersports venue.

conical tower and with its imposing three-storey-high stone walls, the Great Enclosure symbolizes the pinnacle of Shona architecture. For a bird's-eye view of this structure and of Lake Mutirikwi, a climb up the Ancient Ascent to the Hill Complex – once the home of Karanga nobles – is recommended. The ancient citadel can also be viewed from the air from hot-air balloon trips.

The site museum graphically portrays the origins of Great Zimbabwe and displays articles from China, India and Arabia, as well as items from a Karanga king's treasury. In

one room the soapstone Zimbabwe birds that once adorned the walls of the Hill Complex can be seen. Also on site is a reconstructed Shona village with a resident *n'anga* (diviner).

MUTIRIKWI RECREATIONAL PARK Framed by miombo trees and the high peaks of the Beza range, Lake Mutirikwi is the third largest in the country. Black whalebacks of granite rise from the lake, and cottages, camp sites and an interprative centre lie along its shoreline. Boating and sailing are popular pastimes and the lake offers the best black bass fishing in Zimbabwe.

From the viewsite at the dam wall, flocks of egret can be seen returning to their roosts on the lake's rocky islands in the late afternoon. Hippo and crocodile are also sometimes spotted in the waters.

A game park, incorporating a national park rest camp, is located on the northern shore. Although the park is less than one kilometre across the water from the dam wall, it requires a 60-kilometre road journey to reach the entrance and circumvent the dam – either by returning along the road to Masvingo, or continuing eastwards along a scenic

Great Zimbabwe's conical tower is thought to symbolize a giant grain basket.

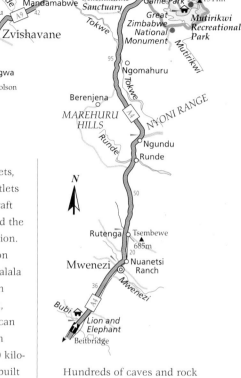

drive that meanders through rocky terrain above the lake. A 64-kilometre road network explores the park and animals that may be seen include white rhino, giraffe, zebra, buffalo and many species of antelope such as tsessebe, reedbuck and sable.

Game-viewing on horseback allows visitors to approach wildlife at close quarters, and walking is allowed on the Mshagashe peninsula surrounding the rest camp. White rhino can often be seen feeding along the shoreline across the bay, and waterbirds such as duck, egret and heron are common. Two picnic sites are situated on the water's edge.

MUSHANDIKE SANCTUARY

Surrounding a 420-hectare dam on the Tokwe River, the Mushandike Wildlife Sanctuary offers excellent bass, barbel and bream fishing, and is also popular for boating and sailing. Mushandike conserves a scenic tract of miombo country, and a network of dirt roads explore the sanctuary. Game-viewing on foot is allowed, and animals such as sable, kudu, waterbuck and grysbok can be seen. Visitors can stay at caravan and camp sites overlooking the dam.

From Mushandike, much of the 260-kilometre journey to Bulawayo passes through unspoilt miombo woodland. The only town between the two is Zvishavane, home of the country's largest asbestos mine.

BULAWAYO Zimbabwe's second-largest city, Bulawayo evokes memories of bygone decades with its wide streets and many historic buildings. Centenary Park – an extensive open space area just two blocks from the City Hall – encompasses the Natural History Museum, aviaries and a theatre. The museum houses an excellent walk-through wildlife display and has a comprehensive section devoted to the region's ancient and recent history. It also boasts the largest collection of animals – 75 000 – in the southern hemisphere. Steam train enthusiasts should visit the open-air Railway Museum, which displays vintage steam locomotives and Cecil Rhodes' private coach. At the Hillside Dams, 6 kilometres south of the city centre, a pleasant walk can be enjoyed around the dams among indigenous trees.

Bulawayo is known for its artists and craftsmen, and the pavements are crowded with entrepeneurs selling soapstone carvings, baskets, pots and crochetwork. Other outlets include the Mzilikazi Art and Craft Centre, Jairos Jiri Craft Shop and the Self-Help Development Foundation.

Several other attractions lie on Bulawayo's outskirts. The Tshabalala Sanctuary, on the city's southern boundary, protects giraffe, zebra, tsessebe and kudu, and visitors can explore the reserve on foot or on horseback. The Khami Ruins, 20 kilometres west of Bulawayo, were built in the 15th to 17th centuries using classic dry-stone building techniques. Some 24 kilometres south of the city, the Chipangali Wildlife Orphanage cares for sick and abandoned animals such as leopard, cheetah, rhino and lion. The centre specializes in breeding duiker, and has a tea room and self-catering accommodation.

MATOBO NATIONAL PARK

A rugged wilderness of granite balancing rocks and hidden valleys, the Matobo National Park is known for its solitude, many San paintings and the spectacular panorama which unfolds from World's View. Atop this huge granite outcrop lies the simple grave of Cecil John Rhodes, who is buried close to his friend and colleague, Leander Starr Jameson.

Several streams rise among the Matobo's tumbled hills and a number of dams have been built. Fishing in these waters for bream and black bass is popular and camp sites overlook the Toghwana, Mtsheleli and Maleme dams. At Maleme, there are also comfortable chalets and lodges tucked between the boulders.

Hundreds of caves and rock shelters display superb examples of San rock art, and those accessible to the public include the Silozwane, Bambata and Inanke caves. At Pomongwe Cave, rock art and Stone and Iron Age implements are on display, while Nswatugi Cave has the best-preserved paintings, including detailed illustrations of giraffe and kudu. The White Rhino Shelter was named for its rhino outlines, and on the strength of the historical evidence found in this cave, 13 white rhino were reintroduced into the Whovi Game Park, in the western quarter of the national park.

Whovi also provides sanctuary for antelope, giraffe, buffalo, zebra and hippo, and horseback trails explore he park. Outside the game park, tsessebe and sable are frequently seen, while the Matobos protect one of the densest leopard, klipspringer and dassie populations in Africa. Often seen are hundreds of multi-coloured rock lizards sunning themselves on the park's giant boulders. Black eagle are common, and birders should look out for Augur buzzard, rock kestrel and lanner falcon.

Nswatugi Cave in the Matobo National Park displays superb examples of San art.

NATIONAL PARKS

Satara, situated in central Kruger, is one of 13 comfortable rest camps in the park.

The discovery of rich deposits of gold and diamonds in the 1860s in the interior of South Africa brought about a rapid influx of settlers and the mass destruction of wildlife. As farms were surveyed and villages established, so wildlife was reduced to relic populations in disease-infested areas or isolated mountain ranges. As late as 1872 the hides of 250 000 wild animals were shipped out of Durban harbour and many species, such as rhino, hippo, elephant, giraffe and lion, were soon on the brink of extinction.

But the wanton destruction of wildlife began much earlier. Although South Africa's indigenous tribes had made little impact on wildlife numbers, with the arrival of Dutch settlers at the Cape in 1652 thousands of seals and seabirds were soon slaughtered and shipped to Europe. In 1657 Jan van Riebeeck promulgated the first wildlife preservation laws. The laws had little effect and by 1680 Simon van der Stel was forced to impose penalties for illegal hunting. But on the advancing frontier of the Cape Colony, little attention was paid to any regulation. By 1875 two animals unique to the Cape – the bluebuck and quagga – had been hunted to extinction. The first steps to halt the carnage were taken in

the 1890s in the Zuid-Afrikaansche Republiek and in Natal. In June 1894 President Paul Kruger declared the first game reserve in Africa, a 174-km² corridor between Natal and Swaziland. Game reserves were gazetted in Natal the following year to protect the last few remaining rhinos in South Africa. On 26 March 1898 Kruger signed a proclamation establishing the Sabie Game Reserve, forerunner of the Kruger National Park. This 4 600 km²-wedge of land between the Sabie and Crocodile rivers was later enlarged until the reserve extended to the Limpopo River. On 31 May

1926, in recognition of Kruger's efforts, the South African Parliament passed the National Parks Act which established the Kuger, the country's first national park. Since its declaration, a further 16 national parks have been created with a total area exceeding 34 560 km² or 2,8% of the country.

In the 1930s several 'species parks' were set up, specifically to protect endangered species such as the Cape mountain zebra, bontebok and the elephants of Addo. But recently the trend has been to declare parks representative of entire ecosystems, and national parks now conserve representative examples of the country's six major biomes.

KRUGER (p. 31, 35-39)

A careful blend of scenery, wildlife, visitor facilities and ambience, the 1 963 268-ha Kruger Park is South Africa's conservation flagship. Widely regarded as Africa's premier national park, Kruger stretches over 352 km from north to south and averages 60 km in width. Seven major

rivers cross this vast wilderness and help to sustain 147 mammal species, 450 bird species, 115 reptile species and 50 fish species. Kruger's abundance of wildlife includes 100 000 impala, 30 000 zebra, 16 000 buffalo, 13 000 blue wildebeest, 8 000 elephant, 5 000 giraffe, 2 000 white rhino, 2 000 lion, 1 000 leopard, 380 wild dog and 170 cheetah. Visitors can explore the park along 2 470 km of all-weather roads, and 8 entrance gates provide easy access to the park's many diverse

A beautiful whitebellied sunbird at the Kruger's Berg-en-dal rest camp.

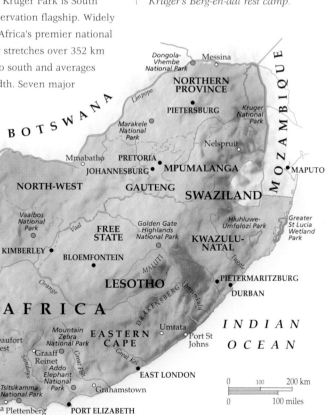

The Kalahari Gemsbok's Twee Rivieren camp (above), *and springbok* (below).

regions. A range of accommodation options is provided by 13 rest camps, 6 bushveld camps, 4 private camps, 2 caravan camps and a tented camp. A total of 7 wilderness trails have been established, and night drives depart from the major camps.

KALAHARI GEMSBOK (p. 138)

An uncharted wilderness of red sand dunes crossed by two dry riverbeds, the 959 103-ha Kalahari Gemsbok is the second largest park in South Africa and arguably its finest wilderness. Home to migratory herds of springbok, eland, gemsbok, red hartebeest and blue wildebeest, the park conserves an intriguing desert ecosystem that has been little affected by human influence. Predators are common in the park and include lion, cheetah, leopard, brown hyaena, spotted hyaena, wild cat, honey badger and bat-eared fox. Over 260 bird species have been recorded and the Kalahari Gemsbok is renowned for sightings of birds of prey. The park adjoins an immense national park in Botswana and the combined park covers almost twice the area of Kruger. Game is free to migrate across the unfenced international boundary in response to scattered rain showers. Twee Rivieren, on the southern boundary, is the largest of three camps and has a restaurant and swimming pool.

AUGRABIES FALLS (p. 138, 141)

The 14 745-ha Augrabies Falls National Park was established in 1966 to protect a spectacular natural feature, a waterfall formed by the Orange River plunging 65 m into a sheer chasm. Augrabies is renowned for its fascinating rock formations and the impressive gorge that stretches for 15 km below the falls. The park's rugged terrain is ideal for hikers and the 39-km Klipspringer Trail traverses all the major landforms present within the park. Other outdoor activities include a hiking, canoeing and mountain biking adventure, and a guided Land Rover tour of the northern section of the park where black rhino are present. Apart from protecting the endangered black rhino, Augrabies is home to baboon, dassie, klipspringer, eland, springbok, gemsbok and giraffe. A rest camp and shady camp site with extensive lawns and three swimming pools is situated near the falls. The main complex contains a restaurant, shop, bar and open-air terrace overlooking the gorge.

KAROO (p. 134)

The 43 261-ha Karoo National Park was established to conserve a portion of the Great Karoo, the immense, semi-arid landscape that is unique to South Africa. The rugged cliffs of the Nuweveld Mountains tower above plains crossed by wooded, dry water courses. Wildlife present includes Cape mountain zebra, springbok, black wildebeest, gemsbok, mountain reedbuck and black rhino. Black eagles are common and over 190 bird species have been recorded. Visitors can explore the park by car, along a 4x4 trail or on foot. The 3-day, 36-km Springbok Hiking Trail, which is closed during summer, and three shorter trails cater for outdoor enthusiasts. The Fossil Trail is suitable for blind visitors. The Karoo Rest Camp offers Cape Dutch-style chalets, a camp site, shop, restaurant and swimming pool, and the Mountain View camp in the Nuweveld Mountains has basic accommodation.

MOUNTAIN ZEBRA (p. 114)

When the Mountain Zebra National Park was established in 1937 it harboured just six highly endangered Cape mountain zebra. Careful protection has increased the population to over 200 and surplus animals have been relocated to other parks. Apart from the mountain zebra, the 6 536-ha park is home to eland, black wildebeest, blesbok, red hartebeest, springbok and mountain reedbuck, and over 200 bird species have been recorded. Facilities at the main camp include a shop, information centre, swimming pool and a camp site. Further down the valley, visitors can stay in a Victorian farmhouse bordering a dam. A three-day, 26-km hiking trail and several short walks are added attractions. The park is one of the country's smallest, but additional land has been donated by the town of Cradock and neighbouring farms will be bought. Once the park has been enlarged, black rhino and cheetah will be re-introduced.

ADDO ELEPHANT (pp. 113, 116)

Originally conceived as a small protected stockade to safeguard the last remaining elephants in the Eastern Cape, the 51 309-ha Addo Elephant National Park has been greatly enlarged and encompasses the former Zuurberg National Park with an extensive tract of the Zuurberg range. It now protects the entire ecosystem of dense, succulent spekboom vegetation. From a nucleus of 15 survivors the elephants have increased to over 220. The park also supports a valuable, Corridor disease-free herd of Cape buffalo, together

A carefully situated bird hide overlooks a water hole at the Karoo National Park.

The suspension bridge over the Storms River at the Tsitsikamma National Park.

with red hartebeest, black rhino, eland and kudu. A total of 180 bird species have been recorded. The main rest camp offers chalet accommodation, camp sites, a restaurant and swimming pool. As the camp overlooks a water hole, visitors can watch game drinking from the comfort of the chalets.

TSITSIKAMMA (pp. 105, 106, 107)

The 63 942-ha Tsitsikamma park, established in 1964, became the country's first marine national park. Tsitsikamma encompasses 90 km of some of South Africa's most spectacular coastline. The park conserves a rocky, rugged coast bordered by steep forested cliffs and extends 5,6 km out to sea. Forest-dwelling animals such as monkeys, bushbuck and blue duiker inhabit the coastal forests, and otters, dolphins and whales are often sighted in the sea. A snorkelling and scuba trail allows visitors to explore the park's rich marine life and there are several short walking trails along the shore. The 42-km Otter Trail, possibly the most beautiful hiking trail in the country, hugs the coastline for 5 days.

WILDERNESS (pp. 104, 109)

The 2 612-ha Wilderness National Park protects a unique system of four coastal lakes, several estuaries and

28 km of coastline in the southern Cape. The picturesque coastal village of Wilderness adjoins the lakes. The National Parks Board controls a buffer area surrounding the park and seeks to maintain a balance between conservation and human activities. Two rest camps are situated near the Touw estuary. The park's lagoons and lakes are the ideal places for rowing, canoeing, swimming, fishing and bird-watching. Two bird hides are situated on the shores of the Langvlei and Rondevlei lakes, and there are several walking trails. A 1-km boardwalk, leading along the bank of the Touw River, is popular among bird-watchers.

BONTEBOK (pp. 95, 101)

The 3 236-ha Bontebok park was established to protect the endemic bontebok from extinction. The relic herd of 61 bontebok flourished in the park and soon increased to about 300. Animals typical of the fynbos such as grey rhebok, grysbok, red hartebeest and Cape mountain zebra are also present. Over 470 plants of the Cape fynbos have been identified including protea, erica and gladiolus species. The Bontebok National Park nestles at the foot of the imposing Langeberg range and borders the Breede River. Spring months are the loveliest and the first bontebok lambs are born in September. A caravan and camping park is situated on

the banks of the river. Swimming and fishing is permitted, and two short walking trails along the river bank provide ideal opportunities for bird-watching and tree identification.

WEST COAST (pp. 81, 90)

The 28 000-ha West Coast National Park was established in 1985 to protect a portion of the coastline, the Langebaan lagoon and four bird islands. Subsequent land purchases have increased its size and the park now surrounds the Langebaan Lagoon, the largest wetland on the West Coast. At low tide, extensive salt marshes and mud flats provide a vital habitat for 30 000 wading birds, including migrants such as the sanderling and knot from Siberia. About 60 000 Cape gannets nest on Malgas Island, and Schaapen Island protects colonies of crowned cormorants. The country's largest jackass penguin colony, and 25 000 breeding pairs of Cape cormorants, inhabit Marcus Island. In spring the Postberg section of the park boasts some of the best wild flower displays along the West Coast. Apart from the 250 species of birds that have been recorded, animals such as red hartebeest, bontebok, blue wildebeest and springbok are present. Black rhino will be re-introduced in the near future. Sailing, canoeing, swimming, fishing and visits to bird islands are some of the leisure activities available. A two-

day hiking trail through the Postberg section is open during the flower season. The Geelbek Environmental Centre offers group accommodation, environment courses and guided trails, and is sited near three bird hides.

TANKWA KAROO

The 27 064-ha Tankwa Karoo park was established to protect the vegetation of the succulent Karoo, a vegetation type covering 3% of South Africa but poorly represented in conservation areas. The Tankwa Karoo lies east of the Cedarberg, in an extremely arid region which often receives an annual rainfall of less than 50 mm. Although six natural springs provide water, only small mammals, birds and reptiles have been recorded. For the park to conserve a viable ecosystem, additional land will have to be obtained. There are no visitor facilities at present.

RICHTERSVELD (p. 128)

A rugged, mountainous desert bordered by a broad meander of the Orange River, the 162 445-ha Richtersveld park was proclaimed in 1991 after an agreement was concluded between the National Parks Board and the Nama people who own the land. The park is managed as a contractual national park and the Parks Board pays a rental fee into a community trust

Swartvlei in the Wilderness National Park provides a peaceful watersporting venue.

Canoeing the Orange River allows tourists to explore the Richtersveld's remote areas.

fund. The Richtersveld is home to many endemic plants including the peculiar halfmens. In spring the rugged mountains and extensive plains are clothed with a carpet of wild flowers. In this harsh wilderness large mammals are scarce, but birds, reptiles and scorpions are common. Three community-owned guest-houses and five camping sites have been completed. The Richtersveld is ideal for 4x4 adventures and three hiking trails have been established. The trails are conducted by trained local guides. Swimming and fishing in the Orange River is permitted.

VAALBOS

The 22 697-ha Vaalbos park, west of Kimberley, is bordered by the Vaal River. The vegetation of Vaalbos represents a transition between three major vegetation types: Kalahari thornveld, Karoo and grassland. Wildlife present includes black rhino, white rhino, buffalo, giraffe, red hartebeest, kudu, eland, springbok and warthog. A total of 160 bird species have been recorded. Vaalbos is open to day visitors, and the Mekala rest camp provides chalet accommodation built in the style of diamond diggers' dwellings. A 40-km network of game-viewing roads explore the park, and there are two picnic sites, one on the banks of the Vaal and the other overlooking a water hole.

GOLDEN GATE HIGHLANDS
(pp. 150, 154)

Embracing spectacular rock formations and unspoilt grassland in the foothills of the Maluti mountains in Free State province, the 11 500-ha Golden Gate Highlands is the only national park in the country that protects a representative sample of the unique Highveld grasslands. Visitor facilities are concentrated in the Little Caledon valley which is dominated by splendid formations of Clarens Sandstone. Animals typical of the Highveld are present and include blesbok, black wildebeest, springbok, eland and mountain reedbuck. Over 140 bird species occur here and bird-watchers can see lammergeyer (bearded vulture), black eagle, bald ibis and orange-throated longclaw. As snow can fall in winter and summers are generally cool, Golden Gate is ideal for active outdoor recreation. A two-day hiking trail and four shorter walks explore the central region of the park. Horses are available for hire and Brandwag has facilities for bowls and tennis.

MARAKELE (p. 25)

Established as recently as 1988, 44 000-ha Marakele is destined to become one of the country's finest national parks. It conserves the highest peaks of the Waterberg, and the towering quartzite cliffs are home to the largest Cape vulture colony in the country. Although the National Parks Board intends to obtain flat land to the north to provide additional wildlife habitat, Marakele already supports elephant, black rhino, white rhino, hippo, giraffe, zebra, eland, sable, tsessebe, roan and leopard. A total of 280 bird species have been recorded. At present the park is accessible only to 4x4 vehicles. A comfortable tented camp overlooks the perennial Matlabas River.

DONGOLA-VHEMBE

Situated in the extreme northwest corner of the country, the 16 000-ha Dongola-Vhembe park protects a corridor of mopane veld adjacent to the Limpopo River and bordering Botswana and Zimbabwe. Wildlife is abundant in the region and lion and elephant occur on the north bank of the Limpopo in Botswana. The park occupies land that once formed part of the Dongola Reserve, a game reserve that was deproclaimed by the government in the 1940s. In future it is hoped that a trans-frontier park will be established that will link Dongola-Vhembe with the Mashatu reserve in Botswana and the Tuli Circle in Zimbabwe.

TABLE MOUNTAIN (p. 78)

In 1995 the Western Cape provincial government announced that Table Mountain would be declared a national park. After negotiations have been concluded, the 28 000-ha park will eventually stretch from Lion's Head to Cape Point, and will safeguard the country's major tourist attraction. A number of walks lead to Table Mountain's summit, or visitors can take the cable car. On top there is a restaurant, a shop, glorious views over Cape Town, and short walks. The Cape Peninsula is one of the richest areas in the world for biodiversity and supports an astonishing 2 285 species of plants, of which 103 species are endangered or vulnerable.

An Addo elephant emerges from a water hole after a cooling swim.

PROVINCIAL NATURE RESERVES

A novel way to enjoy the Drakensberg's magnificent scenery is on horseback.

Over 270 provincial nature reserves are found in South Africa, varying considerably both in size and function. They range from the tiny Duiker Island in Hout Bay, which measures just 150 m in diameter, to the 235 000-ha Natal Drakensberg Park, which is larger than the majority of our national parks. Had it not been for the timeous establishment of provincial reserves, species such as the white and black rhino, black wildebeest, geometric tortoise, Clanwilliam yellowfish, marsh rose and many others would have been destined for extinction. Accommodation ranges from camp sites to comfortable restcamps and exclusive game lodges. Although some are called national parks, they are in fact managed by the relevant provincial authorities.

SUIKERBOSRAND

Suikerbosrand Nature Reserve occupies a prominent range of hills less than 10 km from Johannesburg's southern suburbs. Wildlife is plentiful and includes oribi, blesbok, brown hyena, kudu and cheetah. Over 200 bird species occur here, such as familiar chat, fantailed cisticola and rock

bunting. The sugarbush protea, after which the 13 337-ha reserve is named, is abundant. The reserve offers two rest camps, an interpretative centre, short walks and a network of trails.

PILANESBERG (pp. 146, 149)

The Pilanesberg, an ancient, weathered volcano that rises 500 m above the surrounding plains, is one of the country's leading wildlife reserves. The 55 000-ha Pilanesberg National Park supports the 'Big Five' (*see* p. 171), as well as giraffe, cheetah, hippo, zebra and 17 antelope species. Over 300 bird species have been recorded, among them crimsonbreasted shrike, Cape vulture and black eagle. Visitors can choose from two luxury game lodges, a secluded mountain lodge, three tented camps, a chalet camp and a camp site. Early morning hot-air balloon flights offer visitors a unique game-viewing experience.

BORAKALALO (p. 22)

Surrounding the picturesque Klipvoor Dam, 15 000-ha Borakalalo National Park provides an idyllic retreat for nature enthusiasts, and waterbirds such as heron, coot,

duck and cormorant are common. Silverleaf, combretum and acacia woodlands support an abundance of wildlife including giraffe, white rhino, hippo, roan, sable, kudu and tsessebe. Fishing is allowed in certain parts of the dam, and visitor facilities include a shaded picnic site, a camp site on the northern shore of the dam, a private camp, and a tented camp and camp site situated along the Moretele River.

MADIKWE

Situated in the extreme northwest corner of the North-West province bordering Botswana, the 75 000-ha Madikwe Game Reserve is a wild expanse of hills and bushveld. In total, 10 000 animals have been released in Madikwe, which is home to lion, wild dog, cheetah, spotted hyena, white rhino, giraffe, red hartebeest and elephant, among many others. Birdlife includes black flycatcher, tawny eagle and redeyed bulbul. Two luxury lodges and a bush camp offer accommodation, and conducted game drives and bush walks are available.

BLOEMHOF DAM

Occupying the northern shore of the Bloemhof Dam, this 12 989-ha nature reserve (*see also* Sandveld, p. 175) conserves camelthorn savanna typical of the Kalahari thornveld. Watersports and angling are popular, and the dam attracts many bird species including Egyptian goose, redbilled teal and southern pochard. Game-viewing drives may reveal eland, gemsbok, springbok, blesbok and white rhino.

LOSKOP DAM

Encircled by wooded mountains, 14 800-ha Loskop Dam Nature Reserve is a popular venue for outdoor recreation. Sailing, boating and fishing is allowed, and the dam yields good catches of kurper and carp. The nature reserve surrounding the dam supports

plenty of wildlife, and some of the common species include kudu, zebra, nyala, eland, buffalo, leopard, brown hyena and white rhino. Over 200 bird species have been recorded, such as fish eagle, jackal buzzard, malachite kingfisher and kurrichane thrush. An Aventura resort borders the dam and offers comfortable log cabins, camp sites, mini-golf, tennis, a heated swimming pool and short walking trails.

BLYDERIVIERSPOORT (pp. 26, 40)

The 22 667-ha Blyderivierspoort Nature Reserve was established to conserve the splendour of the Blyde River Canyon. Several vegetation types are present, including grassland, indigenous forest and bushveld. Wildlife typical of both Highveld and Lowveld is present, and visitors can expect to see mountain reedbuck, grey rhebok, oribi, zebra and hippo. Aventura's Blydepoort resort perches on the canyon's edge, and the Swadini resort is situated in the bottom of the canyon on the banks of the Blyde River.

SONGIMVELO

Mpumalanga's largest provincial reserve, the 53 000-ha Songimvelo Game Reserve encompasses mountainous grassland and the bush-covered Komati River valley. A luxury tented camp, hidden by aloes and acacias, is set on the banks of the Komati. Animals restricted to either Lowveld or Highveld habitats are present, and visitors can expect to see black and blue wildebeest, tsessebe, red hartebeest and springbok. Other wildlife present includes elephant, white rhino, buffalo and leopard, and among the birds to be seen are brownhooded kingfisher, lesser kestrel and redbilled oxpecker.

ATHERSTONE

Atherstone Nature Reserve, the largest provincial reserve in the Northern Province, occupies an extensive tract of bushveld near the Botswana border. Elephant, black rhino, white rhino, buffalo, giraffe, and many species of antelope occur. At present, the 24 000-ha reserve's main source of income is derived from controlled hunting in co-operation with neighbouring landowners. A self-catering lodge provides accommodation and conducted game-viewing drives can be arranged.

NYLSVLEY

This 3 121-ha reserve was proclaimed to protect a portion of the 50-km-long Nyl River flood plain. Nylsvley Nature Reserve supports more waterbird species than any other wetland in South Africa and an incredible tally of 423 species of birds, including squacco heron and great white egret, have been recorded. During summer floods, over 80 000 birds have been counted on the wetland. Apart from protecting waterbirds, Nylsvley is home to impala, kudu, reedbuck, waterbuck, blue wildebeest, roan, tsessebe and giraffe.

DOORNDRAAI DAM (p. 24)

Doorndraai Dam Nature Reserve nestles in the foothills of the Waterberg and the prominent Hanglip peak dominates the distant horizon. A two-day hiking trail is perhaps the best means of exploring the 7 229-ha reserve's peaceful bushveld. Fishing and boating is allowed on the dam and several camp sites overlook the water. Trees typical of sour bushveld vegetation, such as boekenhout, combretum and silverleaf, clothe the hillsides. The grasslands bordering the dam attract impala, tsessebe, waterbuck and zebra.

HANS MERENSKY

Set in the mopane veld of the Letaba River Valley, 5 182-ha Hans Merensky Nature Reserve is a popular winter retreat. Aventura's Eiland resort, well-known for its warm mineral baths, is located in the north of the reserve near the Letaba River and offers accommodation in chalets and camp sites. Several short walks explore the reserve, and a 32-km circular hiking trail and horseback trails allow visitors to see game such as impala, sable, zebra and giraffe. A total of 255 bird species have been recorded including lilac-breasted roller and glossy starling.

GREATER ST LUCIA WETLAND PARK (pp. 60, 65)

One of the most important wetlands in South Africa, 368-km² Lake St Lucia is the focal point of a 170 000-ha reserve that encompasses habitats as diverse as mountain, bushveld, sand forest, grassland, wetland, coastal forest, swamp, beach, coral reef and ocean. The lake is a vital nursery for fish, prawns, crabs

Blue wildebeest and Burchell's zebra at an Mkuzi water hole.

and other marine creatures. Hippo and crocodile are common and hundreds of waterbirds such as the white and pinkbacked pelican, Caspian tern, spoonbill, fish eagle and many more are dependent on the lake. The grasslands and forests bordering the lake support nyala, bushbuck, red duiker, waterbuck, samango monkey, buffalo and black rhino, and large herds of game can be seen in the Mkuzi sector. The lake and coastline are popular among fishermen. Visitors can stay in six rest camps, four bush camps, or 10 camp sites, and several short walks and longer hiking trails explore the park.

ITALA (pp. 61, 62)

Grasslands dotted with game, deep river valleys and an imposing escarpment are some of Itala's many natural features. The Itala Game Reserve occupies the catchment of the Phongolo River and altitudes vary from 1 446 m on the plateau to 335 m in the east. The 29 653-ha reserve's diverse habitats support elephant, black rhino, white rhino, leopard, cheetah, giraffe, red hartebeest, kudu, waterbuck and impala, and it is the only reserve in KwaZulu-Natal where tsessebe occur. Ntshondwe Camp commands one of the finest settings in the country. The camp's chalets overlook a reed-fringed

Conducted game drives at Itala may reward the visitor with sightings of giraffe.

dam and the restaurant offers sweeping views. Apart from Ntshondwe, visitors can also stay in three bush camps or a camp site. Guided game drives are available from all the camps.

HLUHLUWE-UMFOLOZI (pp. 61, 64)

Undoubtedly one of the leading game reserves of Africa, the name Hluhluwe-Umfolozi is most often associated with rhino conservation. Over 1 200 white and 300 black rhino inhabit the grasslands, forested hills and bushveld valleys through which several rivers flow. Many wildlife management techniques were pioneered here, and the first wilderness trails in South Africa were initiated in the Umfolozi Section. The 96 453-ha park is also renowned for its five bush camps, three rest camps, game-viewing hides, picnic sites and five wilderness trail camps. Apart from rhino, the reserve supports cheetah, lion, leopard, wild dog, elephant, buffalo, hippo, giraffe, zebra and many species of antelope.

PONGOLAPOORT DAM (p. 62)

The Pongola Game Reserve was the first game reserve on the African continent. Although it was abolished in the 1920s, much of the original reserve has been re-established and extended around the Pongolapoort Dam. In partnership with private game farms, a biosphere of some 22 000 ha has been established. Hippos and crocodiles occur in the dam, fishing is permitted and sundowner cruises are popular. Wildlife includes blue wildebeest, kudu, nyala, giraffe, zebra, white rhino and leopard, and the arid bushveld supports birds such as purplecrested lourie, fish eagle and whitefaced duck.

TEMBE ELEPHANT AND NDUMO (p. 61)

The neighbouring 39 800-ha Ndumo Reserve and Tembe Elephant Park conserve an isolated wilderness along KwaZulu-Natal's northern border and will be amalgamated in the near future. An extensive system of pans, riverine forest, dense woodland and sand forest support a rich diversity of mammals and birds. Tembe was established to conserve the last herds of elephants in the province and the country's largest population of suni antelope. Black and white rhino, hippo, buffalo, nyala, impala and red duiker are also present. Nearly 400 bird species have been identified in Ndumo (compared with 492 species for the entire Kruger Park), including rare waterbirds such as goliath heron, Pel's fishing owl, rufousbellied heron, finfoot and openbilled stork. Both reserves offer game drives and accommodation in chalets or in a tented camp set on the edge of a pan.

WEENEN

This 4 183-ha nature reserve encompasses rolling wooded hills and grassy plains dotted with tall paperbark acacias, with the Bushman's River flowing through a deep valley near its eastern boundary. Weenen is home to black and white rhino, buffalo, giraffe, zebra, red hartebeest and reedbuck, but is renowned for its superb specimens of eland and kudu. It also protects the only roan found in a provincial reserve in KwaZulu-Natal. The bushveld supports many species of birds, and larks, cisticolas and plovers can be seen on the grassland. Picnic sites have been established, and there is a cottage and a camp site near the entrance gate, which overlooks a broad grassveld valley.

SPIOENKOP DAM (p. 57)

Set at the foot of 1 466-m-high Spioenkop, the Spioenkop Dam is the focal point of the 7 283-ha Spioenkop Public Resort Nature Reserve. A camp site, swimming pool and tennis courts lie on the southern shore and a bush camp, accessible only by boat, overlooks the peaceful dam. Fishing and boating are permitted along the southern shore. A network of game-viewing roads traverses the southern shore and wildlife such as waterbuck, giraffe, buffalo and white rhino can be encountered. Visitors can overnight in a secluded tented camp on the northern shore. As there are no roads in this northern region, game can be viewed on foot. The reserve's vegetation, defined as southern tall grassveld, is home to birds such as brownhooded kingfisher, fiscal shrike and Natal francolin. While controlled hunting is occasionally allowed on the northern shore, the camp is closed to the public.

ROYAL NATAL (pp. 51, 57)

Situated in the Drakensberg, the 8 856-ha Royal Natal National Park conserves some of Africa's most spectacular scenery. The breathtaking Amphitheatre, a crescent-shaped ridge that is 6 km wide and towers 1 500 m above the lower valleys, eclipses all of the park's other attractions. Tendele camp provides splendid vistas of the mountain, and the Royal Natal Hotel and Mahai camp site are nearby. A network of paths explore the park and there are mountain streams in which visitors may swim. Visitors can hire horses or fish for trout in the park's dams and streams. From the summit of the Amphitheatre, the Tugela River plummets 948 m into the valley below.

Royal Natal's Tendele camp, superbly situated on a ridge above the Tugela River.

NATAL DRAKENSBERG (p. 51)

The 235 000-ha Natal Drakensberg Park protects South Africa's highest mountain peaks, the vital catchments of several rivers, a treasure house of San rock art, excellent hiking, abundant wildlife and endangered bird species such as the lammergeyer. Large herds of eland can be seen. Mountain reedbuck, grey rhebok, oribi, reedbuck and baboon may be encountered, and small herds of red hartebeest, blesbok and black wildebeest have been introduced. Birders should look for the Gurney's sugarbird, ground woodpecker, orangebreasted rockjumper and a host of raptors including the black eagle, Cape vulture and redbreasted sparrowhawk. Visitors can stay at four rest camps, and hikers can camp in designated camp sites or overnight in caves which were once inhabited by San hunters.

STERKFONTEIN DAM (p. 154)

Located near the summit of the Drakensberg, this 11 000-ha nature reserve conserves unspoilt highland sourveld. Sandstone-crowned *koppies* (hills) punctuate the horizon and the waters of the Sterkfontein Dam flood the lower valleys. The high-altitude dam is ideal for sailing, and a chalet camp and camp site lie on the north-eastern shore. A two-day hiking trail traverses the slopes above the dam, and wildlife typical of high grassland, such as oribi, mountain reedbuck, grey rhebok, blesbok and black wildebeest, can be seen. The rare sungazer lizard is relatively common. Birders should look out for blue crane, ground woodpecker, blue korhaan and bald ibis.

WILLEM PRETORIUS

Encompassing extensive grasslands and wooded hills surrounding the Allemanskraal Dam, this 12 005-ha game reserve preserves a relic of the once game-filled Highveld. Large herds of black wildebeest, blesbok, red hartebeest and springbok occur here, and birds of the grassland, in particular white-quilled korhaan, ostrich and doublebanded courser, are common. In the wooded hills on the northern shore, kudu, eland, giraffe, white rhino and buffalo can be seen. The Aventura resort on the hill crest offers comfortable chalets and a variety of sports such as swimming, tennis, golf and snooker. Boating and fishing are popular, and game-viewing roads explore both sides of the dam.

SOETDORING

The Krugersdrif Dam, 40 km from Bloemfontein, is the focal point of the 6 173-ha Soetdoring Nature Reserve. Cymbopogon and themeda grassveld sustains springbok, black wildebeest, red hartebeest, gemsbok and impala, and as the reserve is not large enough to support free-roaming predators, lion and cheetah are kept in separate enclosures. Birdlife includes guinea fowl, francolin and fish eagle, and boating, water-skiing and fishing are popular pastimes. A conference centre lies near the eastern boundary, and there are camp sites near the picnic areas.

SANDVELD

Tall camelthorn trees are typical of the savanna bordering the Bloemhof Dam

(*see also* Bloemhof Dam, p. 172) which forms part of the 14 700-ha Sandveld reserve. Situated on the eastern edge of the Kalahari thornveld, bird-watchers can expect to see crimsonbreasted shrike, sociable weaver and shaft-tailed whydah, while whitebacked vulture and cattle egret breed in the reserve. The dam supports many waterbirds including redbilled teal, shelduck and yellowbilled duck, and wildlife present includes eland, gemsbok, impala, giraffe and white rhino. Camp sites have been laid out along the dam's 238-km shore, and fishermen may catch mud mullet, carp and mudfish.

TUSSEN-DIE-RIVIERE

Occupying a triangle formed by the confluence of the Orange and Caledon rivers, this 23 000-ha nature reserve is the Free State's largest. Its vegetation consists of the open plains of the upper Karoo dotted with rocky outcrops and *koppies*. Tussen-die-Riviere supports large herds of blesbok, black wildebeest, eland, red hartebeest, kudu, gemsbok and mountain reedbuck, as well as small herds of white rhino and both plains and mountain zebra. Chalets and a camp site overlook the confluence of the rivers, and there are three hiking trails and an overnight hut in the reserve's eastern region. An extensive network of game-viewing roads explore its plains.

The striking Spandau Kop in the Karoo Nature Reserve.

MKAMBATI

Tucked between the Mtentu and Msikaba rivers, this 21 800-ha nature reserve preserves the untamed coastline of the Wild Coast. Coastal forest and Pondoland sourveld comprise the dominant vegetation types, and the endemic Pondoland palm is restricted to Mkambati. Visitors can canoe up the rivers and surf-fishing is permitted. Eland, red hartebeest, gemsbok and blesbok can be seen on the grasslands. Birdlife includes Cape cormorant, swift tern and whitefronted plover, and Cape vultures nest in the gorge. Visitors can stay at the main lodge or in cottages overlooking the Msikaba River mouth.

DWESA

Bounded by the Bashee River in the north, this beautiful 3 900-ha reserve preserves dense forest, grasslands, mangroves and coastline. Lovely beaches, interspersed with rocky shores, run the length of Dwesa and visitors can walk along paths through the forest to the Wild Coast. Animals such as eland, red hartebeest, blesbok, blue duiker and samango monkey inhabit the forests and grasslands, as do birds like chorister robin, mangrove kingfisher and sombre bulbul. A short walk from the beach, log cabins or camp sites provide accommodation.

KAROO (pp. 114, 135)

Surrounding the town of Graaff-Reinet on three sides, this 16 000-ha reserve was proclaimed to conserve Karoo vegetation and wildlife, and its characteristic landforms such as the Valley of Desolation and flat-topped *koppies*. It protects wildlife typical of mountainous regions of the Karoo, and kudu, mountain reedbuck, steenbok and grey duiker are common. Visitors may also see Cape mountain zebra, buffalo, black wildebeest, red hartebeest, springbok and blesbok. Birdlife includes black eagle, greater kestrel and jackal buzzard. In the eastern section of the reserve, visitors can venture on a 26-km hike into the mountainous Drie Koppe region. Roads lead to the Van Ryneveld's Pass Dam's picnic site and the Valley of Desolation viewsite.

DOUBLE DRIFT/SAM KNOTT (p. 125)

Protecting a rugged landscape that has been forged by the Fish River's erosive power, the 44 500-ha nature reserve's deep valleys, blanketed in dense valley bushveld, flank the river's tight bends. Kudu thrive in this type of vegetation and the original core of the reserve was established to protect these stately antelope. Many other wildlife species occur, including buffalo, black rhino, eland, springbok, bushbuck, zebra and giraffe. In total, 185 bird species have been recorded. Picnic sites have been established near to the river, a lodge is situated on its east bank and a bush camp above Double Drift has picnic and fishing sites.

GROOT SWARTBERG

This extensive 89 498-ha nature reserve protects the summit of the dramatic Swartberg range between Ladismith in the west to De Rust in the east. Mountain fynbos is the dominant vegetation, with protea, erica, watsonia and gladioli among the plants that can be seen. Elements of Karoo vegetation occur on the lower slopes. Wildlife includes kudu, klipspringer, steenbok, Cape grysbok, grey rhebok, baboon and leopard. Bird-watchers should look out for raptors such as the black eagle, rock kestrel, steppe buzzard and black harrier. The five-day Swartberg Hiking Trail allows hikers to explore the mountains, and camp sites and cottages are situated in the isolated 25-km-long Die Hel, or Gamkaskloof, valley (*see also* pp. 97 and 99).

ANYSBERG

Situated in mountainous terrain south of Matjiesfontein, the 44 000-ha Anysberg Nature Reserve was proclaimed in 1987 to conserve mountain renosterveld and Karoo vegetation typical of the Succulent Karoo biome (which covers 3% of South Africa). The reserve protects over 500 plant species, and a recent purchase by WWF-SA has extended it south to the Touws River. Over 100 plants of a new species of the resin bush (*Euryops*) group, and 50 specimens of the highly localised succulent, *Gibbaeum nebrownii*, have been located on the additional land. Cape grysbok, leopard, klipspringer, grey rhebok, baboon and steenbok occur, while many raptor species have been recorded, including booted eagle, black eagle, Cape eagle owl and black harrier. A two-day horse trail is conducted over weekends. Accommodation is available in the form of a camp site and a cottage. Although there are no formal hiking trails, walkers are welcome to explore the southern part of the reserve.

DE HOOP (p. 95)

Apart from protecting the lowland fynbos, De Hoop Nature Reserve protects 50 km of coastline, an extensive wetland and rare or endangered species such as Cape vulture, bontebok (the largest population in the country) and Cape mountain zebra. The 35 846-ha reserve is also home to eland, springbok, Cape grysbok, klipspringer and

steenbok, and offers several game-viewing roads. As De Hoop contains many diverse habitats, a total of 260 species of birds have been recorded. The 14-km-long De Hoop vlei provides a vital habitat for the redknobbed coot, Cape shoveller and yellowbilled duck, among many others. A marine reserve extends 5 km out to sea and each year hundreds of southern right whales enter the reserve to calve. Cottages and camp sites provide overnight accommodation and several mountain bike trails have been established. Three walking trails lead along the vlei or ascend the Postberg where the Western Cape's only nesting colony of Cape vultures is specially protected.

HOTTENTOTS-HOLLAND

This 24 500-ha nature reserve protects the majestic Hottentots-Holland, Groot-Drakenstein, Jonkershoek and Franschhoek mountains, which tower above the vineyards, intensively cultivated valleys and the towns of Stellenbosch, Somerset West and Franschhoek. The reserve is only accessible only on foot, and hikers depart on the Boland Trail from the Nuweberg Forest Station near Elgin's apple orchards. The reserve's mountain fynbos is one of the richest localities for plants on earth and contains nearly 1 500 plant species. Between August and December the mountain slopes are splashed with a pallette of flowering

Boosmansbos Wilderness Area (above) *offers good hiking and mountain biking at Grootvadersbosch forest* (below).

daisies, watsonias, restios, ericas, bottle brushes and proteas. Although wildlife is not abundant, baboon, grey rhebok, klipspringer, grey duiker, Cape grysbok and leopard are present. Birds found in the fynbos include ground woodpecker, protea canary and Cape francolin.

HAWEQUAS STATE FOREST (p. 87)

Protecting mountain fynbos in the Du Toits, Slanghoek, Limiet and Elandskloof mountains, this 64 600-ha forest stretches over 76 km from Wolseley in the north to Franschhoek in the south. Many streams arise in the mountains and the catchment of the Wit River, near Wellington, offers some of the finest mountain scenery in the Western Cape. Several hiking trails traverse Hawequas and there is a camp and picnic site on the Wit River at the end of the Bain's Kloof Pass. Wildlife and birds typical of mountain fynbos reserves can be seen, such as Cape francolin and protea canary.

GOEGAP (p. 160)

This 15 000-ha nature reserve conserves the flat plains and rough granite hills of the Namaqualand Broken Veld, a vegetation type characterised by succulents and tall quiver tree aloes (or kokerbooms). Over 600 plant species have been identified here, many of which are on display in the wildflower garden. Hikers can explore the reserve along three hiking trails, and game-viewing roads provide an opportunity for observing desert wildlife such as gemsbok, springbok, klipspringer, Hartmann's mountain zebra and black-backed jackal. Bird-watchers should watch for the Karoo korhaan, Namaqua sandgrouse, redeyed bulbul and Namaqua dove.

Wilderness Areas
WOLKBERG (p. 33)

Folded quartzite cliffs, hidden forest patches, montane grassland and countless streams are among the attractions of this isolated 19 000-ha wilderness area. The highest peak, 2 050-m-high Serala, dominates the northern region, and south of the peak, the dense Lost Forest blankets the valley. In another valley, an estimated 4 000 cycads can be found. Hikers are free to explore the higher slopes of the wilderness or venture into the deep valleys. Wildlife typical of mountains is present and includes klipspringer, grey rhebok, mountain reedbuck and leopard, and about 160 species of birds have been recorded, such as African hawk eagle, steppe buzzard and African goshawk. Puff-adder, mamba and python occur here, as well as the rare ghost frog.

NTENDEKA (p. 63)

One of the finest surviving indigenous forests in KwaZulu-Natal, Ntendeka's most impressive feature is its dolerite cliffs which tower above forested valleys. The most common forest trees are the forest waterberry, silver oak, red currant and knobwood. Orchids are abundant and forest tree ferns grow to record heights of 8 m. Forest-dwelling animals, such as samango monkey, blue duiker, bushbuck, bushpig and the rare red squirrel, can be seen on walks through the forest. About 200 bird species have been recorded in the 5 230-ha wilderness area, including the rare bald ibis and blue swallow. A camp site provides accommodation.

BAVIAANSKLOOF

This vast 172 000-ha wilderness area extends 120 km in an east-west direction and encompasses the craggy Kouga and Baviaanskloof mountains. The Kouga Dam, near Patensie, marks the eastern boundary of the wilderness area. Three rivers flow through the wilderness, and the spectacular gorge cut by the Groot River is bordered by towering cliffs. Wildlife present includes kudu, mountain reedbuck, baboon and leopard, and eland and Cape mountain zebra have been released in the eastern section. Six vegetation types are protected within the wilderness area, and these attract over 300 bird species. Near the rivers, birders should look out for giant kingfisher and fish eagle; sombre bulbul and southern boubou occur in dense bush; the forests are home to forest canary and bleating warbler; black harriers hover over mountainous

De Hoop's marine reserve extends 5 kilometres out to sea.

grassland; and malachite sunbird and Cape sugarbird can be seen on the protea-dotted slopes. The endangered redfin minnow is found in mountain streams. Three camp sites lie in the valley, there is a picnic site at Smitskraal and five chalets, surrounded by yellowwood forests, at Geelhoutbos.

DORINGRIVIER

This 9 395-ha wilderness area conserves the higher slopes of the Outeniqua Mountains near George and protects the catchments of the Doring, Witels, Groot Brak and Kandelaars rivers. The area is rich in mountain fynbos plants and forest patches occur on the southern slopes of the mountains. The Knysna woodpecker and Knysna lourie inhabit forest patches and the fynbos is home to the Cape siskin, malachite sunbird, protea canary and greybacked cisticola. Wildlife present includes baboon, leopard, klipspringer, bushbuck and blue duiker.

BOOSMANSBOS (p. 101)

The crest of the Langeberg and the range's highest peak, 1 637-m-high Grootberg, are protected by this 14 200-ha wilderness which was named after an isolated patch of forest. In total, 65 km of trails

King proteas thrive in the Hottentots-Holland Nature Reserve.

encourage hikers to traverse its high peaks and deep valleys. A second forest, Grootvadersbosch, located on the southern boundary, is the largest remaining indigenous forest in the Langeberg and hikers can explore the forest along a 10-km trail. It was in this forest that the bushbuck first became known to European zoologists, when Anders Sparrman visited the area in 1776. Bushbuck still inhabit the forest, and Boosmansbos also supports grysbok, grey rhebok, leopard, klipspringer and baboon. Over 180 bird species have been recorded, among them Knysna woodpecker, grey cuckoo shrike and olive bush shrike. Two huts provide basic accommodation.

GROENDAL

Situated near the town of Uitenhage, this 29 916-ha wilderness area conserves the catchment of the Swartkops River. Its highest peak is 1 180-m-high Strydomsberg in the west, and the varied vegetation comprises elements of grassy fynbos, mountain fynbos, valley bushveld and forest. The wilderness area is accessible only on foot and its rugged terrain is home to mountain reedbuck, grey rhebok, baboon and leopard. Blue duiker, bushbuck and bushpig inhabit the thickets and valley forests, as do birds such as sombre bulbul, Knysna lourie and black harrier.

GROOT WINTERHOEK

This extremely rugged wilderness conserves the high peaks of the Groot Winterhoek Mountains, which tower 1 900 m above the town of Tulbagh. The summit of the range, at 2 078 m, is the second highest peak in the Western Cape. The 23 615-ha wilderness area is accessible only to hikers, and the entrance is found north of Porterville. Many tributaries of the Berg River arise in the mountains and the deep valley to the west of the high peaks is aptly-named Vier-en-twintig Riviere ('twenty-four rivers'). At the bottom of the valley, the river plunges down a waterfall into a deep pool. Hikers can explore 90 km of trails, and three huts overlook the Vier-en-twintig Riviere valley. Although wildlife is not easily seen in the mountain fynbos, baboon and klipspringer are present and birdwatchers will observe raptors, the lesser doublecollared sunbird, Cape rock thrush and yellow canary.

CEDARBERG (pp. 129, 130)

The Western Cape's largest wilderness area, the Cedarberg is an uncharted expanse of surrealistic rock formations, secret valleys, streams and towering peaks. The 72 000-ha wilderness protects the catchment of eight rivers and offers some of the best hiking opportunities in South Africa. As the entire area is managed as a wilderness, visitor facilities have been deliberately excluded. Apart from two camp sites and a few crude shelters, hikers explore the wilderness along a 250-km network of trails and sleep under the stars. The wilderness area, which is named after the Clanwilliam cedar, protects valuable pockets of this rare tree. The snow protea, which is endemic to the mountains, grows on the slopes of 2 028-m-high Sneeuberg, the highest peak in the range. Although wildlife is not common, animals such as baboon, grey rhebok and klipspringer occur, and the wilderness is also an important sanctuary for the Cape leopard.

PRIVATE RESERVES

Sabi Sabi offers personalised service, and their guided game drives are a highlight.

Private reserves offer an exclusive wildlife experience limited to small groups of visitors, and usually provide luxury accommodation with the emphasis on personal attention. Experienced rangers are on hand to guide visitors on game-viewing drives, night drives and bush walks. Typically, the reserves provide lavish meals, including outdoor cookouts and game dishes.

KAGGA KAMMA

Situated in the rugged Cedarberg north of Ceres, the 5 600-ha Kagga Kamma reserve is known for its magnificent scenery, rock formations and its band of resident San. Many of the rock features are adorned with San rock art estimated to be up to 6 000 years old. Several hikes explore the reserve and 4x4 game-viewing drives are offered. Wildlife present includes kudu, bontebok, caracal, gemsbok and springbok, and black eagles are commonly seen. Day visitors are welcome and overnight guests stay in traditional accommodation or in a luxury tented camp.

BUSHMANS KLOOF (p. 130)

One of the Western Cape's eco-tourism attractions is the 7 200-ha Bushmans Kloof near Wupperthal. Wildlife typical of dry mountain fynbos and the Karoo occurs here and includes bontebok, springbok, gemsbok and black wildebeest. The reserve protects a herd of rare Cape mountain zebra and the Western Cape's only wild dog population, and raptors such as black and martial eagles are often seen. Over 120 San rock art sites have been located and a resident expert conducts guests on walks to the rock shelters. Mountain hikes, game drives, river walks, swimming in rock pools and a restaurant are some of Bushmans Kloof's other attractions, and visitors stay in comfortable Cape cottages.

SHAMWARI (p. 116)

The leading private reserve of the Eastern Cape, 8 000-ha Shamwari supports a wide variety of wildlife including black and white rhino, lion, buffalo, elephant, hippo, giraffe, eland, wildebeest and zebra. Game drives and walks are provided in valley bushveld, and guests stay in a two-storey Edwardian mansion or in self-catering farmsteads. Shamwari's cultural village, Kaya Lendaba ('house of stories'), gives visitors an insight into traditional African culture through music, dancing, storytelling and sport.

TWALU

Managed by the Conservation Corporation, Twalu is situated at the foot of the Korrana Mountains in the Kalahari Desert. The 75 000-ha retreat, characterised by its red dunes and wide-open desert grasslands, is the largest private reserve in South Africa and has been stocked with elephant, black rhino, lion, cheetah, leopard, spotted hyena, roan, buffalo, giraffe, sable, eland, kudu and gemsbok. Visitors are accommodated in a luxury lodge that has its own landing strip, and activities include game-viewing drives and rhino tracking.

PHINDA RESOURCE RESERVE

The Conservation Corporation's 17 000-ha Phinda Resource Reserve is the leading eco-tourism reserve of KwaZulu-Natal and borders the Greater

Shamwari's Edwardian mansion provides luxurious accommodation.

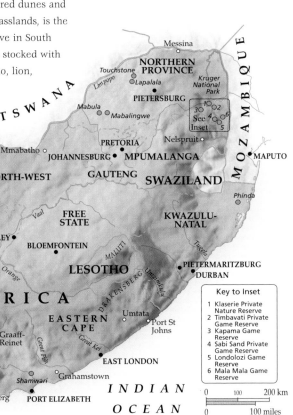

Key to Inset
1 Klaserie Private Nature Reserve
2 Timbavati Private Game Reserve
3 Kapama Game Reserve
4 Sabi Sand Private Game Reserve
5 Londolozi Game Reserve
6 Mala Mala Game Reserve

St Lucia Wetland Park (*see* pp. 60, 65 and 173). Not only does the reserve support elephant, white rhino, lion, cheetah and giraffe, but Phinda also caters for outdoor activities such as canoeing, river-boat cruises, game drives and guided bush walks. Black rhino tracking in the adjacent Mkuzi Game Reserve and scuba diving at Sodwana Bay are also offered. Over 300 species of birds occur at Phinda, among them fish eagle, emeraldspotted dove and goliath heron. Visitors stay in Phinda Nyala Lodge or Forest Lodge.

MABULA (p. 22)

Occupying 12 000 ha of sour bushveld west of Warmbaths, Mabula is crossed by a range of hills which offer superb views of the distant Waterberg. The main lodge is managed by the Protea Hotels chain and three smaller time-share camps also cater for guests. Mabula is rich in wildlife and visitors can go on game drives, walks or on horseback to see some 18 species of antelope, giraffe, lion, elephant, white rhino, buffalo and hippo. Birdlife includes ostrich, goldenbreasted bunting and forktailed drongo.

MABALINGWE (p. 23)

Covering 6 400 ha of bush-covered hills in the foothills of the Waterberg, Mabalingwe is home to 17 antelope species, hippo, white rhino and elephant. Game drives or walks explore the reserve, and birds which may be seen include crested barbet and Burchell's coucal. The largest camp, Ingwe, is beautifully sited on a hilltop overlooking a dam, one of many built on the river flowing through the reserve.

LAPALALA (p. 24)

Preserving 35 000 ha of wilderness in the Waterberg, Lapalala was the first private reserve in South Africa to obtain black rhino, and other animals found here include kudu, Burchell's

A staff member at Ulusaba drums guests to dinner.

zebra, roan and blue wildebeest. Over 200 bird species occur here, such as secretary bird, helmeted guineafowl and black eagle. Visitors stay in six exclusive camps overlooking the Lephalala River. A tented camp and small lodge are located further south in an area where black rhino are specially protected. Visitors are encouraged to explore the wilderness on foot.

TOUCHSTONE (p. 24)

Covering 6 500 ha of undulating bushveld, Touchstone offers wilderness trails on horseback and game drives in open vehicles. Wildlife that may be seen includes elephant, buffalo, leopard, cheetah and sable, while black eagles and falcons soar above the cliffs bordering the river. Up to a dozen visitors can be accommodated in each of Touchstone's three intimate camps.

KLASERIE

The 62 000-ha Klaserie reserve borders the Olifants River and the Kruger Park. The Klaserie River, fringed by woodland, flows through the centre of this vast retreat, which is the second-largest private reserve in South Africa. The luxurious Buffalo Lodge overlooks a floodlit water hole, and activities include game drives in open vehicles

and guided walks. Animals that may be seen include elephant, giraffe, lion, leopard and spotted hyena, and birds such as blackheaded oriole, glossy starling and coqui francolin are common.

KAPAMA

The 12 000-ha Kapama reserve offers game-viewing drives and night drives through the Lowveld, and visitors can expect to see white rhino, lion, buffalo, zebra, giraffe and antelope. Birdlife includes arrowmarked babbler, crested barbet and yelloweyed canary. Kapama accommodates visitors in a double-storey guest house, luxury tented camp or in the self-catering Lion Den. The Hoedspruit Research and Breeding Centre adjoining Kapama offers educational videos, tours to see wild dogs and the over 70 cheetahs raised here, and a visit to a 'vulture restaurant'.

TIMBAVATI (p. 39)

Timbavati is situated in the best game-viewing country in South Africa and is renowned for sightings of lion, buffalo and elephant. Over 200 bird species occur here, including whitebacked vulture, lilacbreasted roller and saddle-billed stork. Visitors can choose from a variety of lodges, each one with restricted access to a portion of the reserve and offering game drives, guided walks and game-viewing hides.

The M'Bali tented camp and Umlani Bush Camp are situated in the north, the luxurious Kambaku and Tanda Tula lodges are found in the central region, and Timbavati Wilderness Trails lies in the southwestern corner.

SABIE SAND COMPLEX

The 70 000-ha Sabie Sand Complex – incorporating the Mala Mala, Londolozi and Sabi Sabi reserves – is one of the leading private reserves in the country. It adjoins the Kruger Park, and, as the dividing fence has been removed, the wildlife is free to migrate. Visitors are almost assured of sightings of the 'Big Five' animals (*see* p. 171), and cheetah, wild dog and spotted hyena are also regularly seen. Day and night game-viewing drives are conducted in open vehicles. Some of the reserve's well-known lodges include Djuma, Chitwa Chitwa, Leadwood, Hunter's Safari, Idube, Inyati, Ulusaba, Singita and Savanna in Sabie Sand; Main, Tree and Bush camps in Londolozi; Mala Mala, Harry's and Kirkman's in Mala Mala; and the Notten's, River and Bush lodges in the southern Sabi Sabi region.

Plush accommodation at Mala Mala (top), *and a leopard at Londolozi* (above).

BOTANIC GARDENS

Flagship of the National Botanic Institute, Kirstenbosch has a remarkable setting.

South Africa is home to an astonishing variety of plants, and it has been estimated that about 21 000 species occur in the country. Table Mountain alone – in an area covering just 57 km² – has nearly 1 500 plant species, more than occur throughout Great Britain. Table Mountain and the mountains of the Western Cape form part of the Cape Floral Kingdom, more commonly referred to as Cape fynbos (*see* p. 183), which supports 6 800 species. Of the world's six plant kingdoms, fynbos is the smallest and covers just 0,04% of the earth's landmass. The remainder of South Africa is classified under the Paleotropical Floral Kingdom.

KIRSTENBOSCH (pp. 78, 84)

Widely recognised as one of the leading gardens in the world, Kirstenbosch is the principal botanic garden in South Africa, and houses the headquarters of the National Botanic Institute. Nestling against the eastern slopes of Table Mountain, the gardens were founded in 1913 and are dedicated to the protection and propagation of South Africa's indigenous flora. The property extends over 560 ha and visitors will delight in the 6 000 plant species arranged in the cultivated beds and an additional 900 species that grow wild. Some of the garden's many attractions include a section of a bitter almond hedge planted by Jan van Riebeeck in 1660, a sunken pool known as Lady Anne Barnard's Bath, a cycad collection, the JW Mathews Rock Garden, and the Fragrance Garden, which caters for blind visitors.

Many paths and trails explore the beautiful surroundings. The restaurant near the entrance is popular for breakfast, tea and lunch, and in summer, sunset concerts are held on Sundays. Kirstenbosch runs an educational programme for school children at the Goldfields Environmental Education Centre and the DG Murray Children's Discovery Centre. The Compton Herbarium, the scientific heart of the garden and whose function is to identify and classify plants, preserves over 250 000 specimens of South African plants. A spacious glasshouse, known as the Botanical Society Conservatory, houses a permanent exhibit of plants from the country's arid regions that would otherwise not survive the Western Cape's wet winters. Tours of the conservatory are conducted daily.

CALEDON

This 214-ha garden is renowned for its displays of spring flowers, and an annual flower show is staged in September when the Caledon bluebell can be seen. Nearly 60 ha has been cultivated and the remainder consists of mountain fynbos.

Trees indigenous to fynbos have been planted and a dam forms an attractive feature in the valley. Short walks explore the garden which also has a tea room and picnic sites.

HAROLD PORTER (p. 89)

Left as a bequest to the National Botanic Institute in 1959, this 189-ha garden in Betty's Bay occupies a narrow valley backed by mountain slopes clothed in fynbos. The 916-m-high Platberg guards the head of the valley and trails crisscross the mountain. Many indigenous mountain fynbos plants are on display, including proteas, ericas, gladiolus, watsonias and red disas. A walk from the formal beds through dense forest leads to a waterfall which plunges into a pool. A restaurant offers refreshments at the garden's entrance.

Aloes add vibrant splashes of colour to the Karoo National Botanic Garden.

KAROO

Backed by the Hex River Mountains, the Karoo National Botanic Garden in Worcester displays plants indigenous to the Succulent Karoo and semi-desert regions, such as succulents and vygies (*Mesembryanthemaceae*). The succulent collection is the largest in South Africa, and in spring and summer the display beds are ablaze with colour.

VAN STADEN'S

The best time to visit the Van Staden's Wild Flower Reserve is from April to September when the gardens are a riot of colour. Situated on the east bank of the Van Staden's River, about 40 km west of Port Elizabeth, about 60 ha of the total area of 286 ha has been devoted to formal beds and the remainder consists of unspoilt fynbos and Alexandria Forest veld type. A total of 213 species of plants and over 100 bird species have been identified, among them olive thrush, chorister robin and olive bush shrike. The garden is noted for its abundance of proteas and orchids, and the endemic fire lily. Several trees restricted to the area, including the Cape star-chestnut and Cape wing-nut, can be seen. Picnic sites are available and a walking trail leads down to the Van Staden's River.

WITWATERSRAND (p. 16)

This 225-ha garden is one of the finest in the country. The 70-m-high Witpoortjie Waterfall is visible from many of the paths traversing the garden, and visitors explore dense patches of woodland and riverine forest. The interpretative centre near the cycad beds contains mammal and bird displays, and a short history of the garden. The Sasol dam and bird hide is located near the entrance, and in total, 180 species of birds have been recorded, including whitebellied sunbird, brownhooded kingfisher and a nesting pair of black eagles. During weekends the restaurant serves breakfast under shady trees.

PRETORIA

Situated in the eastern Pretoria suburb of Silverton, the 76-ha Pretoria National Botanical Garden displays over 5 000 species of indigenous plants which are arranged according to major vegetation types, such as savanna, fynbos and forest. The over 500 species present here represnt more than half of the indigenous tree species of South Africa. A botanical research centre occupies the centre of the garden.

LOWVELD (pp. 30, 36)

The tropical town of Nelspruit is an ideal setting for the Lowveld National Botanic Gardens, established in 1969 on 154 ha of land. The garden borders the Crocodile River and a 2-km walk along the river bank reveals many species of Lowveld trees, including marula, wild fig and combretum. Another short walk leads to a cascade on the river. Water pumped from the river is sprayed from towers to create a dense band of riverine forest.

NATAL (p. 50)

The Natal National Botanical Garden, founded in 1870, occupies a pretty site

at the base of a hill clothed in indigenous forest. The Dorpspruit flows through the reserve and a large water body, formed by damming the stream, is home to many species of waterbirds, such as Egyptian goose, grey heron and hamerkop. The original garden displayed an extensive array of trees from around the world, but the emphasis has shifted to displaying indigenous plants. From the restaurant, a path leads past a duck pond and a wetland to a forest of yellow fever trees, and several walking trails lead up through dense forest to the crest of the hill. An avenue of plane trees has been declared a national monument.

DURBAN (p. 49)

The 15-ha Durban Botanical Gardens, established in 1849, became known worldwide when the *Encephalartos woodii* cycad from Ngoye Forest was successfully transplanted in these gardens (*see* p. 67). The first jacaranda trees, imported into South Africa from Argentina, were planted in the gardens, and the Ernest Thorp orchid house became famous as the country's first naturalistic display house. Other attractions include a garden for the blind, a sunken garden and an ornamental lake.

HARRISMITH (p. 154)

The 2 395-m-high Platberg forms a backdrop to the Harrismith Botanic Gardens which displays plants typical of high-altitude grasslands. Over 1 000 species of plants indigenous to the Drakensberg region can be seen, including Drakensberg agapanthus, *clivia* sp., fire lily, blue squill and poker. Two dams are situated in the centre of the 114-ha garden and visitors can wander along a network of trails.

FREE STATE

Situated north of Bloemfontein, the Free State National Botanical Garden

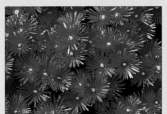
displays plants indigenous to the Highveld, including buffalo thorn, cabbage tree and lilies. Large specimens of the karee tree (*Rhus* sp.) provide ample shade. Apart from acacias and karee species, wild olives and white stinkwood trees grow in the areas of natural bush. The garden's wooded *koppies* (hills) and formal beds, as well as a tributary of the Modder River, attract over 90 bird species, including all three species of mousebird. A dam supports many waterbird species, such as Egyptian goose, redknobbed coot and purple gallinule, while weavers nest in the reeds of the adjacent vlei.

HIKING TRAILS

BLYDERIVIERSPOORT (p. 40)

 5 days, 65 km

This one-way trail provides hikers with an unparalleled view of the Blyde River Canyon. The trail begins at God's Window, at an altitude of 1 700 m, and ends at 600 m in the hot, bush-covered canyon. Much of this relatively easy trail crosses rolling mountainous grassland that is watered by several streams. The hike affords glorious views over the Escarpment and Lowveld and passes the impressive Bourke's Luck Potholes. The last day descends into the canyon, passing through dense riverine forest and bushveld before ending at Aventura's Swadini resort.

FANIE BOTHA (p. 40)

 5 days, 77 km

The one-way Fanie Botha trail traverses pine plantations in the Mauchsberg between Sabie and Graskop. Hikers climb steeply to the higher slopes of Mount Anderson, descend the Escarpment and pass the Mac-Mac Falls. On the last day, the trail hugs the edge of the Escarpment and ends at God's Window where viewsites provide magnificent vistas over the Lowveld.

GIANT'S CASTLE – TWO HUTS

 3 days, 37 km

Giant's Castle is renowned for its dramatic surroundings, unspoilt rivers, sheltered valleys and San rock art. The circular walk to the Giant's and Bannerman huts allows hikers to experience some of the area's most beautiful scenery. This fairly undemanding trail passes the San cave museum and follows Two Dassie Stream to Giant's Hut. On the second day, a contour path follows the base of the sheer basalt peaks to Bannerman's Hut. The return journey leads down a ridge to the Bushman's River and the rest camp. Hikers in the Giant's Castle

Rustic huts on the Giant's Castle trail provide hikers with overnight accommodation.

region can expect to see large herds of eland, as well as blesbok, mountain reedbuck, grey rhebok and oribi.

GIANT'S CUP

 5 days, 59 km

The Giant's Cup trail meanders through lovely grassland valleys in the foothills of the Drakensberg. Six rivers surge through the valleys and the overnight huts are all near to water. The Giant's Cup, the cup-shaped mountain after which the trail is named, dominates the horizon on the first two days. Hikers can expect to see mountain reedbuck, grey duiker and oribi, and the mountains are also home to many raptors, including black eagle, bearded vulture and mountain buzzard. The hike ends at Bushman's Nek.

AMATOLA (p. 119)

6 days, 105 km

Traversing the Amatola Mountains in the Eastern Cape, the one-way Amatola trail begins at Maden Dam, near King William's Town, although there are four other starting points as well. The trail meanders through magnificent patches of indigenous forest, and crosses pine plantations and grassland. The hike provides panoramic views over the surrounding countryside, especially on the fourth day when it climbs Mnyameni Valley and Geju Peak. Although the trail is strenuous, hikers will delight in its sylvan forests,

waterfalls, shaded pools and streams. Bushpig, bushbuck and samango monkey are present, and trumpeter hornbill, chorister robin and cinnamon dove are found in the forests. The trail ends at Zingcuka Forest Station.

ALEXANDRIA (p. 117)

 2 days, 36 km

Beginning at the forest station south of Alexandria, the relatively easy Alexandria trail first passes through the Alexandria Forest, one of the finest surviving indigenous forests in the Eastern Cape. Bushbuck, blue duiker, bushpig and vervet monkey occur, and the forest represents the most southerly distribution of the trumpeter hornbill. Before reaching the overnight hut, the trail runs parallel to a wild section of the coast. On the second day the hike crosses the Alexandria dunefield, South Africa's largest active dune system, before returning to the forest station.

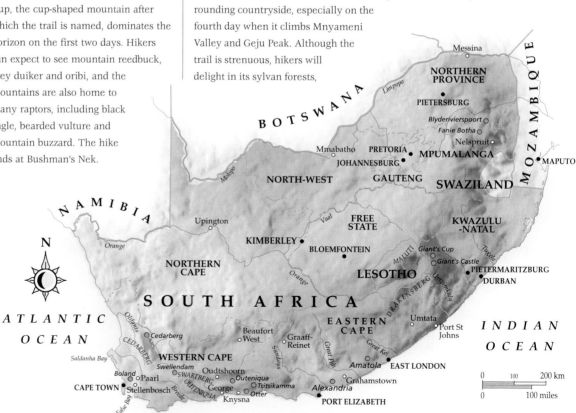

OTTER (pp. 105, 107)

 5 days, 41 km

Beginning at Storms River Mouth, the one-way Otter Trail in the Tsitsikamma National Park is one of the most beautiful in South Africa. The undulating trail hugs the rugged shore, crosses coastal fynbos and enters patches of coastal forest. The hike follows the unspoilt coastline and the distances each day are short (the longest day is only 14 km), allowing sufficient time for relaxing in the unspoilt surroundings, swimming in the rivers and the ocean, and observing seabirds, whales and dolphins. Cape clawless otter,

FYNBOS

The vegetation of the folded sandstone mountains and sandy coastal plains of the Western Cape is commonly known as fynbos – an Afrikaans name referring to the small, delicate leaves of many of the species. Although the soils of the mountains and coastal plains of the Western Cape region are low in nutrients, an estimated 6 800 species of fynbos plants occur. Fynbos species comprise 80% of all plants found in the Cape Floral Kingdom, the smallest of the world's six floral kingdoms and which covers just 0,04% of the earth's landmass. An estimated 70% of the fynbos plants are endemic and some are so limited in distribution that they occur only on a single mountain peak.

Fynbos vegetation can be divided into Mountain Fynbos and Lowland Fynbos. Plants of the mountains can be classed mainly under the genera protea, restio, leucadendron, erica, leucospermum, watsonia, brunia and ixia. Lowland Fynbos can be broadly divided into Coastal Fynbos (found on sand and limestone) and Coastal Renosterveld, vegetation dominated by renosterbos (Elytropappus).

Fynbos is home to several endemic birds, such as Cape rockjumper, Protea canary and Cape sugarbird, and large mammals include Cape grysbok and bontebok.

Beautiful ericas form part of the Mountain Fynbos grouping.

Hikers on the Tsitsikamma trail may come across patches of brilliant watsonias.

bushbuck, vervet monkey and blue duiker can also be seen. Both the Lottering and Bloukrans rivers have to be crossed, either by swimming or wading. The trail ends at Nature's Valley.

TSITSIKAMMA (p. 105)

 5 days, 61 km

The one-way Tsitsikamma trail, a logical inland extension to the Otter Trail, starts at Nature's Valley and heads north to the Tsitsikamma Mountains. It traverses a variety of habitats including moist forest, pine plantation and tall fynbos typical of high-rainfall regions. Each of the four overnight huts are sited near to streams that course down the high mountain slopes. Although provision has been made for shorter routes, hikers doing the entire trail continue to the end point at the Paul Sauer Bridge.

OUTENIQUA (p. 108)

 5 days, 90 km

The one-way Outeniqua trail begins at the Beervlei Forest Station and climbs through mountain fynbos and pine plantations to the upper slopes of the Outeniqua Mountains. It then descends to the extensive indigenous forests and plantations that blanket the lower slopes. On the final three days, the trail passes through the largest indigenous forests in South Africa. Bushpig, bushbuck, blue duiker, vervet monkey

and leopard may be seen, and birds present in the forest include crowned eagle, Knysna lourie and Knysna woodpecker. The hike ends at Diepwalle.

SWELLENDAM (p. 100)

 6 days, 74 km

The circular Swellendam trail explores the Marloth Nature Reserve in the scenic Langeberg and is rated as one of the loveliest hikes in the country. This fairly strenuous trail traverses mountain fynbos and enters patches of forest in secluded valleys, and, from the higher slopes, affords superb views across the Breede River Valley. The hike also passes Middelrivierberg (1 628 m), one of the highest peaks in the Langeberg. Hikers will detect birds typical of fynbos, such as Cape sugarbird and protea canary.

BOLAND

 3 days, 47 km

Situated in the Hottentots-Holland Nature Reserve (*see also* p. 176), the Boland trail traverses the spectacular mountains that soar above the valley vineyards, orchards and the towns of Stellenbosch, Somerset West and Franschhoek. It begins in the plantations of the Nuweberg State Forest near Grabouw, and hikers can complete a circular route or proceed to Stellenbosch or Franschhoek. The mountains offer an ideal opportunity to study the fascinating fynbos vegetation, and almost 1 500 plant species occur. Klipspringer, baboon, Cape grysbok and leopard are present. Birds that can be seen in the fynbos include ground woodpecker, Victorin's warbler and Cape francolin.

CEDARBERG (pp. 129, 130 and 177)

2-7 days

The unspoilt Cedarberg Wilderness Area provides some of the best hiking opportunities in South Africa. Although there are no equipped overnight huts, there are two camp sites and several basic shelters within the rugged wilderness. Hikers traverse an extensive network of paths and explore many of the Cedarberg's magnificent natural landforms including the Maltese Cross, Wolfberg Arch, several waterfalls and the 2 026-m-high Sneeuberg, the highest peak in the range. Animals such as baboon and klipspringer are present.

The craggy Cedarberg provides unrivalled hiking experiences.

WINE FARMS

Vergelegen's elegant manor house is shaded by 300-year-old camphor trees.

Wine was first produced in South Africa by Jan van Riebeeck. The original stock of grape cuttings arrived from France in 1655 and on 2 February 1659 Van Riebeeck wrote in his diary, "Today, praise be the Lord, wine was made for the first time from Cape grapes." Three centuries later South Africa is ranked among the world's top wine-producing nations. South African wines are exported throughout the world, have won numerous international awards, and compete against the best European wines. Although vineyards have been extended into the Little Karoo and Orange River regions, most wine farms are found within a 100-kilometre radius of Cape Town.

GROOT CONSTANTIA (pp. 79, 85)

The farm Groot Constantia was presented to Governor Simon van der Stel in 1685, who planted the first vines for which Constantia became well-known. Today the main homestead is devoted to a cultural museum, the old cellar houses a wine museum, and the Jonkershuis, the dwelling traditionally built for the oldest son, is a restaurant. Wine-tasting is offered at the modern cellar near the entrance to the estate.

BUITENVERWACHTING (pp. 79, 85)

The estate is open for wine-tasting and sales on weekdays and Saturday mornings, and tours of the cellars are conducted on weekdays. Connoisseurs of fine food rate Buitenverwachting's restaurant as one of the finest in the Western Cape.

VERGELEGEN (p. 88)

Nestling at the foot of the imposing Helderberg, Vergelegen was once the home of Governor Wilhelm Adriaen van der Stel who planted 500 000 vines on the estate. Vergelegen's many attractions include its beautiful historic buildings, the Lady Phillips Tea Garden, a museum, gift shop, wine-tasting, cellar tours and magnificent grounds.

SPIER (p. 86)

Apart from wine-tasting and a full selection of wines for sale, the Spier estate offers visitors superb cuisine, music festivals, craft markets and pony rides for children. The estate has three restaurants, and pre-packed picnic baskets can be booked, or visitors can make up their own at the estate's farm stall. During summer, orchestras perform in the open-air amphitheatre.

BLAAUWKLIPPEN (p. 86)

This estate produces grapes from some 15 cultivars and its fine wines have won many awards. Blaauwklippen is open for cellar tours, wine-tasting and sales from Monday to Saturday, and from October to the end-April, horse-drawn coach rides and lunch platters are offered daily except Sundays. The main homestead was completed in 1789. A collection of antique Cape furniture is displayed in the museum, and the estate's country shop specialises in Cape Malay preserves and relishes.

DELHEIM (p. 86)

High on the slope of the Simonsberg, Delheim affords lovely views across to Table Mountain. Its cellar provides a cosy setting for tasting Delheim's excellent wines, and in summer cheeses, bread and pâtè are served each day in the garden. During the winter, visitors can enjoy hot soup and home-made bread from Monday to Saturday.

SIMONSIG (p. 86)

This estate has a reputation for producing innovative wines that are rated among the country's best, among them Chardonnay, Pinotage and Chenin Blanc. Simonsig is open for sales and wine-tasting from Monday to Saturday, and cellar tours Mondays to Fridays.

DELAIRE (p. 86)

Situated on the summit of Helshoogte Pass, Delaire offers visitors splendid views of the surrounding mountains. The estate is renowned for its Late Harvest, Sauvignon Blanc, Weisser Riesling and Chardonnay white wines, and dry Cuvee Rouge and Barrique reds are also produced. Lunches are served throughout the year and picnics are available in spring and summer. Delaire is open for sales and wine-tastings from Monday to Saturday. Visitors can overnight in two mountain chalets.

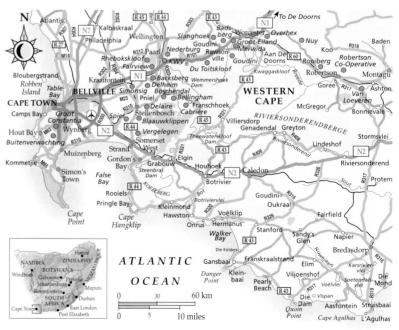

BOSCHENDAL

Backed by the Groot Drakenstein mountains, the estate's impressive manor house is a national monument and displays antique furniture and historic artifacts. The Boschendal Restaurant is well-known for its buffet lunches, and Le Café serves light meals under oak trees. Visitors can also enjoy Le Pique-Nique, a French-style picnic under pine trees. Apart from the vineyard tours, Boschendal has a self-guided, 15-minute walking tour of an exhibition vineyard next door to the Taphuis. From Monday to Friday, and daily during summer, wine-tasting can be enjoyed in the Taphuis.

BELLINGHAM (p. 87)

One of the region's leading wine producers, Bellingham has a tradition for excellence that dates back to 1693. This innovative estate produced the first Shiraz, Rosé and Premier Grand Cru wines in the country, and Bellingham's Premier Grand Cru pioneered a new extra-dry wine category in the local market. The estate is open on weekdays, and on Saturdays during spring and summer, for wine-tasting and sales, light lunches and vineyard tours.

CABRIÈRE

Cabrière produces the Pierre Jourdan range of wines. Only Chardonnay and Pinot Noir vines have been planted over the past 15 years. Wine-tasting at the Haute Cabrière Cellar, opened in 1995 to commemorate 300 years of French influence in the Cape, is complemented by the Haute-Cabrière Cellar Restaurant.

BACKSBERG

Backsberg specialises in classic red wines and is known for its Cabernet Sauvignon. The estate is open for wine sales and cellar tours on weekdays and

Saturday mornings, and its museum displays early wine-making equipment.

NEDERBURG

Nederburg stocks the biggest range of quality wines in the country, and the annual Nederberg Wine Auction has become a prominent event on the wine connoisseur's calendar. Regular cellar tours and wine-tasting are conducted in five languages and wine can be bought from Monday to Saturday. In summer picnic lunches can be booked.

KWV

The Ko-operatiewe Wijnbouwers-vereeniging (KWV) is the largest wine co-operative in the world, and is famous for its award-winning wines and brandies. Cellar tours, slide shows and wine-tasting are presented in English, Afrikaans, German and French from Monday to Saturday. KWV is famous for its huge Cathedral Cellar and contains the five largest vats in the world. But as the wines are for export only, purchases cannot be made.

FAIRVIEW

A variety of goat's milk cheeses and wine-tasting are some of the attractions of the Fairview estate. Goats are milked on the estate and visitors can

observe these animals climbing a ramp around a tower. The estate is open from Monday to Saturday for tastings and sales of both cheese and wine.

RHEBOKSKLOOF

Situated north of Paarl Mountain, Rhebokskloof is known for its fine wines, excellent cuisine and estate tours. The Victorian Restaurant offers á la carte meals and light lunches are served on the terrace. The Cape Dutch Restaurant caters for weddings, special functions and Sunday buffets. Rhebokskloof is open throughout the week.

ROOIBERG

Owned by 36 wine producers, Rooiberg Co-operative's cellar, specialising in the production of superb dry wines, was opened in 1964. Winner of countless trophies and gold medals, the cellar has produced no fewer than 28 wines which have been awarded the coveted Superior classification. The co-op is open for wine sales and tastings on weekdays and on Saturday mornings.

ROBERTSON CO-OPERATIVE

The Robertson Co-Operative Winery was established in 1941, and about 25 000 tons of grapes are processed each year. Apart from producing

Resident goats at Fairview provide the milk for the estate's famous cheeses.

various dry white wines, the cellar also makes dry red, semi-sweet, late harvest and sweet Muscadel wines. The winery is open for wine-tasting and sales on weekdays and Saturday mornings, and offers conducted tours of the cellar.

VAN LOVEREN

Situated at the confluence of the Cogmanskloof and Breede rivers, Van Loveren's favourable climate and good soils encourage the production of superb white wines. The estate is well-known for its Blanc de Noir wines as well as Blanc de Blanc and Premier Grand Cru. Tastings and sales take place from Monday to Saturday.

Worcester

The Worcester district accounts for one-quarter of the total national wine production, and in terms of sheer volume Worcester is the most important wine-producing district in South Africa. Co-ops which are easily accessible from the N1 include Du Toits Kloof, Badsberg, Slanghoek, Goudini, Merwida, Nuy, Groot Eiland, Aan-de-Doorns and Overhex. With a few exceptions, all of the wineries in the district are open to the public from Monday to Saturday, and some also offer cellar tours.

The Cabrière estate is renowned for the elegance of its dry wines.

THE COUNTRY

The Twelve Apostles overlooking Camps Bay beach.

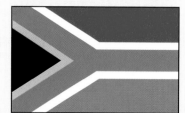

The new, brightly coloured South African flag was first raised at midnight on 26 April 1994.

Provinces	Area	Capital
Western Cape (WC)	129 370 km²	Cape Town
Eastern Cape (EC)	169 600 km²	Port Elizabeth
Northern Cape (NC)	361 800 km²	Kimberley
Free State (FS)	129 480 km²	Bloemfontein
KwaZulu-Natal (KN)	92 180 km²	Pietermaritzburg
North-West (NW)	116 190 km²	Mmabatho
Gauteng (GP)	18 810 km²	Johannesburg
Mpumalanga (MP)	78 370 km²	Nelspruit
Northern Prov. (NP)	123 280 km²	Pietersburg

Surface Area - 1 223 201 square kilometres

THE LAND

Significant Caves / Importance

Significant Caves	Importance
Cango (Oudtshoorn, WC)	Dolomitic/Tourism
Sudwala (Nelspruit, NP)	Dolomitic/Tourism
Sterkfontein (Krugersdorp, GP)	Prehistoric
Makapansgat (Potgietersrus, NP)	Historical
Boomslang (Kalk Bay, WC)	'Urban' caves
Echo (Ohrigstad, MP)	Resonance
Eland (Drakensberg, KN)	139 San paintings
Wolkberg (Tzaneen, NP)	Geological structures

Dams	Capacity
Gariep (Colesberg, EC/FS)	5 673 x 10⁶ m³
Vaal (Vereeniging, FS)	2 400 x 10⁶ m³
Grootdraai (Standerton, MP)	364 x 10⁶ m³
Sterkfontein (Harrismith, FS)	2 617 x 10⁶ m³
Woodstock (Bergville, KN)	381 x 10⁶ m³
Vanderkloof (Petrusville, FS)	3 236 x 10⁶ m³
Katse (Lesotho)	1 950 x 10⁶ m³
Hartbeespoort (Pretoria, GP)	212 x 10⁶ m³
Loskop (Middelburg, MP)	200 x 10⁶ m³
Pongolapoort (Mkuze, KN)	2 336 x 10⁶ m³

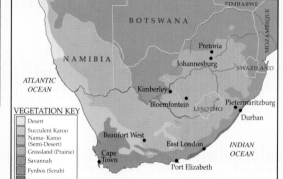

VEGETATION KEY
- Desert
- Succulent Karoo
- Nama- Karoo (Semi-Desert)
- Grassland (Prairie)
- Savannah
- Fynbos (Scrub)
- Subtropical Forest

Longest Rivers	Length
Orange	2 340 km, drains 47% surface area.
Vaal	1 210 km
Limpopo	900 km

Mountains / Highest Peaks

Mountains	Highest Peaks
Lesotho Drakensberg	Thaba Ntlenyana 3 482 m
KwaZulu-Natal Drakensberg	Injasuthi Peak 3 459 m
Eastern Cape Drakensberg	Ben Macdhui 3 001 m
Rooiberg (FS)	Ribbokkop 2 837 m
Witteberg (EC)	Avoca Peak 2 769 m
Swartberg (WC)	Seweweekspoort 2 325 m
Hex River Mts. (WC)	Matroosberg 2 209 m
Wolkberg (NP)	Iron Crown 2 126 m
Grootwinterhoek (WC)	Grootwinterhoek Peak 2 078 m
Cedarberg (WC)	Sneeuberg 2 026 m
Dutoitsberge (WC)	Dutoits Peak 1 995 m
Transvaal Drakensberg (MP)	Mariepskop 1 944 m
Amatolas (EC)	Gaika's Kop 1 963 m
Magaliesberg (GP & NW)	1 852 m
Soutpansberg (NP)	Letsumbe 1 747 m
Langeberg (WC)	Misty Point 1 710 m
Tsitsikamma (EC)	Formosa Peak 1 675 m
Outeniqua (WC)	George Peak 1 580 m
Table Mountain (WC)	Maclear's Beacon 1 086 m

THE CLIMATE

Rainfall

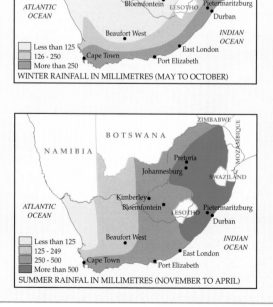

Less than 125
126 - 250
More than 250
WINTER RAINFALL IN MILLIMETRES (MAY TO OCTOBER)

Less than 125
125 - 249
250 - 500
More than 500
SUMMER RAINFALL IN MILLIMETRES (NOVEMBER TO APRIL)

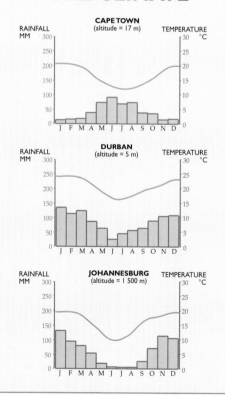

CAPE TOWN (altitude = 17 m)

DURBAN (altitude = 5 m)

JOHANNESBURG (altitude = 1 500 m)

Temperature

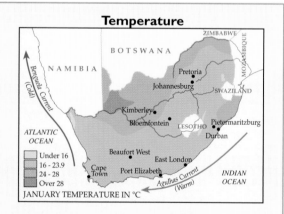

Under 16
16 - 23.9
24 - 28
Over 28
JANUARY TEMPERATURE IN °C

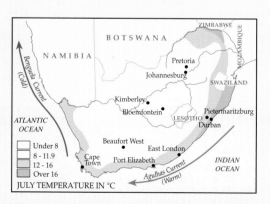

Under 8
8 - 11.9
12 - 16
Over 16
JULY TEMPERATURE IN °C

AGRICULTURE AND RESOURCES

Agricultural Production (%)

Animal Products		Field Crops		Horticultural	
Livestock slaughtered	37,7	Maize	39,8	Deciduous fruits	27,6
Wool	2,9	Wheat	15,5	Citrus	10,7
Poultry	38,3	Sugar	16,3	Viticulture	13,0
Fresh milk	10,6	Tobacco	5,3	Vegetables	34,2
Dairy products	5,6	Other	23,1	Other	6,3
Other	2,7				

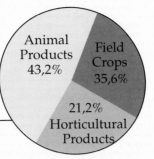

Animal Products 43,2%
Field Crops 35,6%
21,2% Horticultural Products

Agriculture's Contribution to GDP (R million)
GDP - Gross Domestic Product

Year	GDP	Agriculture's contribution	
1991	278 137	13 324 -	4,8%
1992	309 085	11 963 -	3,9%
1993	344 917	14 147 -	4,1%
1994	384 152	17 329 -	4,5%

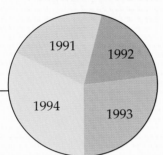

1991 1992 1994 1993

Mineral Production by value 1994 (R million)

No.	Mineral	1994
1	Gold	24 953
2	Coal	10 412
3	Platinum-group metals	5 747
4	Iron ore	1 398
5	Copper	1 255
6	Manganese ore	644
7	Limestone & dolomite	589
8	Aggregate & sand	560
9	Nickel	550
10	Chrome ore	396
11	Granite	242
12	Other	6 800
Total		53 550

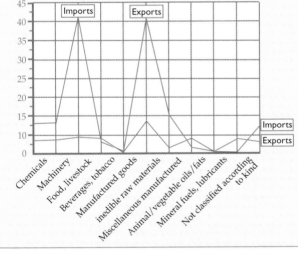

GDP 1994 (by sector)

No.	Sector	1994
1	Agriculture, forestry	17 930
2	Mining, quarrying	33 168
3	Manufacturing	89 766
4	Construction	12 265
5	Electricity, gas, water	15 751
6	Transport, communication	28 976
7	Trade, commerce	61 648
8	Other	123 057
Total		382 561

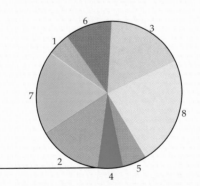

Gross Value of Agricultural Production
(1994 - R in millions)

Field Crops	Rand	%Sector	%Total
Maize	4 358	44,5	15,9
Wheat	1 481	15,3	5,5
Hay	1 078	11,1	3,9
Grain sorghum	227	2,3	0,8
Sugar-cane	1 123	11,4	4,2
Groundnuts	202	2,1	0,7
Tobacco	350	3,5	1,2
Sunflower seed	362	3,7	1,4
Cotton	105	1,0	0,3
Other	490	5,1	1,7
Subtotal	**9 776**	**100,0**	**35,6**
Horticulture	**Rand**	**%Sector**	**%Total**
Viticulture	780	13,5	2,8
Citrus	662	11,5	2,4
Subtropical fruit	290	5,1	1,0
Deciduous and other	1 641	28,3	6,0
Vegetables	1 143	19,6	4,3
Potatoes	692	12,0	2,5
Other	577	10,0	2,2
Subtotal	**5 785**	**100,0**	**21,2**
Animal	**Rand**	**%Sector**	**%Total**
Wool	371	3,1	1,4
Dressed poultry & eggs	4 518	38,6	16,6
Cattle, calves slaughtered	2 898	24,8	10,6
Sheep, goats slaughtered	915	7,8	3,4
Pigs slaughtered	491	4,2	1,8
Fresh milk	1 250	10,7	4,6
Dairy products	698	5,9	2,7
Other	568	4,9	2,1
Subtotal	**11 709**	**100,0**	**43,2**
Total	**27 270**	**-**	**-**

Imports and Exports
(1995 - Rands in millions)

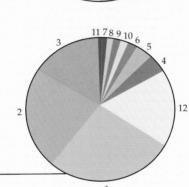

Imports Exports

Chemicals, Machinery, Food, livestock, Beverages, tobacco, Manufactured goods, inedible raw materials, Miscellaneous manufactured, Animal/vegetable oils/fats, Mineral fuels, lubricants, Not classified according to kind

Imports
Exports

ANIMAL KINGDOM

Largest Mammals | Mass/Height

Elephant (*Loxodonta africana*)	6 t
White rhinoceros (*Ceratotherium simum*)	2,3 t
Hippopotamus (*Hippopotamus amphibius*)	2 t
Black rhinoceros (*Diceros bicornis*)	1,8 t
Buffalo (*Syncerus caffer*)	750 kg
Eland (*Taurotragus oryx*)	730 kg
Giraffe (*Giraffa camelopardalis capensis*)	5,5 m

The 'Big Five'

Lion (*Panthera leo*)	200 kg
Leopard (*Panthera pardus*)	80 kg
Elephant (*Loxodonta africana*)	6 t
Rhinoceros (*Diceros bicornis*)	1,8 t - 2,3 t
Buffalo (*Syncerus caffer*)	750 kg

POPULATION (1994)

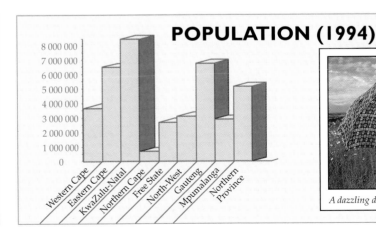

Western Cape, Eastern Cape, KwaZulu-Natal, Northern Cape, Free State, North-West, Gauteng, Mpumalanga, Northern Province

A dazzling display of cosmos near Harrismith.